The First Book of

The Norton Utilities® 6

The First Book of

The Norton Utilities® 6

Joseph Wikert

Revised by Lisa Bucki

International Standard Book Number: 0-672-27384-5
Library of Congress Catalog Card Number: 91-62480

Screen reproductions in this book were created by means of the program Collage Plus from Inner Media, Inc., Hollis, NH.

Printed in the United States of America

Publisher:
Richard K. Swadley

Publishing Manager and Acquisitions Editor:
Marie Butler-Knight

Managing Editor:
Marjorie Jo Hopper

Manuscript Editor:
Sara Black

Cover Artist:
Held & Diedrich Design

Indexer:
Susan VandeWalle

Production Team:
*Sandra Grieshop, Phil Kitchel, Sarah Leatherman, Laurie Lee,
Anne Owen, Howard Peirce, Cindy L. Phipps, Bruce Steed,
Johnna VanHoose, Mary Beth Wakefield, Vicki West, Phil Worthington*

Special thanks to C. Herbert Feltner for assuring the technical
accuracy of this book.

Contents

viii

4   Enhancing Your Batch Files, *85*

5 Managing Your Disks with the Utilities, *109*

X

6 Maintaining Your Hard Disk Drive, *133*

xi

xii

xiv

13 Protecting Your System with The Norton AntiVirus, *315*

XV

Introduction

Who This Book Is For

Congratulations on your purchase of one of the fine software packages from Peter Norton Computing, Inc.! This book explains how to use the following Norton products:

> The Norton Utilities Version 6.0
>
> The Norton Commander Version 3.0
>
> Norton Backup Version 1.2
>
> The Norton AntiVirus Version 1.0

If you're just starting out with any of these popular products you'll appreciate the way topics are covered in *The First Book of The Norton Utilities 6*—this book takes you by the hand and leads you step by step through all the fundamental features of each software package. As a more knowledgeable user, you will appreciate the way important operations are summarized with quick steps in this book.

Conventions Used in This Book

As you read through *The First Book of The Norton Utilities 6* you'll notice certain conventions we've used to make the book easier for your to use.

Any text that you should type is shown in `special computer type like this`. Also, certain operations require depression of two keys simultaneously. For example, the expression Alt-C tells you to press the Alt and C keys simultaneously to perform a command.

This book also uses the following shorthand terms for common mouse operations:

Point means to move the mouse pointer over an object on-screen.

Click means to point to an object and click the left mouse button. Unless told otherwise, you should always use the left mouse button.

Double-click means to point to an object and press the left mouse button twice rapidly.

 Quick Steps

1. Look for these lists of step-by-step instructions for frequently used procedures.

The first column will tell you something to do. The second column will tell you the results of your action.

 **Tip:** Helpful tips, notes, and shortcuts are included in tip boxes throughout this book.

 Caution: Cautionary notes, also in boxes, warn of possible dangers.

Acknowledgments

I would like to thank Kraig Lane with Peter Norton Computing, Inc., for all his assistance throughout the development of *The First Book of The Norton Utilities 6*. Thanks also to Richard Swadley, Marie Butler-Knight, Joe Kraynak, and Herb Feltner for all their contributions to this book.

Trademarks

All terms mentioned in this book that are known to be trademarks or service marks are listed below. In addition, terms suspected of being trademarks or service marks have been appropriately capitalized. SAMS cannot attest to the accuracy of this information. Use of a term in this book should not be regarded as affecting the validity of any trademark or service mark.

Clipper is a registered trademark of Nantucket, Inc.

Commander Mail, Commander Link, and The Norton Editor are trademarks of Peter Norton Computing, Incorporated.

COMPAQ is a registered trademark of COMPAQ Computer Corporation.

CompuServe is a registered trademark of CompuServe Incorporated.

dBASE, dBASE II, dBASE III, dBASE IV, and MultiMate are registered trademarks of Ashton-Tate.

dBXL is a trademark of WordTech Systems, Inc.

DESQview is a trademark of Quarterdeck Office Systems.

FoxBASE is a registered trademark of Fox Software, Inc.

IBM, IBM PC ST, and PS/2 are registered trademarks of International Business Machines Corporation.

Lotus, Symphony, and 1-2-3 are registered trademarks of Lotus Development Corporation.

MCI Logo and MCI Mail are registered service marks of MCI Communications Corporation.

Mosaic Twin is a registered trademark of Mosaic Software, Inc.

MS Word, MS-DOS, MS Works, MS Windows Write, and Excel are trademarks of Microsoft Corporation.

The Norton Backup and The Norton Commander are registered trademarks of Peter Norton Computing, Incorporated.

The Norton Utilities, Norton Disk Doctor, WipeFile, Wipe Disk, and UnErase are registered trademarks and Speed Disk, Disk Monitor, Calibrate, Diskreet, and WipeInfo are trademarks of Peter Norton Computing, Incorporated.

PC Paintbrush is a registered trademark of ZSoft Corporation.

An Introduction to The Norton Utilities

In This Chapter

▶ What the utilities are and what they do
▶ Utility integration
▶ How to get help

This first chapter explains how The Norton Utilities can simplify your life as a PC user. We briefly discuss each utility in general, then take a close look at the Norton Integration program. If you need to install The Norton Utilities on your system, see Appendix A, "Installation and Configuration," for complete instructions.

Picking Up Where DOS Left Off

As a PC user you have encountered situations where DOS was not as friendly as you might expect. For example, what about the potentially dreadful DEL command? Have you ever accidentally deleted a very important file? As far as DOS is concerned, once you've deleted a file, it's gone for good. There is no DOS command to recover a deleted file.

Fortunately, as an owner of The Norton Utilities, you now have access to tools for solving this and many other DOS-related shortcomings.

The programs included in The Norton Utilities can help you

▶ *Recover* files and data when problems occur, and help head off similar losses of data

▶ Improve the *speed* of your system

▶ *Secure* against data loss or having data altered or viewed by unauthorized users

▶ Complete common computing *tasks* more efficiently and effectively

The Norton Utilities will run on any IBM PC or 100% compatible PC running DOS 2.0 or later (including DOS 4.xx with large hard-disk partitions) with a minimum of 512K of available RAM. The Utilities support the popular display configurations including Hercules, CGA, EGA, and VGA. Although a hard disk is not required, one is recommended. (As you can see in Appendix A, installation and execution to/from a floppy disk can be rather awkward.) In short, if your computer runs DOS, it will probably run The Norton Utilities! Now let's explore the utility programs.

2

Summarizing the Utilities

The inside back cover of this book lists all the Norton utilities and tells where to look in this book for a detailed explanation of each of them. Following are descriptions of some of the utilities you're most likely to use in your day-to-day operations.

BE: Batch Enhancer

The BE utility adds a great deal of flexibility to the already powerful DOS batch file feature. If you are tired of dull and dreary batch files, you will enjoy using BE to enhance them with color, pop-up windows, sound, and more. New features, such as the GOTO, JUMP, and EXIT commands, give you more control over batch file execution. Other new commands enable you to work with the system clock, reboot your system, or check the status of certain keys. Perhaps the most important benefit of BE, however, is that it lets you easily create interactive menu-driven batch files.

CALIBRAT: Calibrate

The CALIBRAT utility performs several tests on your PC's hard disk. This powerful utility also has the ability to rewrite the data on your hard disk to improve the disk's efficiency and performance.

DISKEDIT: Disk Editor

This DISKEDIT utility allows you to locate, view, and edit virtually all areas of a disk, including RAM, and print selections of the information you're viewing to facilitate editing. You can also use DISKEDIT to learn more about important DOS system files and the layout of DOS disks.

3

DISKMON: Disk Monitor

The DISKMON utility lets you monitor all disk activity on your system and can prevent computer viruses from destroying the contents of your hard disk.

DISKREET: Diskreet

Use the DISKREET utility to prevent others from viewing the contents of your personal/private files. DISKREET encodes files with password protection so only you can decode and understand them.

DISKTOOL: Disk Tools

Norton's DISKTOOL utility is actually several tools in one! DISKTOOL lets you perform several disk-related functions including making a disk bootable, reviving a defective diskette, and saving/restoring important system configuration information.

FILEFIND: File Find

As its name implies, the FILEFIND utility helps you find files that may be located anywhere on your disk, but that's only part of FILEFIND's functionality. DOS maintains a set of file attributes and date/time stamps for every file on a disk. In addition to other useful operations, FILEFIND can easily modify a file's attributes and date/time stamps.

FILEFIX: File Fix

FILEFIX is an intelligent file repair tool that can fix damaged Lotus 1-2-3, Symphony, and dBASE files. FILEFIX builds a new copy of the damaged file containing as much recoverable data as possible.

4

EP: Erase Protect

This utility is a powerful tool that can prevent deleted file data from being overwritten so that files can be recovered long after they are deleted.

IMAGE: Image

Use IMAGE to prepare for an inadvertent file erasure or disk format. IMAGE writes important disk information to a special file that Norton's file recovery utilities (UNERASE and UNFORMAT) use.

NCACHE: Norton Cache

The Norton Cache utility expedites disk operations by maintaining frequently accessed disk data in a fast memory buffer. This cache utility is easily tailored for any PC configuration. NCACHE is also compatible with Windows 3.X, particularly when you're running Windows in enhanced mode.

NCC: Norton Control Center

The NCC utility provides a centralized function for setting and adjusting everything from DOS's display colors to your keyboard's repeat rate.

This utility also allows you to configure up to four serial ports, set your PC's time and date, and more.

NCD: Norton Change Directory

This utility is Norton's answer to DOS's cryptic CHDIR command, which changes the active directory. It is easy to forget where a subdirectory is located, especially when you have subdirectories off of subdirectories (for example, C:\UTILITY\SHELLS\NU). NCD offers a graphical representation, or tree structure, of your disk's directory layout as well as a speed search option to locate specific entry quickly. You can easily "prune and graft" to move a directory and its contents (including subdirectories) to a new location.

NDD: Norton Disk Doctor

The NDD utility can diagnose and even correct many common disk problems. NDD is the first utility you should consult when you encounter problems with unreadable and damaged files.

5

NORTON: Norton Integration

Later in this chapter, you will see how the NORTON utility provides a menu from which all the other Norton utilities may be executed. NORTON doesn't just provide access to the other utilities; it also provides detailed help (including syntax for each utility) and help with common DOS and application errors (including the utility that may solve the problem) through the Help feature and Advise menu.

SFORMAT: Safe Format

SFORMAT is a powerful utility that provides a safe and fast means to format hard and floppy disks. As noted in Appendix A, which covers installation, you can (and should) let the Installation program replace DOS's FORMAT with Norton's SFORMAT. SFORMAT offers an easy-to-use menu feature for selecting different format modes.

SPEEDISK: Speed Disk

Disks develop inefficient unused areas, or become *fragmented*, as a result of writing, changing, and deleting files. Fragmented hard disks are a common cause of poor PC performance. Use SPEEDISK to unfragment and optimize your hard disk with one of several different optimization methods.

SYSINFO: System Information

The System Information utility is perhaps best known for calculating common benchmarks for PC performance comparison. This utility also provides PC configuration details, including microprocessor, memory, video, and disk drive information.

6

UNERASE: UnErase

This cornerstone of The Norton Utilities allows you to quickly and easily recover accidentally deleted files. The sooner you run UNERASE after deleting a file, the better your chances are of complete data recovery. This utility now works for 1-2-3 and dBASE files.

UNFORMAT: UnFormat

UNFORMAT is a lifesaver for the "Oops, I just formatted the wrong disk!" syndrome. UNFORMAT recovers as many files as possible from an accidentally formatted disk. Be sure to use the IMAGE utility (discussed earlier) regularly to assist UNFORMAT in its recovery process.

WIPEINFO: Wipe Info

With all of Norton's wonderful data recovery utilities (for example, UNFORMAT and UNERASE), you may be wondering how to remove data from a disk. Norton's WIPEINFO utility overwrites all data in a file or disk so that it cannot be recovered; this is an important utility to use when working with confidential files. Use WIPEINFO with extreme caution, because even the most powerful Norton utility cannot recover data from a disk after you run WIPEINFO.

Utility Integration

Now that you've been briefly introduced to each of the Norton utilities, let's take a closer look at NORTON, the utility integration tool that provides a friendly interface to all the other utilities.

 Running NORTON, the Utility Integration Tool

1. Type the command **NORTON** at the DOS prompt (usually C> or C:\>).

2. Press Enter.

7

This starts the NORTON utility (Figure 1.1).

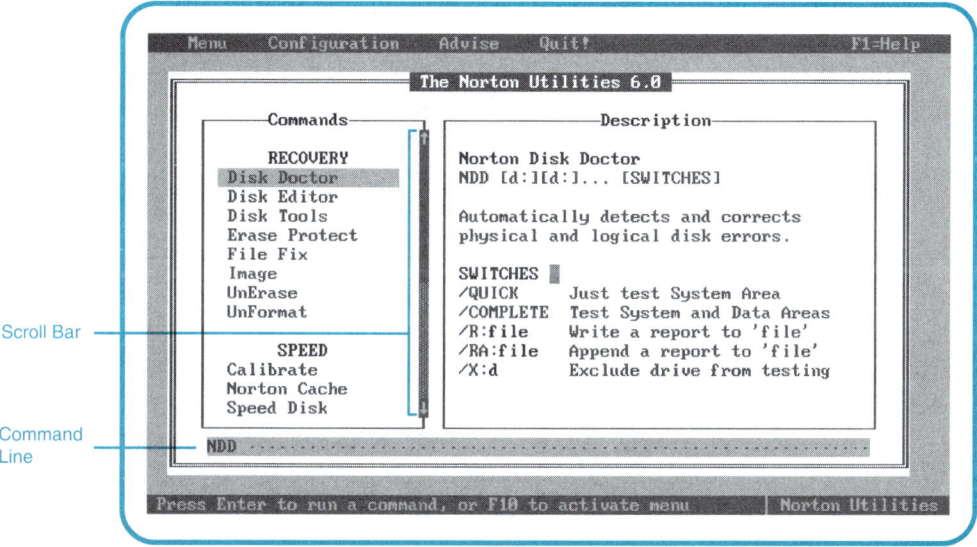

Figure 1.1   NORTON provides easy access to many utilities.

> **Tip:** If the message "Bad command or file name" is displayed after you type `NORTON` and press Enter, you may have incorrectly installed The Norton Utilities. The configuration portion of the Installation program can (and should) be used to place the Norton directory in your AUTOEXEC.BAT file's PATH statement (for example, `PATH=C:\NU`). This permits you to run any of the utilities from any directory/subdirectory. However, for this change to the AUTOEXEC.BAT file to take effect, you must reboot your PC after installation. For more information, see Appendix A, "Installation and Configuration."

The screen in Figure 1.1 is divided into three sections. The left side of Figure 1.1 shows a list of several of the Norton utilities split into categories like Recovery and Speed. Press the down arrow key or click with the mouse to highlight the Disk Doctor entry. The right side of the screen now provides a description of the Norton Disk Doctor (NDD) utility, including syntax and usage. The bottom line of Figure 1.1 contains the letters NDD and a blinking cursor. Press the down arrow key a few times or click on other utility names and notice three things:

1. Each time you press the down arrow key, the next utility name down the list on the left side of the screen is highlighted.
2. A description of the newly highlighted utility on the left side of the screen is shown on the right side of the screen.
3. The bottom line of the screen changes to show the program name of the highlighted utility.

> **Tip:** Notice that the Commands list in Figure 1.1 has a *scroll bar* along the right side. Use the mouse to click on the up and down arrows at the ends of this and any other scroll bar in The Norton Utilities to move through the list.

For example, the screen in Figure 1.2 shows what is displayed when you highlight `System Info`. (NOTE: The list of utilities on the left side of the screen in Figure 1.1 scrolls up/down when you reach the bottom/top of the exposed portion of the list. The System Information (SYSINFO) utility appears at the very end of the tools list.) Note that when you select System Info from the NORTON screen, the command for starting it, SYSINFO, appears in the command line. You can add switches to this command line that will be active when you start the highlighted program.

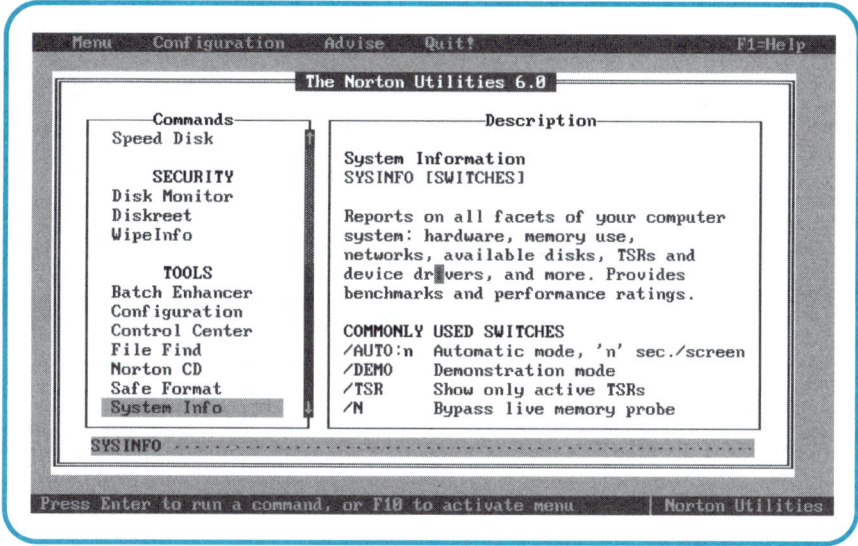

Figure 1.2   You can select SYSINFO from the NORTON screen.

9

You can run any of the other utilities within NORTON by selecting it, entering any necessary parameters, then pressing Enter. Or, you can double-click on the utility name in the list to run the utility. Select System Info (as shown in Figure 1.2) and press Enter to run SYSINFO and display the System Summary screen in Figure 1.3.

We will examine SYSINFO specifics in Chapter 2, so for now, press Escape twice to return to the screen in Figure 1.2. We did not specify any parameters when we ran SYSINFO. As you can see in Figure 1.2, the syntax for SYSINFO is

SYSINFO [*switches*]

where the *switches* are either /AUTO:n, /DEMO, /TSR, or /N as described below in the same panel. Now let's run SYSINFO with a /DEMO parameter by selecting System Info in the NORTON screen (Figure 1.2) and typing /DEMO on the command line as shown in Figure 1.4.

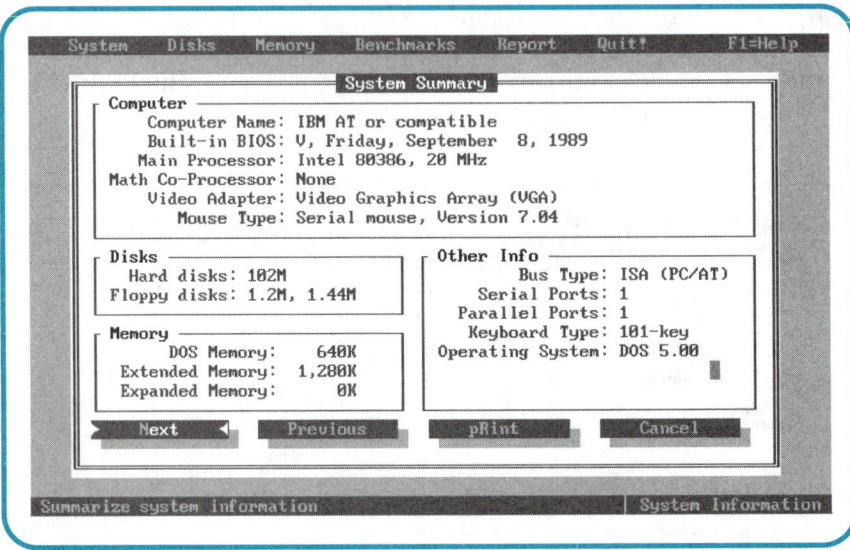

Figure 1.3 **The System Summary screen is the first SYSINFO screen displayed.**

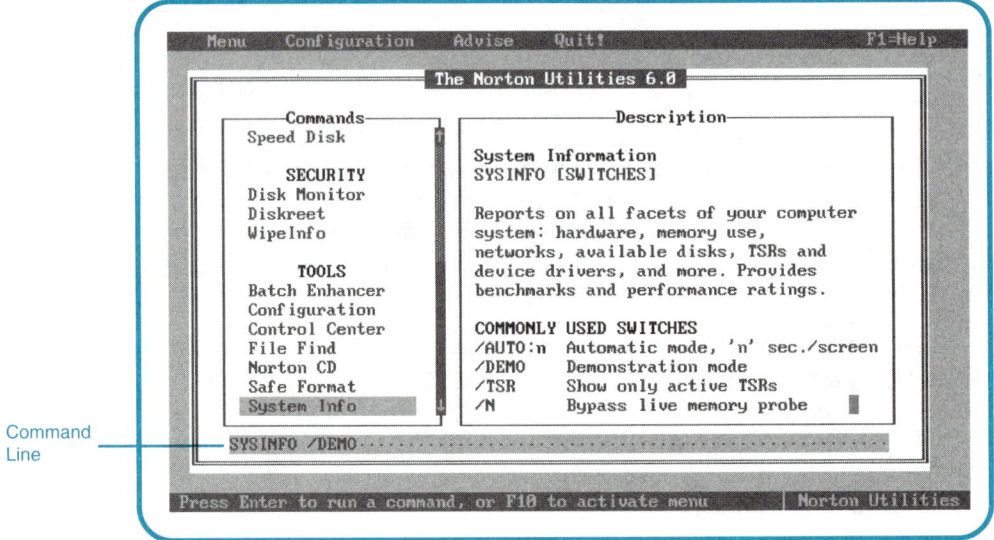

Figure 1.4 **NORTON provides a command line to enter parameters.**

Notice that the /DEMO parameter appears at the bottom of the SYSINFO screen as you type it in. The bottom line of the NORTON screen is a pseudo-DOS command line. It will display and allow you to edit the highlighted utility's name and parameters. Now you can press Enter to run SYSINFO with the /DEMO parameter. The /DEMO parameter tells SYSINFO to run in a demonstration mode where each screen is displayed for approximately 10 seconds. Press Esc to return to the NORTON utility.

Using Menus and Dialog Boxes

Most of the Norton utilities include pull-down menus that offer access to additional utility features and settings. Press F10 when the NORTON screen in Figure 1.1 is displayed to pull down the NORTON Menu menu (Figure 1.5). (NOTE: If your PC is configured with a mouse, you can pull down a menu by positioning the mouse cursor over the menu name [for example, Menu] and clicking.)

11

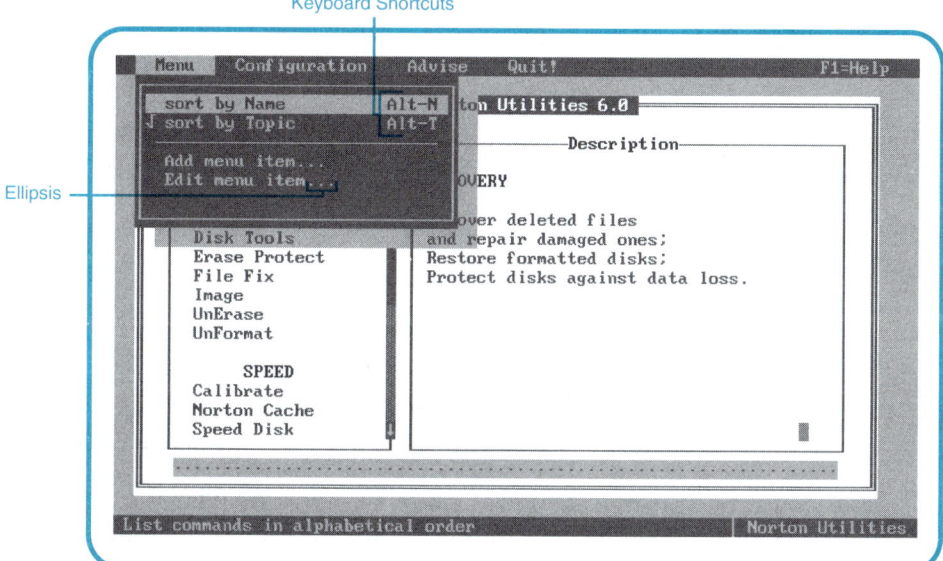

Figure 1.5   The Menu menu is one of three pull-down menus available to customize the program.

Some menu commands include keyboard shortcuts that you can use to select the command without using the menu. The ellipsis (. . .) following other command names means that selecting the command displays a dialog box where you specify additional choices.

With the Menu menu displayed, press the right arrow key or click on Configuration with the mouse to pull down the Configuration menu. The first option, Video and mouse..., is highlighted. Press Enter or click on the Video and mouse... option to get Figure 1.6.

12

Radio Button

Check Box

Command Button

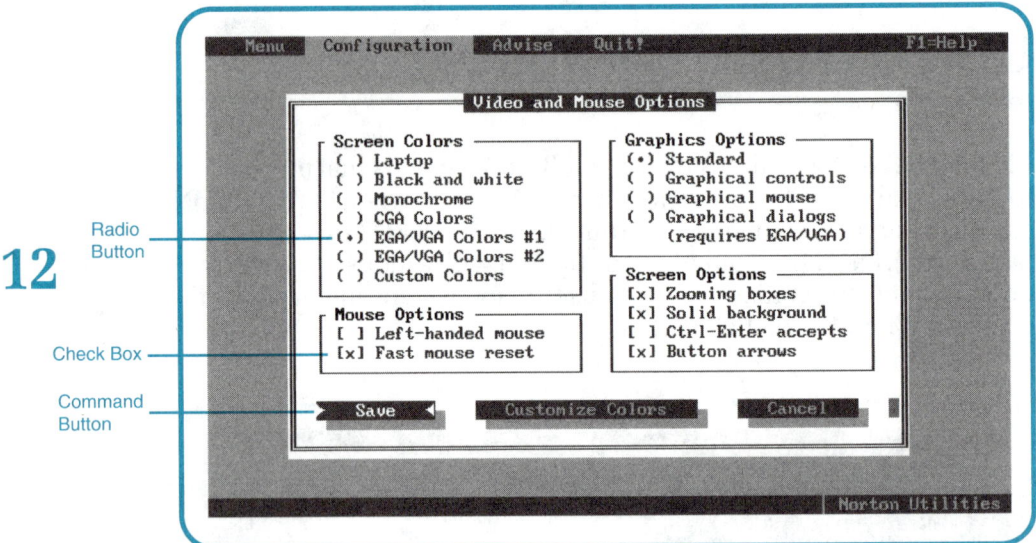

Figure 1.6   Use the Video and Mouse Options dialog box to set mouse and display options.

 Tip: You can also press the highlighted (and capitalized) letter in a command choice to select it.

The dialog box shown in Figure 1.6 lets you set up The Norton Utilities for your PC's video and mouse configuration. It contains many of the components that appear in a typical dialog box.

> **Note:** Your Norton screens (especially the ones that contain dialog boxes) may look different from the ones in this book, depending on the Graphics Option you select when you configure The Norton Utilities during installation or with NUCONFIG. See Appendix A for more information.

The Norton dialog boxes have check boxes, radio buttons, text boxes, and command buttons. Following are highlights of how to move among and select dialog box options.

▶ Select an option by pressing the highlighted letter in its name or by clicking with the mouse.

▶ Or, use Tab or the arrow keys to move the cursor among the options, then perform a second step to select the option:

When the cursor is in a check box, press Enter to select that option.

Move to a text box, and type your entry.

Move to a command button, and press Enter to perform the command.

▶ You can select only one option button at a time.

▶ Select the `Cancel` command button to close a dialog box without invoking its choices.

13

> **Note:** Much of this book will give the keystroke method of selecting commands. If you have a mouse, you may find it easier to continue pointing, then clicking or double-clicking to make selections.

The Advise Menu

The NORTON utility also includes an Advise menu, which offers easy-to-read suggestions for solving common hard and floppy disk problems, DOS and CHKDSK error messages, and error messages from the

application programs on your system. For example, if you pull down the
Advise menu and select Application error messages, the screen shown
in Figure 1.7 appears. The screen lists the program type and the error
messages. Highlight the error message you're getting, then select the
Expand command button for an explanation of what might be wrong and
a suggested course of action (using one of the Norton utilities, if
appropriate). You can select one of the command buttons that appear
at the bottom of the screen to run the suggested utility.

14

Application

Error
Message

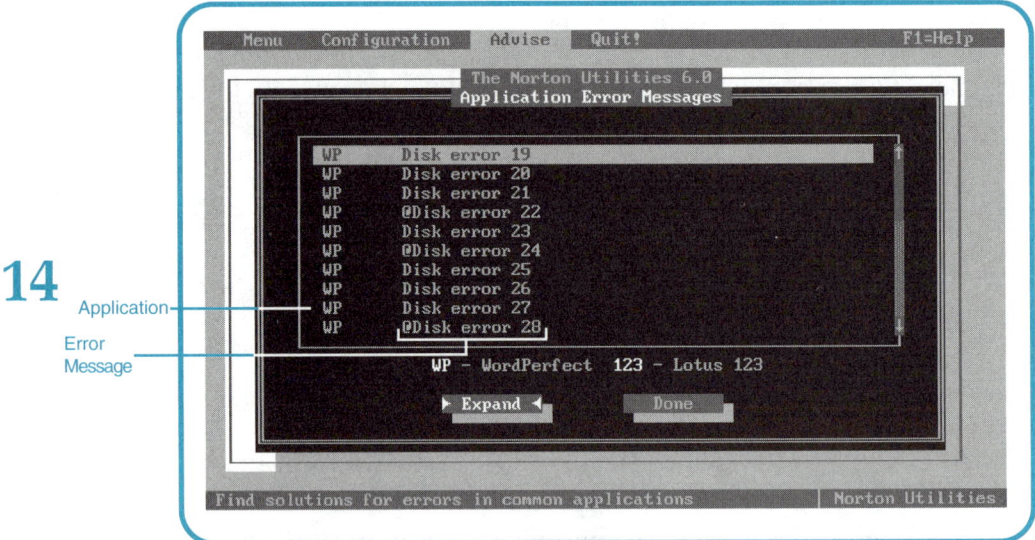

Figure 1.7   The Advise screen for application error messages.

The last choice on the Advise menu, Search..., enables you to
check for error messages if you enter part of the message or key words
from the message. Choosing Search displays the dialog box shown in
Figure 1.8. The *cursor* (a blinking underline or box) appears in a *text
box*, where you can type the full or partial error message. After you
do so, press Tab and then Space Bar (or click with the mouse) to
select the following check box if you would like to search for
application error messages, as well. Then select the Start Search
command button to perform the search. When Search finds the
message, it will present you with information about the problem and
probable solution.

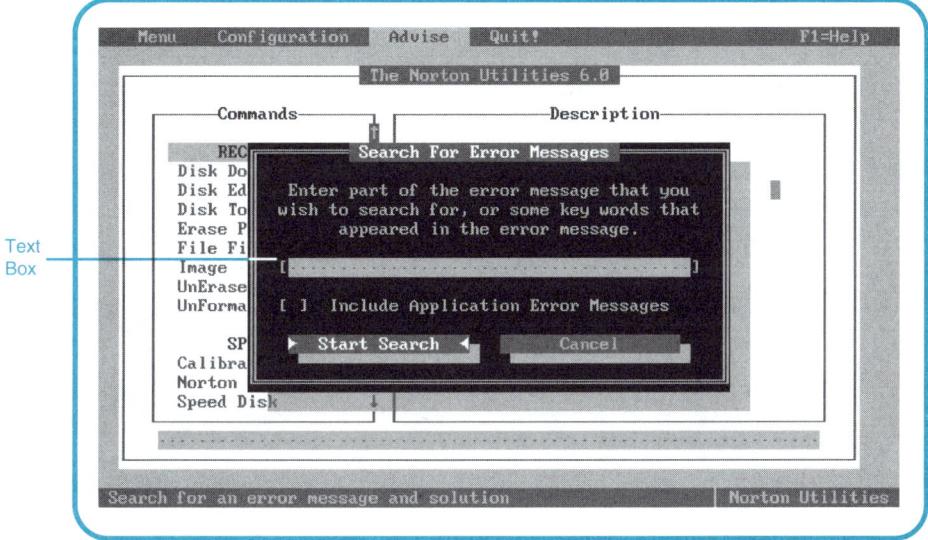

Text
Box

Figure 1.8   The Search For Error Messages dialog box.

15

Utility Help

The Norton Utilities offer two different types of on-screen help: help within a utility and utility syntax help.

Help Within a Utility

The Help screen in Figure 1.9 is displayed if you press F1 while the NORTON screen is displayed (Figure 1.1).

The screen in Figure 1.9 describes many of the NORTON features we already discussed. Use the up or down arrow keys to scroll through the Help screen and learn more about the NORTON utility. Click on any highlighted topic for more information about it. Most of the Norton utilities display a help screen when you press F1. These help screens provide information about how to use the utility, special keys, and other important points. If you require help within a utility and you don't feel like reaching for the documentation, press F1, and you might find what you need!

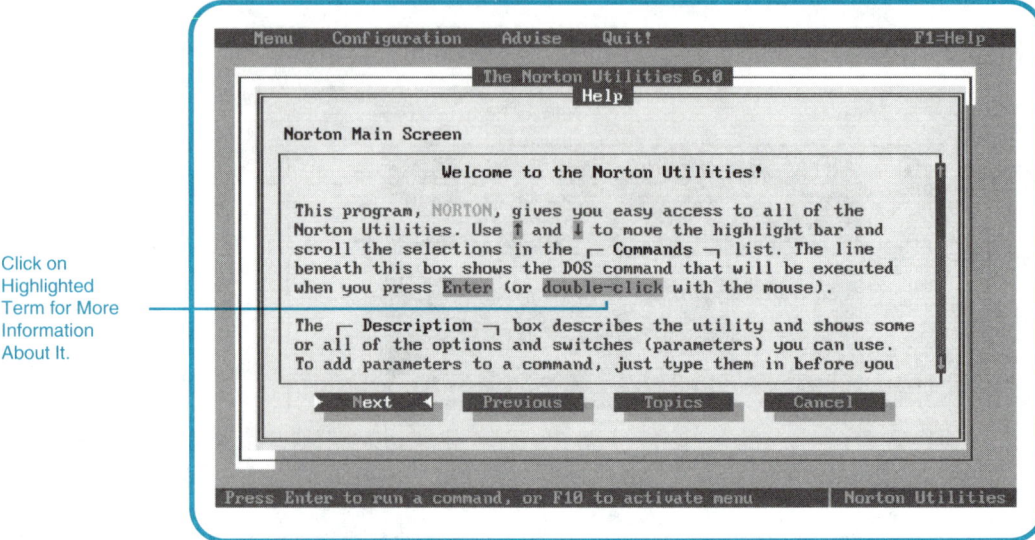

Click on
Highlighted
Term for More
Information
About It.

16

Figure 1.9 NORTON's Help screens provide general informa-
tion about the program, as well as specific help for each utility.

Utility Syntax Help

It's convenient to have help within a utility via the F1 key. But what if
you can't remember a utility's syntax and you don't want to hunt
through the documentation? The answer is simple: In the command
line of the NORTON screen, type in the utility name with a question
mark switch and press Enter. For example, if you want to see SYSINFO's
syntax, type `SYSINFO /?`, and press Enter (Figure 1.10).

The help information in Figure 1.10 might look familiar to you.
Similar information was displayed in the NORTON utility for
SYSINFO (see Figure 1.2). The /? help feature is handy when you
want to quickly see a utility's syntax without running NORTON or
thumbing through documentation.

```
C:\NU>sysinfo /?
System Information, Gemini p02, Copyright 1991 by Symantec Corporation

Display system configuration information, and performance statisitics.

SYSINFO [/AUTO:n] [/N] [/SOUND]
SYSINFO /DEMO
SYSINFO /TSR
SYSINFO [drive:] /SUMMARY
SYSINFO [drive:] /DI

  /AUTO:n    Automatically cycle through all information screens
             (delay n seconds between screens).
  /N         Suppress Memory Scan.
  /SOUND     Beep between CPU tests.
  /DEMO      Cycle through benchmark tests only.
  /TSR       Print list of TSR programs.
  drive      Drive on which information is desired.
  /SUMMARY   Print SysInfo Summary screen.
  /DI        Print information on current or specified drive.

C:\NU>
```

Figure 1.10   When you type /? after a command, NORTON shows you the proper syntax for the command.

17

Setting Up The Norton Utilities to Run with Windows

If you choose, you can run The Norton Utilities from Microsoft Windows version 3.0. Norton's Installation program copies the icon files (with .ICO extensions) for various utilities to the same directory as the rest of Norton's program files. The following Quick Steps describe how to use Windows' Program Manager to set up The Norton Utilities to run with Windows.

 Creating a Program Icon for The Norton Utilities

1. At the Program Manager, choose **File** by clicking or pressing Alt-F.

    The File menu appears.

18

2. Choose **New** by clicking or pressing Enter.

The New Program Object dialog box appears.

3. Press **G** or click on **Program Group**. Press Enter, or click **OK**.

The Program Group Properties dialog box appears.

4. Type **Norton** or another short name in the Description: text box, and select **OK**.

Windows displays a new window called title Norton, as shown in Figure 1.11. Next, you'll need to place the utilities in the window, one by one.

5. Choose **File** again by clicking or pressing Alt-F.

The File menu appears.

6. Choose **New** by clicking or pressing Enter.

The New Program Object dialog box appears.

7. Press **I** or click on **Program Item**. Press Enter, or click **OK**.

The Program Item Properties dialog box appears.

8. Type a Description: for the utility you're installing (for example, type **Norton** for the main Norton utility) in the text box and press Tab.

The cursor moves to the Command line: text box.

9. Type the drive and directory where your Norton program files are, followed by the file name of the PIF file for the utility you're setting up. For example, type **C:\NU\NORTON.EXE**.

10. Press Alt-I or click the **Change Icon...** button.

The Select Icon dialog box appears, with the default icon name in the File Name: text box.

11. Type the drive and directory where your program files for The Norton Utilities are, followed by the name of the .ICO file for the utility you're setting up. For

The Select Icon dialog box closes.

example, type
`C:\NU\NORTON.ICO`. Press
Enter.

12. Press Enter, or click **OK**.

The Program Item
Properties dialog box
closes. An icon for the
utility you specified
appears in the Norton
window. Figure 1.12 shows
the Norton Utilities icon
installed in the Norton
Window.

13. Repeat Steps 5 through 12
for each utility you would
like to install in the Norton
window.

□

19

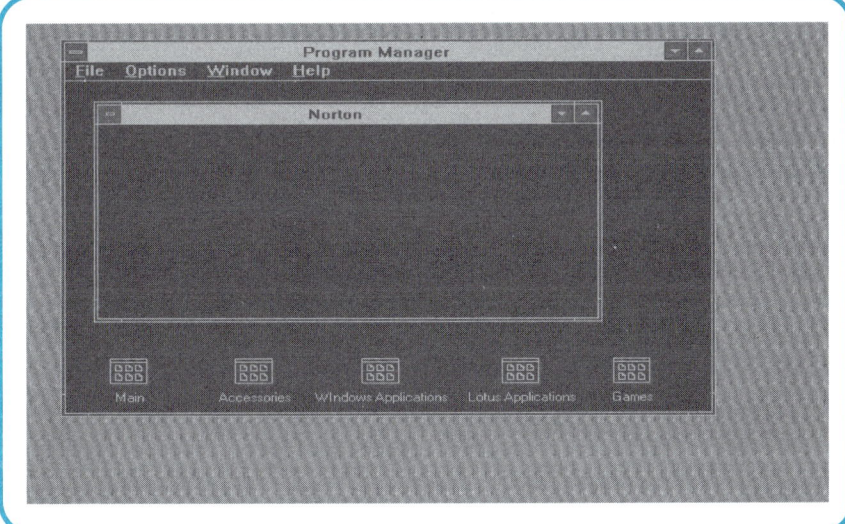

Figure 1.11   The new Norton window.

To run a utility from the Norton window, simply double-click
on its icon, or highlight the icon name and press Enter.

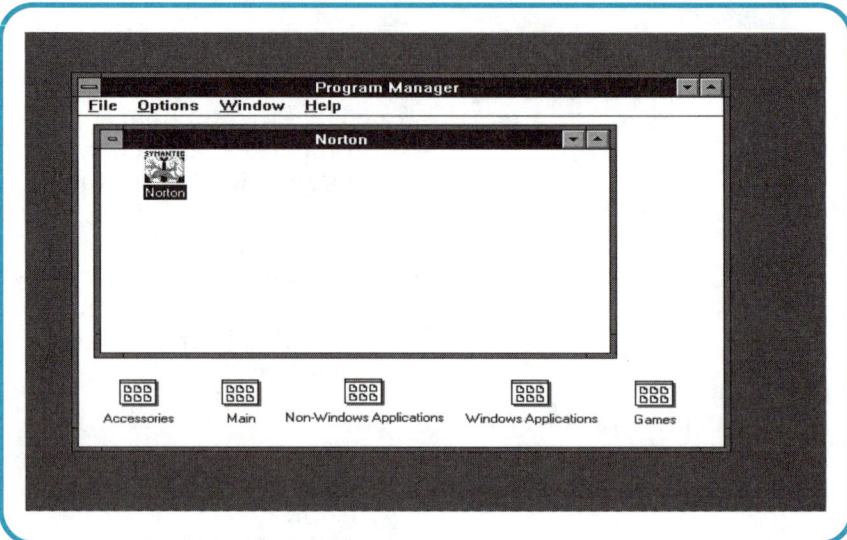

Figure 1.12   The Norton Utilities icon.

20

What You Have Learned

In this chapter you learned some fundamentals of The Norton Utilities. You also learned:

► If your computer runs DOS, it will also run The Norton Utilities.

► It is fairly easy to install The Norton Utilities to either a floppy or hard disk-based PC. Norton's Installation program is very user friendly.

► The NORTON utility is a handy tool that provides information about (and easy access to) all the other utilities.

► The Norton Utilities offer two different types of on-screen help: help within a utility (using F1) and utility syntax help (using the ? parameter).

► You can set up the utilities to run from Windows 3.X.

DOS and Utility Basics

In This Chapter

▶ *Understanding DOS and PC hardware*
▶ *Obtaining configuration data with SYSINFO*
▶ *Configuring PC attributes with NCC*

This chapter explains some DOS and PC hardware fundamentals. You will need to understand these concepts before you can appreciate all the information The Norton Utilities can provide.

This chapter also introduces you to two special utilities, SYSINFO and NCC, which provide operations that are either difficult or impossible to perform via DOS. Most of the Norton utilities can be classified as either file utilities or disk utilities, but SYSINFO and NCC do not fall into either of these categories.

What Is DOS?

Your PC's hardware does not directly understand the commands you type at your keyboard. When you enter the command `DIR C:*.*`, an interface translates the command so your PC's hardware can understand it. The primary interface between you and your hardware is the Disk Operating System, or DOS, for short.

Regardless of whether your PC is floppy or hard disk-based, it relies on DOS to perform fundamental operations. DOS is simply a collection of special tools that allows you to copy, delete, and rename files, format disks, view directories, and the like. Although DOS provides a multitude of useful commands, many of them are cryptic and cumbersome to use. The Norton Utilities is less cryptic and cumbersome, and that is one of the reasons The Norton Utilities is so popular.

Several different versions of DOS have been distributed since the original DOS for the IBM PC. To see which version of DOS your PC is running, type **VER** at the DOS prompt and press Enter. The VER command is another of DOS' many built-in tools. When I run DOS' VER command, it indicates my PC is running MS-DOS Version 3.30. The "MS" in MS-DOS stands for Microsoft, the company that developed and distributes the DOS package I use.

DOS 4.x allows very large hard disk partitions. (Hard disk partitions are discussed later in this chapter in the PC Disks section.) DOS 4.x also offers a built-in DOS "shell," which substitutes a graphic command interface for the traditional DOS command line (for example, `c:\>`). This version of The Norton Utilities also supports the latest version of DOS 5.0. Particularly, version 6.0 supports DOS 5.0's task-switching, deletion-tracking, format recovery, and LOADHIGH (loads and runs programs in upper memory) features. When you installed The Norton Utilities on your system, you also had the option of adding help about the utilities to the DOS 5.0 help information. Like DOS 4.x, DOS 5.0 offers a shell to create a more friendly and useful interface for users.

Chapter 8 introduces a new component of The Norton Utilities program, NDOS. NDOS is compatible with DOS versions 2.1 and later and serves as a replacement for the COMMAND.COM file. It enables you to work at the command line, using numerous switches to enhance command flexibility. Chapters 9, 10, and 11 of this book cover a very popular DOS shell, the Norton Commander. I feel that the Commander is a much more powerful shell than the one available with DOS, and I think you will agree after reading these chapters and testing the Commander's abilities.

DOS relies on many different components of your PC to do its job. Let's take a look at what I feel is the most important of these components, the microprocessor.

Microprocessors

The microprocessor is the "brains" of your PC and is often referred to as a Central Processing Unit, or CPU, because it controls virtually all processing within the computer.

As is true with DOS, several different models of microprocessors have been used in PCs since the IBM PC was introduced. The original IBM PC featured the Intel 8088, an 8-bit microprocessor. The 8088 did a pretty good job of managing most processing needs, but it soon became apparent that additional horsepower would be required to handle more sophisticated software. The next generation of PCs, the IBM PC XTs and compatibles, also used the Intel 8088 microprocessor and featured hard disks.

As software packages became more elegant and complex, the 8088 had to give way to the faster, more powerful 80286 microprocessor. The 80286 is the microprocessor found in IBM PC ATs and compatibles. Besides offering faster throughput than 8088s, the 80286 family of microprocessors was the first to allow *multitasking* on PCs. Multitasking means the computer can run two or more programs, or tasks, concurrently. This multitasking feature allows products like Microsoft Windows and Quarterdeck's DESQview to run more than one application at a time.

But even the fastest 80286s are not quick enough to handle the more processor-intensive programs like graphics design and three-dimensional modeling applications. These power-hungry programs require the 80386, a 32-bit microprocessor. The 80386 can process larger pieces of data than any of its predecessors and offers more sophisticated multitasking capabilities than the 80286.

23

Note: A microprocessor's speed is expressed in megahertz, or MHz, for short. The original IBM PC's microprocessor ran at 4.77 MHz. Today you can purchase an 80386-based PC running at 16, 20, 25, or even 33 MHz.

The 80386's cousin, the 80386SX, is a cross between the 80286 and 80386 CPUs. The 80386SX has many of the same features as the 80386. The primary difference between the two is in the amount of data they can exchange with external devices. If you think of this data exchange as a highway, you could say the 80386 offers a four-lane expressway and the 80386SX is restricted to a two-lane country road, like the 80286. In more technical terms, the 80386 uses a 32-bit data bus whereas the 80386SX and 80286 microprocessors use a 16-bit data bus.

It seems that every day brings a newer, faster microprocessor. Several PC manufacturers are now distributing 80486-based systems, which blow the socks off the fastest 80386 PCs.

What about the older 80286/8088 computers? Are they obsolete and totally useless in today's computer marketplace? Absolutely not! The vast majority of PC users do not need the horsepower of an 80486, or even an 80386. Further, new applications that run on all types of IBM compatible PCs, regardless of the CPU, are being written every day.

With this microprocessor knowledge under your belt, let's now take a look at the types of memory your PC uses to store and manipulate data.

24

PC Memory

The smallest piece of data a computer can store is called a **bi**nary digit, or bit. A binary digit is either a one or a zero; no other values are allowed. A bit is very similar to a light switch, which also has two possible states: on or off. When a bit holds a value of one, we say that the bit is *on*. Alternatively, a bit that is *off* holds a value of zero.

The amount of memory in your PC is expressed in *bytes*; 1 byte is made up of 8 bits. Large amounts of memory are expressed in kilobytes (or K, for short). One kilobyte of memory equals 1,024 bytes. For example, if your PC has 640K of memory, it can store up to $640 \times 1,024$ (655,360) bytes.

There are actually two different types of memory in your PC: RAM and ROM.

RAM Versus ROM

RAM is short for Random-Access Memory, which means your PC can access different RAM locations without having to traverse every location in between. Actually, your PC can access both RAM and ROM in a random manner, so this is not what differentiates the two.

ROM is an acronym for Read-Only Memory. Your PC can read from ROM memory, but it cannot write to ROM. The primary difference between RAM and ROM is that data can be read from and/or written to RAM; the information held in ROM is fixed and cannot be overwritten. In addition, RAM is sometimes referred to as volatile memory. That is, the information stored in RAM is lost when you turn your PC off. In contrast, the contents of ROM are not lost or changed when you turn off your computer. Most ROM chips contain important programs that control fundamental device operations on your PC (for example, disk drive reads/writes).

When someone says a PC has 640K of memory, they are usually referring to the amount of RAM. Your PC uses RAM to hold your applications programs and their data while the programs are active. Although microprocessors can address more than 1 megabyte of memory (1 megabyte [Mb] equals 1,048,576 bytes) of memory, MS-DOS provides access to a total of only 640K of RAM. That is why it is so common to find PCs with a total of 640K of RAM.

25

If DOS can access only 640K, why do so many PCs come with more than 1 Mb of RAM? This additional memory is generally referred to as either expanded or enhanced memory. Several different applications that allow you to take advantage of this additional memory are available today. For instance, Quarterdeck's DESQview program allows you to run several applications simultaneously (multitasking) using expanded or extended memory.

TSRs

TSR is an acronym for Terminate-and-Stay-Resident. Once a TSR program has been loaded, it becomes almost invisible until you press a special key to use it. This special key or key combination is also called a *hot key*.

TSR programs are executed from the DOS command line like any other program. Once you load a TSR program, it requires a portion of DOS's 640K of accessible RAM to remain resident. Although each TSR program may take up only a few kilobytes of RAM, the 640K pool may be significantly reduced when several TSR programs are loaded. That is when you will start running into problems executing non-TSR programs that require almost all of DOS' 640K of memory.

Fortunately, there are several commercially available utilities that allow you to place your TSR programs in expanded or extended memory rather than DOS' 640K of RAM. Some TSR programs offer this option as a standard feature so you do not need to purchase a special utility to free up DOS' RAM space.

Now let's take a look at another PC storage medium, disks.

PC Disks

Several brands and models of disk drives are on the market. Table 2.1 shows storage information about the four most popular floppy disk types.

Table 2.1   Floppy Disk Specifications

Disk Size	Type	Storage Capacity
5¹/₄"	Double-sided, double-density	360K
5¹/₄"	Double-sided, high-density	1.2 Mb
3¹/₂"	Double-sided, double-density	720K
3¹/₂"	Double-sided, high-density	1.4 Mb

Caution: You can use the full capacity of both double- and high-density diskettes in a high-density disk drive, but *do not format double-density diskettes in a high-density drive.* This could cause corrupted or unreadable data on your diskettes.

In the early days of PCs, data storage was limited to slow, low-density floppy disks. The door was opened for hard disk-based PCs when DOS 2.0 and the IBM PC XT architecture were introduced. The original PC hard disks stored from 5 to 30 Mb of data. Today's hard disks are much faster than those earlier models and offer up to several hundred megabytes of storage in one unit.

If you are using DOS 2.x or 3.x, you are limited to a maximum hard disk partition size of 32 Mb. When you partition a hard disk via DOS' FDISK command, you are telling DOS how to configure the disk as one or more logical drives. Although you have only one physical hard disk in your PC, you can have DOS treat it as several logical disk drives (for example, C:, D:, and E:). For example, if you have a 100-Mb hard disk, you could use FDISK to partition it as follows:

Logical Drive	Size (in megabytes)
C:	32
D:	32
E:	32
F:	4

Versions 4.0 and 5.0 of DOS allow unlimited logical disk partition sizes. With DOS 4.0 and 5.0, the 100-Mb disk above can be set up via FDISK as one 100-Mb partition.

Disks and disk formats are fairly complex subjects, and we have only scratched the surface of the subject so far. More advanced disk concepts, as well as the disk-based Norton utilities, are covered in Chapters 5, 6, and 7.

27

SYSINFO: System Information

We briefly discussed SYSINFO in Chapter 1, and you saw how it can be invoked from the NORTON utility. Now let's use our newly found DOS and hardware knowledge to see exactly what SYSINFO reports. You can also invoke SYSINFO directly from the DOS prompt as shown in the following Quick Steps.

 Using SYSINFO to Obtain System Information

1. At the DOS prompt, type the command **SYSINFO** and press Enter.

   The System Summary screen is displayed (Figure 2.1).

2. Press Enter.

   The Video Summary screen is displayed.

3. Press Enter.

   The Hardware Interrupts screen is displayed.

4. Keep pressing Enter to browse through the rest of SYSINFO's screens. When you want to leave SYSINFO, press Esc twice or select the Quit menu.

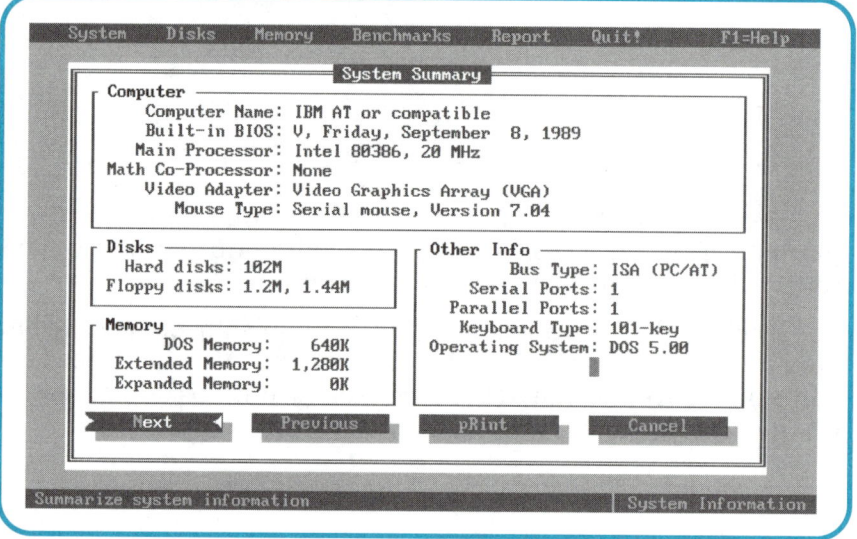

Figure 2.1   The System Summary screen contains general system information.

SYSINFO provides five types of information: System, Disks, Memory, Benchmarks, and Report. If you keep pressing Enter to view the next screen, all the System menu screens are displayed first, followed by all the Disks menu screens, and so on. These five information types also correspond to pull-down menus at the top of each screen. If you don't want to display all the SYSINFO screens, you can quickly jump from one SYSINFO screen to any other one by using the pull-down menus.

The System Menu

The System menu consists of six selections: System summary, Video Summary, Hardware interrupts, Software interrupts, Network information, and CMOS status.

System Summary

The System Summary screen (Figure 2.1) provides details about your computer system, including disk/memory size and other interesting facts. The screen is split into four areas: Computer, Disks, Memory, and Other Info. Most of the information displayed is self-explanatory, but I would like to note a couple of important items.

The second line in the Computer section, Built-in BIOS:, indicates the date of my PC's Basic Input/Output System (BIOS) ROM. The BIOS provides an interface to your PC's hardware for input/output activities. The BIOS date could be important if you are having problems running certain programs on your PC. Check with your PC dealer to determine if your BIOS is out-of-date and needs to be upgraded.

The System Summary screen is also an excellent reference for quickly determining a PC's configuration. For example, in Figure 2.1, you can see that my PC is an 80386-based model with a 102-Mb hard disk and 1.2- and 1.44-Mb floppy disk drives. Further, I have a Video Graphics Array (VGA) monitor, a mouse, and a 101-key keyboard.

29

Video Summary

The Video Summary screen (Figure 2.2) shows information about your PC's video configuration. This information includes details about your PC's display adapter, character specifics, and video memory.

Hardware Interrupts and Software Interrupts

The next two SYSINFO screens provide information about hardware and software interrupts. An interrupt causes the microprocessor to stop what it is currently doing and perform some special task. The interrupt information provided on these screens is useful for programmers writing sophisticated applications.

Network Information

The Network Information screen is accessible only if your PC is connected to a Novell network. This screen reports miscellaneous network and network-user details.

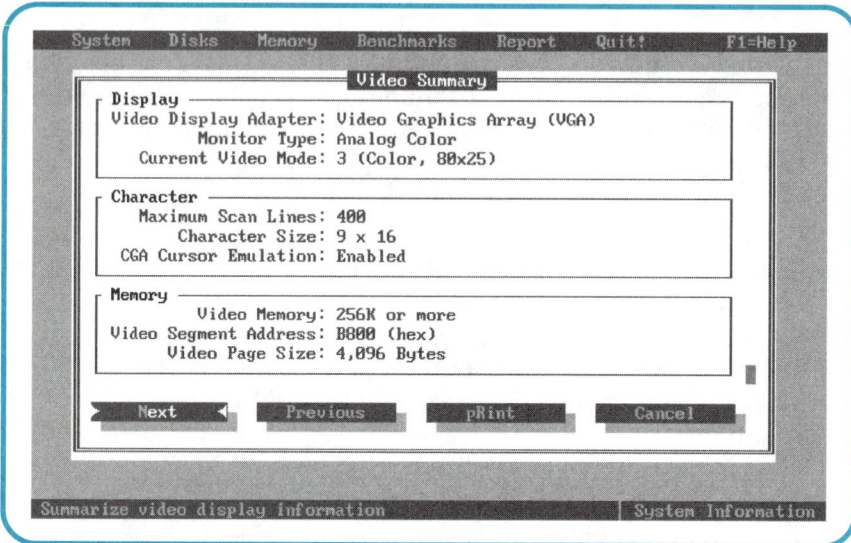

Display
Video Display Adapter: Video Graphics Array (VGA)
Monitor Type: Analog Color
Current Video Mode: 3 (Color, 80x25)

Character
Maximum Scan Lines: 400
Character Size: 9 x 16
CGA Cursor Emulation: Enabled

Memory
Video Memory: 256K or more
Video Segment Address: B800 (hex)
Video Page Size: 4,096 Bytes

30

Figure 2.2 *The Video Summary screen reports your PC's video configuration.*

CMOS Status

The last SYSINFO screen in the System category, the CMOS Values screen, provides specifics about your PC's memory and hard/floppy disk drives and appears when you select CMOS Status.

CMOS is an abbreviation for Complementary Metal-Oxide Semiconductor. CMOS RAM chips require less power than non-CMOS RAM chips, so that the small battery within your PC is enough to preserve their contents even after the computer is turned off. Your PC's hardware configuration information is stored in CMOS memory.

The CMOS Values screen shows the contents of this memory in a readable form. If any invalid or incorrect results are shown in the CMOS Status portion of the CMOS Values screen, you should consult your PC owner's manual and/or run the SETUP utility that accompanied your PC. (NOTE: SETUP is not a Norton utility. It is a hardware configuration utility that should have been delivered with your PC. If you cannot find your SETUP utility, contact your PC dealer.)

The Disks Menu

For information about The SYSINFO Disks menu, refer to Chapter 6—
Maintaining Your Hard Disk Drive.

The Memory Menu

The Memory menu contains six selections: Memory usage summary,
Expanded memory (EMS), eXtended memory (XMS), memory Block
list, TSR programs, and Device drivers.

Memory Usage Summary

The screen in Figure 2.3 is displayed when you select the Memory Usage
Summary option from the Memory menu.

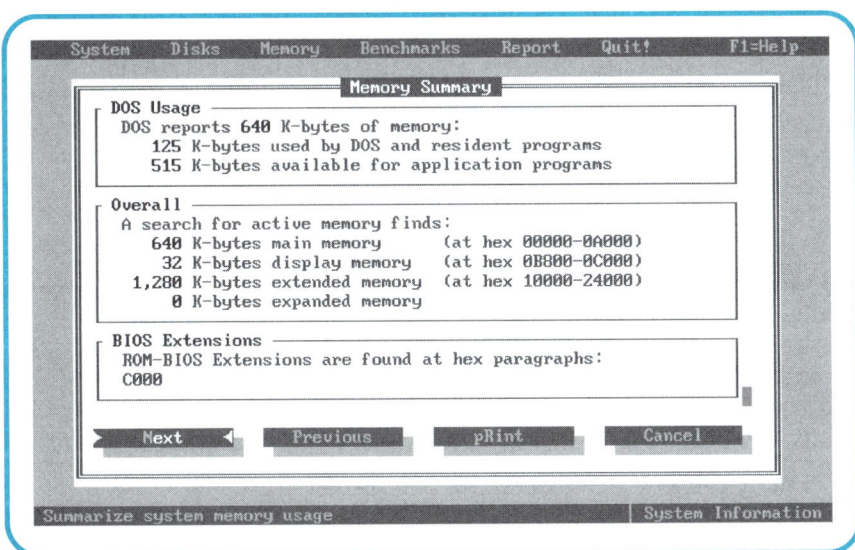

*Figure 2.3   The Memory Summary screen shows how your PC's
memory is being used.*

The Memory Summary screen in Figure 2.3 displays information about the various types of memory in your PC. This memory
information is reported in three categories: DOS Usage, Overall, and
BIOS Extensions.

The DOS Usage section in Figure 2.3 shows the amount of memory used by and accessible to DOS. The total amount of memory reported by DOS is then split into two areas: memory used by DOS and resident programs (for example, TSR programs) and memory available for application programs.

In the Overall section of Figure 2.3, SYSINFO reports the total size and location of four memory areas: main memory, display memory, extended memory, and expanded memory.

> The total amount of *main memory* is generally equal to the amount of DOS memory already reported. (One exception to this rule is if you are using an application switcher like SoftLogic Solutions' Software Carousel, which lets you keep several applications loaded in memory simultaneously.)
>
> The amount of *display memory* reported by SYSINFO depends on what type of video adapter (CGA, EGA, VGA, etc.) you are using.
>
> The amount of *expanded/extended memory* should reflect the total expanded or extended memory installed on your PC.

32

The BIOS Extensions section in Figure 2.3 indicates the memory locations of any ROM BIOS extensions (for example, special add-on boards).

Expanded and Extended Memory Summaries

The Expanded Memory summary screen is available only if you've added an expanded memory board to your system that lets it use memory beyond 640K. When available, select eXtended memory (EMS) from the Memory menu to display the summary of how much expanded memory is available, how it's allocated, and how it's managed.

Extended memory (available on 80286 and newer generation PC compatibles) is memory above 1 Mb used by DOS and the internal system. When you select the eXtended memory (XMS) choice from the Memory menu, the summary screen that appears tells you how much extended memory is available and gives you details about how it's allocated.

Memory Block List

The DOS Memory Blocks screen is displayed when you select the memory Block list option from the Memory menu. This screen displays information about DOS memory allocation, including the memory size, owner, and type (data, environment, or program).

TSR Programs

The TSR Programs screen shown in Figure 2.4 lists information about any active TSR applications.

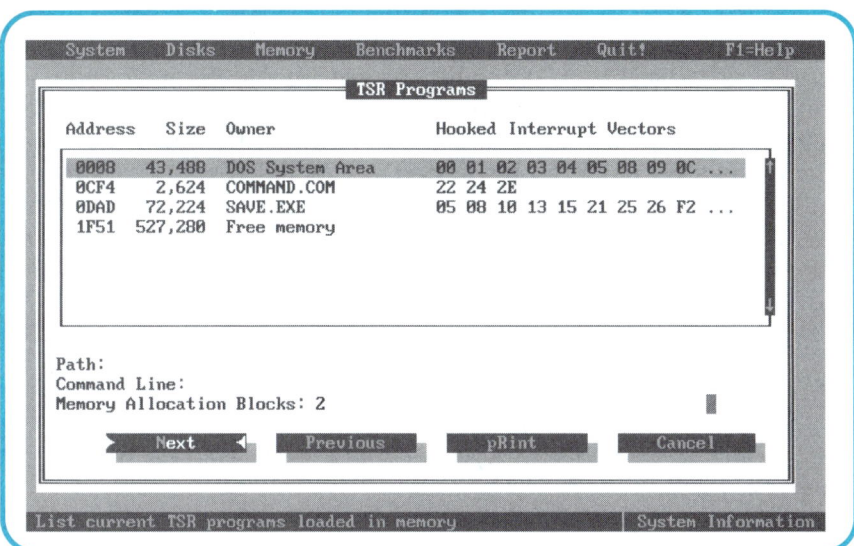

Figure 2.4   All active TSR programs are listed on the TSR Programs screen.

You can use the up and down arrow keys to scroll through the list of TSR programs and obtain additional information about each application. This additional information includes the TSR program's directory path (for example, C:\MYTSRS), the command line used to invoke it (for example, ATSR.EXE), and how much memory it occupies.

Device Drivers

Device drivers are applications that allow DOS to recognize and interface with special hardware devices such as a mouse. The Device Drivers screen lists memory locations, names, and descriptions for all device drivers currently loaded in your PC.

33

The Benchmarks Menu

Norton's System Information (SI) utility, SYSINFO's predecessor, was perhaps best known for its benchmark (PC performance comparison) reporting.

SYSINFO continues in the tradition of SI by providing very interesting benchmark data. If you are an old SI user, you will probably be surprised at the results that SYSINFO reports— SYSINFO's benchmark numbers are significantly *lower* than those previously reported by SI. SI tended to overstate benchmark results, and the SYSINFO comparisons are more realistic. The Benchmarks menu offers four comparison selections: CPU Speed, Hard Disk Speed, Overall Performance Index, and Network Performance Speed.

CPU Speed

34

The CPU Speed screen (Figure 2.5) shows the CPU benchmark results of the PC being tested, along with the results of three other computers: a Compaq 386/33 MHz, an IBM AT 286/8 MHz, and an IBM PC XT 88/4.77 MHz.

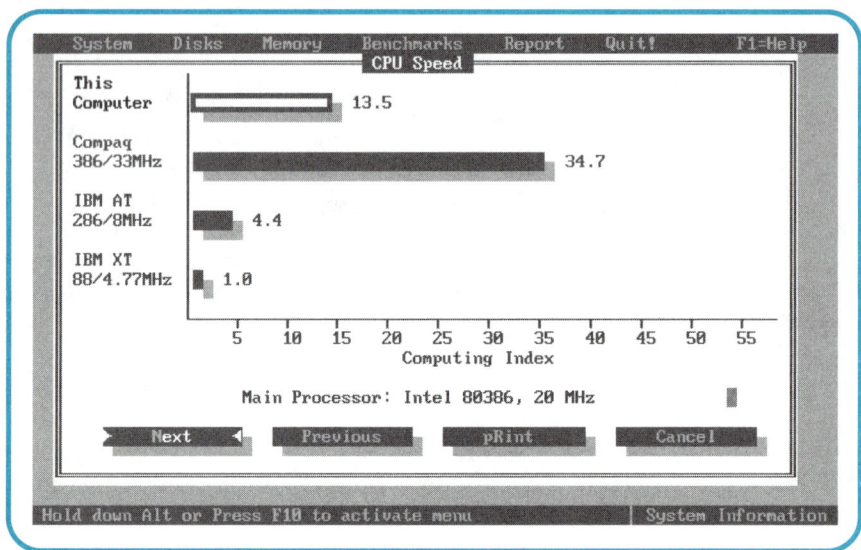

Figure 2.5   Microprocessor benchmark results are reported on the CPU Speed screen.

The CPU speed information shown in Figure 2.5 is fairly easy to interpret. The IBM PC XT 88/4.77 MHz computer listed is an IBM PC XT with an 8088 microprocessor running at 4.77 MHz. SYSINFO's benchmark calculations show a comparison of the PC being tested to the IBM PC XT. Figure 2.5 reports a 1.0 CPU rating for the IBM PC XT 88/4.77 MHz computer and a 4.4 rating for the IBM AT 286/8 MHz computer. So according to SYSINFO, the IBM AT's (286/8 MHz) microprocessor is 4.4 times as fast as the IBM PC XT's (88/4.77 MHz) microprocessor. Further, the Compaq's (386/33 MHz) microprocessor is 34.7 times as fast as the IBM PC XT's (88/4.77 MHz) microprocessor.

The CPU rating for This Computer, shown at the top of Figure 2.5, is for my PC. As you can see, the SYSINFO CPU speed rating for my PC is 13.5, which places it between the performance of an IBM AT 286/8 MHz and a Compaq 386/33 MHz. The bottom of Figure 2.5 also shows that my PC has an Intel 80386 microprocessor running at 20 MHz.

35

Disk Speed

The SYSINFO Disk Speed screen shown in Figure 2.6 compares the performance of my PC's hard disk with a Compaq 386 disk, an IBM AT disk, and an IBM PC XT disk.

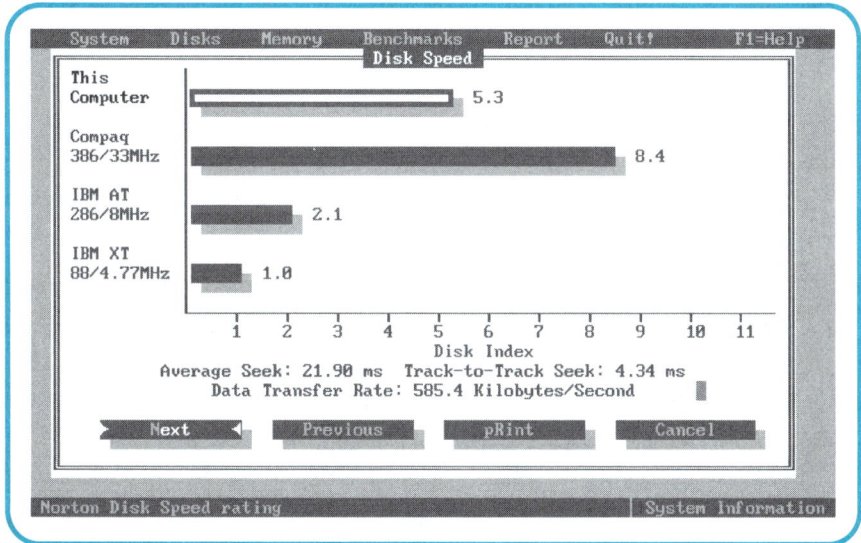

Figure 2.6   The Disk Speed screen shows the benchmark results for my PC's hard disk.

The speed rating for the IBM PC XT's disk in Figure 2.6 is 1.0. Because the IBM AT's disk speed rating is 2.1, we can say that the AT's disk is 2.1 times as fast as the XT's disk. Further, the Compaq's disk is 8.4 times as fast as the XT's disk. SYSINFO reports my PC's disk speed to be 5.3, which ranks it more than twice as fast as an IBM AT's disk. The Disk Speed screen in Figure 2.6 also reports other technical disk statistics, including average seek time, track-to-track seek time, and data transfer rate.

Overall Performance Index

The performance values reported in the CPU Speed and Disk Speed screens (Figures 2.5 and 2.6) are averaged and presented in the Overall Performance Index screen (Figure 2.7).

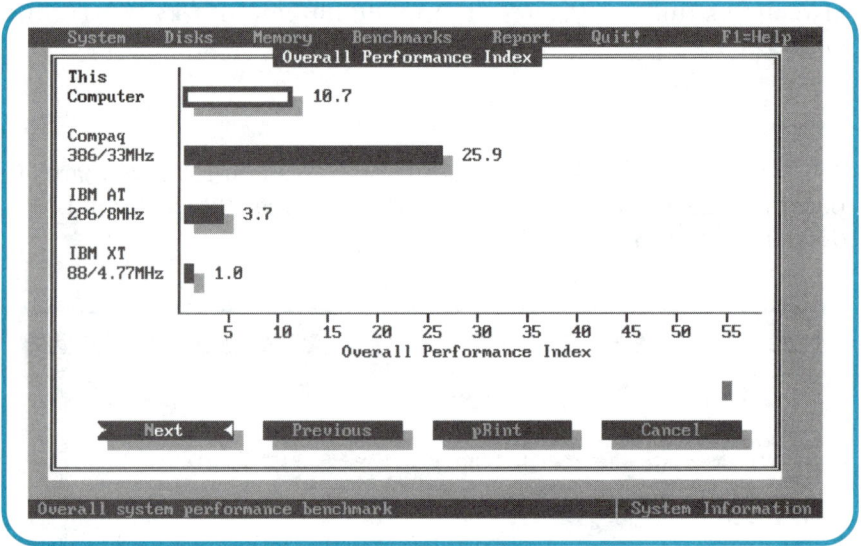

Figure 2.7   Results of the overall performance benchmark are reported on the Overall Performance Index screen.

Once again, in Figure 2.7, my PC's performance is compared against the performance of a Compaq 386, an IBM AT, and an IBM PC XT.

Network Performance Speed

The Network Performance Speed screen is the last screen displayed in the SYSINFO Benchmarks area. This screen reports network read/write throughput values if your PC is connected to a Novell network.

The Report Menu

The Report menu allows you to view a couple of special files and print a SYSINFO report.

View CONFIG.SYS

CONFIG.SYS is an important file, containing configuration information for special devices or device drivers used with your PC (for example, an extended memory driver or a mouse driver). The View CONFIG.SYS option in the Report menu lets you look at the contents of your CONFIG.SYS file.

37

View AUTOEXEC.BAT

AUTOEXEC.BAT is a special type of file called a *batch file*. (Batch files are thoroughly discussed in Chapter 4—Enhancing Your Batch Files.) AUTOEXEC.BAT contains the set of commands that are executed every time you turn on or reboot your PC. The View AUTOEXEC.BAT option in the Report menu lets you look at the contents of your AUTOEXEC.BAT file.

Print Report

If you would like a printout of all SYSINFO's statistics, you can select `Print report` option in the Report menu. This displays the Report Options screen (Figure 2.8).

The Report Options screen lets you construct customized SYSINFO reports by choosing among each of the options listed. You can even specify a report header and/or special notes you want to appear at the bottom of the report. The SYSINFO report can be sent directly to your printer or written to a file.

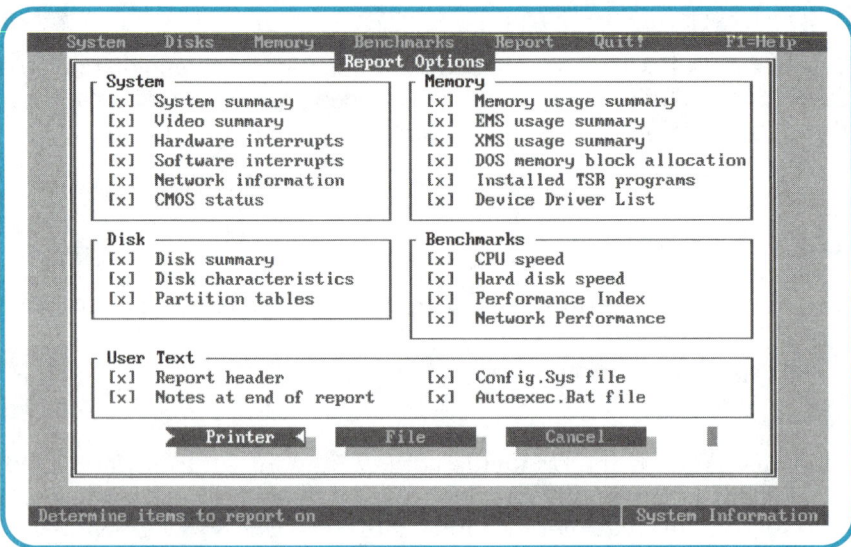

Figure 2.8 *You can customize your SYSINFO report with the Report Options screen.*

NCC: Norton Control Center

The other utility we discuss in this chapter allows you to control and configure several attributes of your PC. The Norton Control Center (NCC) provides an easy interface for configuring display, keyboard, mouse, serial port, and other functions.

 Running Norton Control Center (NCC)

1. At the DOS prompt, type the command **NCC**.

2. Press Enter.

The Norton Control Center screen is displayed (Figure 2.9). ☐

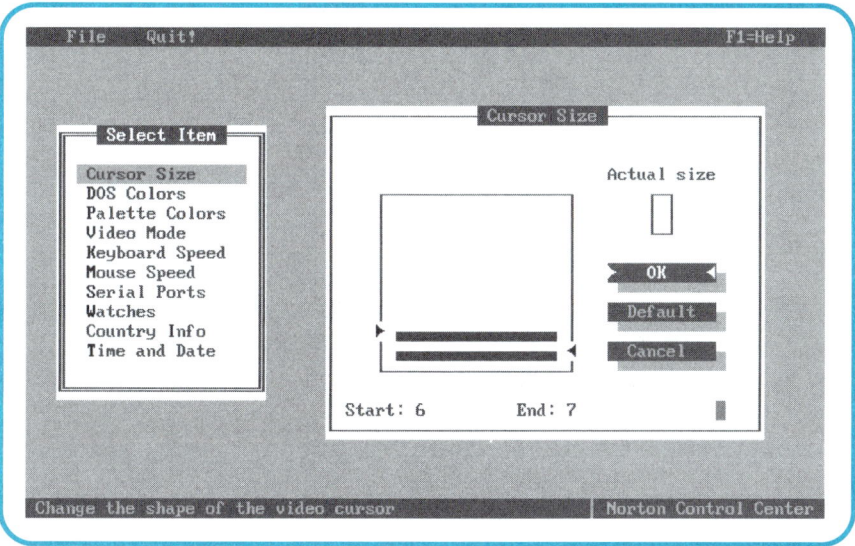

Figure 2.9 Norton Control Center screen provides access to ten customizable items.

As you can see in Figure 2.9, the Norton Control Center provides access to ten different items: Cursor Size, DOS Colors, Palette Colors, Video Mode, Keyboard Rate, Mouse Speed, Serial Ports, Watches, Country Info, and Time and Date.

Cursor Size

Through the NCC interface (Figure 2.9), you can modify your cursor's appearance. You configure your cursor size by specifying two values: where the cursor starts and where it ends. The range of possible start/end values depends on your video adapter (CGA, EGA, etc.). The values on my VGA range from 0 to 7.

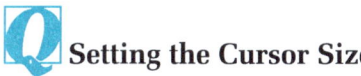 **Setting the Cursor Size**

1. Press Tab.   This deactivates the left
                                panel (Select Item) of Figure
                                2.9 and makes the right
                                panel (Cursor Size) active.

2. Press the up or down arrow key to move the cursor to the desired Start position, and press Tab. Or, drag the arrowhead along the left side of the box with the mouse.

This sets the starting position of the cursor.

3. Press the up or down arrow key to move the cursor to the desired End position, and press Enter. Or, drag the arrowhead on the right side of the box to the desired end position, then click OK.

This sets the cursor size and reactivates the Select Item panel (Figure 2.9).

☐

40

DOS Colors

NCC's DOS Colors option allows you to set the text color, background attributes, and border color for DOS screens.

 Setting the DOS Colors

1. Press the down arrow key or click with the mouse to highlight the DOS Colors selection and press Enter. Or, press **D**.

This selects the DOS Colors option and displays the screen in Figure 2.10.

2. Press the up or down arrow key to select the desired text color or click with the mouse. Use the mouse with the scroll arrows along the right side of the box to see more choices.

3. Press the Space Bar to toggle between the available text options of Blink and Bright.

4. When you are satisfied with your selection, press Tab or click to move to the background attributes selection.

5. Press the Space Bar to toggle between the available background options, Blink or Bright.

6. When you are satisfied with your background selection, press Tab or click to move to the Border Color selection.

7. Select the desired border color, and press Enter or click OK.

This ends the DOS Color selection process and reactivates the Select Item panel.

41

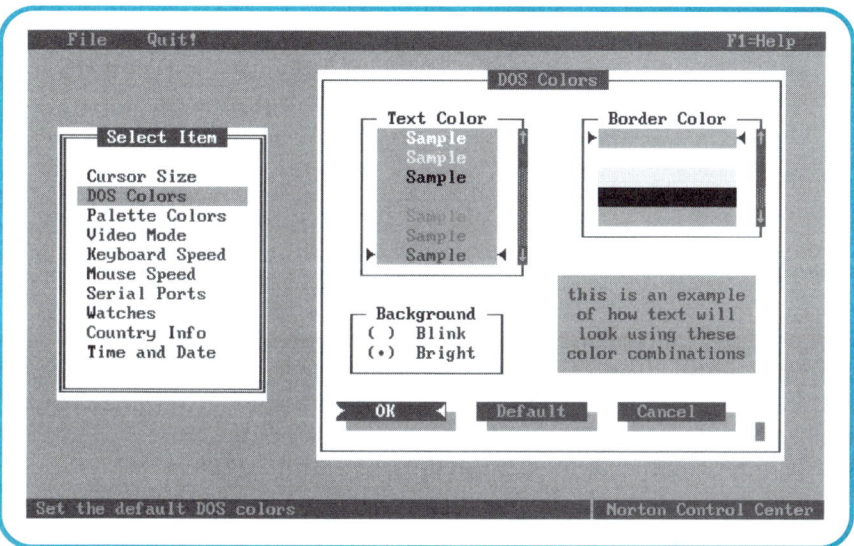

Figure 2.10   You can change your DOS color settings with the DOS Colors screen.

Palette Colors

If your PC is equipped with either an EGA or VGA monitor, you can use the Palette Colors selection to specify the 16 colors available for display use.

 Setting the Palette Colors

1. Press the down arrow key or click with the mouse to highlight the Palette Colors selection and press Enter. Or press P.

   This selects the Palette Colors option and displays the screen in Figure 2.11.

2. Press the up and down arrow keys to select the desired palette color, or click on the color you want.

   This scrolls through the 16 palette colors used in the Norton screens.

3. Select the Change box at the bottom of the screen, and press Enter (Figure 2.11).

   The Change Color Dialog box is displayed.

4. Select the desired color, and press Enter or click OK.

   This selects the new palette color, ends the Palette Color selection process, and reactivates the Select Item panel.   □

42

Video Mode

The Video Mode feature allows you to select which video mode to use if your monitor supports more than one mode. As you experiment with different display modes, the compressed characters used in a compact mode (for example, 52 line EGA display) are sometimes difficult to read—most people stay with the default 25 line mode.

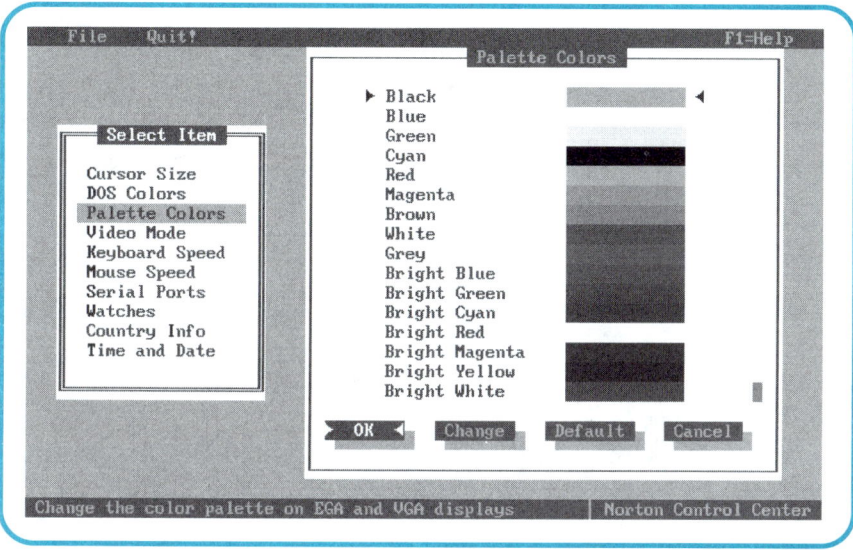

Figure 2.11 The Palette Colors Selection screen lets you customize your colors.

43

 Setting the Video Mode

1. Press the down arrow key or click with the mouse to highlight the Video Mode selection and press Enter. Or, press **V**.

   This selects the Video Mode option and displays the screen in Figure 2.12.

2. Select the desired Display Lines value.

3. Press Tab or click to move to the `Display Mode` selection.

4. Press Space Bar or click to select either the `Black and White` or `Color` mode option.

5. Press Enter, or click `OK`.

   This ends the Video Mode selection process and reactivates the Select Item panel.

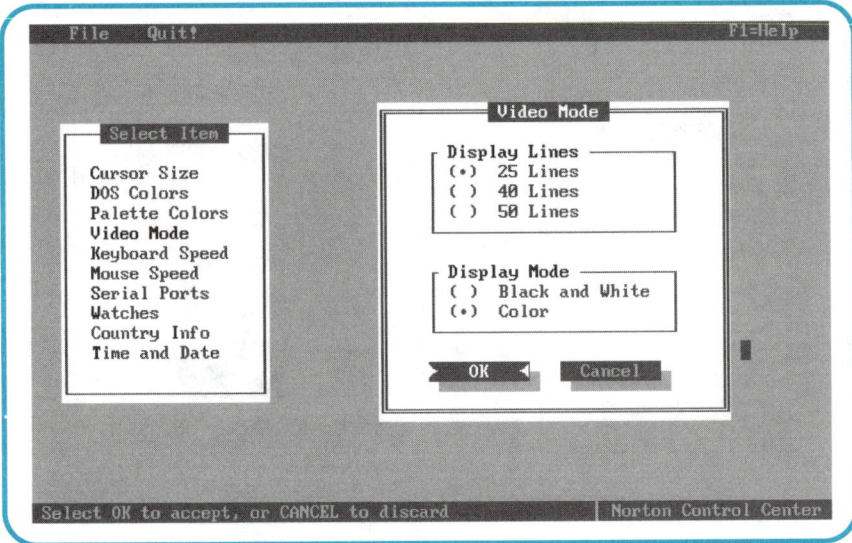

Figure 2.12   You can set up your monitor to operate in any of its available modes using the Video Mode screen.

Keyboard Speed

If your PC's microprocessor is an 80286, 80386, or 80486, you can use the Keyboard Speed utility to alter two keyboard characteristics: *keyboard repeat rate* and the *delay before auto repeat*. The keyboard repeat rate is the number of times a depressed key will repeat per second. The delay before auto repeat is the amount of time to wait after you press and hold down a key before it will automatically repeat.

 Setting the Keyboard Speed

1. Press the down arrow key or click with the mouse to highlight the Keyboard Speed selection, and press Enter. Or, press **K**.

This selects the Keyboard Speed option and displays the screen in Figure 2.13.

2. Use the left and right arrow keys or mouse to move the keyboard repeat rate indicator to the desired setting.

3. Press Tab or click the delay slider on the display bar.

The cursor moves to the repeat selection area of the screen.

4. Use the left and right arrow keys or mouse to move the delay before auto repeat indicator to the desired setting.

5. Press Enter or click OK when you are satisfied with the keyboard rate settings.

This ends the Keyboard Speed selection process and reactivates the Select Item panel.   ☐

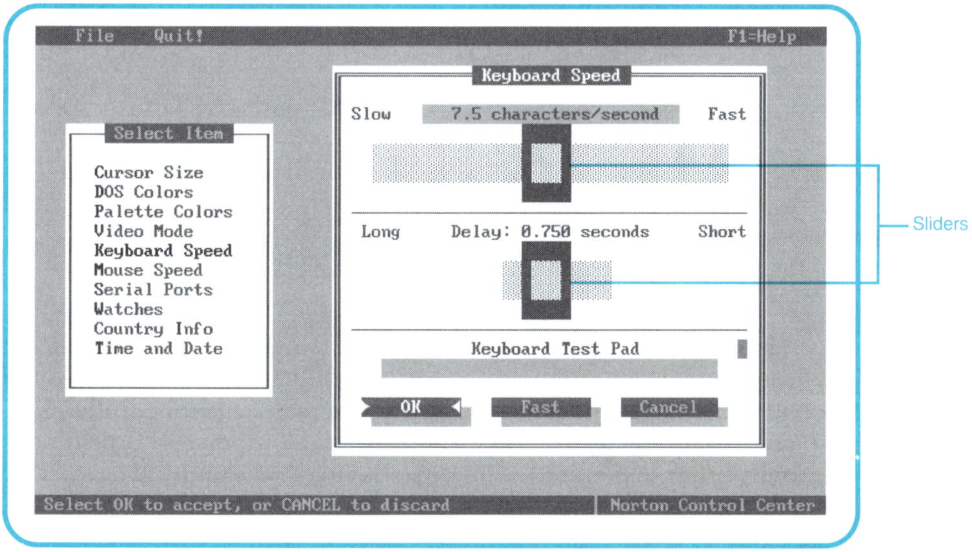

45

Figure 2.13   Use the Keyboard Speed screen to change your keyboard's speed and repeat rate.

Mouse Speed

If your PC is configured with a mouse, you can use NCC to set the mouse's sensitivity value. A high sensitivity value causes slight mouse movement to result in broad cursor movement. On the other hand, a low sensitivity value causes substantial mouse movement to result in slight cursor movement.

Q Setting the Mouse Speed

1. Press the down arrow key or click with the mouse to highlight the Mouse Speed selection, and press Enter. Or, press M.

   This selects the Mouse Speed option and displays the screen in Figure 2.14.

2. Use the left and right arrow keys or mouse to move the mouse sensitivity indicator to the desired setting.

3. Press Enter, or click OK.

   This ends the Mouse Speed selection process and reactivates the left panel. □

46

Serial Ports

A *port* is an outlet on your PC that provides a plug-in interface for various peripheral devices (such as a mouse, modem, or printer). Your PC probably has several different ports, including serial and parallel ports. Typical serial devices include a mouse, modem, or serial printer—a parallel printer is generally the only device you would ever see connected to a parallel port.

NCC allows you to specify communications protocol for each of your PC's serial ports. This communications protocol includes: baud rate, parity, number of data bits, and number of stop bits.

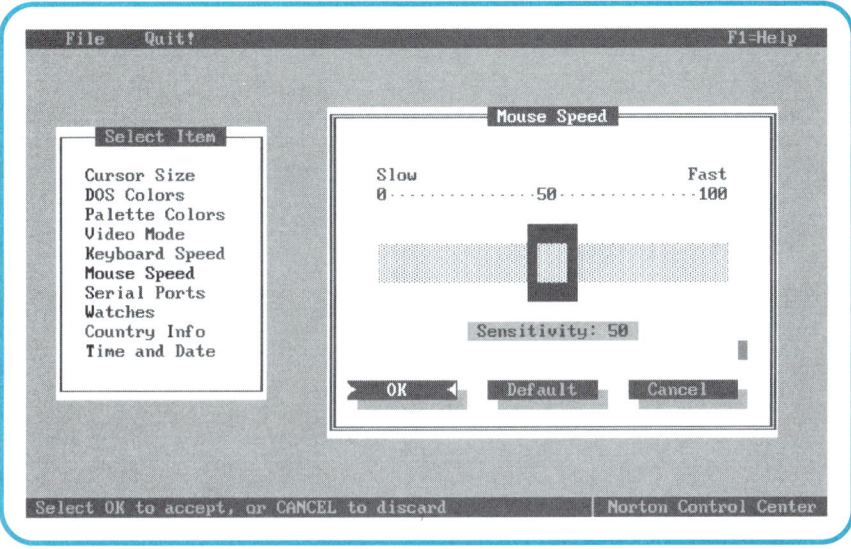

Figure 2.14 Change the sensitivity of mouse movement with the Mouse Speed screen.

 Configuring Serial Ports

1. Press the down arrow key or click with the mouse to highlight the `Serial Ports` selection and press Enter. Or, press **S**.

   This selects the Serial Ports option and displays the screen in Figure 2.15.

2. Press the up or down arrow keys to select a communications port (COM1, COM2, etc.) to configure.

3. Press Tab or click to move to the `Baud` selection area.

4. Select a different baud rate.

5. Press Tab or click to move to the `Stop Bits` selection area.

6. Select a different stop bits value.

7. Press Tab or click to move to the `Parity` selection area.

8. Select a different parity value.

9. Press Tab or click to move to the `Data Bits` selection area.

10. Select a different data bits value.

11. Press Enter, or click `OK`.

This ends the Serial Ports selection process and reactivates the Select Item panel. □

48

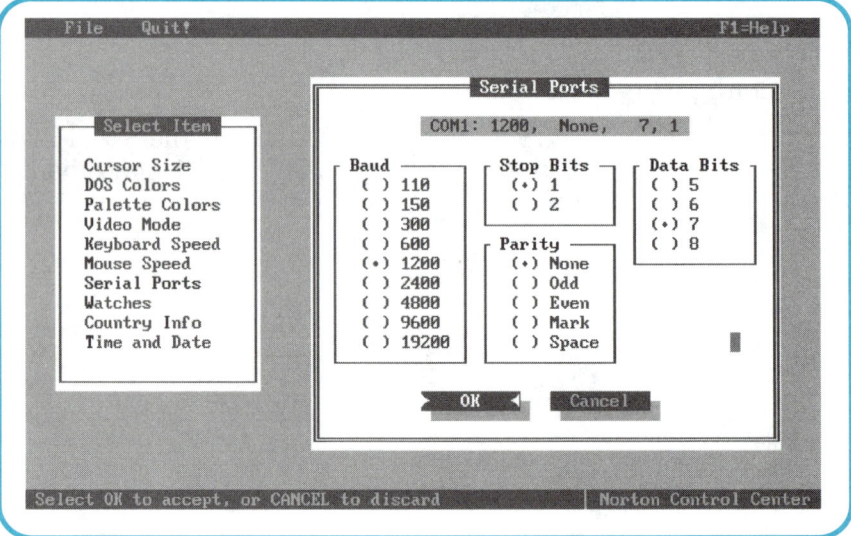

Figure 2.15   The Serial Ports screen displays and lets you modify the current serial port configuration.

Watches

As you probably know, your PC has an internal clock that keeps track of the current time and date. The DOS TIME and DATE commands allow you to display and/or set the clock's time and date. The Norton Utilities takes timekeeping one step further. The NCC utility offers four independent stopwatches for tracking elapsed times. These stopwatches allow you to easily determine how long it took a program to run, a batch file to execute, and other similar duties.

Using the Stopwatches

1. Press the down arrow key or click with the mouse to highlight the Watches selection, and press Enter. Or, press W.

   This selects the Watches option and displays the screen in Figure 2.16.

2. Select the desired watch.

3. Select the Start, Reset, or Pause box at the bottom of the Watches screen. (NOTE: The Start box is replaced by the Pause box if an active watch is selected.)

   This starts, pauses, or resets the selected watch.

4. Select OK.

   This reactivates the left panel.

49

The Norton stopwatches also offer another, more useful method of tracking time. You can run NCC with a command line parameter to start or stop a specific watch without having to go through all the NCC menus and screens. When you type the command NCC /START:1 and press Enter, NCC resets and starts stopwatch #1 and displays the information shown in Figure 2.17.

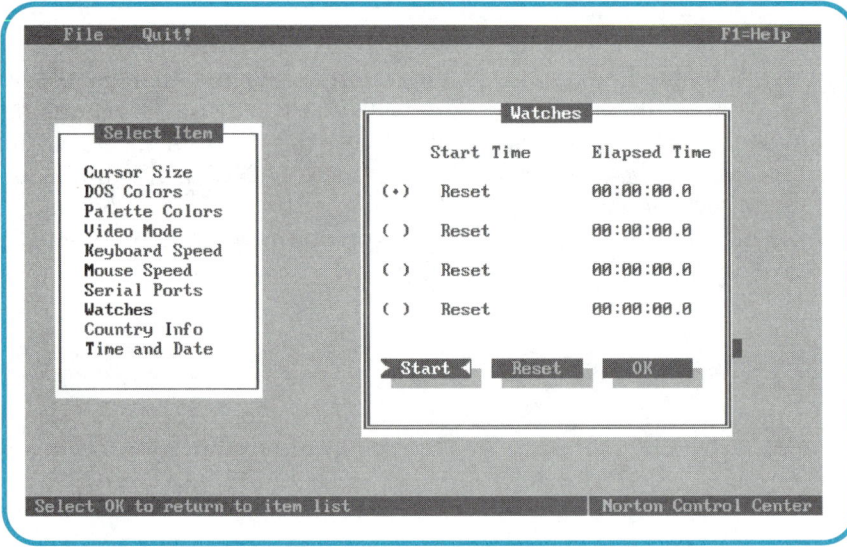

50

Figure 2.16   The Watches screen provides access to four separate stopwatches.

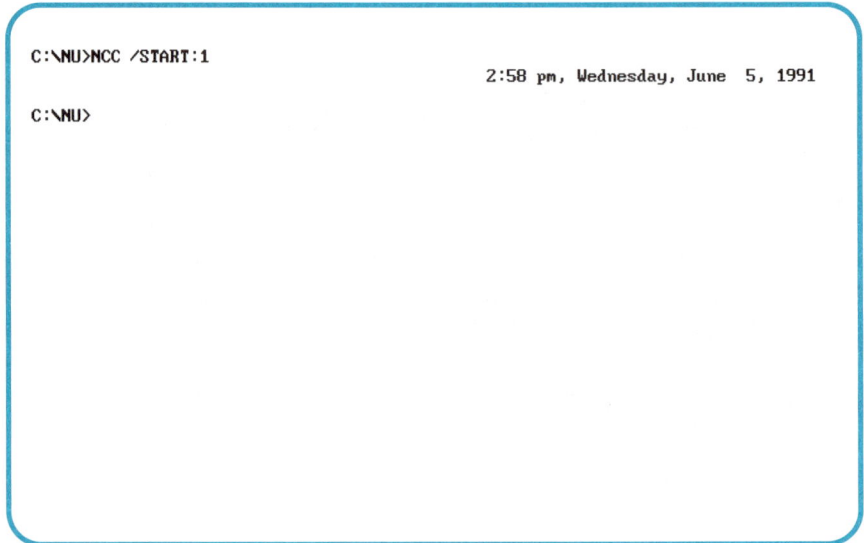

Figure 2.17   You can also start, stop, or pause a stopwatch from the command line.

If you then type the command **NCC /STOP:1** and press Enter, you can see how much time has elapsed since you started the stopwatch (Figure 2.18).

```
C:\NU>NCC /START:1
                                        2:58 pm, Wednesday, June  5, 1991

C:\NU>NCC /STOP:1
                                        2:59 pm, Wednesday, June  5, 1991

                                                             44 seconds
C:\NU>
```

51

Figure 2.18   Tracking elapsed time can also be accomplished from the command line.

Country Info

The Country Info selection in NCC allows you to configure your PC for use in foreign countries. With Country Info you can set up the following formats: Time, Date, Currency, List, and Numbers.

> **Note:** Before you can use this feature, you must run the utility NLSFUNC from the DOS command line. Refer to *The Waite Group's MS-DOS Bible,* 3rd ed. for a detailed explanation of the NLSFUNC command.

Setting Country Formats

1. Press the down arrow key or click with the mouse to highlight the Country Info selection, and press Enter. Or, press **I**.

   This selects the Country Info option and displays the screen in Figure 2.19.

2. Select the desired country, and press Enter or click OK.

   This sets the country formats, ends the Country Info selection process, and reactivates the left panel. □

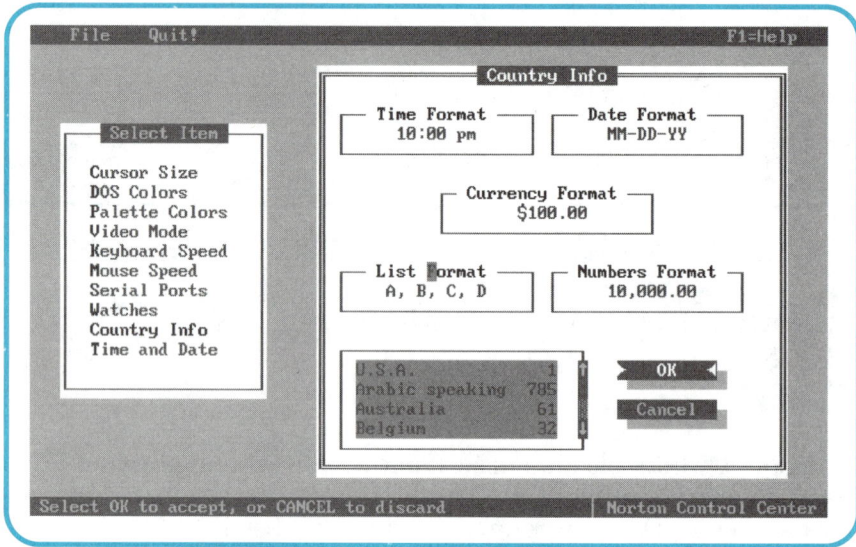

Figure 2.19   Reconfigure a PC for a different country using the Country Info screen.

Time and Date

The NCC Time and Date selection offers a visually pleasing alternative to DOS' TIME and DATE functions.

Setting the System Time and Date

1. Press the down arrow key or click with the mouse to highlight the Time and Date selection, and press Enter. Or, press **T**.

   This selects the Time and Date option and displays the screen in Figure 2.20.

2. Enter the current month, day, and year in numeric format (for example, **09 13 91** for September 13, 1991).

   If you want to set the system time only, skip this step and press Enter.

3. Enter the current hour, minute, and second (for example, **08 23 59**).

   If you do not want to set the system time, press Enter and skip Step 4.

4. Enter either **A** or **P** (for A.M. or P.M.), and press Enter or click OK.

   This ends the Time and Date selection process and reactivates the left panel.

53

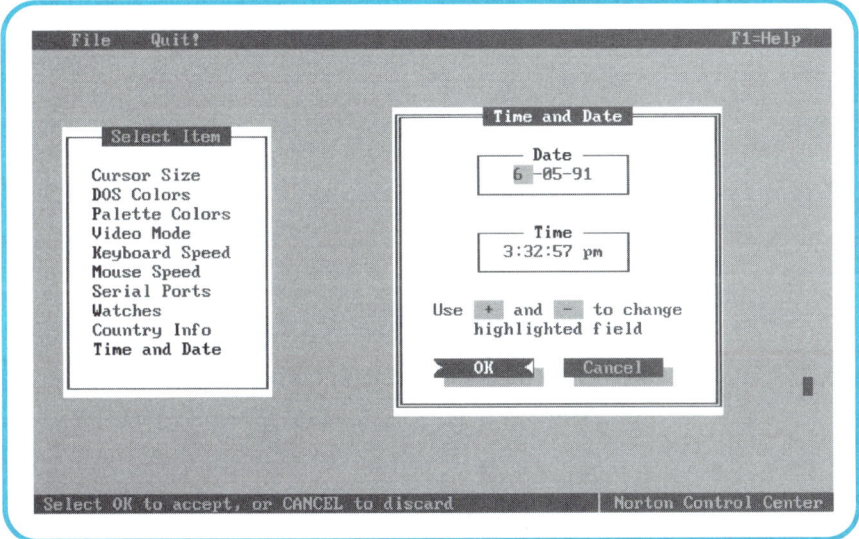

Figure 2.20   Use NCC's Time and Date screen to set your system's time and date.

What You Have Learned

In this chapter you learned about DOS and a few of the important hardware components within your PC. You also learned:

▶ The System Information (SYSINFO) utility provides information about DOS, hardware configuration, memory layout, and benchmark results.

▶ SYSINFO's benchmark calculations show a comparison of your PC to an IBM PC XT.

▶ The Norton Control Center (NCC) provides an easy interface for configuring display, keyboard, mouse, serial port, and other functions.

54

Using Norton File Utilities

In This Chapter

▶ *Using FILEFIND to simplify file operations*
▶ *Quickly recovering an erased file*
▶ *Preserving deleted files*
▶ *Repairing special files*
▶ *Removing files from a disk*

This chapter explains many of The Norton Utilities' features that compensate for DOS's file-handling shortcomings. One of these utilities, FILEFIND, is quite useful for many of your everyday PC tasks. If you are concerned with file security on your PC, you will definitely want to examine the WIPEINFO utility, which goes beyond the DEL command for file erasure.

Lotus 1-2-3, Symphony, and dBASE users will be pleased to know that version 6.0 of The Norton Utilities offers a FILEFIX utility that is intelligent enough to know how to repair damaged data files for these popular business applications.

But for most PC users, no one Norton utility may be as important as UNERASE, which can resurrect previously deleted files. When teamed up with the ERASE PROTECT utility, UNERASE provides the capability to recover files long after they have been deleted.

File Attributes and FILEFIND

DOS maintains special status information for each file on a disk. This information indicates the state of several important file attributes, including read-only, archive, system, and hidden (see Table 3.1). The DOS ATTRIB command allows you to change a file's read-only and archive attributes, but it does not provide access to the system and hidden attributes. Norton's FILEFIND lets you display, set, or clear any of the four file attributes, including those inaccessible to ATTRIB.

Table 3.1 File Attribute Definitions

Attribute	Meaning
Archive	Indicates file has not been backed up
Hidden	Indicates file is not visible via the DOS DIR command
Read-only	Indicates file cannot be modified
System	Indicates operating system (DOS) file

56

Displaying File Attributes Using FILEFIND

1. At the DOS prompt, type **FILEFIND**, and press Enter.

   This starts the FILEFIND utility and displays the FileFind screen in Figure 3.1.

2. Type a file specification in the File Name: field (for example, **C:*.***), and press Enter.

   This tells FILEFIND to start looking for all files in C:.

3. If you want to stop the list as it scrolls, select the Stop command button. Use the Start command button to resume scrolling.

   When the desired files are found, a search completion message appears.

4. Press Enter or click OK to acknowledge the search completion message.

   This displays the list of files that match the search criteria (Figure 3.2). ☐

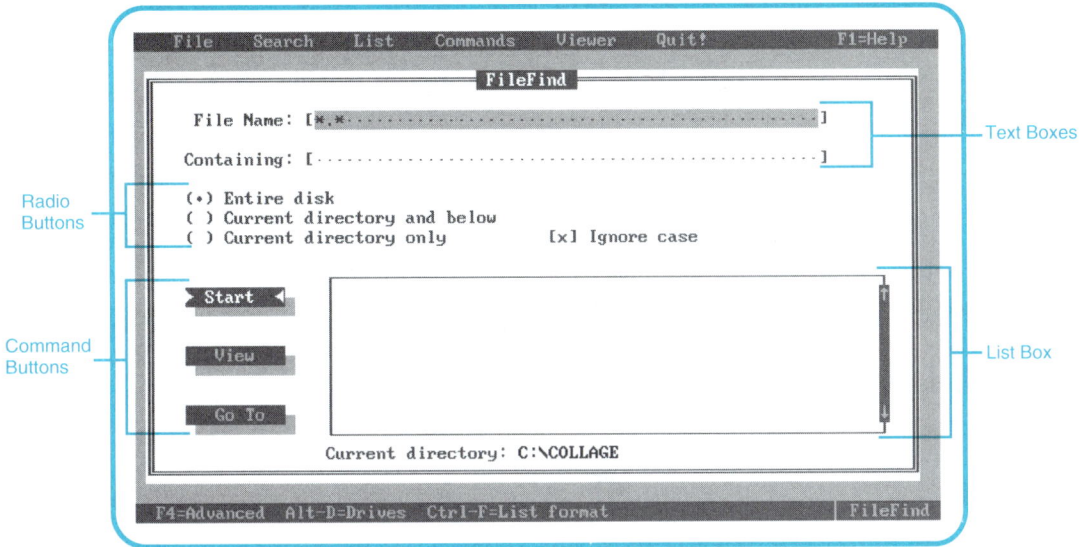

Text Boxes

Radio
Buttons

Command
Buttons

List Box

Figure 3.1 **The FileFind screen provides access to several file-handling tools.**

57

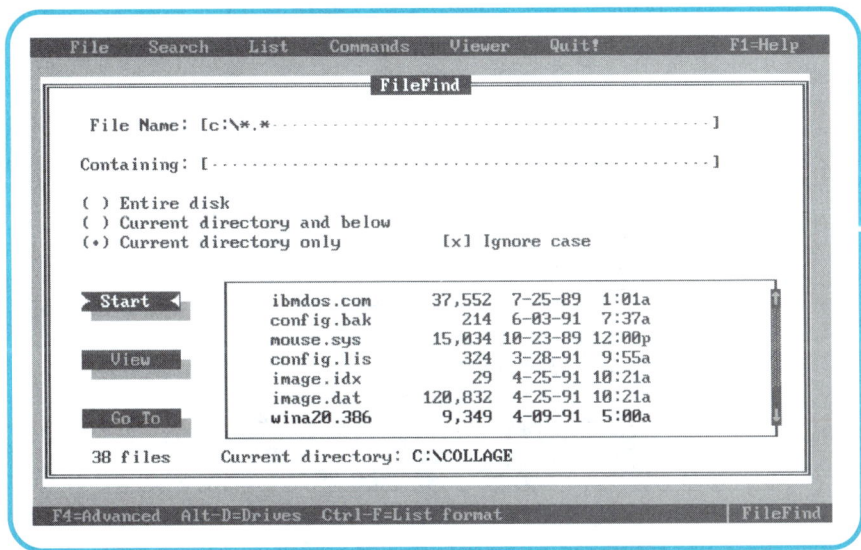

Figure 3.2 **FILEFIND displays a list of files matching the search criteria.**

> **Note:** The FileFind screen works just like a dialog box. See Chapter 1 for more information on working with screens like this.

The FILEFIND listing in Figure 3.2 shows all files in the root directory of drive C:. The contents of this box can be scrolled by using either the up and down arrow keys or the mouse scroll bar along the right side of the box.

A file attribute is either on or off. FILEFIND displays an identifier for each attribute that is on.

Setting and Clearing File Attributes

58

You can use the Commands menu to set or clear any of the four file attributes. For example, let's clear the archive attribute for all files in C:'s root directory. (See Chapter 5 for more information about root directories.) The Change Attributes dialog box is displayed when you select the Set Attributes option in the Commands menu (Figure 3.3).

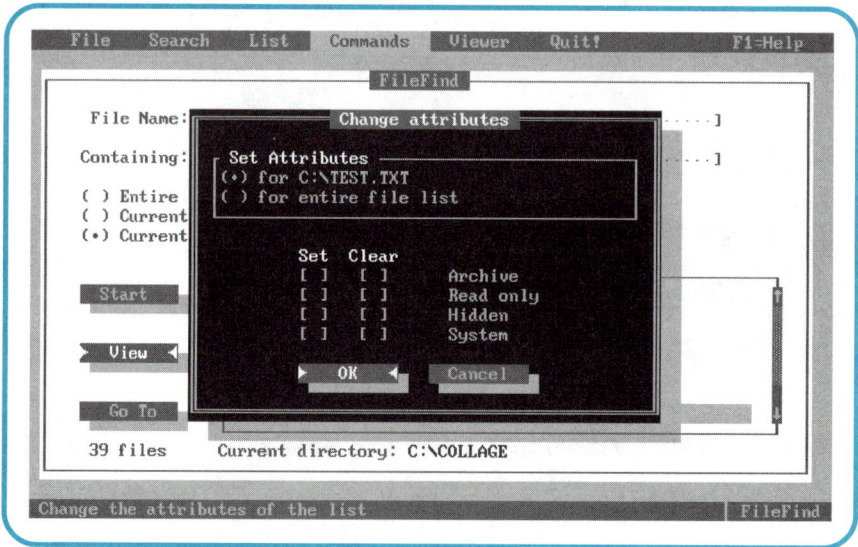

Figure 3.3   The Change Attributes dialog box lets you assign one or more of the four file attributes to any file.

Press the Space Bar or click to select the for entire file list option in the Set Attributes portion of the Change Attributes dialog box. Then press Tab twice followed by the Space Bar or click to place an X in the Clear column next to the archive attribute (Figure 3.4).

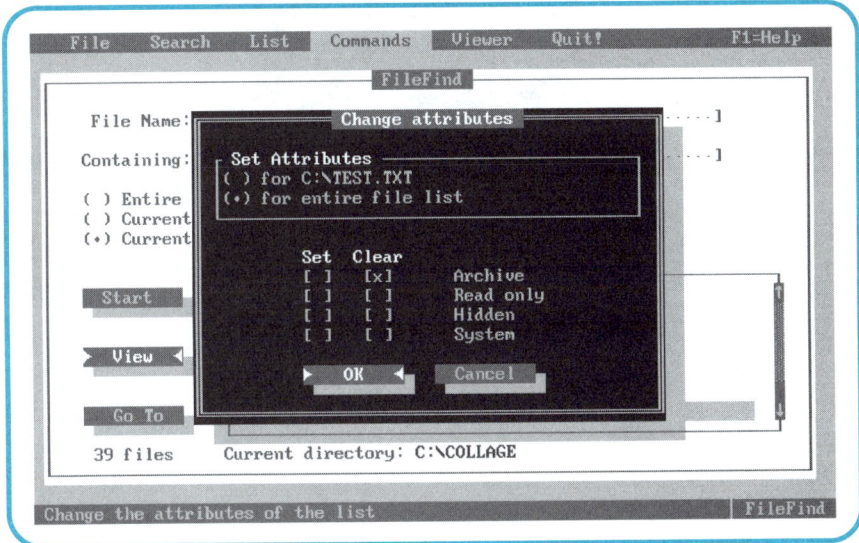

Figure 3.4   You can clear an attribute from a file by placing an X in the Clear column.

Press Enter to initiate the file attribute change. When FILEFIND is finished changing the attributes, the summary screen in Figure 3.5 is displayed.

The summary information in Figure 3.5 shows how many files were affected and which attributes were set or cleaned.

Modifying File Attributes from the Command Line

FILEFIND also lets you set file attributes directly from the DOS command line if you desire. This technique is a time-saver and lets you avoid all the menu and dialog box selections discussed previously. When you type **FILEFIND** from the command prompt, it finds the specified files and displays them in the FILEFIND screen. Table 3.2 shows the four file attributes and their corresponding FILEFIND command line identifiers.

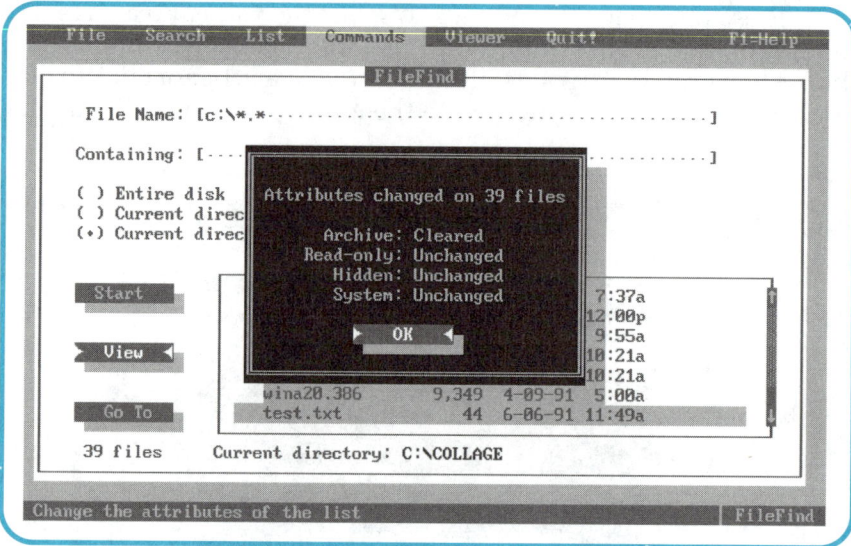

Figure 3.5   FILEFIND displays a summary of the changes made.

60

Table 3.2   FILEFIND Identifiers

File Attribute	Identifier
Archive	/A
Hidden	/HID
Read-only	/R
System	/SYS

Use a plus sign (+) after the file attribute identifier to turn on an attribute. For example, the command `FILEFIND C:\TEST.TXT /HID+` turns on the hidden attribute for the file TEST.TXT in the root directory. Place a minus sign (–) after a file attribute identifier to turn off an attribute. For example, `FILEFIND C:\TEST.TXT /R-` turns off TEST.TXT's read-only attribute.

You can use combinations of identifiers to set or clear several attributes with one command. For example, the command `FILEFIND C:\TEST.TXT /A+/HID+/R-` turns on the archive and hidden attributes and turns off the read-only attribute.

If you run FILEFIND with command line parameters as already shown, you will notice that the summary screen in Figure 3.5 is always displayed when FILEFIND is finished. Use the /BATCH option if you want FILEFIND to skip the summary screen and automatically return to the DOS prompt (for example, `FILEFIND TEXT.TXT /R-/BATCH`).

Clearing All Attributes

Although the command `FILEFIND *.* /A-/HID-/R-/SYS-` clears attributes for all files in the current directory, FILEFIND offers the /CLEAR option as a shortcut alternative. Therefore, `FILEFIND *.* /CLEAR` is equivalent to `FILEFIND *.* /A-/HID-/R-/SYS-` but is much easier to type.

> **Tip:** The DOS DEL command cannot find hidden/system files and will not delete read-only files. I use FILEFIND with the /CLEAR option to turn off the hidden and read-only attributes so I can delete an entire directory with DEL. FILEFIND can be used with Norton's WIPEINFO utility (discussed later in this chapter) to remove files in directories/subdirectories quickly and easily.

61

Filtering File Selections

In the previous examples, you have seen how to use the * wild-card character to select specific files for FILEFIND. DOS's? wild-card character may be used for more restrictive file selections as well. But what if you want to hide *all* archived files in a directory? No combination of * and ? will accomplish this. In this situation, you need to use file attribute identifiers as file filters.

The command `FILEFIND C:\*.* /HID` lists all hidden files in C:'s root directory. The /HID identifier in this command acts as an additional file filter for the C:*.* specification. We can use this feature to set or clear file attributes based on the values of other file attributes. For example, here is the command to hide all archived files in the root directory: `FILEFIND C:\*.* /A/HID+`. Since the file selection (C:*.*) is modified by the archive filter (/A), this command turns on the hidden attribute for archive files only.

Measuring File Size and Disk Space for Backup

Backing up data files onto floppy disks is an important routine, which should be performed regularly, but which is often skipped for one reason or another. It's not necessary to use a sophisticated program like Norton Backup to maintain backup copies of your data files; DOS's BACKUP utility works well for this purpose. In addition, many backup operations can be accomplished with DOS's COPY and XCOPY commands. However, Norton does offer some utilities that make the job easier.

The available data storage space on your target disk is an important consideration. Before starting a backup, you must determine whether your floppy disk has enough space available to hold the files you wish to copy. Since the DIR command shows file sizes and available disk space, you could use it to decide whether a group of files will fit on a floppy disk. This solution is not very user-friendly because it requires you to add up the individual file sizes and compare the total to the available space on the floppy. Fortunately, The Norton Utilities offer a more elegant alternative.

Determining File Size and Disk Space with FILEFIND

You can use the FILEFIND utility to report the size of one or more files and determine whether the files will fit on another disk (that is, the target floppy disk).

 Determining Available Disk Space for File Copy

1. At the DOS prompt, type **FILEFIND**, and press Enter.

   This starts the FILEFIND utility and displays the screen in Figure 3.1.

2. Type a file specification in the File Name: field (for example, **C:*.***), and press Enter. message appears.

   This tells FILEFIND to start looking for all files in C:. When the desired files are found, a search completion

3. Press Enter or click OK to acknowledge the search completion message.

The list of files that match the search criteria (C:*.*) is displayed (Figure 3.2).

4. Click on the Commands menu, then the Target Fit command. Or, press Alt-C, then the down arrow key twice, and finally Enter, to select the Target Fit option from the Commands menu.

This displays the Target Fit dialog box shown in Figure 3.6.

5. Press the up or down arrow key or click to select the target drive (for example, A:), and press Enter.

FILEFIND reports whether the selected files will fit on the target disk (Figure 3.7).

□

63

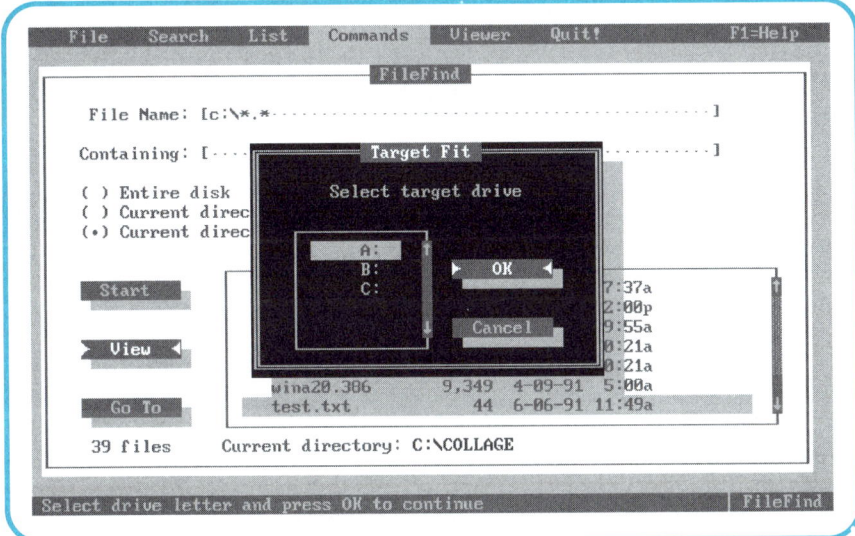

Figure 3.6 Select the target copy drive with the Target Fit dialog box.

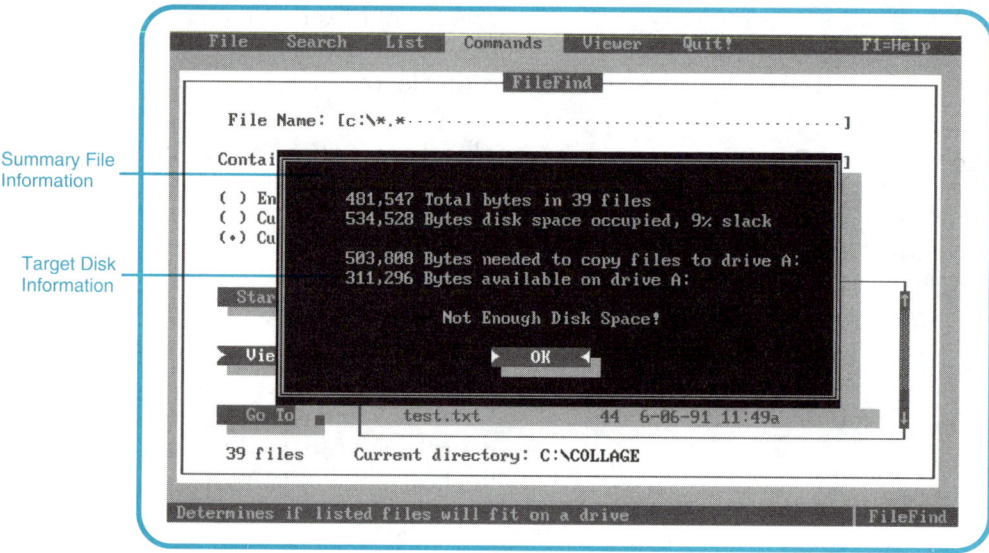

Summary File
Information

Target Disk
Information

**Figure 3.7   The target fit report indicates whether the selected
files will fit on the target disk.**

The information shown in Figure 3.7 can be split into two areas:
summary file information and target disk information.

Summary File Information

The Summary File Information portion of FILEFIND's target fit report
includes a total of the individual file sizes and the total disk space they
occupy.

At first, you may wonder why these two figures would differ.
After all, if the size of a group of files is X bytes, why wouldn't they
also occupy X bytes on the disk? To understand the answer to this
question, you must first understand how DOS stores files on a disk.
Disk storage specifics are discussed in Chapter 6—Maintaining Your
Hard Disk Drive, but a brief introduction to one of these concepts—
clusters—is provided here to help you understand the information
reported by FILEFIND.

The DOS DIR command and Norton's FILEFIND show file sizes
in bytes. For example, DIR reports that my AUTOEXEC.BAT file is
832 bytes in size. In order to quickly and easily address an entire
disk's data area, DOS works with larger, more manageable chunks of
data called *clusters*. A cluster is the smallest block of space DOS will

reserve for a file on a disk. The number of bytes in a cluster depends on the size and format of the disk in question. Table 3.3 shows cluster sizes for four most common floppy disk drive formats.

Table 3.3 *Floppy Disk Cluster Sizes*

Disk Size	Disk Format	Bytes per Cluster
5¼"	360K	1,024
5¼"	1.2 Mb	512
3½"	720K	512
3½"	1.4 Mb	512

The number of bytes per cluster for a hard disk depends on the version of DOS in use. For example, for DOS 3.3, each cluster on a hard disk consists of 2,048 bytes.

If it required only 832 bytes of storage space, the AUTOEXEC.BAT file would occupy one cluster on that hard disk. Even though AUTOEXEC.BAT uses only 832 of the 2,048 bytes in that cluster, the remaining 1,216 bytes are not available for another file's use. This unused area in a cluster is referred to as slack. The following formula may be used to determine the percent of slack space for one or more files:

65

$$\% \text{ Slack} = \frac{(\# \text{ Cluster Bytes}) - (\# \text{ Data Bytes})}{(\# \text{ Cluster Bytes})}$$

where *# Cluster Bytes* is the number of bytes allocated for the file(s) and *# Data Bytes* is the number of bytes actually used by the file(s). Using this formula, we can plug in the values for the AUTOEXEC.BAT file on the example hard disk:

$$\frac{(1 \text{ Cluster} * 2,048 \text{ Bytes/Cluster}) - (832 \text{ Bytes})}{(1 \text{ Cluster} * 2,048 \text{ Bytes/Cluster})}$$

which simplifies to

$$\frac{2,048 \text{ Bytes}}{1,216 \text{ Bytes}}$$

or 59% slack.

Target Disk Information

The target disk information reported by FILEFIND shows

1. How much disk space is required for the specified files
2. How much space is available on the target disk
3. Whether enough disk space is available on the target disk for the specified files

FILEFIND checks the slack characteristics of both the source and target disks. The disk space requirements in this portion of FILEFIND's report therefore indicate the total number of bytes, including slack, required on the target disk.

Determining Target Fit from the Command Line

66

If you want to bypass the menus and dialog boxes of FILEFIND, you can specify command line parameters to determine whether a set of files will fit on a target disk. For example, the command `FILEFIND C:\*.*` `/TARGET:A` tells FILEFIND to determine whether the files in the root directory of C: will fit on the disk in drive A:. When FILEFIND completes this task, the target fit report in Figure 3.7 is displayed.

Date/Time Stamps

The date/time stamps shown in a DIR or FILEFIND listing typically indicate when a file was created or last modified. DOS does not offer a command to easily modify a file's date/time stamps, but fortunately, The Norton Utilities do.

> **Note:** DOS's COPY command does not change a file's date/time stamps. For example, the command `COPY` `TEST.TXT TESTBACK.TXT` creates a new file TESTBACK.TXT with the same date/time stamps as TEST.TXT.

Using FILEFIND to Set Date/Time Stamps

The versatile FILEFIND utility provides an easy way to set a file's date/time stamps. Shown in the following Quick Steps is an example of setting date/time stamps using FILEFIND.

 Setting a File's Date/Time Stamps

1. At the DOS prompt, type **FILEFIND**, and press Enter.

   This starts the FILEFIND utility and displays the screen in Figure 3.1.

2. Type a file specification in the File Name: field (for example, C:\AUTOEXEC.BAT), and press Enter.

   FILEFIND locates the specified file and displays a search completion message.

3. Press Enter or click OK to acknowledge the search completion message.

   FILEFIND then displays the list of files that match the search criteria.

67

4. Select the Commands menu, then select Set Date/Time.

   The Set Date/Time dialog box shown in Figure 3.8 is displayed.

5. Press Tab then the Space Bar or simply click to select the Set the time to: field.

   This moves the cursor to the Set the time to: field and places an X next to it.

6. Press Tab or click on the text box to the right of the Set the time to: field. Enter the current time (for example, 2:00 PM).

7. Press Tab then the Space Bar, or click to select the Set the time to: field.

   This moves the cursor to the Set the date to: field and places an X next to it.

8. Press Tab, then enter the current date (for example, 3-30-90), and press Enter.

   FILEFIND changes the date/time stamps for the AUTOEXEC.BAT file to the values you specified. A completion message is displayed when the date/time change is made.

9. Press Enter or click OK.   This returns you to
the FileFind screen. □

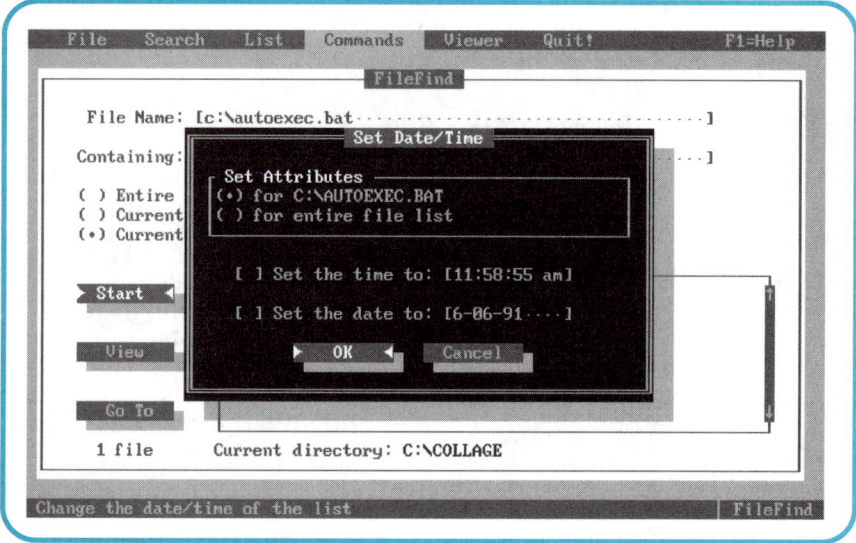

*Figure 3.8   Specify the file's new date and time using the
Set Date/Time dialog box.*

Setting Date/Time Stamps from the Command Line

Use the /D and /T options with FILEFIND to set file date/time stamps
from the command line. For example, the command

```
FILEFIND C:\AUTOEXEC.BAT /D03-30-92 /T14:20:00
```

sets the date/time stamps for the AUTOEXEC.BAT file to 3-30-90
2:00 PM.

 Caution: FILEFIND lets you set dates only from 1980 on.

The preceding example showed you how FILEFIND can set both the date and time, but you can also use this utility to set just one of those values (for example, `FILEFIND C:\AUTOEXEC.BAT /D03-30-90` or `FILEFIND C:\AUTOEXEC.BAT /T14:20:00`). In addition, you can use the DOS wild-card characters in FILEFIND's file specification (for example, `FILEFIND C:\*.* /T14:20:00`).

When setting date/time stamps with FILEFIND from the command line, the date and time formats are mm-dd-yy and hh:mm:ss, respectively. The time value is expressed in 24-hour clock format, so 15:20:00 is 3:20 PM. And you can omit leading zeroes, so /D3-3-90 is the same as /D03-03-90.

Using the Default Date and Time

One of the most useful applications for FILEFIND is to have it set a file's date/time stamp to the current date/time. This is accomplished via the /NOW option (for example, `FILEFIND C:\*.* /NOW`). Use DOS's DATE and TIME commands to make sure your PC's internal date and time are correct before using this option.

69

Clearing the Date and Time

In the PC world, the origin of time is 12:00 AM on January 1, 1980—at least that's as far back as DOS's DATE and TIME commands will let you go. You can use FILEFIND to reset file date/time stamps to 12:00 AM on January 1, 1980 by specifying /D and /T with no date and time values. For example, the command `FILEFIND C:\*.* /D /T` sets the date and time values for all files in C:'s root directory to 12:00 AM, January 1, 1980.

Quickly Recovering an Erased File

So far, you have learned about several of the file-based tools available in The Norton Utilities. These tools allow you to change file attributes, determine whether a set of files will fit on another disk, and more. But for my money, no one file-based utility is as important as Norton's UNERASE.

Caution: If you want to recover deleted files from your hard disk and you haven't installed The Norton Utilities, *do not* install the utilities now! The Norton installation program copies all the utilities to your hard disk and may overwrite the deleted files you wish to recover. Instead, insert the Norton Emergency Disk 2 into your A: (or B:) drive and substitute `A:UNERASE` (or `B:UNERASE`) for `UNERASE` in the Quick Steps that follow.

The UNERASE utility gives you the ability to easily recover previously deleted files from your hard or floppy disks.

Note: When DOS deletes a file, it still remembers all but the first character of the deleted file's name. UNERASE displays a question mark (?) as the first character of a deleted file's name. As part of the UNERASE procedure, you must provide the real first character of the deleted file's name.

70

Recovering Deleted Files

1. At the DOS prompt, type `CD` and the name of the directory where the deleted file resided (for example, `CD C:\WORK`), and press Enter.

2. Type `UNERASE`, and press Enter.

   This starts the UNERASE utility and displays the screen in Figure 3.9.

3. Press the up or down arrow key to highlight the file you wish to recover (for example, `?axmemo.txt`).

4. Press `U` or click the `UnErase` button.

   This displays the first character dialog box shown in Figure 3.10.

5. Type the first character of the deleted file's name (for example, **T**).

This recovers the deleted file.

☐

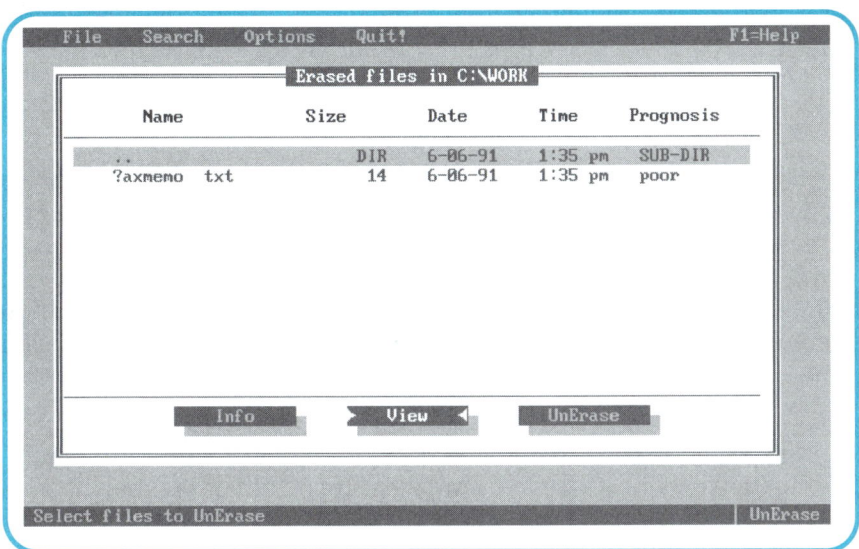

Figure 3.9   UNERASE lists all erased files in the current directory.

71

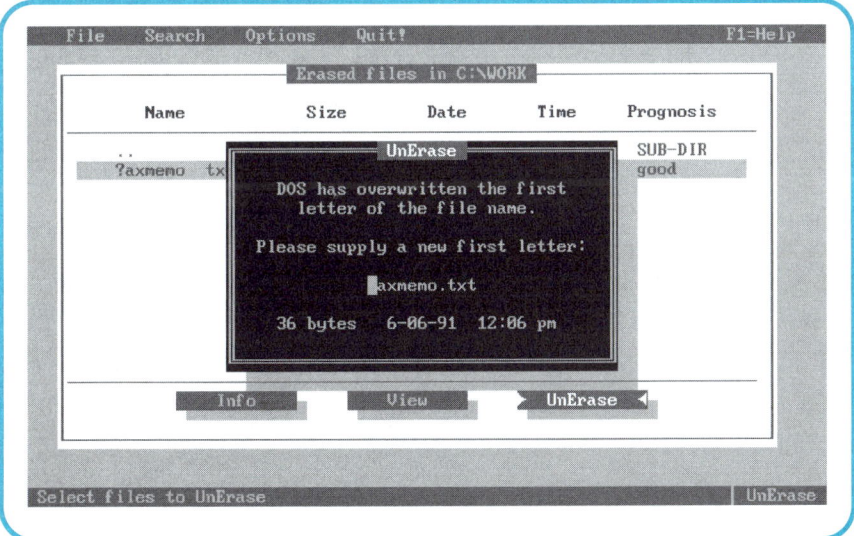

Figure 3.10   Specify the first character of the deleted file's name in the first character dialog box.

UNERASE: The Inside Story

One of the DOS DEL command's nicest features is that it does not destroy a file's contents; rather, DEL tells DOS to make the specified file's disk space available for other storage. For example, let's say the file C:\WORK\TAXMEMO.TXT is 950 bytes large and therefore occupies only one cluster on a hard disk on which each cluster consists of 2,048 bytes. For additional clarity, let's say that cluster #20 is where C:\WORK\TAXMEMO.TXT resides.

The command `DEL C:\WORK\TAXMEMO.TXT` does not affect cluster #20. All the data in C:\WORK\TAXMEMO.TXT still resides on the disk, at cluster #20, even after I use DEL to remove the file. The only thing DEL does is inform DOS that the cluster(s) occupied by the deleted file(s) are now available for use by other files. Although the contents of C:\WORK\TAXMEMO.TXT still exist on the disk, it is now unprotected by DOS and could be overwritten the next time something is copied to the disk.

72

The UNERASE utility is fairly effective at recovering deleted files because it knows how to analyze unused clusters. Keep in mind that every time you COPY a file, save a file from a word processor, or perform a similar operation, you run the risk of overwriting the unprotected data of a deleted file. Therefore, the chances of recovering an accidentally deleted file are best if you run UNERASE immediately after the deletion.

What To Do If UNERASE Fails . . .

The Prognosis column in Figure 3.9 indicates whether UNERASE thinks it can recover the specified files. A "good" prognosis means that UNERASE can probably resurrect the file with no manual intervention. However, a file with a "poor" prognosis may be more difficult to recover. Regardless of the prognosis listed, you should first try the Quick Steps for Recovering Deleted Files to recover the deleted file. The message shown in Figure 3.11 is displayed if UNERASE cannot recover the specified file.

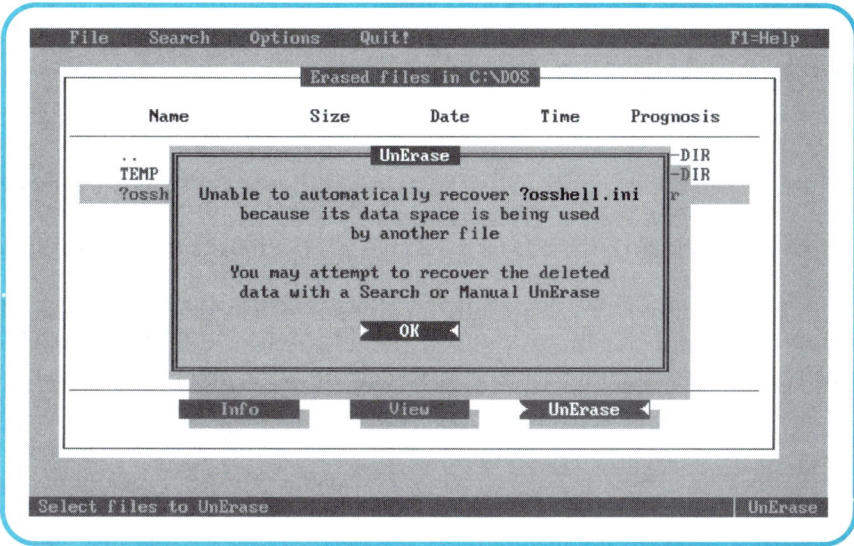

Figure 3.11 Sometimes UNERASE may not be able to recover a file.

73

There are many reasons why UNERASE may be unable to recover certain files automatically, and most of them can be circumvented manually. So if you encounter a problem while automatically recovering a file with UNERASE, don't give up hope! UNERASE offers a manual recovery feature that you may be able to use to reconstruct the deleted file. This advanced feature is covered in Chapter 7—Advanced Disk Management.

Note: Another important utility, IMAGE, is covered in Chapter 6—Maintaining Your Hard Disk Drive. Regular use of IMAGE can increase UNERASE's ability to recover accidentally deleted files. Be sure to read about IMAGE in Chapter 6 to see how it can guard against accidental data loss.

Now let's discuss the ERASE PROTECT utility, which can be instrumental in allowing an automatic UNERASE of older deleted files.

Preserving Deleted Files with ERASE PROTECT

Although Norton's UNERASE utility can often recover recently deleted files, it is not always 100% successful. By itself, UNERASE can fully recover only those deleted files that have not been overwritten by other files. Since you never know when a COPY command is going to overwrite a deleted file, you might consider using the ERASE PROTECT utility to extend the life of deleted files. ERASE PROTECT is a TSR utility that can prevent deleted file data from being overwritten so that files may be recovered long after they are deleted.

 Using ERASE PROTECT to Protect Deleted File Data

1. At the DOS prompt, type **EP**, and press Enter.

   This starts the ERASE PROTECT utility and displaysthe initial screen shown in Figure 3.12.

2. Press Enter or click on Choose drives.

   The Choose Drives dialog box is displayed.

3. Use the Tab and Space Bar or click to specify which drives you want ERASE PROTECT to protect, then press Enter.

   This selects drives to protect and updates the initial screen. Notice that the number of drives selected in this step is now indicated in the Status: field next to the Choose drives dialog box.

4. Press the down arrow key to highlight the File Protection dialog box, and then press Enter or click on File protection.

5. Press Tab three times, enter the maximum amount of deleted file data you wish to retain.

   For example, you might enter 1000, which is 1000K or approximately 1 Mb.

6. Press Enter.

This accepts the default ERASE PROTECT settings, at which all files (*.*) are retained for 5 days, with a maximum of 1 Mb of deleted file data. The initial screen is redisplayed with updated information.

7. Select Quit.

This concludes ERASE PROTECT configuration and terminates the utility. Remember that ERASE PROTECT is a TSR utility, however. So although it has been terminated, it is still resident in memory and ready to preserve data each time you delete a file. □

75

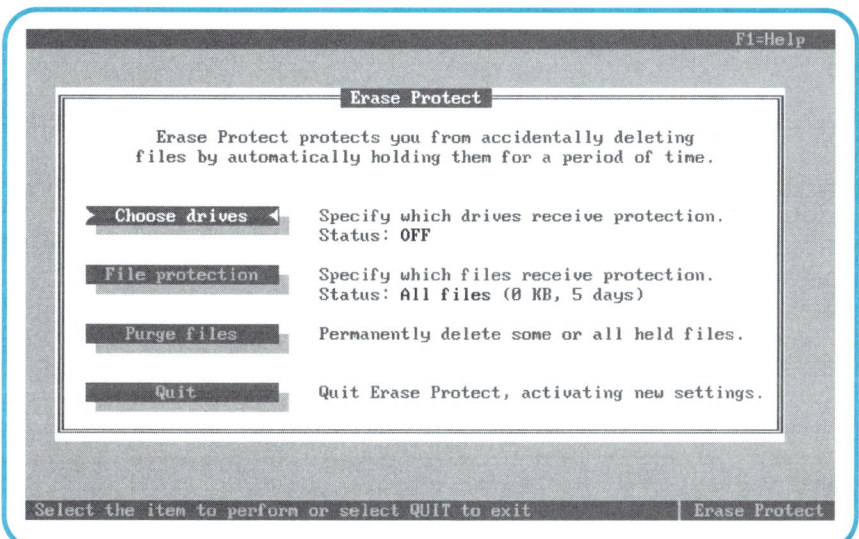

Figure 3.12   The initial ERASE PROTECT screen lets you configure the utility for your PC.

After you complete these Quick Steps, the ERASE PROTECT utility is configured and loaded as a TSR program. Each time you delete a file, ERASE PROTECT places the contents of the deleted file in a special directory called TRASHCAN. To ensure that ERASE PROTECT has been properly loaded, use DOS's DIR command to see if a TRASHCAN directory exists on each drive you specified in Step 3 of the preceding Quick Steps.

Using the ERASE PROTECT parameter settings as directed in the Quick Steps, the TRASHCAN directory will retain files up to 5 days after they are deleted. We have also specified a size limit for the TRASHCAN directory—no more than 1 Mb of deleted files will be maintained in the TRASHCAN directory. When this size limit is reached, ERASE PROTECT will begin to delete, or purge, the oldest files in the TRASHCAN directory to make room for newly deleted files. You may wish to adjust this size limit based upon the size of your hard disk, how much space is available on your hard disk, how often you delete files, and so on.

76

When you turn your PC off today and turn it back on tomorrow, you don't need to go through the Quick Steps to restart ERASE PROTECT. ERASE PROTECT stores your configuration information in a file called EP.INI.

To restart ERASE PROTECT with your configuration information, use the /ON option and run `EP /ON` from the DOS command line.

ERASE PROTECT also offers an option that uninstalls the utility. The command `EP /OFF` disables the utility and removes it from memory. Another command line option, /STATUS, lets you check the current condition of the ERASE PROTECT utility. If you enter the command `EP /STATUS`, ERASE PROTECT indicates whether it is enabled or disabled and shows the current configuration settings.

Recovering Files from the TRASHCAN

Norton's UNERASE utility is used to recover deleted files that ERASE PROTECT has saved in the TRASHCAN directory. The UNERASE utility checks to see if a TRASHCAN directory exists on the active drive. If this special directory does exist, UNERASE uses the information in the .SAV and EP.MAP files to quickly and easily recover any deleted files that have been retained.

Purging Files from the TRASHCAN

Once a file has been deleted, it may remain in the TRASHCAN directory for several days, depending upon your ERASE PROTECT configuration. Don't expect the deleted file's name to show up in a directory listing of TRASHCAN, however. When you delete a file, ERASE PROTECT places it in the TRASHCAN directory and gives it a special file name. The deleted files retained in the TRASHCAN directory have a .SAV extension but the rest of their file names are fairly meaningless. A special file in the TRASHCAN directory called EP.MAP is ERASE PROTECT's cross reference between these meaningless file names and the original file names.

When you are certain that you want to delete a file and completely remove it from your disk, you can use ERASE PROTECT's purge feature to erase it. When you select the Purge files command button in Figure 3.12, the Purge Deleted Files screen in Figure 3.13 is displayed.

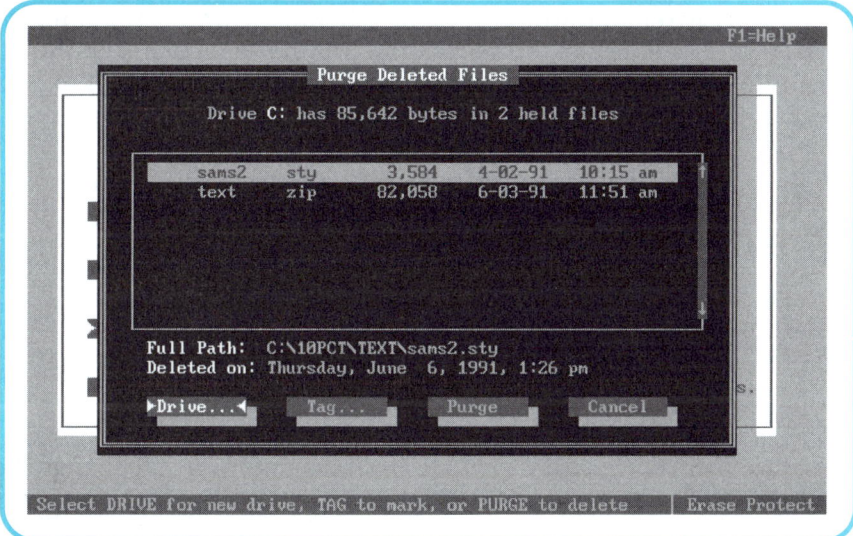

Figure 3.13   The Purge Deleted Files screen shows a list of all deleted files that may be purged.

The Purge Deleted Files screen shows a list of the files currently in the TRASHCAN directory. You can use the up and down arrow keys to scroll through this list and use the Space Bar to mark a highlighted file for deletion. After you have marked all the files you wish to purge from the TRASHCAN directory, highlight the Purge button in Figure 3.13 and press Enter to erase the files. Remember that once a file has been purged from the TRASHCAN directory there is no guarantee that you will be able to recover it with UNERASE.

Repairing Special Files with FILEFIX

If you use Lotus 1-2-3, Symphony, or dBASE, you will be happy to know that The Norton Utilities includes a tool to help you repair corrupt data files for these popular business applications. A data file can become corrupted for one of several reasons including a malfunctioning disk or a software bug.

78

If you are having problems with a Lotus 1-2-3 (Versions 1A and 2.x), Symphony, or dBASE data file, you should consider letting FILEFIX try to repair the damage. FILEFIX creates a new, undamaged version of the data file and leaves the original damaged file intact. The following Quick Steps explain how to repair a Lotus 1-2-3 data file, but the steps are similar for Symphony and dBASE data files.

 Repairing a Lotus 1-2-3 Data File

1. At the DOS prompt, type **FILEFIX**, and press Enter.	This starts the FILEFIX utility and displays the File Fix screen in Figure 3.14.
2. Press Enter or click to accept the 1-2-3 selection highlighted.	The Choose File to Repair screen is displayed.
3. Press Tab and use the up and down arrow keys to select a 1-2-3 file (for example, sales.wk2) from the list displayed.	If needed, you can change the active directory/drive using the Dirs/Drives selectors.
4. Press Enter.	The Repair Lotus 1-2-3 File screen is displayed.

5. Press Enter to accept the default fixed file name (fixed.wk2) and repair mode (recovering all data).

6. Press the left or right arrow key to highlight one of the report selection boxes, and press Enter.

The recovery process begins and the repair summary screen shown in Figure 3.15 is displayed.

Based on your selection, FILEFIX either prints a report, writes a report to a file (you specify a report file name on a subsequent screen), or skips the report process. □

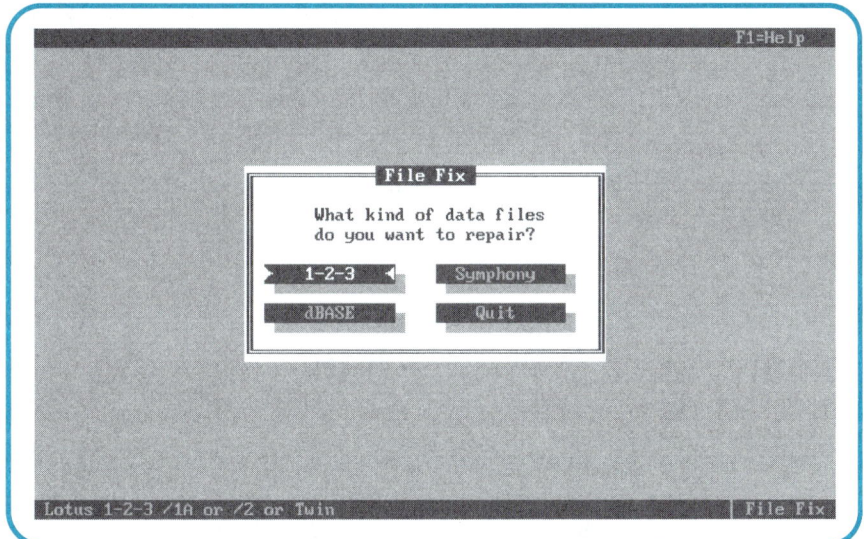

79

Figure 3.14   Select the type of damaged file with the FILEFIX type selection screen.

The FILEFIX utility has the intelligence to know what may be wrong with a damaged Lotus 1-2-3, Symphony, or dBASE data file. Because FILEFIX knows the internal structure of these data file types, it can make an educated guess at how to repair the damage. After you use FILEFIX to repair a data file, you should immediately test the repaired data file to see if the damage has been corrected. Do *not* delete the original damaged data file until you are satisfied with the contents of the repaired data file created by FILEFIX.

```
                                                              F1=Help

                 ┌──────── Repair Lotus 1-2-3 File ────────┐
                 │   Repair of file sales.wk2 to fixed.wk2  │
                 │                is complete.              │
                 │                                          │
                 │      Bytes recovered:         21         │
                 │      Bytes discarded:      1,203         │
                 │                                          │
                 │    Select a destination for the report:  │
                 │                                          │
                 │  ►No report ◄    Printer        File     │
                 └──────────────────────────────────────────┘

    A report will show which bytes of the file were removed     File Fix
```

Figure 3.15   FILEFIX repair results are shown on the repair summary screen.

Removing a File Permanently with WIPEINFO

Earlier in this chapter, I explained how the UNERASE utility can recover deleted files. Is there any way to actually remove a file from a disk so it cannot be recovered? Although it is convenient to have a recovery feature available, sometimes you really want to delete a file so no one else can see what it contained (for example, personnel records or top secret memos).

If you COPY enough files to a disk, you may eventually overwrite the unprotected clusters of all deleted files. But this could take a long time (especially if you have a large hard disk partition), and there is no way to guarantee that it would overwrite all the deleted files. If you are really determined to obliterate a file you may even consider FORMATting the disk. This approach is a bit drastic and may not work anyway since files can often be recovered from recently formatted disks (thanks to Norton's UNFORMAT utility!).

If you truly need to eradicate a file from a disk you should use Norton's WIPEINFO utility.

Norton's WIPEINFO utility overwrites a file's clusters, thereby removing the file's data from a disk.

> **Caution:** Use WIPEINFO with extreme caution because it overwrites a file's data clusters and makes recovery via UNERASE impossible.

Q Wiping a File from a Disk

1. Type **WIPEINFO**, and press Enter.

   This starts the WIPEINFO utility and displays the screen shown in Figure 3.16.

2. Press Enter.

   This selects the default Files selection in Figure 3.16 and displays the Wipe Files screen.

3. Type the drive, directory, and name of the file to be wiped (for example, **C:\WORK\JUNK.DOC**), and press Enter.

   A warning message is displayed.

4. Press **W** or click on Wipe to acknowledge the warning message.

   The Wiping Files screen is displayed.

5. Select the file, then press **W** or click on Wipe to wipe the file selected.

   WIPEINFO wipes the file and displays a completion message. □

81

WIPEINFO Configuration

WIPEINFO overwrites each byte in every cluster of the specified file with the default value, 0. Therefore, if you look at the clusters previously occupied by JUNK.DOC, all you will see is a bunch of zeroes. If you want, you can change this value to any other number. You can also select the number of times you want the file wiped, for extra security. Select the Configure button on the WIPEINFO screen shown in Figure 3.16 to access the Wipe Configuration screen (Figure 3.17).

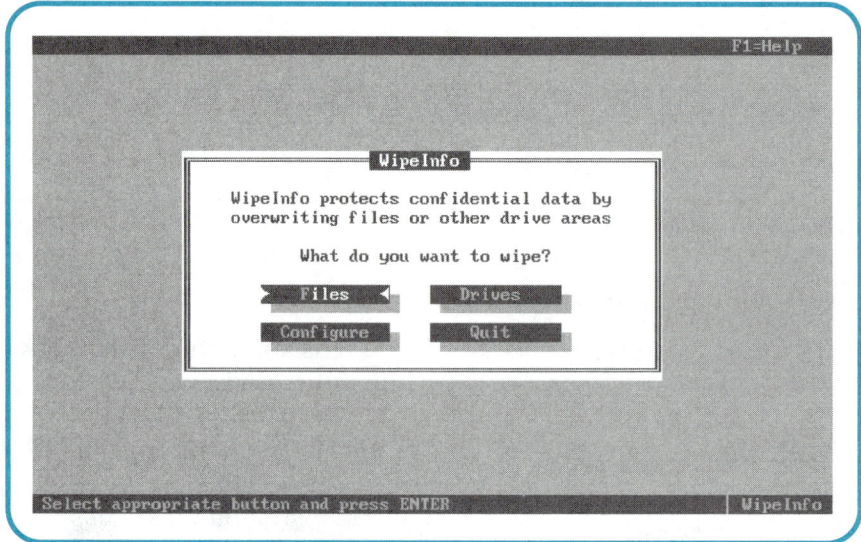

Figure 3.16   The initial WIPEINFO screen.

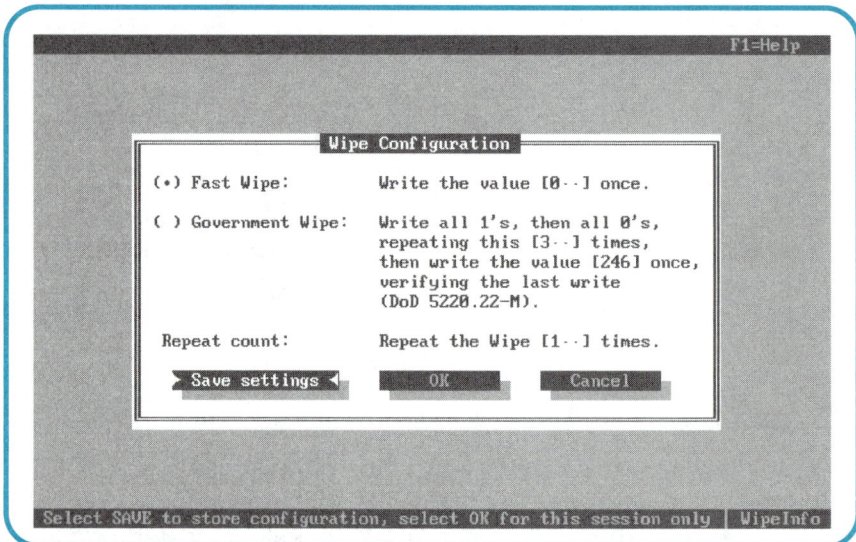

Figure 3.17   Select the desired WIPEINFO settings with the Wipe Configuration screen.

There are two Wipe options available in WIPEINFO: Fast Wipe and Government Wipe. WIPEINFO was configured with the Fast Wipe option when we eradicated the JUNK.DOC file in the previous Quick Steps. WIPEINFO overwrites each byte in a file one time with the specified value (0). You can change the 0 to another value: Press Tab or click to move the cursor to the Fast Wipe default value field, and type a new value. After you change the overwrite value, press Enter to save the new WIPEINFO configuration setting.

If you use WIPEINFO with the Government Wipe option shown in Figure 3.17, each wiped file is overwritten seven times with the following overwrite values:

Overwrite #	Overwrite Value
1	1
2	0
3	1
4	0
5	1
6	0
7	246

The Wipe Configuration screen in Figure 3.17 lets you change the number of times the 1/0 overwrite combination will be performed (the default is three times). You can also specify a different overwrite value for the final overwrite (the default value is 246). Press the down arrow then the Space Bar or click to place a dot next to the Government Wipe selection to use the Government Wipe option instead of the Fast Wipe option.

If you are the kind of person who worries whether the refrigerator light goes off when the door closes, you will appreciate the repeat count option shown in Figure 3.17. The default repeat count is 1, but you can tell WIPEINFO to repeat the wipe as many as 999 times! So if you use the Government Wipe option and change the repeat count to 4, each file will be overwritten 28 times ($4 \times 7 = 28$)!

You can also use WIPEINFO to wipe entire disks. We'll see how to use WIPEINFO to eradicate a disk in Chapter 6—Maintaining Your Hard Disk Drive.

What You Have Learned

In this chapter, you learned about Norton's file-related utilities. Specifically, you learned:

- ▶ DOS maintains a special status indicator for each file on a disk. This status indicates the state of several important file attributes, including read-only, archive, system, and hidden.
- ▶ Norton's FILEFIND utility lets you display, set, or clear any of the four file attributes listed previously, including those inaccessible to DOS's ATTRIB command.
- ▶ The FILEFIND utility also reports the size of one or more files and (optionally) determines whether the files will fit on another disk.
- ▶ In order to quickly and easily address an entire disk's data area, DOS works with larger, more manageable chunks of data called clusters. A cluster is the smallest block of space DOS will reserve for a file on a disk. The unused area of a cluster is referred to as slack.
- ▶ The FILEFIND utility allows you to set or clear a file's date and time stamp value.
- ▶ Norton's UNERASE utility gives you the ability to easily recover previously deleted files from your hard or floppy disks. The chances of recovering an accidentally deleted file are best if you run UNERASE immediately after the deletion.
- ▶ ERASE PROTECT is a TSR utility that can prevent deleted file data from being overwritten so that files may be recovered long after they are deleted.
- ▶ The FILEFIX utility can repair corrupt Lotus 1-2-3, Symphony, and dBASE data files.
- ▶ Norton's WIPEINFO utility overwrites a file's clusters, thereby removing the file's data from a disk. WIPEINFO overwrites each byte in every cluster of the specified file with the default value, 0.

Enhancing Your Batch Files

In This Chapter

▶ *Using batch files for automation*
▶ *Batch file syntax*
▶ *Improving batch files with BE: Batch Enhancer*

This chapter begins by explaining DOS batch file syntax and continues with an explanation of Norton's Batch Enhancer utility. Even if you are a batch file expert, you will appreciate what the Batch Enhancer can do for you—BE can make the simplest batch file look like a sophisticated windowing application.

Automation: The Key to Batch Files

Many PC operations require the same commands to be performed over and over again. For example, I have two subdirectories, WORK\MEMOS and WORK\REPORTS, that contain important work-related files. At the end of each week I have to place the contents of each subdirectory on separate floppy disks for my boss. The DOS commands I execute to perform this operation are shown in Table 4.1.

Table 4.1   DOS Commands for File Backup

DOS Command	Result
CD WORK\MEMOS	Moves to the WORK\MEMOS subdirectory
COPY *.* A:	Copies the contents of WORK\MEMOS to a floppy disk in the A: drive (when the COPY is complete I place a new floppy in the A: drive)
CD ..\REPORTS	Moves to the WORK\REPORTS subdirectory
COPY *.* A:	Copies the contents of WORK\REPORTS to the floppy disk in the A: drive

Using a DOS batch file, I can consolidate all four commands in Table 4.1 into one command.

Creating a Batch File

A batch file is an ASCII text file that contains one or more DOS commands. DOS can get confused if it encounters non-ASCII characters in a batch file. Therefore, you must be careful when determining what text editor to use for writing batch files. Even though DOS' EDLIN editor creates ASCII text files, I do not recommend using it—EDLIN is an antiquated, hard-to-use line editor (which means you can edit only one line at a time). Even the most modest shareware editors look fully featured when compared to EDLIN!

> **Tip:** Some word processors (for example, WordStar) offer a nondocument mode for creating/modifying ASCII text files. Use the DOS TYPE command (for example, **TYPE AUTOEXEC.BAT**) to see if a file contains only ASCII characters. If TYPE does not beep or display strange symbols, it's a good bet the file consists of ASCII characters only.

If you are looking for a good text editor, I suggest using either the Norton Editor or the built-in editor with the Norton Commander. The Norton Commander's built-in editor cannot handle large files, but you would have to write a very large batch file to exceed its limitations. The Norton Editor can edit virtually any size file and provides more bells and whistles than the Commander's built-in editor.

A Simple Batch File

When you have selected a text editor, you are ready to start creating batch files. It's not as hard as it sounds; all you have to do is type a list of commands that are to be carried out consecutively. To try it, use your text editor to create a batch file called ONE.BAT using the commands shown in Listing 4.1.

Listing 4.1   ONE.BAT Batch File Listing

```
ECHO OFF
REM This is a simple batch file called ONE.BAT.
REM It performs a DIR of the current directory.
DIR *.*
ECHO ON
REM This is the end of the ONE.BAT batch file.
PAUSE
```

To execute the ONE.BAT batch file, type the command `ONE.BAT` or just `ONE` and press Enter (see Figure 4.1).

Each line of the ONE.BAT batch file in Listing 4.1 is an executable DOS statement. Some of the special batch file statements used in ONE.BAT may not be familiar to you, however, so let's discuss each command separately.

The ECHO Command

DOS displays, or echoes, each statement on the screen as it executes a batch file. The ECHO OFF command causes DOS to suppress display of subsequent command lines in a batch file. DOS continues to suppress command line displays until it encounters an ECHO ON command.

```
EP        EXE      64424 04-29-91    6:00a
TS        EXE      18984 04-29-91    6:00a
IMAGE     EXE      11144 04-29-91    6:00a
FILEFIX   EXE      93704 04-29-91    6:00a
TROUBLE   HLP      44401 04-24-91   12:16p
NDOS      HLP     169547 04-09-91   10:37p
NU        HLP     336847 04-25-91    4:14p
NORTON    INI        530 06-03-91    7:45a
EP        INI         37 06-06-91    1:28p
READ      ME         511 04-29-91    6:00a
NORTON    OVL      62246 04-29-91    6:00a
NUCONFIG  OVL        908 04-29-91    6:00a
NDOS      OVL      73186 04-29-91    6:00a
SCREEN    SCR        596 06-08-91    4:45p
DISKREET  SYS      52846 04-29-91    6:00a
PCSHADOW  SYS        833 04-29-91    6:00a
KEYSTACK  SYS       1123 04-29-91    6:00a
        55 file(s)    2524294 bytes
                     23926784 bytes free

C:\NU>REM This is the end of the ONE.BAT batch file.

C:\NU>PAUSE
Press any key to continue . . .
```

88

Figure 4.1   The ONE.BAT batch file displays the contents of the current directory.

The REM Command

You can include comments or notes in a batch file by using the REM command. When DOS encounters a REM command in a batch file, it ignores everything else on that line. The second, third, and sixth lines of ONE.BAT are comment lines. Comment lines can be used to document a batch file's purpose and explain what is happening at a certain point within the batch file.

The ECHO OFF command at the start of ONE.BAT causes DOS to not display the first two comment lines when the batch file is executed. The comment on line 6 of ONE.BAT is displayed when the batch file is executed because the ECHO feature is turned back on at line 5 (ECHO ON).

The DIR Command

You can run an executable program (for example, files with the .EXE or .COM extensions), or a DOS command, in a batch file by specifying the program name/command followed by any required parameters. For example, the DIR command is invoked at the fourth line of ONE.BAT. The next statement in ONE.BAT, ECHO ON, is not performed until DIR finishes execution.

The PAUSE Command

The two lines after the DIR command in Listing 4.1

```
ECHO ON
REM This is the end of the ONE.BAT batch file.
```

turn the ECHO feature back on and note the end of the ONE.BAT batch file. Actually, the next statement, PAUSE, is the last one in ONE.BAT. The PAUSE command causes DOS to suspend execution of a batch file until you press a key. PAUSE is useful for suspending batch file execution while a user reads a screen, inserts a diskette, and so on.

Batch File Parameters

You have seen examples of some of The Norton Utilities that use command line parameters (for example, the /ON in EP /ON). Many other DOS applications support command line parameters as well. Because batch files represent a special type of executable file, it should be no surprise that they also support command line parameters. Our next batch file, TWO.BAT (Listing 4.2) shows how to incorporate command line parameters in a simple batch file.

89

Listing 4.2   TWO.BAT with a Parameter

```
ECHO OFF
REM This is a simple batch file called TWO.BAT.
REM It starts up ERASE PROTECT (EP) with a user-specified parameter.
EP %1
ECHO ON
REM This is the end of the TWO.BAT batch file.
PAUSE
```

When you run TWO.BAT, you should include one of the ERASE PROTECT parameters discussed in Chapter 3 (/ON, /OFF, or /STATUS). For example, if you type `TWO.BAT /STATUS` and press Enter, TWO.BAT will run ERASE PROTECT with a /STATUS parameter, thus showing the status of the ERASE PROTECT TSR program. The /STATUS parameter on the TWO.BAT command line is passed to ERASE PROTECT via the %1 operator in the statement `EP %1`.

DOS offers ten unique operators for using command line parameters in batch files: %0 through %9. The leftmost command line parameter is referred to as %0, the next leftmost parameter is %1, and so on.

> **Note:** Refer to *The Waite Group's MS-DOS Bible,* Fourth Edition for an explanation of how to use the SHIFT command to access more than ten command line parameters.

The next batch file, THREE.BAT (Listing 4.3), illustrates how two parameters can be used in a batch file.

Listing 4.3   THREE.BAT with Two Parameters

```
ECHO OFF
ECHO Hello, %2 !
REM This is a simple batch file called THREE.BAT.
REM We start off by greeting the user.
REM Next, THREE.BAT starts up ERASE PROTECT (EP) with a
REM user-specified parameter.
REM The batch file concludes with another brief
REM message to the user.
EP %1
ECHO ON
REM This is the end of the THREE.BAT batch file, %2 !
PAUSE
```

When you run THREE.BAT you must specify two parameters: the parameter for ERASE PROTECT and your name. For example, I might try `THREE.BAT /STATUS Joe`.

The second line in THREE.BAT displays a greeting to the user. Even though the ECHO feature is turned off by the first line of THREE.BAT, we can use ECHO to display a string of characters on the screen. For example, the statement in Listing 4.3 `ECHO Hello, 2% !` echoes the message "Hello, Joe." regardless of whether ECHO is ON or OFF.

The next-to-last line in THREE.BAT also uses %2: `REM This is the end of the THREE.BAT batch file, %2 !` This statement displays a batch file termination message with the user's name and illustrates two important points:

1. Batch file command-line parameters may be incorporated in remark (REM) statements.

2. A parameter can be used in as many different statements within a batch file as is necessary.

Looping Within a Batch File

Creating a batch file is similar to writing a computer program in a language like C, Pascal, or BASIC. Computer programming languages offer a means for user input, output, and comments. We have seen how DOS batch files offer these features as well with PAUSE, ECHO, and REM commands. Another important feature common to programming languages and batch files is the capability to perform the same operation over and over again, or loop. Listing 4.4 illustrates how to use a loop in a batch file.

91

Listing 4.4   FOUR.BAT with a Looping Construct

```
ECHO OFF
REM This is a simple batch file called FOUR.BAT.
REM FOUR.BAT runs ERASE PROTECT (EP) twice...
REM once for each parameter entry in the FOR loop.
FOR %%a IN (ON STATUS) DO EP /%%a
ECHO ON
```

FOUR.BAT uses a FOR loop to run the ERASE PROTECT utility twice. The syntax of a FOR loop is

```
FOR %%x IN (set) DO statement %%x
```

In short, this syntax means that the specified *statement* will be executed once with each item listed in set. Each item in the set is a parameter for the statement. Therefore, the FOR loop in Listing 4.4 first executes EP /ON, followed by EP /STATUS.

You may wonder why the slash (/) appears before the second %%a and not with the ON and STATUS parameters. We must write the parameters without slashes because DOS strips the slash off the parameters in the FOR loop. So if you try to use: **FOR %%a IN (/ON /STATUS) DO EP %%a**, DOS will try to run EP ON (that is, without the slash preceding ON).

The two %%a's in the FOR loop syntax are referred to as dummy parameters. A dummy parameter acts as a place holder in the FOR statement. The dummy parameter is replaced by each item in the set for every iteration through the loop. In FOUR.BAT, I chose to use the letter "a" (%%a) as the dummy parameter. Actually, you can use any letter in the alphabet after the two percent signs. Perhaps the most important rule to remember is that both dummy parameters in the FOR loop must use the same letter. For example, FOR %%a IN (ON STATUS) DO EP /%%z is not a valid FOR loop. In fact, this erroneous FOR loop causes DOS to try to execute ERASE PROTECT twice with a /%z parameter.

Conditional Execution (IF and GOTO)

One of the minor annoyances with DOS' COPY command is that it lets you overwrite files without warning. The command COPY MYMEMO.DOC YOURMEMO.DOC copies the file MYMEMO.DOC to YOURMEMO.DOC. If a file named YOURMEMO.DOC existed before executing COPY, it is overwritten by MYMEMO.DOC and, probably, is gone forever! You can use a batch file like the one shown in Listing 4.5 to copy individual files and reduce the chance of overwriting important data.

Listing 4.5   C.BAT—An Individual File Copy Utility

```
ECHO OFF
REM This batch file helps you avoid accidentally
REM overwriting important files when using the
REM COPY command.
IF NOT EXIST %2 GOTO end
ECHO WARNING...%2 ALREADY EXISTS!!!
ECHO PRESS CTRL-C TO ABORT THIS COPY...
ECHO PRESS ANY OTHER KEY TO OVERWRITE %2...
PAUSE
:end
ECHO ON
COPY %1 %2
```

I have named the batch file in Listing 4.5 C.BAT as an abbreviation for DOS' COPY command. Rather than using DOS' COPY command to copy MYMEMO.DOC to YOURMEMO.DOC I can use C.BAT with the following parameters: C MYMEMO.DOC YOURMEMO.DOC.

If C.BAT determines that YOURMEMO.DOC already exists, the batch file suspends execution (via PAUSE) and lets you abort the copy by pressing the Ctrl-C key combination. You can press any other key to let MYMEMO.DOC overwrite YOURMEMO.DOC. C.BAT uses a couple of special commands to perform this intelligent copy process: IF and GOTO.

The IF command in Listing 4.5 IF NOT EXIST %2 GOTO end is read "if the file specified by the second command line parameter (%2) does not exist, go to the 'end' label." In all the previous batch files, we have seen that DOS executes one command after another without skipping any in between. The IF . . . GOTO construction allows us to branch around one or more statements within a batch file. This branching feature illustrates yet another commonalty between programming and batch file languages.

Why is it so important to allow branching within a batch file? One of two different situations may arise when running C.BAT: Either the destination file already exists or it does not. C.BAT must act differently depending upon the existence of the destination file.

93

If the destination file does not exist, we want to copy the source file to the destination file with no further intervention by the user. In this case, the GOTO clause of the IF statement causes control to jump to the next statement after the "end" label. A *label* is an identifier that is preceded by a colon (:) and appears on a line by itself. The ECHO ON statement is the first line executed after this branch (since ECHO ON is the first statement after the ":end" identifier). Then, the file is copied via the COPY %1 %2 statement.

If the destination file does exist, we want to display a message and suspend batch file execution until the user decides whether the file should be overwritten. In this case, the GOTO clause of the IF statement is not executed. Because the condition of the IF statement is not true, the next line in the batch file is executed. More specifically, the three ECHO statements are executed followed by the PAUSE command. At this point, the user can press Ctrl-C to abort the batch file or any other key to overwrite the destination file. If you press a key other than Ctrl-C, the ECHO ON and COPY %1 %2 statements are executed. (Notice that the ":end" identifier line is treated like a REMark and is skipped.)

Note: This is a very simple example of the IF and GOTO commands. For a more detailed explanation of IF and GOTO, refer to *MS-DOS Bible,* Fourth Edition.

Interactive Batch Files

You have seen how PAUSE can be used to suspend batch file execution until the user presses a key. The previous C.BAT example took PAUSE one step further: It offered a point where the user could press Ctrl-C and gracefully abort batch file execution. PAUSE is the only mechanism DOS provides for user interaction with batch files. What if you want to write a menuing batch file that lets you select from a list of applications to run like the one in Figure 4.2?

It would not be too difficult to write a batch file to display the text shown in Figure 4.2. Further, you could use PAUSE to wait for the user to make a selection. But since there is no way to know what key the user pressed, how would you know which application to start? The answer is simple: Use Norton's Batch Enhancer utility.

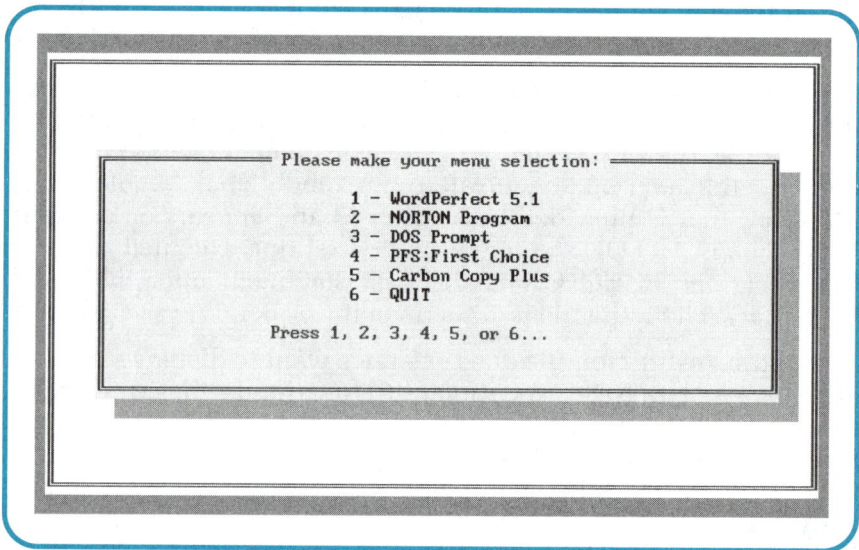

```
┌───────── Please make your menu selection: ─────────┐
│                                                    │
│              1 - WordPerfect 5.1                   │
│              2 - NORTON Program                    │
│              3 - DOS Prompt                        │
│              4 - PFS:First Choice                  │
│              5 - Carbon Copy Plus                  │
│              6 - QUIT                              │
│                                                    │
│         Press 1, 2, 3, 4, 5, or 6...               │
│                                                    │
└────────────────────────────────────────────────────┘
```

Figure 4.2   This sample application menu selection screen was created using a batch file.

BE: Batch Enhancer

The Batch Enhancer utility is different from the other Norton utilities we have discussed so far. As its name implies, BE can enhance dull and dreary batch files, thus making them more aesthetically pleasing. For my money, however, BE's most important attribute is its ability to handle user entries and permit a batch file to process menu selections. The MENU.BAT listing shown in Listing 4.6 shows how BE can be used in an interactive menuing batch file.

Listing 4.6   *The MENU.BAT Batch File*

```
ECHO OFF
REM Display application menu
:menu
BE CLS
BE SA WHITE ON MAGENTA
BE WINDOW 1 1 23 78 BRIGHT WHITE ON BLUE ZOOM
BE WINDOW 6 6 18 74 BRIGHT CYAN ON GREEN SHADOW
BE ROWCOL 6 24 " Please make your menu selection: " BRIGHT WHITE
BE ROWCOL 8 32 "1 - WordPerfect 5.1" BRIGHT YELLOW
BE ROWCOL 9 32 "2 - NORTON Program" BRIGHT YELLOW
BE ROWCOL 10 32 "3 - DOS Prompt" BRIGHT YELLOW
BE ROWCOL 11 32 "4 - PFS:First Choice" BRIGHT YELLOW
BE ROWCOL 12 32 "5 - Carbon Copy Plus" BRIGHT YELLOW
BE ROWCOL 13 32 "6 - QUIT" BRIGHT YELLOW
BE ROWCOL 15 24
REM Request input from the user
BE ASK "Press 1, 2, 3, 4, 5, or 6..." 123456 BRIGHT WHITE
REM Process the user's entry
IF ERRORLEVEL 6 GOTO quit
IF ERRORLEVEL 5 GOTO ccplus
IF ERRORLEVEL 4 GOTO first
IF ERRORLEVEL 3 GOTO prompt
IF ERRORLEVEL 2 GOTO norton
REM NOTE: No GOTO for WordPerfect is required since it is
REM      started by default with the next executable
REM      statement.
REM WordPerfect 5.1 selection
:wp51
CD C:\wp51
WP
GOTO menu
```

```
REM NORTON Program selection
:norton
CD C:\NU
NORTON
GOTO menu
REM DOS Shell selection
:prompt
REM Inform user how to leave the DOS prompt
BE CLS
BE BOX 5 15 19 65 DOUBLE CYAN
BE ROWCOL 8 25 "YOU HAVE SELECTED TO EXECUTE THE" BRIGHT WHITE
BE ROWCOL 9 25 "DOS PROMPT. THE DOS PROMPT ALLOWS" BRIGHT WHITE
BE ROWCOL 10 25 "YOU TO RUN ANY DOS COMMAND OR" BRIGHT WHITE
BE ROWCOL 11 25 "PROGRAM. WHEN YOU WANT TO RETURN" BRIGHT WHITE
BE ROWCOL 12 25 "TO THE APPLICATION MENU, TYPE" BRIGHT WHITE
BE ROWCOL 13 25 "'EXIT' AND PRESS ENTER." BRIGHT WHITE
BE ROWCOL 16 25 "THIS MESSAGE WILL SELF-DESTRUCT" BRIGHT RED
BE ROWCOL 17 33 "IN 5 SECONDS!!" BRIGHT RED
BE BEEP
REM Delay 5 seconds (90 / 18 = 5 secs.)
BE DELAY 90
BE CLS   C:\COMMAND.COM
GOTO menu
REM PFS:First Choice selection
:first
CD C:\CHOICE
FIRST
GOTO menu
REM Carbon Copy Plus selection
:ccplus
CD C:\CCPLUS
CC
GOTO menu
:quit
BE SA NORMAL
BE CLS
ECHO ON
```

When MENU.BAT is executed, it displays the menu selection screen shown in Figure 4.2. You may have noticed the various BE statements throughout MENU.BAT. For example, the fourth line in MENU.BAT is BE CLS, which illustrates the general syntax for the BE utility. In short, the BE utility name is always followed by a subcommand and, optionally, subcommand parameters. In the BE

CLS statement (Listing 4.6), CLS is referred to as the subcommand. Let's look more closely at MENU.BAT and discuss each of the BE subcommands it uses.

The CLS Subcommand

CLS is a BE subcommand that clears the screen and moves the cursor to the *home position* (the top left corner of the screen). I use CLS in MENU.BAT to provide a fresh, blank screen to display my application menu. The DOS CLS command is functionally identical to BE's CLS subcommand.

The SA Subcommand

Note: You need to install the DOS device driver ANSI.SYS before you can use the SA subcommand.

1. Check your DOS directory for ANSI.SYS. (Since my DOS directory is called DOS, this explanation uses the C:\DOS directory. If your ANSI.SYS file resides elsewhere, substitute that location for my C:\DOS specification.)

2. Look for a file named CONFIG.SYS in the root directory of your C: drive or on your DOS diskette.

   If you cannot find CONFIG.SYS, create in the root directory a CONFIG.SYS file with
   `DEVICE=C:\DOS\ANSI.SYS` in it. Or, if your PC does not have a hard disk, use `DEVICE=A:\DOS\ANSI.SYS` instead.

   If CONFIG.SYS does exist, examine it to see if a
   `DEVICE=ANSI.SYS` line exists. If no such line exists, add it.

3. Reboot to install the ANSI.SYS driver.

97

The SA subcommand, which is an acronym for Screen Attributes, allows you to set the foreground and background colors on your PC's display. The first example of SA in MENU.BAT sets the foreground color (text) to WHITE and the background color to MAGENTA. The syntax for this usage of SA is

```
BE SA forecolor ON backcolor
```

where *forecolor* and *backcolor* are the foreground and background colors, respectively. There are eight foreground/background colors available with SA:

Black	Magenta
Green	Yellow
White	Cyan
Blue	Red

You may use any combination of these colors for either the foreground or background in SA. Be careful not to set the foreground and background colors to the same value or you will wind up with "invisible" text on your screen.

You may modify the foreground color with either of the two intensity values BRIGHT or BLINKING. For example, the statement BE SA BRIGHT WHITE ON BLUE changes the foreground color to BRIGHT WHITE and the background color to BLUE.

98

As you can see, the SA subcommand lets you customize your screen using your favorite foreground/background colors. You can use the other form of the SA subcommand when you want to return the screen to the default colors. The syntax for this other SA form is

```
BE SA main-setting
```

where *main-setting* is either NORMAL, REVERSE, or UNDERLINE.

The second-to-last statement in MENU.BAT BE SA NORMAL resets the foreground and background colors to their default values (for example, on some EGA monitors, the default values are WHITE on BLACK). Also, NORMAL turns off the REVERSE and UNDERLINE main-setting switches if they are on. You should experiment with different foreground/background colors and main-setting values to see what combination you prefer.

The WINDOW Subcommand

The next two lines in MENU.BAT

```
BE WINDOW 1 1 23 78 BRIGHT WHITE ON BLUE ZOOM
BE WINDOW 6 6 18 74 BRIGHT CYAN ON GREEN SHADOW
```

use the WINDOW subcommand to place two windows on the screen. The syntax for the WINDOW subcommand is

```
BE WINDOW top left bottom right attributes
```

where *top*, *left*, *bottom*, and *right* are the window coordinates and *attributes* specifies characteristics about the window. Valid attributes include any of the colors in Listing 4.6 and the special window options SHADOW and ZOOM.

Window coordinates are specified by row and column where the top left corner of the screen is row 0 column 0. Column values increase from left to right across the screen and row values increase from top to bottom.

Window colors are specified with the format

```
BE WINDOW border-color ON fill-color
```

where *border-color* is the color BE will use to draw the window border and *fill-color* is the color BE will use to fill the window.

When BE draws a window with the SHADOW option, it places a see-through shadow along the bottom and right sides of the window to create the illusion of a three-dimensional object. Windows drawn with the other special option, ZOOM, appear to explode onto the screen.

With this knowledge, we can now analyze the statement

```
BE WINDOW 1 1 23 78 BRIGHT WHITE ON BLUE ZOOM
```

which draws a window from row 1 column 1 to row 23 column 78. This BLUE window is drawn with a BRIGHT WHITE border. Finally, the ZOOM option is used to create the exploding visual effect.

The ROWCOL Subcommand

The next several statements in MENU.BAT use the ROWCOL subcommand to place colored text on the screen. The syntax for ROWCOL is

```
BE ROWCOL row column text color
```

where *row* and *column* specify where the *text* should be located and *color* is any one of the colors in Listing 4.7. These colors may also be modified by the intensity values BRIGHT or BLINKING. So the statement

```
BE ROWCOL 6 24 " Please make your menu selection: " BRIGHT WHITE
```

places the BRIGHT WHITE text " Please make your menu selection: " on the 6th row starting in the 24th column. Several ROWCOL statements are used together to create the application menu shown in Figure 4.2. The last ROWCOL command used for the menu is BE ROWCOL 15 24, which places the cursor on row 15 column 24 but does not display any text. This cursor placement is important for the next statement in MENU.BAT which uses the ASK subcommand.

The ASK Subcommand

The ASK subcommand is the key to interactive batch files with the BE utility. The syntax for ASK is

```
BE ASK text keys color
```

where *text* is the prompt to display in *color* and *keys* are the valid keys that the user may press. For example, the statement

```
BE ASK "Press 1, 2, 3, 4, 5, or 6..." 123456 BRIGHT WHITE
```

displays the BRIGHT WHITE prompt Press 1, 2, 3, 4, 5, or 6... and waits for the user to press one of the numeric keys 1 through 6 (123456). BE sounds an error tone if you try to press a key not listed in the "keys" list. When you press a valid key, BE places a value in a special location called ERRORLEVEL.

The ERRORLEVEL Variable

ERRORLEVEL is a variable whose value may be set by either DOS or an executable program, such as Norton's BE utility. Once a program like BE sets ERRORLEVEL, a batch file may perform conditional operations based upon ERRORLEVEL's value. BE sets ERRORLEVEL to

1—if the first key in the "keys" list was pressed

2—if the second key in the "keys" list was pressed, and so on.

The five IF statements

```
IF ERRORLEVEL 6 GOTO quit
IF ERRORLEVEL 5 GOTO ccplus
IF ERRORLEVEL 4 GOTO first
IF ERRORLEVEL 3 GOTO prompt
IF ERRORLEVEL 2 GOTO norton
```

branch to different parts of MENU.BAT depending upon the value of ERRORLEVEL. Because of a quirk with the ERRORLEVEL feature, you must always list the "IF ERRORLEVEL . . . GOTO . . ." statements in descending order of ERRORLEVEL value. Also note that there is no IF statement to check for an ERRORLEVEL value of 1.

Since the batch file commands for menu selection #1 (WordPerfect 5.1) appear immediately after the last IF statement, there is no need to perform a GOTO. DOS automatically executes the next sequential batch file statement if ERRORLEVEL is not 2 when the IF ERRORLEVEL 2 GOTO norton statement is executed.

101

Each block of application statements in MENU.BAT is fairly straightforward. In general, a CD is performed to switch to the application's directory, the application is executed, and the menu is redisplayed. The only exception to this general flow is the DOS Shell menu selection, which uses a few more BE subcommands.

The BOX Subcommand

When option #3 (DOS Prompt) is selected in MENU.BAT, the screen is cleared and a box is displayed with the BOX subcommand whose syntax is

```
BE BOX top left bottom right attributes
```

where *top*, *left*, *bottom*, and *right* are the box coordinates and *attributes* specifies characteristics about the box. Valid attributes include any of the colors in Listing 4.7 and the special box border options SINGLE and DOUBLE. By default, boxes are drawn with a SINGLE line border.

For example, the statement

```
BE BOX 5 15 19 65 DOUBLE CYAN
```

draws a DOUBLE-line border CYAN box from row 5 column 15 to row 19 column 65. Several ROWCOL statements are then used to display information about the DOS Prompt option.

The BEEP Subcommand

The BEEP subcommand is also used within the batch file logic for the DOS Shell selection. The statement BE BEEP plays a tone through your PC's internal speaker. If you are musically inclined, you can use BEEP to play a simple song or just a few random notes. The syntax for BEEP is

```
BE BEEP /D# /F# /R# /W#
```

and each option is defined as shown in Table 4.2.

Table 4.2   BEEP Subcommand Options

Option	Meaning
/D#	Duration or length of tone to play in 18ths of second (for example, /D9 equals $^9/_{18}$ or $^1/_2$ second)
/F#	Frequency of the tone in cycles per second (for example, /F262 represents a frequency of 262 cycles per second [Hz] or a musical note "C")
/R#	Number of times to repeat the tone (for example, /R4 repeats the tone four times)
/W#	How long to pause, in 18ths of a second, after playing the specified tone (for example, /W18 equals a pause of 1 second)

The DELAY Subcommand

The DELAY command offers an easy-to-use method of freezing a screen for a period of time without waiting for the user to press a key to continue. The syntax for DELAY is

```
BE DELAY time
```

where *time* is expressed in 18ths of a second. So, the statement in Listing 4.6

```
BE DELAY 90
```

causes the MENU.BAT batch file to suspend execution for 90/18 or 5 seconds.

> **Tip:** You can customize MENU.BAT to work with the applications on your system. Just edit all the lines corresponding to the entry you want to replace. For example, to replace the PFS:First Choice entry, you would edit lines 12, 21, and 56 through 59.

Batch Enhancer Script Files

When you run the MENU.BAT batch file, the menu lines appear on-screen one at a time, with a slight pause before each line appears. This is because it takes DOS time to find and execute the BE commands included in MENU.BAT. You can, however, make it easier to execute a series of BE commands by including them in a script file. When you include the BE commands in a script file, the Batch Enhancer can execute them much more quickly. Let's revisit the MENU.BAT example to explore the power of script files.

103

Look at Listing 4.6. The lines of MENU.BAT included in Listing 4.7 build the menu's lines on-screen and request the user's input.

Listing 4.7   The SCREEN.SCR Script File

```
BE SA WHITE ON MAGENTA
BE WINDOW 1 1 23 78 BRIGHT WHITE ON BLUE ZOOM
BE WINDOW 6 6 18 74 BRIGHT CYAN ON GREEN SHADOW
BE ROWCOL 6 24 " Please make your menu selection: " BRIGHT WHITE
BE ROWCOL 8 32 "1 - WordPerfect 5.1" BRIGHT YELLOW
BE ROWCOL 9 32 "2 - NORTON Program" BRIGHT YELLOW
BE ROWCOL 10 32 "3 - DOS Prompt" BRIGHT YELLOW
BE ROWCOL 11 32 "4 - PFS:First Choice" BRIGHT YELLOW
BE ROWCOL 12 32 "5 - Carbon Copy Plus" BRIGHT YELLOW
BE ROWCOL 13 32 "6 - QUIT" BRIGHT YELLOW
BE ROWCOL 15 24
REM Request input from the user
BE ASK "Press 1, 2, 3, 4, 5, or 6..." 123456 BRIGHT WHITE
```

If you remove these lines from MENU.BAT and save them as a separate script file, you can include a command for MENU.BAT to run that script file, which will build the menu screen much more quickly. To do so:

1. Use your text editor to remove the lines in Listing 4.7 from MENU.BAT and save them as a file called SCREEN.SCR. Or, you can simply use the text editor to create and name that file.

2. Open the MENU.BAT file and delete the lines shown in Listing 4.7, if you haven't done so.

3. In place of the lines you've deleted (immediately following the command BE CLS), type the command BE C:\NU\SCREEN.SCR. (Substitute the drive and directory where you've saved SCREEN.SCR for C:\NU.)

4. Save the updated MENU.BAT. Listing 4.8 shows the new MENU.BAT file.

104

Listing 4.8   The Revised MENU.BAT File

```
ECHO OFF
REM Display application menu
:menu
BE CLS
BE C:\NU\SCREEN.SCR
REM Process the user's entry
IF ERRORLEVEL 6 GOTO quit
IF ERRORLEVEL 5 GOTO ccplus
IF ERRORLEVEL 4 GOTO first
IF ERRORLEVEL 3 GOTO prompt
IF ERRORLEVEL 2 GOTO norton
REM NOTE: No GOTO for WordPerfect is required since it
REM       started by default with the next executable
REM       statement.
REM WordPerfect 5.1 selection
:wp51
CD C:\wp51
WP
GOTO menu
REM NORTON Program selection
:norton
CD C:\NU
NORTON
GOTO menu
```

```
REM DOS selection
:prompt
REM Inform user how to leave the DOS prompt
BE CLS
BE BOX 5 15 19 65 DOUBLE CYAN
BE ROWCOL 8 25 "YOU HAVE SELECTED TO EXECUTE THE" BRIGHT WHITE
BE ROWCOL 9 25 "DOS PROMPT. THE DOS PROMPT ALLOWS" BRIGHT WHITE
BE ROWCOL 10 25 "YOU TO RUN ANY DOS COMMAND OR" BRIGHT WHITE
BE ROWCOL 11 25 "PROGRAM. WHEN YOU WANT TO RETURN" BRIGHT WHITE
BE ROWCOL 12 25 "TO THE APPLICATION MENU, TYPE" BRIGHT WHITE
BE ROWCOL 13 25 "'EXIT' AND PRESS ENTER." BRIGHT WHITE
BE ROWCOL 16 25 "THIS MESSAGE WILL SELF-DESTRUCT" BRIGHT RED
BE ROWCOL 17 33 "IN 5 SECONDS!!" BRIGHT RED
BE BEEP
REM Delay 5 seconds (90 /18 = 5 secs.)
BE DELAY 90
BE CLS
C:\COMMAND.COM
GOTO menu
REM PFS:First Choice selection
:first
CD C:\CHOICE
FIRST
GOTO menu
REM Carbon Copy Plus selection
:ccplus
CD C:\CCPLUS
CC
GOTO menu
:quit
BE SA NORMAL
BE CLS
ECHO ON
```

Now, when you run MENU.BAT, the initial menu screen appears much more quickly. In addition to creating script files to include in batch files, you can create ones for use from the DOS prompt.

 Caution: Batch Enhancer script files can contain only BE commands. DOS commands are not recognized.

Other Batch Enhancer Commands

In addition to those BE commands we've already described, there are several others you'll find particularly helpful when creating batch and script files. Table 4.3 lists these commands and gives a brief description of each. A complete discussion of these commands is beyond the scope of this book but can be found in The Norton Utilities User's Guide.

Table 4.3   Other BE Commands

Command	Use to
EXIT	End execution of a BE script file
GOTO	Control the starting point for executing a script file (works only with BE script files)
JUMP	Specify branching in BE script files
MONTHDAY	Return the system day and month as a code for use by the batch file
PRINTCHAR	Display the specified characters on-screen in the specified colors
REBOOT	Have a batch file execute a warm boot of your computer
SHIFTSTATE	Report to the file whether the Shift, Alt, or Ctrl key is depressed
TRIGGER	Pause a batch file and restart it at the specified time
WEEKDAY	Return the system day of the week as a code for use by the batch file

106

What You Have Learned

In this chapter you learned some of the fundamental concepts behind DOS batch files. Specifically, you learned:

► A batch file is an ASCII text file that contains one or more DOS commands.

► Batch files represent a special type of executable file and support command line parameters (for example, %1 and %2). Batch files also offer looping and conditional constructs similar to the ones supported by programming languages.

▶ Besides PAUSE, DOS batch files offer no useful means for accepting user input. Further, PAUSE does not allow the batch file programmer to execute certain blocks of statements based upon a specific key depression.

▶ The Batch Enhancer utility can enhance dull and dreary batch files thus making them more aesthetically pleasing. Through the use of subcommands, BE can add color, sound, and windows and manage user interaction within batch files.

▶ The ASK subcommand is the key to interactive batch files with the BE utility. ASK allows the batch file programmer to execute specific blocks of batch file statements based on user keyboard entries/selections.

▶ You can create script files that quickly execute BE commands. Include script files in batch files.

107

Managing Your Disks with the Utilities

In This Chapter

▶ *Working with directories and tree structures*
▶ *Using NCD: Norton Change Directory to simplify directory operations*
▶ *Using Prune & Graft*
▶ *Recovering a deleted directory*
▶ *Sorting files*
▶ *Finding your way through the forest*

This important chapter discusses a few of the Norton utilities that help you manage your disks. The disk-based utilities covered in this chapter will help you with everything from working with directories and subdirectories to locating text strings.

We begin with an explanation of the DOS directory tree structure. Then we discuss the Norton Change Directory (NCD) utility, which offers a visual alternative to several of the DOS directory commands. You learn how to organize your disk with the Prune & Graft feature of NCD and the Directory Sort utility. Finally, we cover two important features of the FILEFIND utility that help you locate files and text strings on your disks.

Directories and Tree Structures

Modern hard disk drives are capable of storing hundreds of megabytes of data. DOS allows you to break a disk down into smaller, more manageable areas known as directories and subdirectories. As you may already know, a disk is similar to a filing cabinet because they both are used to store data. We can take that analogy one step further and say that a disk directory is comparable to a folder within the filing cabinet. A subdirectory is merely a directory within a directory, or, a folder within a folder.

A special directory, called the *root directory,* exists on all disks (for example, C:). All other directories on a disk are either a direct or indirect descendent of the root directory. For example, in the path name C:\TEMP, TEMP is a first-level directory from the root C:. In the path name C:\TEMP\WORK, WORK is a subdirectory from the first-level directory C:\TEMP. Figure 5.1 shows the relationship between the root directory and other directories/subdirectries.

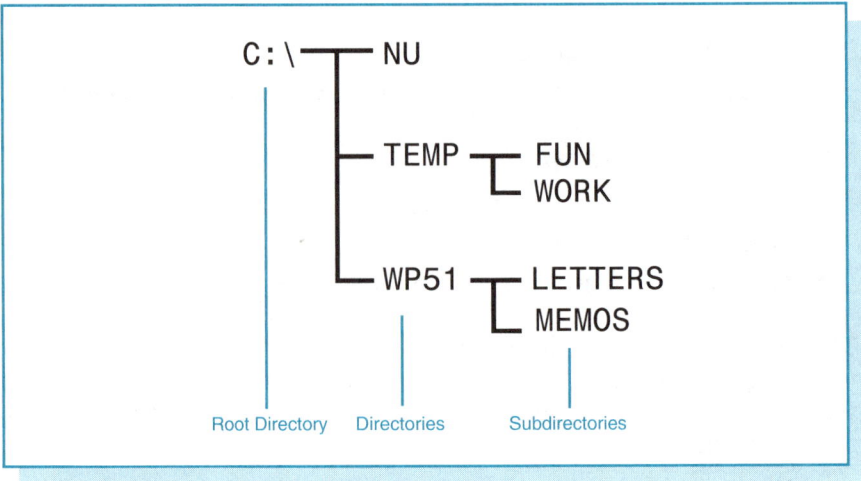

Figure 5.1   Directories on a disk form a tree structure, with multiple branches and levels.

In Figure 5.1, there are three directories off the root: TEMP, NU, and WP51. Further, the TEMP and WP51 directories have subdirectories associated with them. Figure 5.1 is a graphical representation of DOS' directory tree structure—each descendent directory is shown as a branch off its parent directory. Unlike a real tree, however, the root of a DOS directory tree is at the *top* of the diagram.

The DOS MD and RD commands are used to make and remove directories, respectively. For example, the TEMP directory shown in Figure 5.1 can be created with the command `MD C:\TEMP`. And, if the MEMOS directory in Figure 5.1 is empty (that is it contains no files or subdirectories), it may be removed with the command `RD C:\WP51\MEMOS`.

Once you have created a few directories on your disk, how do you move from one directory to another? The DOS CD command is the basic vehicle for jumping from one directory to another. For example, the command `CD C:\TEMP\WORK` changes the active directory to C:\TEMP\WORK.

111

> **Tip:** Use DOS's PROMPT command to include the active directory in the DOS prompt. The command `PROMPT $P$G` changes the command prompt from C> to C:\> when in the root directory. The advantage of using this type of prompt is more apparent when another directory or subdirectory is active. For example, when the C:\TEMP\WORK directory is active, the DOS prompt becomes C:\TEMP\WORK>. You can add `PROMPT $P$G` to your AUTOEXEC.BAT file to make this feature automatic. (For more on AUTOEXEC.BAT, see "View AUTOEXEC.BAT in Chapter 2. Chapter 4 gives more information on editing batch files like AUTOEXEC.BAT.)

NCD: Norton Change Directory

Although the DOS CD command is adequate for moving about from directory to directory, the Norton Change Directory (NCD) utility offers a fast graphical approach to directory navigation.

Changing Directories with Norton Change Directory (NCD)

1. At the DOS prompt, type the command **NCD**, and press Enter.

   This starts the NCD utility and displays a directory tree structure like the one shown in Figure 5.2.

2. Press the right arrow key or click to highlight the destination directory (for example, **WP51**), and press Enter.

   The destination directory becomes the active directory, and the NCD utility is terminated. ☐

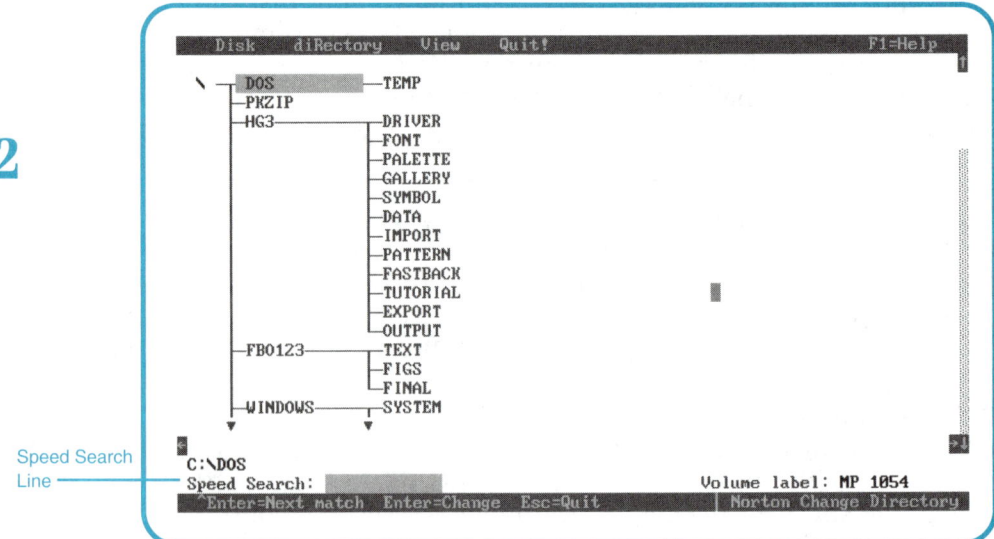

Speed Search Line ————

Figure 5.2   The NCD utility provides many useful directory tools.

The screen in Figure 5.2 shows the directory tree structure horizontally. In other words, the root directory is on the left, and the first level of directories appears to the right of the root. In Figure 5.2, the root is the current directory; NCD denotes the current directory with an inverse block around it (see the root [\] in Figure 5.2).

As shown in the Quick Steps, you can use the arrow keys or mouse to move from one directory to another with NCD. In general, the up and down arrow keys will move vertically through the tree, and the left and right arrow keys will move horizontally. You may also use the Home and End keys to jump to the top (root) and bottom (lowest directory/subdirectory) of the tree, respectively. The PgUp and PgDn keys are handy for quickly moving up and down through the tree a screenful at a time.

Although the selection block moves from one directory to another when you press the arrow keys, the active directory is not changed until you press Enter (as shown in Step 2 of the Quick Steps). You can press Esc at any time within NCD to quit the utility and return to DOS without changing directories.

The NCD Speed Search

A Speed Search box appears in the bottom left portion of the NCD screen in Figure 5.2. The Speed Search feature allows you to quickly jump from one directory to another without having to search for your destination with the arrow keys. For example, to move the highlight to the WINDOWS directory in Figure 5.2, I can press W and the selection block moves to WINDOWS (Figure 5.3).

113

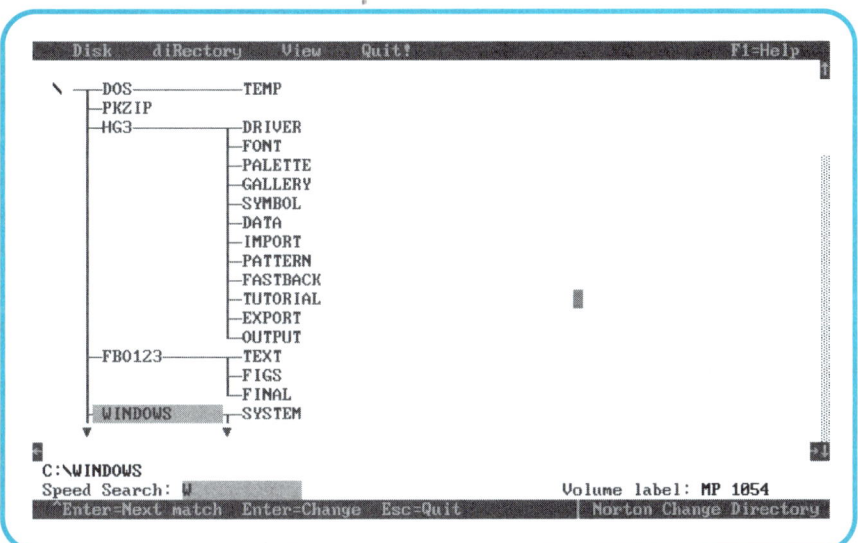

Figure 5.3   Using Speed Search with NCD.

Now I can press Enter to make WINDOWS the active directory. The Norton Speed Search feature is very simple to use: just keep typing the letters of the name you wish to locate until you find a match. Depending on how you name your directories, Speed Search needs from one to eight keystrokes to locate the desired directory.

The NCD Function Keys

The NCD utility isn't just a visual replacement for DOS's CD command; NCD offers several other features as well, which are accessible through the Disk, Directory, and View menus. I find it easier to use these other features via function keys rather than the pull-down menus. NCD supports eight function keys: F1, F2, F3, and F6–F10.

F1—Help

114

Pressing F1 provides helpful information about the NCD utility (Figure 5.4).

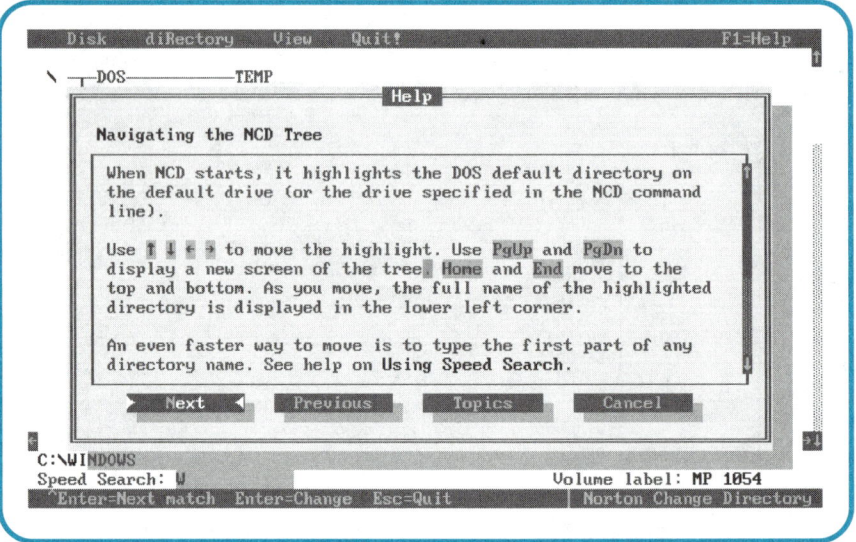

Figure 5.4   Pressing F1 accesses the Help screen.

F2—Rescan

The first time you run NCD, it scans your disk to create a list of the directories/subdirectories. This information is stored in a file called TREEINFO.NCD in the root directory. Each subsequent time you run NCD, it uses the TREEINFO.NCD file to generate the directory tree on your monitor. Unfortunately, DOS directory commands do not keep TREEINFO.NCD up to date. So if you create or remove directories with MD or RD after the TREEINFO.NCD file is created, NCD may report erroneous directory information. If you suspect the TREEINFO.NCD file is out of sync with your disk's directory structure, press F2 to rescan the disk and update TREEINFO.NCD.

F3—Select Drive

Press F3 to switch from one disk drive to another within NCD. When you press F3, the screen in Figure 5.5, which lists all the valid drive selections, is displayed.

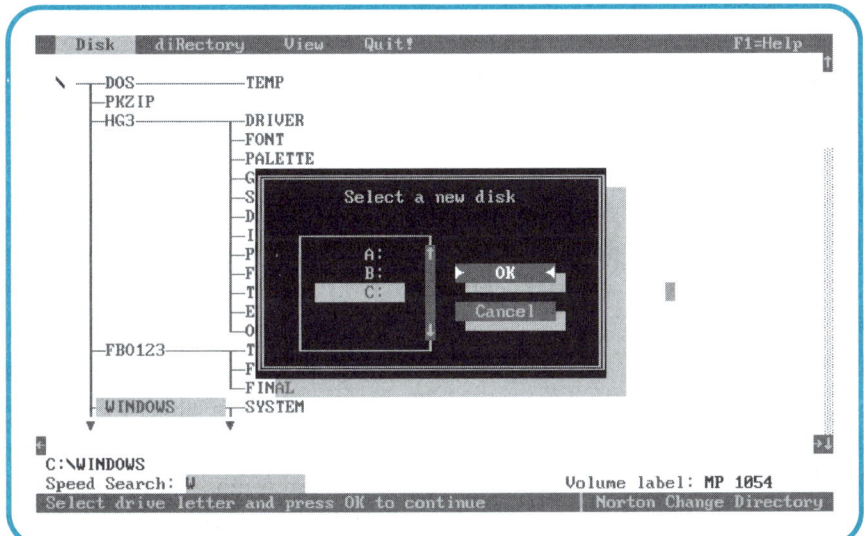

Figure 5.5   The NCD drive selection box lets you change the active drive.

Use the up or down arrow keys or click the mouse to move the selection block to the desired drive, then press Enter or click OK. Or, just type the drive letter (for example, C) and NCD immediately switches to that drive.

F6—Rename

The Rename key, F6, gives you the ability to rename a directory or subdirectory. Move the selection block to the directory/subdirectory you wish to rename, and press F6 (Figure 5.6).

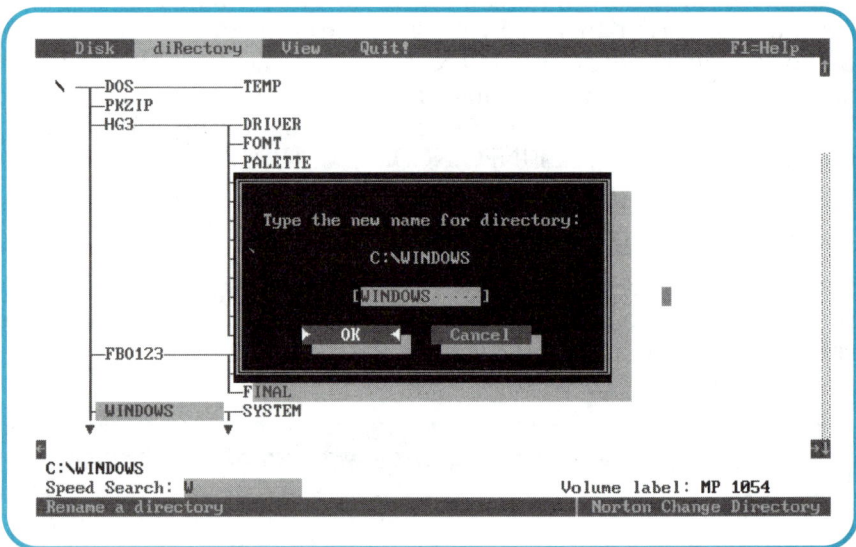

Figure 5.6   Pressing F6 lets you rename a directory.

Type the new name over the old one, and press Enter to rename the directory/subdirectory.

F7—MkDir

The MkDir key, F7, provides an easy way to add directories to your disk. To create a directory off the root, first move the selection block to the root, and press F7. The screen displays an empty directory block, where you can enter the new directory name (Figure 5.7). Type the new name, and press Enter or click OK.

F8—Delete

Using NCD utility, you can delete empty directories with the F8 key. Move the selection block to the directory you wish to delete, and press F8. If the directory is empty, NCD will delete it and remove it from the tree display. As is the case with DOS' RD command, it is impossible to

116

remove a nonempty directory in NCD. NCD displays an error message if you try to delete a directory that contains files.

If you use NCD to create (F7) and remove (F8) your directories, you won't need to rescan the disk with F2. NCD automatically updates the TREEINFO.NCD file when you use F7 or F8 to create or remove directories.

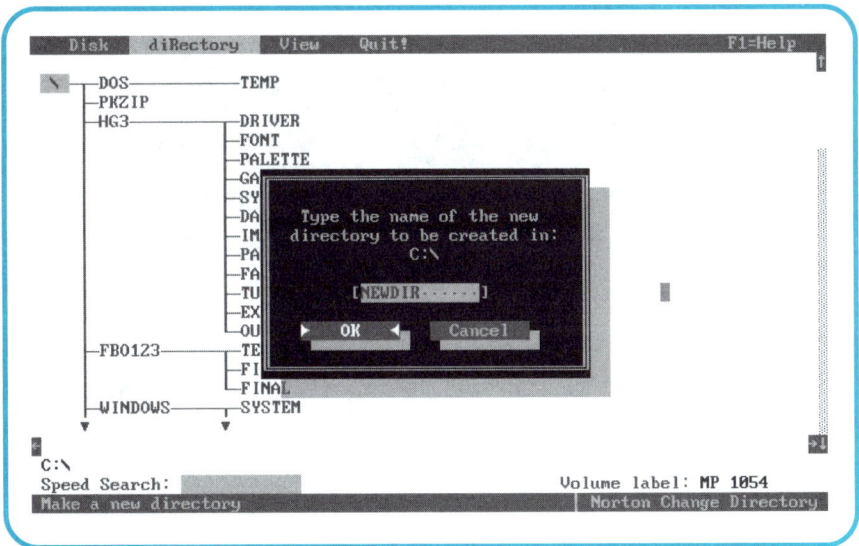

Figure 5.7   Using MkDir (F7) to create a new directory.

117

F9 and F10—Menu Bar

Press F9 or F10 when you want to use any of the commands on NCD's pull-down menus, such as the Print tree command on the diRectory menu.

Volume Label Maintenance

DOS allows you to assign a special name, or volume label, to each disk you use. For example, you could assign the volume label MY C DISK to your C: disk or MY FLOPPY to a floppy disk. The DOS LABEL command lets you specify a volume label of up to 11 characters. Norton's NCD utility lets you specify volume labels up to 12 characters long and provides volume label maintenance help. The active disk's volume

label is displayed at the bottom right corner of the NCD screen
(Figure 5.8). Press Ctrl-V to display the Volume Label dialog box shown
in Figure 5.8.

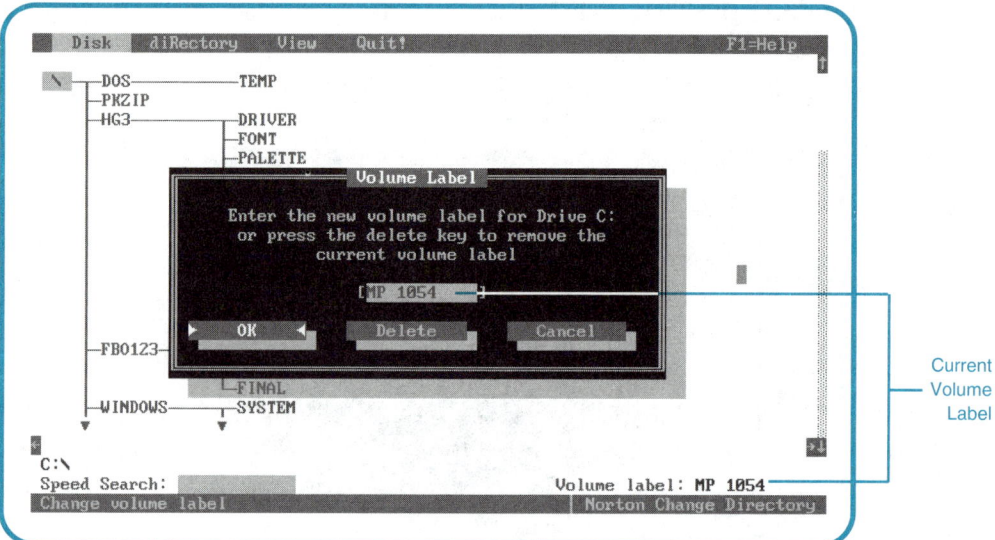

Figure 5.8   Pressing Ctrl-V shows the Volume Label dialog box.

When the dialog box in Figure 5.8 is displayed you can either

▶ Change the label by typing over the existing one and pressing
Enter

▶ Press the Delete button to delete the volume label

After you make your selection, the dialog box in Figure 5.8 is closed and
the new volume label is shown at the bottom of the NCD screen.

Pruning and Grafting Directories

Moving a directory and its contents, including subdirectories, can be a
time-consuming procedure if you use DOS' MD (Make Directory) and
COPY commands. Fortunately, NCD offers a Prune & Graft feature that
lets you remove (prune) a directory from one location and insert (graft)
it at another location on the directory tree.

By default, the Prune & Graft feature is not active. To make it
active, press Alt-R or click on diRectory in the NCD menu bar. Select
Configure. The NCD Configuration dialog box, shown in Figure 5.9,
appears. Select Enable Prune & Graft and press Enter or click OK.

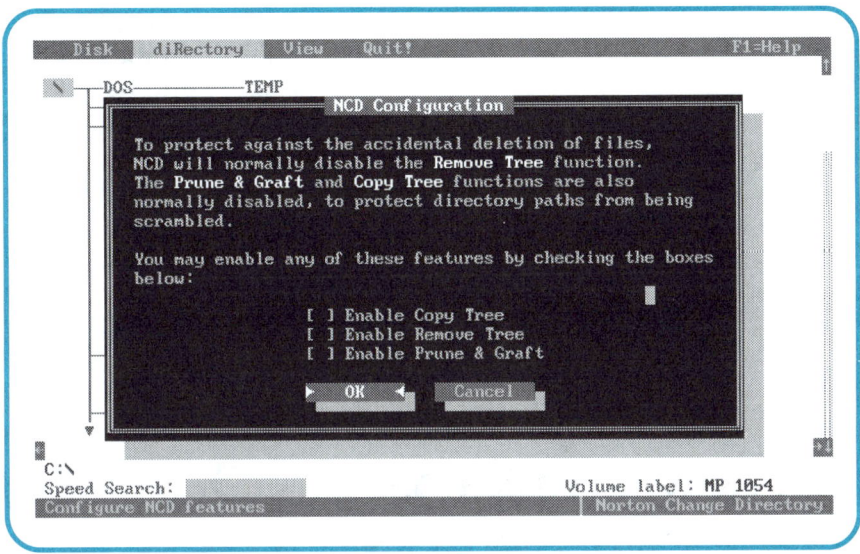

Disk   diRectory   View   Quit!   F1=Help

```
DOS         TEMP
┌─────────────── NCD Configuration ───────────────┐
│ To protect against the accidental deletion of files, │
│ NCD will normally disable the Remove Tree function.  │
│ The Prune & Graft and Copy Tree functions are also   │
│ normally disabled, to protect directory paths from being │
│ scrambled.                                           │
│                                                      │
│ You may enable any of these features by checking the boxes │
│ below:                                               │
│                                                      │
│            [ ] Enable Copy Tree                      │
│            [ ] Enable Remove Tree                    │
│            [ ] Enable Prune & Graft                  │
│                                                      │
│         ▶ OK ◀        Cancel                         │
└──────────────────────────────────────────────────┘
C:\
Speed Search:                        Volume label: MP 1054
Configure NCD features               Norton Change Directory
```

Figure 5.9   Activating Prune & Graft.

119

Once you've activated Prune & Graft, you can put it to use with the following Quick Steps.

Pruning & Grafting Directories

1. At the main NCD screen, press Alt-G.

   The Prune & Graft screen appears.

2. Use the up and down arrow keys or click with the mouse to highlight the name of the directory you want to move.

3. Press Enter or click on **Prune**.

   The Prune command button changes to the Graft command button.

4. Use the up and down arrow keys or the mouse to specify the new location for the directory and its contents.

   The highlighted directory name moves to the new location.

5. Press Enter or click on **Graft**.

   The Graft command button once again becomes the Prune command button.

6. Use Steps 2 through 5 to move other directories, if you wish.

7. To end the Prune & Graft session, press Tab twice and then Enter to select the **Close** button, or simply click on the **Close** button.

   The Prune & Graft screen closes. NCD automatically updates the directory tree.

   □

Recovering a Deleted Directory

120

In Chapter 3, we discussed Norton's UNERASE utility, which allows you to recover accidentally deleted files. As you may already know, DOS has a built-in safeguard that prevents you from accidentally deleting a directory that contains files. However, you could write a batch file that automates the process of first deleting a directory of files and then removing the directory. Regardless of how you lose a directory full of files, to recover those files you must first recover their directory.

Recovering Deleted Directories with UNERASE

1. Use the NCD utility to move to the parent of the deleted directory. Press Esc.

   For example, if you are trying to recover C:\TEMP, you should use NCD to make the root directory C: active.

2. Type the command **UNERASE**, and press Enter.

   This starts the UNERASE utility and displays the initial UNERASE screen shown in Figure 5.10.

   The first character dialog box is displayed.

3. Press the up or down arrow key or click with the mouse to highlight the directory you wish to recover (for example, **?YMEMO**), then press **U** or click on the UnErase command button.

4. Type the first character of the deleted directory's name (for example, M).

This recovers the deleted directory and displays the screen in Figure 5.11. □

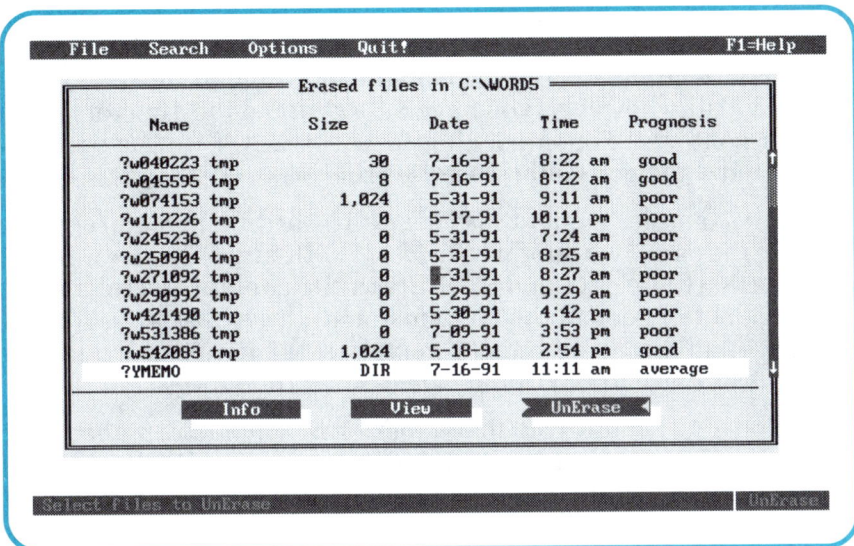

Figure 5.10   The initial UNERASE screen lets you choose the directory to recover.

121

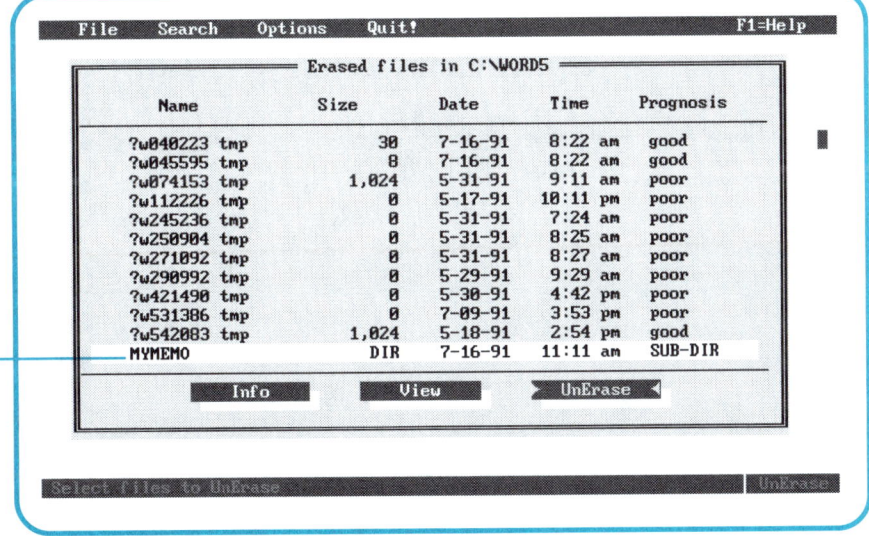

The First Letter in the Directory Name Reappears After It's Recovered

Figure 5.11   When a directory has been successfully unerased, the directory name's first letter appears instead of a question mark.

In Chapter 3's discussion of the UNERASE utility, we saw that a deleted file's name (except for the first character) remains intact in a special table maintained by DOS. The same rule is true for deleted directories; that is why you must supply UNERASE with the first character of the directory you wish to recover.

After recovering a deleted directory, you might think that you would have automatically recovered everything in the directory as well. In reality however, you have only restored the directory name, *not* its contents. You must then use UNERASE to resurrect the recovered directory's subdirectories/files.

For example, let's assume I have a TEMP directory that contains several files and two subdirectories: WORK and FUN. Let's further assume that the WORK and FUN directories contain several files too. If I accidentally delete the contents of all three directories (TEMP, WORK, and FUN) and the directories themselves, I must use UNERASE twice to recover all the deleted directories.

The first UNERASE that I perform will recover the TEMP directory. Then I must use UNERASE to recover the WORK and FUN subdirectories within TEMP. Once all three directories are recovered I must use UNERASE to recover all the files in TEMP, WORK, and FUN. After I have successfully UNERASEd the directory (Figure 5.11), I can select the recovered directory and press Enter to see what files in that directory can be UNERASEd (Figure 5.12).

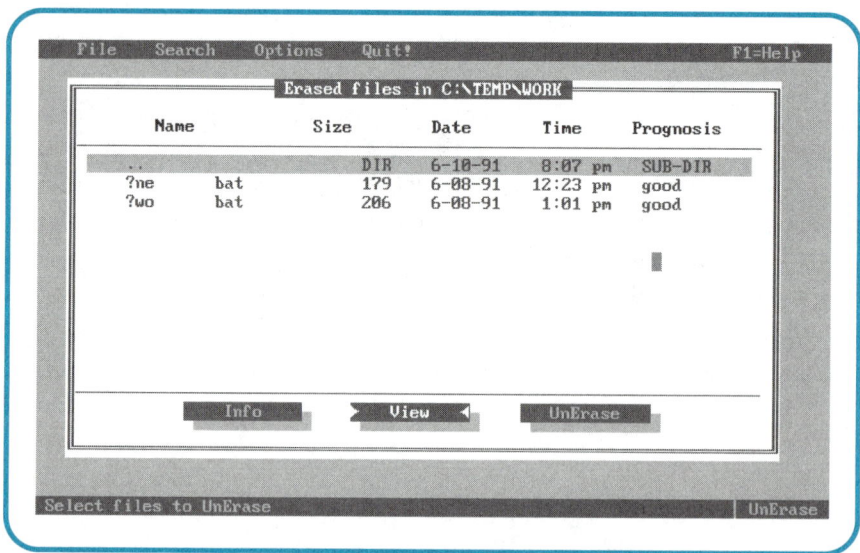

Figure 5.12   Using UNERASE displays a list of recoverable files in the UNERASEd directory.

I can then use the steps outlined in Chapter 3 to recover all the deleted files shown in Figure 5.12. Or, I can use the Quick Steps outlined earlier in this chapter to recover subdirectories from the recently recovered directory.

Changing the Order of Directories and Files

When you use DOS's DIR command, it scrolls a list of files and directories on-screen. Unfortunately, it does not order the directories and files alphabetically or in any other way to make it easier for you to find the files you're looking for.

The Directory Sort utility places files and directories in order according to the *sort-keys* you select: date, extension, name, size, or time. You can specify more than one sort-key. In that case, Directory Sort orders the files by the *primary* (first) sort-key first, then uses the second sort-key to break ties, and so on. If the directory you sort (the current directory) contains subdirectories, Directory Sort groups the subdirectories first, then the files. Hidden or system files are not sorted so as not to disturb any protection methods. Table 5.1 lists the default sort orders for the different sort-key types.

123

Table 5.1   Directory Sort Defaults

Sorting by This Sort-Key...	Orders the Files/Directories . . .
Date	From least recent to most recent
Extension	In alphabetical order
Name	In alphabetical order
Size	From smallest to largest
Time	From least recent to most recent

You can display the full Directory Sort dialog box by typing **DS** at the DOS prompt. (Appendix B explains how to use Directory Sort as a command line utility.) Figure 5.13 shows the Directory Sort screen.

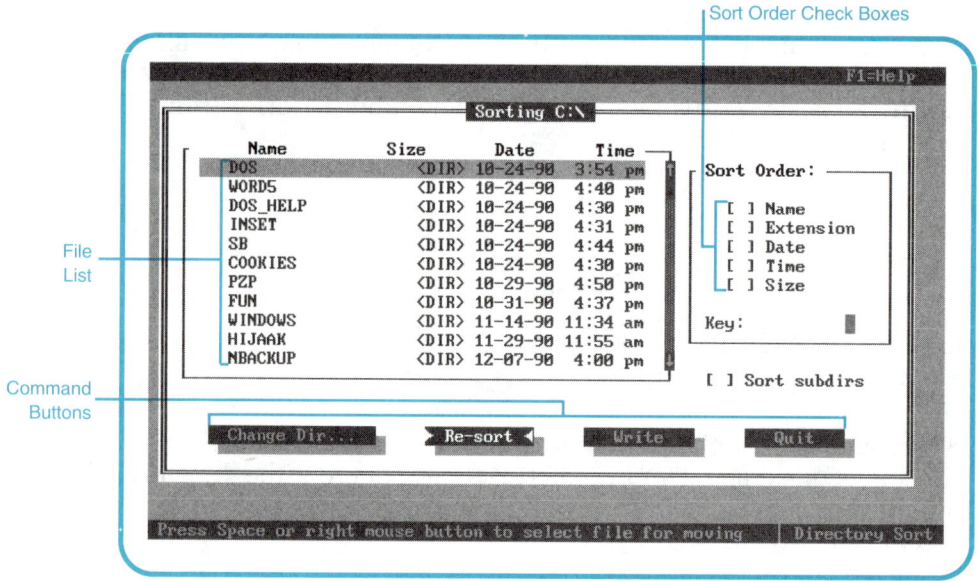

Sort Order Check Boxes

File List

Command Buttons

Figure 5.13   The Directory Sort screen.

The following Quick Steps explain how to use the Directory Sort utility.

Using the Full Directory Sort Utility

1. Type **DS** at the DOS prompt or in the command line at the bottom of the main Norton program screen. Press Enter.

   The Directory Sort dialog box appears. The file list box displays the files in the current directory.

2. If necessary, specify another drive and directory by selecting the **Change Dir...** button (press **C** or click on the button).

   Directory Sort displays the Change Directory dialog box.

3. Type the name of the drive and directory you want to sort (for example, **D:\CLIENTS**). Press Enter or click **OK**.

   You return to the Directory Sort dialog box, which now displays in the file list box the files and subdirectories in the new drive and directory.

4. Select the sort-keys you want to use in the Sort Order: area by pressing the first letter in the sort-key name or clicking with the mouse. Press - at a sort key to sort in reverse order.

A check appears next to each sort-key you choose. The numeral that appears indicates the sort-key's precedence. That is, the first key you choose becomes 1, the primary sort-key, and so on.

5. To sort the files in the subdirectories of the selected directory, tab to the Sort subdirs line and press Space Bar to select it.

A check appears next to the Sort subdirs line.

6. Press R, or click Re-sort.

Directory Sort orders the files according to the sort-key(s) you specified and displays the new order in the file list box.

125

7. If you wish, repeat steps 2 through 6 to sort files in another directory or resort the files in the current directory.

8. Press W or click Write to write the new file order to disk.

Directory Sort stores the new file order on disk.

9. Press Q, or click Quit.

The Directory Sort dialog box closes, and depending on where you were when you started Directory Sort, the DOS prompt or the main Norton screen appears. □

Finding Your Way Through the Forest

After you have created many directories and subdirectories, it is very easy to become lost in the "disk forest." Even if you practice the best disk management techniques, it is possible to forget where you placed a file or two! Fortunately, the FILEFIND utility discussed in Chapter 3 includes two powerful features that let you locate files and text strings. Let's take a look at the file location feature first to see how you can use it to locate quickly a file on your disk.

FILEFIND Revisited

126

If you misplace a file on your hard disk, you could use DOS's DIR command to locate it. However, since the DIR command cannot report on more than one directory/subdirectory at a time, you would have to execute one DIR command for each directory/subdirectory on your disk. For example, if I am looking for the file MYSTUFF.DOC and my disk contains the following six directories:

```
C:\TEMP
C:\TEMP\WORK
C:\TEMP\GAMES
C:\MEMOS
C:\MEMOS\FUN
C:\MEMOS\SERIOUS
```

I may have to execute up to six DIR commands (for example, `DIR C:\TEMP\*.*` `DIR C:\TEMP\WORK\*.*` `DIR C:\TEMP\GAMES\*.*`, and so on) to locate the missing file. You may not think that six commands is too much work when you are looking for a misplaced file, but what if your disk has 100 directories? Or 1000 directories? Norton's FILEFIND utility lets you search for a misplaced file on one or more disks with only one command—regardless of how many directories your disks contain.

 Searching for a File with FILEFIND

1. Type the command **FILEFIND** followed by the name of the file you wish to locate (for example, **FILEFIND MYSTUFF.DOC**).

2. Press Enter.   This starts the FILEFIND
                                   utility and searches for
                                   the specified file.   □

The screen in Figure 5.14 shows the result of searching for
MYSTUFF.DOC on my hard disk. As you can see in Figure 5.14,
FILEFIND has determined that MYSTUFF.DOC is located in my
MEMOS\SERIOUS subdirectory.

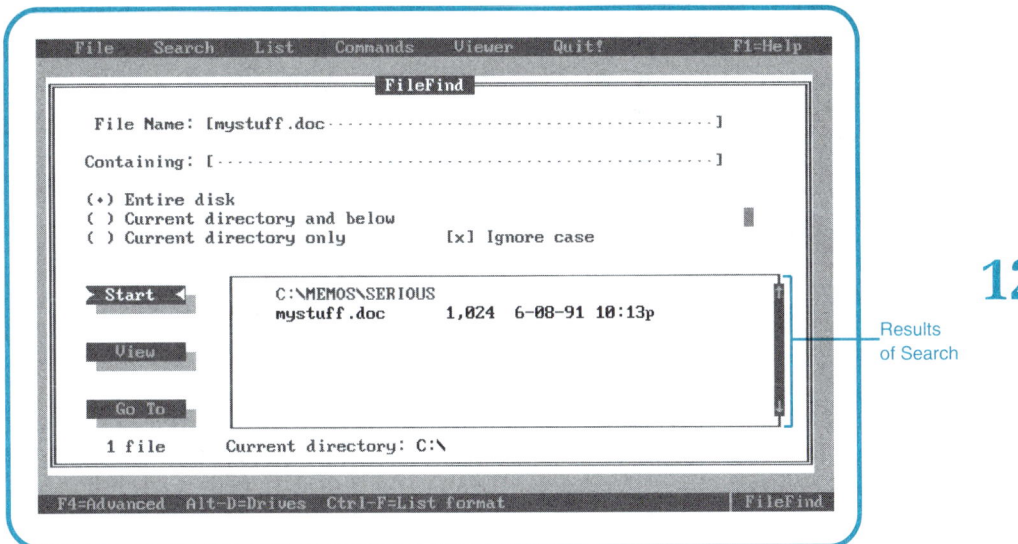

127

*Figure 5.14   I can use FILEFIND to locate the file
MYSTUFF.DOC no matter where it is on my disk.*

The FILEFIND utility searches through all directories and
subdirectories on the currently active drive. You can use the wild-
card character * with a colon (that is *:) to force FILEFIND to search
for the specified file on all drives. For example, the command FF
*:MYSTUFF.DOC instructs FILEFIND to look for MYSTUFF.DOC on all
hard and floppy drives. This feature is especially handy if your hard
disk is split into more than one logical partition and you wish to
search the entire physical disk (for example, C:, D:, and E:). Don't
worry about not having a disk in your floppy drive when using the
*: feature. If FILEFIND does not find a disk in a floppy drive when
*: is used, it simply continues with the next drive.

FILEFIND supports the DOS wild-card characters * and ? for
full or partial file name specifications. So if you cannot recall the full

name of a misplaced file, you can still use FILEFIND to locate it (for example, `FILEFIND MY*.DOC` or `FILEFIND CHAPT?.BK`).

Searching for Text with FILEFIND

The FILEFIND utility does a fine job of locating misplaced files. Even if you know only part of the misplaced file's name, you can use FILEFIND to locate it. But what if you are looking for a file that contains information about a trip you recently took to California? Was the file named TRIP.RPT or CALIFOR.TRP? You have no idea what name you gave the trip report file, but you do know the file contains the string "trip report." FILEFIND can look inside each file on the disk and tell you which files contain your specific text string.

Searching for a Text String with FILEFIND

1. Type **FILEFIND**, and press Enter.

   This starts the FILEFIND utility and displays the screen shown in Figure 5.15.

2. Press Tab, enter the text string you wish to locate (for example, **trip report**), and press Enter or click Start.

   This initiates a search for the text string "trip report" and displays a search completion message when finished.

3. Press Enter to acknowledge the search completion message.

   This displays a list of files containing the specified text string (Figure 5.16).

4. Use the up and down arrow keys or the mouse to highlight a file shown in the list, and press Enter or View.

   This displays the viewer screen, which shows the contents of the selected file and highlights the search text.

5. Press F6 to see if there are any other occurrences of the specified text string in the file being viewed.

   This highlights the next occurrence of the specified text string or displays a message if there are nomore occurrences in the file. □

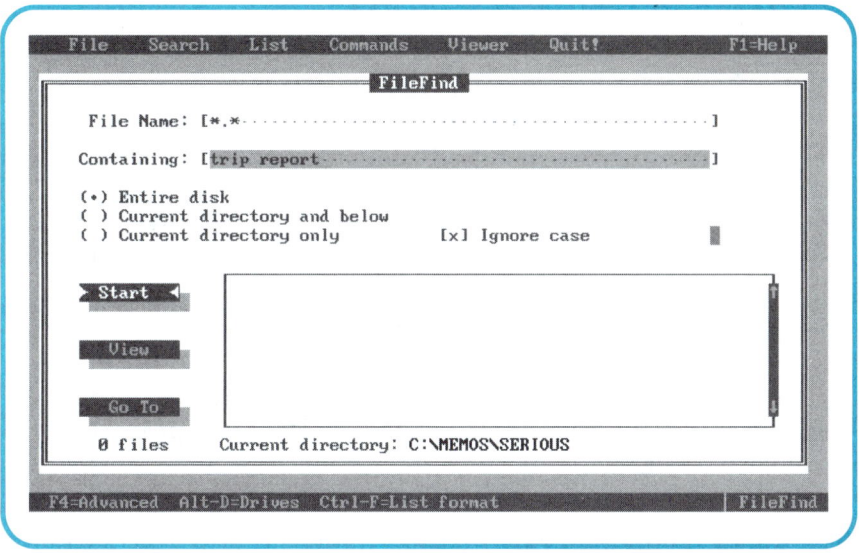

Figure 5.15   Initial FILEFIND screen.

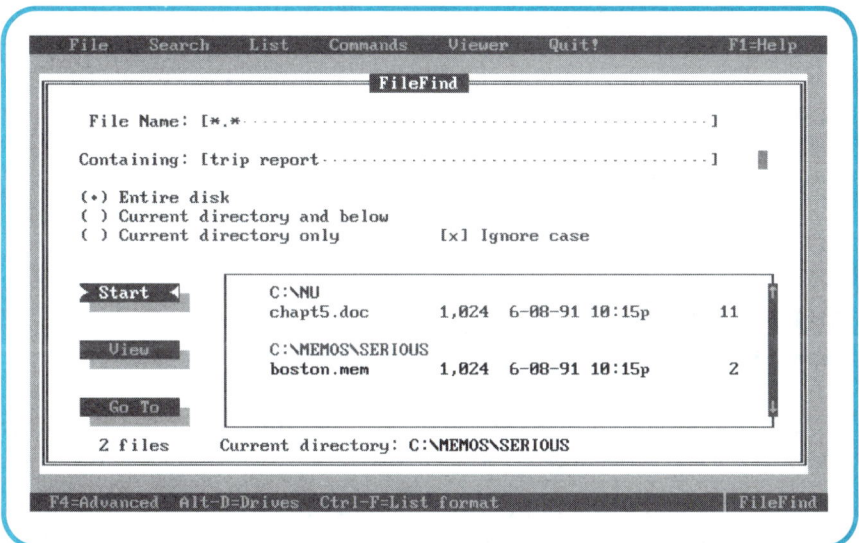

Figure 5.16   List of files containing a specified text string.

Press Esc when the viewer screen is displayed if you want to return to the list. You can then highlight a different file and press Enter to view it.

The list screen in Figure 5.16 shows file name, size, and date for all files containing the specified text string. The number of occurrences of the specified text string is also indicated after the time. For example, in Figure 5.16 we can see that the string "trip report" occurs twice in the file BOSTON.MEM and 11 times in the file CHAPT5.

By default, FILEFIND is not case sensitive, so the steps above would find the string "Trip Report," "TRIP REPORT," or even "TrIp RePoRt." Although I almost never use it, FILEFIND does offer a case sensitivity option, `/CS`. If we had used the /CS option in the Quick Steps example, FILEFIND would locate files containing only the lowercase string "trip report."

The text search feature of FILEFIND is a fast and powerful tool. The Quick Steps described earlier show how to run FILEFIND interactively. Once you are comfortable with FILEFIND, you may want to specify all parameters on the command line to save time.

130

The command `FILEFIND C:\*.* "trip report" /S` provides the same results as the earlier Quick Steps. The /S option tells FILEFIND to search through all subdirectories. Notice that the text string *trip report* is enclosed in quotes here. When running FILEFIND from the command line, you must place the text string in quotes if it contains spaces. Without the quotes (that is, `FILEFIND C:\*.* trip report /S`), FILEFIND searches for the string *trip* and ignores *report*.

What You Have Learned

In this chapter you learned about directories and tree structures. More specifically, you learned:

▶ A special directory called the root directory exists on all disks (for example, C:). All other directories on a disk are either a direct or indirect descendent of the root directory.

▶ Although the CD command is adequate for moving about from directory to directory, the Norton Change Directory utility offers a fast graphical approach to directory navigation.

► NCD offers a Speed Search feature so you can quickly jump from one directory to another without having to search for your destination with the arrow keys.

► DOS allows you to assign a special name, or volume label, to each disk you use. Norton's NCD utility lets you specify volume labels up to 12 characters long and offers a mechanism for volume label maintenance.

► You can use NCD's Prune & Graft feature to move a directory and its contents to a new tree location on a disk without arduous copy procedures.

► Norton's UNERASE utility lets you recover deleted directories. Once a directory has been recovered, you can then use UNERASE again to recover deleted files/subdirectories within that directory.

► You can use the Directory Sort utility to organize files and directories by name, date, time, extension, or size.

► Norton's FILEFIND utility lets you search for a misplaced file on one or more disks with only one command, regardless of how many directories your disks contain.

► FILEFIND's text search feature can show you what files contain a specific text string.

131

Maintaining Your Hard Disk Drive

In This Chapter

▶ *Understanding disk structures*
▶ *Preserving important disk information*
▶ *Recovering data from an accidentally formatted disk*
▶ *Wiping files from a disk*
▶ *Diagnosing and correcting disk problems*

This second chapter on disk utilities shows you how to avoid accidental data loss and explains the physical layout of DOS disks. First you learn about the fundamental components and structure of DOS disks and how to interpret the disk information reported by Norton's SYSINFO utility. Then we cover disk formatting and erasure utilities—and how to recover data from accidentally formatted disks. Chapter 6 concludes with coverage of Norton's Disk Doctor (NDD) utility, which allows you to diagnose and correct disk problems.

Understanding Disk Structures

As the saying goes, "you don't have to know how the engine works before you can drive a car." The same rule holds true for PC users—you don't have to understand the internal workings of a computer to use a PC. A bit of technical insight certainly doesn't hurt, though. In fact, a basic knowledge of PC inner workings is almost mandatory before you can interpret and appreciate the information reported by the more advanced tools in The Norton Utilities.

To work with some of Norton's disk utilities, you must first understand the structure of a DOS disk. You have already been introduced to a few of the terms I will use in this discussion, so let's quickly review those first.

134

Bits, Bytes, Sectors, and Clusters

You may recall from Chapter 2 that a binary digit, or *bit*, is the smallest piece of data a computer can store. The discussion in Chapter 2 continued by defining a *byte* as a collection of 8 bits. A bit is very simple, and can have a value of only 0 or 1. As many as 256 different values can be indicated by combinations of 1s and 0s in an 8-bit byte.

The computer industry has created a standard for assigning specific 8-bit values for a slew of characters, including all the ones that appear on your PC's keyboard. This standard is called the *ASCII character set*. (ASCII is an acronym for American Standard Code for Information Interchange.)

If a group of bits is called a byte, what do you call a group of bytes? How about a sector? A *sector* consists of 512 bytes. To address an entire disk's data area quickly and easily, DOS works with even larger, more manageable chunks of data called *clusters*.

The number of sectors in a cluster differs among disk types. For example, each cluster on my PC's hard disk is made up of four sectors, but on a high-density 5¼" floppy disk there is only one sector per cluster. It's not too important to understand why different disk types have different numbers of sectors per cluster. However, you should understand that 8 bits constitute a byte, 512 bytes make up a sector, and a cluster contains one or more sectors (depending on the disk type).

Tracks and Cylinders

Now that you know what sectors and clusters are, let's try to visualize them on a disk. The illustration in Figure 6.1 shows the circular disk platter inside a $5^1/_4$" disk.

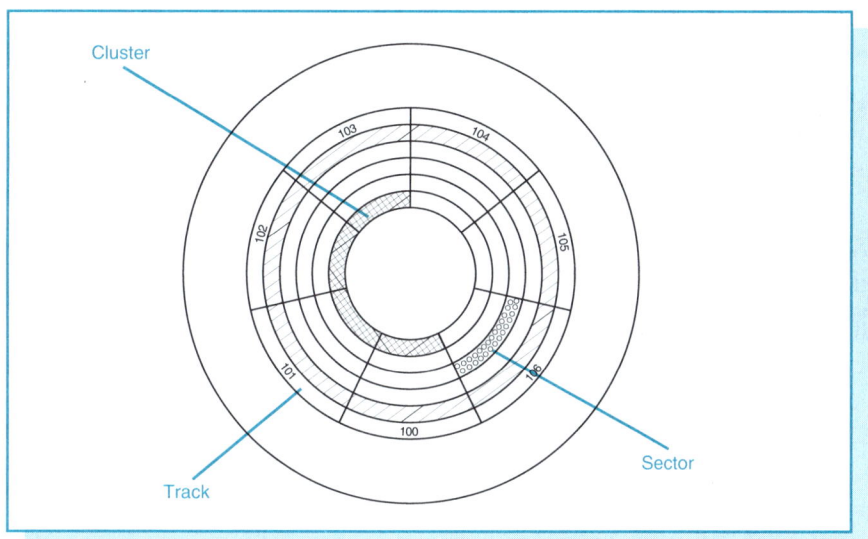

Figure 6.1   Groups of sectors form tracks around the surface of a disk.

As you can see in Figure 6.1, the sectors and clusters are arranged in a circular format; this format resembles the layout of the grooves in a record album. In Figure 6.1, sectors 100 through 106 form a circle on the disk surface. This circle of sectors is called a *track*. These days, virtually all floppy disks are double-sided, so we can say that there are tracks on both sides of the disk platter.

Now let's expand the discussion to include hard disks. The illustration in Figure 6.2 shows the surface of a hard disk.

Hard disks typically contain more than one platter. The hard disk in Figure 6.2 consists of three platters. The platters in a hard disk are stacked fairly close together, and each platter contains tracks, clusters, and sectors just like floppy disks. In Figure 6.3, we've added an imaginary cylindrical object that appears to cut through the three platters in the hard disk.

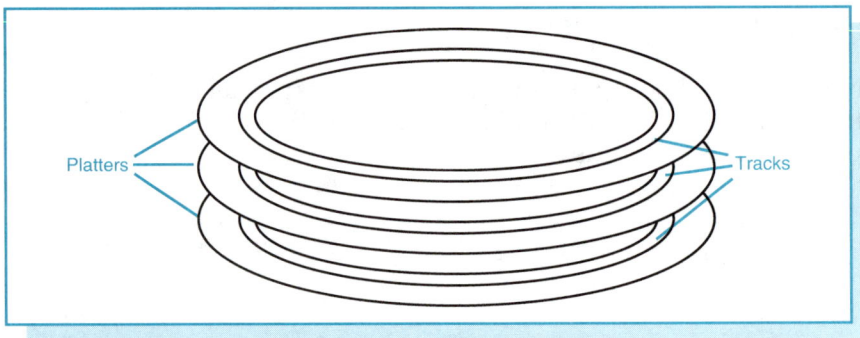

Figure 6.2   Hard disks contain several disk platters.

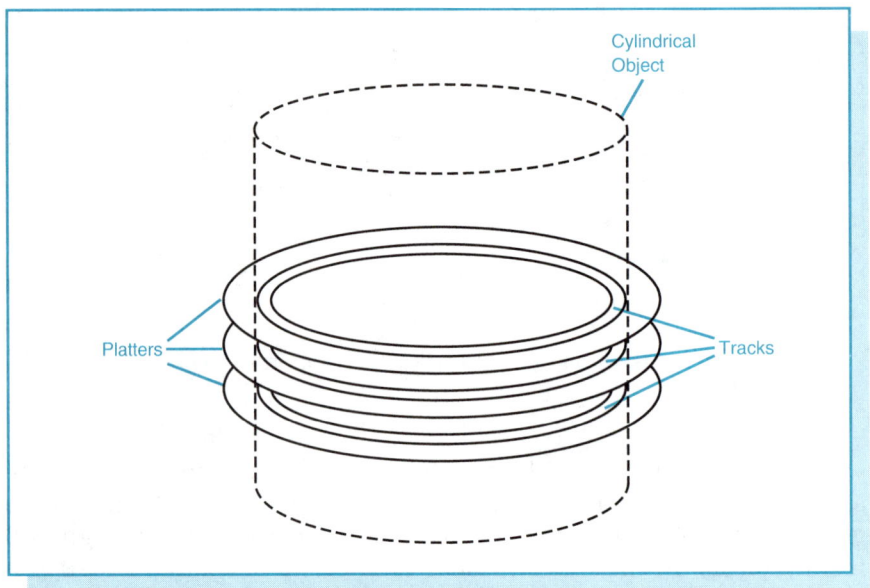

Figure 6.3   Vertically stacked tracks form cylinders.

The cylindrical object passes through six tracks on the hard disk in Figure 6.3. (Remember, each platter has two sides!) The collection of vertically stacked tracks intersected by the object in Figure 6.3 is known as a *cylinder*.

Disk Areas

The terms and concepts discussed so far in this chapter apply to all regions of a DOS disk—that is, the entire disk is made up of bits, bytes, sectors, and so on. There are special regions or areas on a DOS disk where certain pieces of information must reside. These areas are known as the *system area* and the *data area*. Three components make up the system area: the boot record, the root directory, and the file allocation table (or, FAT, for short).

Boot Record

The boot record resides in the *boot sector*, which is the first sector of the first track on the first side of a bootable DOS disk. The boot sector exists on all DOS disks regardless of whether the disk is bootable or not. (When you FORMAT a DOS disk, you can make it bootable by using the /S option, which causes the system files to be copied to the newly formatted disk.) The information contained in the boot record of a bootable disk instructs DOS on how to bring itself up "by the bootstraps" and prepare for your commands.

Root Directory

The root directory area contains information about all the files and directories that reside in the root directory (for example, C:). Each file and directory in the root has an entry in this area that contains information such as name, size, and date/time of creation. One of the most important items in a directory entry is a number that indicates the file or directory's offset in the file allocation table.

File Allocation Table

The file allocation table indicates the status of all the clusters on a DOS disk. The information contained in the FAT is so important that DOS actually maintains two copies of the FAT on a disk, just in case something happens to the first copy. Unlike directories, the FAT is organized by clusters rather than by files. There is one entry in the FAT for each cluster on the disk. The illustration in Figure 6.4 shows the relationship between the root directory area and the FAT.

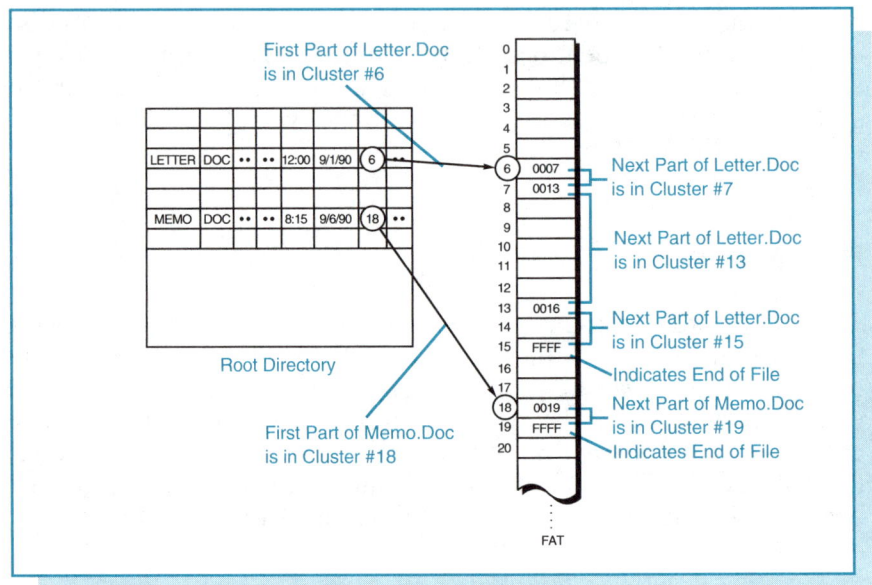

Figure 6.4 Relationship between the root directory area and FAT.

As you can see in Figure 6.4, the contents of the file LETTER.DOC start in cluster #6. Looking at the 6th offset of the FAT in Figure 6.4, we can see that LETTER.DOC continues into cluster #7. The 7th offset of the FAT tells us that cluster #13 is the next cluster in the sequence for LETTER.DOC. Skipping down to the 13th offset of the FAT, we see that the next portion of LETTER.DOC resides in cluster #15. Finally, the 15th offset of the FAT contains the special value 'FFFF', which indicates the end of the file. So LETTER.DOC occupies four clusters on the disk: clusters #6, #7, #13, and #15. Figure 6.4 also shows a directory entry for a file named MEMO.DOC, which occupies two clusters: #18 and #19.

The FAT in Figure 6.4 illustrates an important point about how DOS allocates clusters for a file. Although it is possible for a file to occupy sequential clusters (for example, MEMO.DOC uses clusters #18 and #19), quite often DOS may wind up utilizing nonsequential, or noncontiguous, clusters for a file. (For example, LETTER.DOC, which uses clusters #6, #7, #13, and #15.) A file that is stored in noncontiguous clusters is called a *fragmented file*. File fragmentation is a leading cause of disk inefficiency because it takes DOS longer to manipulate a file whose data is scattered across the disk. In Chapter 7 you'll see how to use Norton's SPEEDISK utility to determine if your disk contains a high percentage of fragmented files. SPEEDISK also lets you defragment your disk by rewriting all the files in contiguous clusters.

Data Area

The last area of a DOS disk is known as the *data area*. The data area is where all the data for your files and subdirectories is located. All sectors that are not part of the boot record, root directory, or FAT are part of the data area.

Now that you know some of the details behind DOS disk structures, let's revisit the SYSINFO utility and discuss the disk information it reports.

139

Obtaining Disk Information

Chapter 2's discussion of SYSINFO explained four of the five areas reported by this informative utility. The menu for SYSINFO's fifth area, Disks, offers three useful selections: Disk Summary, Disk Characteristics, and Partition Tables.

 Looking at Disk Information with SYSINFO

1. Type the command **SYSINFO**, and press Enter.

   This runs the SYSINFO utility and displays the System Summary screen.

2. Press Alt-D or click on Disks in the menu bar. Then press Enter or click on Disk Summary.

   This activates the Disks menu,selects the Disk summary option, and displays the Disk Summary screen (Figure 6.5).

3. Press Enter or click on Next.	This displays the Disk Characteristics screen (Figure 6.6).
4. Press Enter or click on Next.	This displays the Partition Tables screen (Figure 6.7).□

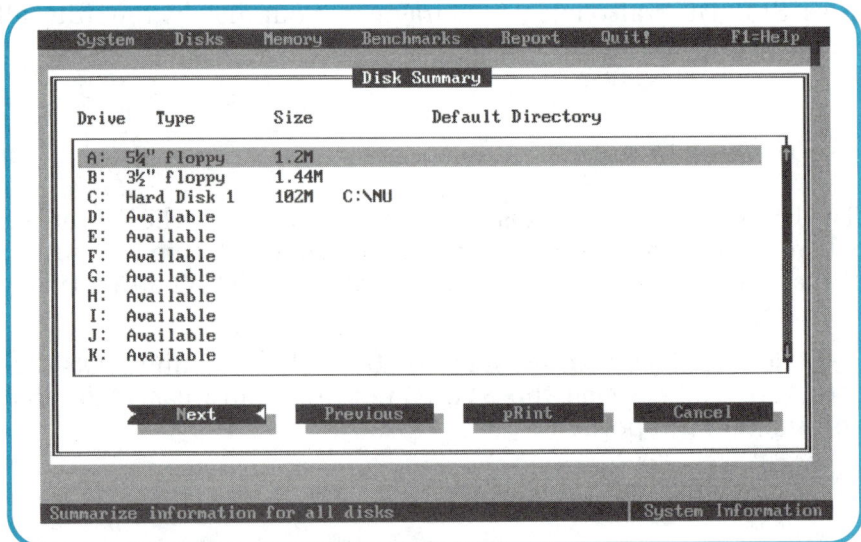

Figure 6.5 *The Disk Summary screen shows information about all disk drives on your PC.*

Disk Summary

The Disk Summary screen shown in Figure 6.5 shows four pieces of information, or fields, for each drive defined on your PC: Drive, Type, Size, and Default Directory. The first three fields are fairly self-explanatory; they show the drive's one-letter ID (for example, A:), the drive type (for example, 5-1/4"), and the drive's capacity (for example, 1.2M). The Default Directory field indicates the drive's default (active) directory. For example, if I change to the WORK directory of my C: drive using CD C:\WORK, WORK becomes the default directory for C:. Even if I move to my D: drive, WORK is still C:'s default directory.

140

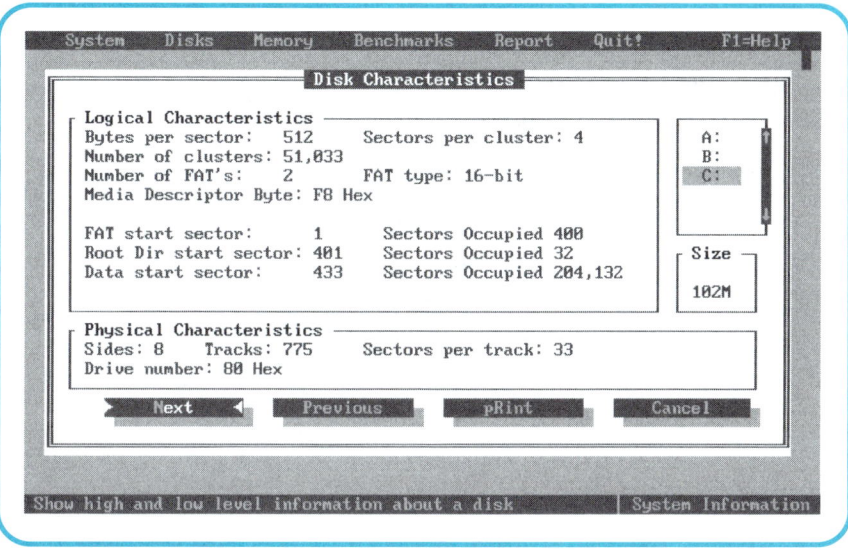

Figure 6.6   The Disk Characteristics screen reports both logical and physical disk information.

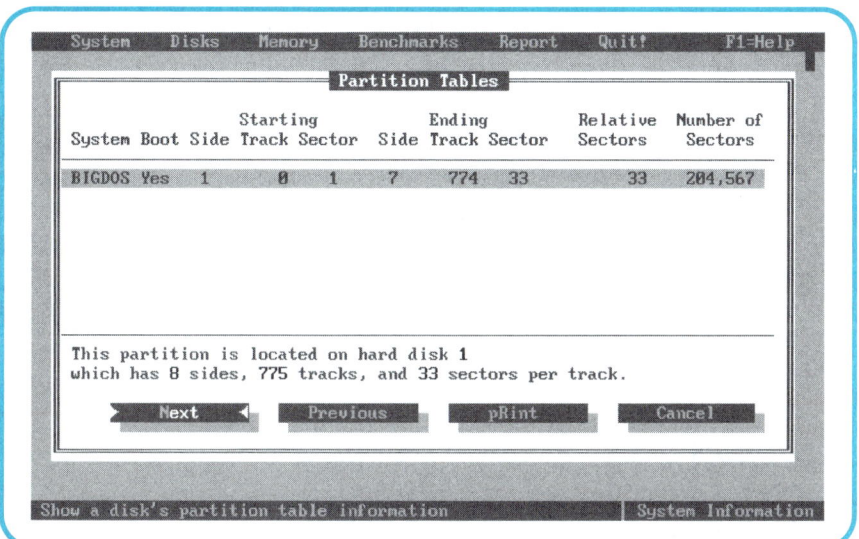

Figure 6.7   Starting and ending partition positions are indicated on the Partition Tables screen.

Disk Characteristics

The Disk Characteristics screen shown in Figure 6.6 has two main areas: Logical Characteristics and Physical Characteristics.

As you can see in the Logical Characteristics portion of Figure 6.6, my C: drive has 512 bytes per cluster and each cluster contains four sectors. Further, there are 51,033 clusters on the C: drive. Using these figures, we can determine exactly how many bytes can be stored on C:. The formula for total capacity is

$$\text{Total Capacity} = \frac{\text{\# of Bytes}}{\text{Sector}} \times \frac{\text{\# of Sectors}}{\text{Cluster}} \times \text{\# of Clusters}$$

Now let's insert the values for the C: drive in Figure 6.6 to determine its total capacity:

$$\text{Total Capacity} = \frac{512 \text{ Bytes}}{\text{Cluster}} \times \frac{4 \text{ Sectors}}{\text{Cluster}} \times 51{,}033 \text{ Clusters}$$

$$\text{Total Capacity} = 104{,}515{,}530 \text{ Bytes}$$

The value shown in the Size area of Figure 6.6, 102M, is an approximation of the exact capacity we calculated.

The rest of the information shown in Figure 6.6 is not very fascinating unless you are interested in more low-level details about a disk. The Logical Characteristics portion also contains information about a disk's system and data areas, including the starting sector and number of sectors occupied by the FAT, root directory, and data area. The Physical Characteristics section reports a few other disk-related tidbits including the number of sides, tracks, and sectors per track.

Partition Tables

The Partition Tables screen (Figure 6.7) shows detailed information about each of the partitions defined on your hard disk. You learned in Chapter 2 that hard disks are partitioned using the FDISK command. When you partition a hard disk with DOS's FDISK command, you are telling DOS how to configure the disk as one or more logical drives. Although you may have only one physical hard disk in your PC, you can have DOS treat it as several logical disks (for example, C: and D:). Each partition on your hard disk is shown as a line in the Partition Tables screen. The Partition Tables screen reports three important pieces of information: whether the partition is bootable (Boot), the partition's starting/ending side/track/sector, and the total number of sectors used by the partition.

The three disk-related screens in SYSINFO report several interesting facts about your PC's disk configuration. Now let's see how to use another Norton utility to format floppy or hard disks safely and quickly.

Formatting Disks

One of the first rules you learn when working with PCs is that all disks, whether hard or floppy, must be formatted (using DOS's FORMAT command) before you can save files on them. DOS's FORMAT command is fairly simple to use. For example, to format the disk in drive A: you use the command FORMAT A:

143

As with most DOS commands, FORMAT offers a wide variety of options, and sometimes the meaning of these options is not completely obvious. As mentioned before, the /S option causes FORMAT to place the special system files on the formatted disk to make it bootable. Perhaps "B" (for "bootable") would have been a better choice for that feature, but the /B option is used for a totally different purpose! Fortunately for us, The Norton Utilities includes a tool that offers a safe and friendly approach to disk formatting.

SFORMAT: The Safe Format Alternative

The SFORMAT utility provides an easy-to-use alternative to DOS's FORMAT command. Although SFORMAT supports many of FORMAT's command line options, you don't need to remember them because SFORMAT allows you to interactively select formatting options on-screen.

Q Formatting a Floppy Disk with SFORMAT

1. Type the command **SFORMAT** and a disk drive identifier **SFORMAT A:**), and press Enter.

   This starts the SFORMAT utility and displays the initial SFORMAT screen shown in Figure 6.8.

2. Press Enter to accept the default SFORMAT settings shown in

   If files/directories currently exist on the specified disk, a warning message is displayed; otherwise, SFORMAT begins formatting the specified disk.

3. If the warning message is displayed, press Enter to continue. Otherwise, wait until a completion message is displayed.

4. Press Esc twice.

   The screen in Figure 6.8 is displayed the first time you press Esc. The SFORMAT utility is terminated the second time you press Esc. □

144

🖎 **Note:** In Chapter 1 you read how The Norton Utilities Installation program will optionally replace DOS's FOR-MAT command with the Norton SFORMAT utility. If you instructed the Installation program to make this replacement, you can invoke the SFORMAT utility (in Step 1) using either the FORMAT or SFORMAT command.

SFORMAT Options

The SFORMAT utility offers several formatting options. The current status of each of these options is shown on the screen in Figure 6.8. Use Tab or the mouse to position the cursor in one of the six option areas of Figure 6.8: Drive, Size, System Files, Format Mode, Volume Label, and Save UnFormat Info.

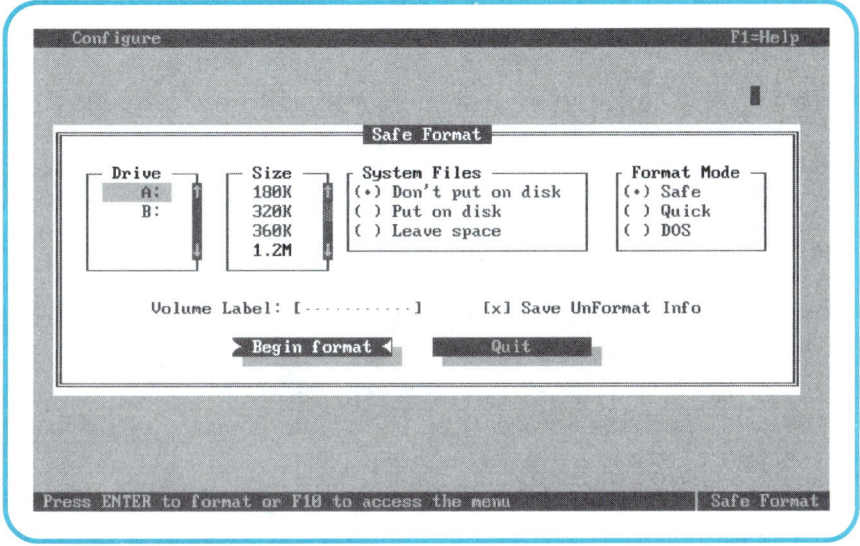

Figure 6.8   SFORMAT offers several disk-formatting options.

145

The Drive portion of Figure 6.8 lists all the disk drives SFORMAT can access. (SFORMAT can also support the 2.88-Mb disk drive if one is attached to your system.) Use the up and down arrow keys or the mouse to highlight a drive to format. The Drive list might show only floppy disk drives, since SFORMAT can be configured to prevent formatting of hard disks. If you wish to allow SFORMAT to format hard disks, select the Hard Disks... option of the Configure menu, and the screen in Figure 6.9 is displayed.

Press the Space Bar or click to place an X next to the Allow Hard Disk Formatting option (shown in Figure 6.9), and press Enter. The initial SFORMAT screen (Figure 6.8) is redisplayed, and the Drive portion includes a list of all formattable hard disks. Select the Save Settings option from the Configuration menu if you want to save the hard disk formatting option for future SFORMAT use.

In Chapter 2 you read about the difference between double- and high-density floppy disks. If your PC is equipped with a high-density disk drive, you have the option of formatting either high-, low-, or double-density diskettes. However, keep in mind the warning in Chapter 2: It is not a good idea to format double-density diskettes in a high-density drive.

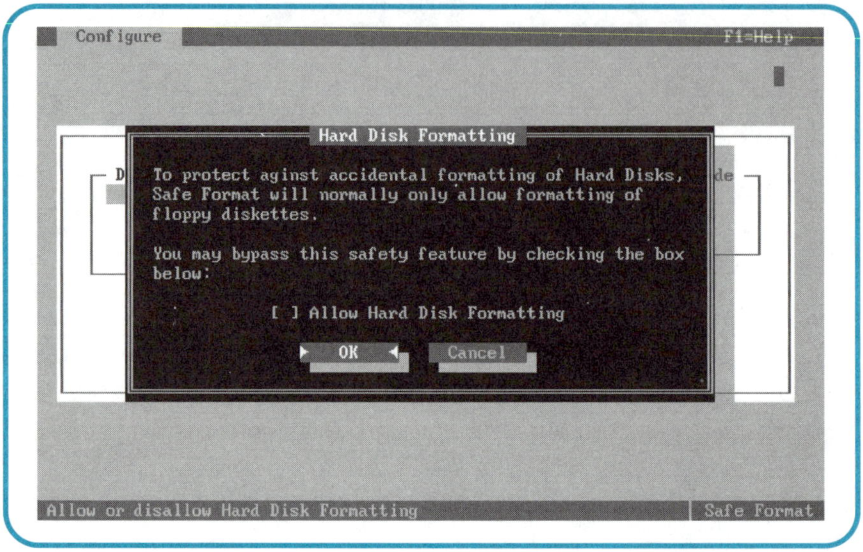

Figure 6.9   SFORMAT contains a hard disk safety feature that can be bypassed via the Hard Disk Formatting dialog box.

The SFORMAT utility has the intelligence to know whether the specified drive is either $3^1/_2$" or $5^1/_4$". As a result, only valid disk format sizes for the specified drive are displayed in Figure 6.8. After pressing Tab, use the up or down arrow keys or the mouse to select a different format size.

The System Files portion of the screen in Figure 6.8 lets you specify whether or not the system files should be copied to the formatted disk. The system files include all the files that make a disk bootable. You have three options for this selection. You can create

▶ A bootable disk

▶ A nonbootable disk with room reserved for the system files

▶ A nonbootable disk with no room reserved for the system files

There is an advantage to creating a nonbootable disk with room reserved for the system files: You have the option of easily making the disk bootable in the future (via DOS's SYS command) without having to reformat it. Use the up and down arrow keys and press Space Bar to select a different System Files option.

SFORMAT offers three different methods of formatting a disk: Safe mode, Quick mode, and DOS mode. Use the up and down arrow keys and press Space Bar or click to select a different Format Mode option.

Safe mode is safe because it does not affect a disk's data areas: It just resets the system area and performs some tests. This allows the Norton UNFORMAT utility (discussed later in this chapter) to easily recover all files from an accidentally formatted disk. Safe mode also happens to be faster than DOS's FORMAT command. Use Safe mode when working with disks that have not previously been formatted.

When you select Quick mode, SFORMAT simply clears the disk's file allocation table and root directory; it performs no tests. Use Quick mode whenever you are working with a previously formatted disk. You cannot use Quick mode on disks that have not previously been formatted.

If you select DOS mode, SFORMAT emulates DOS's own FORMAT algorithm. This means that any files/subdirectories on the disk will be wiped out and unrecoverable after the format. Use this destructive format option with extreme caution!

The Volume Label option lets you attach a name (up to 11 characters) to a newly formatted disk. This volume label is displayed every time you use DIR to list the disk's contents. Type in the desired volume label using any of the alphanumeric or symbol keys.

147

If you select the Save Unformat Info option, SFORMAT will automatically run another utility, IMAGE. IMAGE saves a copy of the disk's system information in a special hidden file called IMAGE.DAT that another Norton utility (UNFORMAT) can use to recover files if you ever accidentally reformat the disk. (We talk more about IMAGE and UNFORMAT later in this chapter.) Press Space Bar to select this valuable file recovery feature.

If you do select any of these special options, be sure to use the Save Settings option of the Configure menu to preserve your choices for the next time you use SFORMAT.

Preserving Important Disk Information

In Chapter 3 you learned how to use UNERASE to quickly recover accidentally deleted files. You also learned that you can increase the chances of a successful file recovery by using UNERASE as soon as possible after an accidental deletion. In reality, however, that's not always possible. You may need to recover a file you accidentally deleted yesterday or last week. In addition, recovery of badly fragmented files can be very difficult if not impossible, even with a powerful tool like UNERASE. To keep the odds of file recovery in your favor, I suggest regular use of the Norton IMAGE utility.

Maintaining a Good "Image"

The Norton Utilities tool IMAGE can be used to assist UNERASE and UNFORMAT (discussed later) in data recovery. The IMAGE utility saves a copy of a disk's system area (boot record, FAT, and root directory) in a hidden file called IMAGE.DAT. You may recall that SFORMAT can optionally create an IMAGE.DAT when you format a disk. The IMAGE utility gives you the ability to create/update the IMAGE.DAT file to make sure it reflects the most up-to-date system area information.

148

 Using IMAGE to Guard Against Data Loss

1. Type the command **IMAGE** and a disk drive identifier (for example, **IMAGE C:**).

2. Press Enter.

This starts the IMAGE utility. IMAGE runs by itself and displays the screen shown in Figure 6.10 when it is finished. □

I highly recommend that you use IMAGE regularly to keep an updated IMAGE.DAT file on each partition of your PC's hard disk. The easiest way to do this is to include the IMAGE command in your AUTOEXEC.BAT file, which executes every time you boot your computer.

You can specify multiple disk drives on IMAGE's command line to update the IMAGE.DAT files for more than one disk partition. For example, the command **IMAGE C: D:** will update the IMAGE.DAT files on both the C: and D: drives. If IMAGE finds an IMAGE.DAT file on the specified disk, it first renames IMAGE.DAT to IMAGE.BAK and then creates a new IMAGE.DAT file. If you include IMAGE in your AUTOEXEC.BAT file, your hard disks will always contain two generations of system area information that can be used by UNERASE and UNFORMAT.

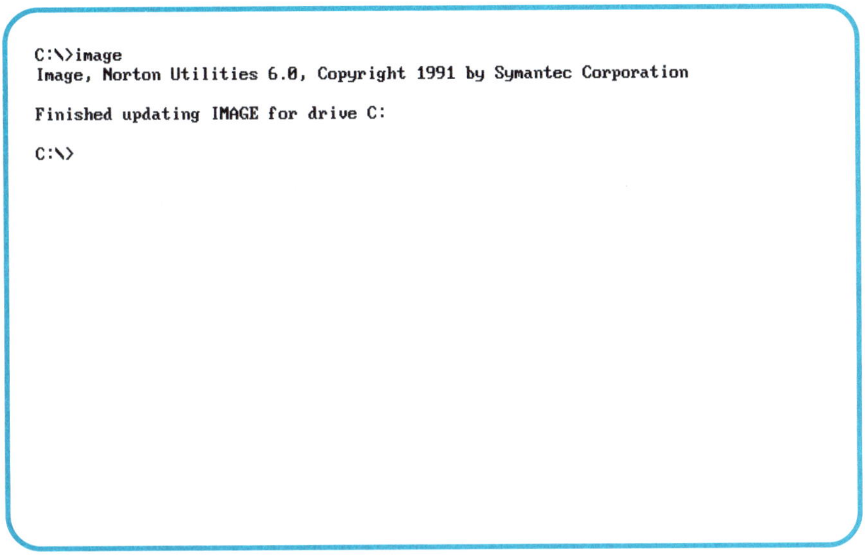

```
C:\>image
Image, Norton Utilities 6.0, Copyright 1991 by Symantec Corporation

Finished updating IMAGE for drive C:

C:\>
```

Figure 6.10 IMAGE screen.

149

Recovering Data from an Accidentally Formatted Disk

It's much easier to delete a file accidentally than it is to accidentally format a disk. But since both scenarios are possible, The Norton Utilities include two important tools for data recovery: UNERASE for resurrecting deleted files and UNFORMAT for rescuing data from an accidentally formatted disk. We explored UNERASE in Chapter 3, and you will read more about it in Chapter 7. Now, let's see how to recover files with the powerful UNFORMAT utility.

> **Caution:** If you want to recover files from an accidentally formatted hard disk and you haven't installed The Norton Utilities, *do not* install the utilities now! The Norton installation program copies all the utilities to your hard disk and may overwrite the files you wish to recover. Instead, insert the Norton Emergency Disk 1 into your A: (or B:) drive and substitute A:UNFORMAT (or B:UNFORMAT) for UNFORMAT in the Quick Steps that follow.

Q UNFORMATting a Disk

1. Type the command **UNFORMAT** and a disk example, **UNFORMAT A:**), and press Enter.

   This starts the UNFORMAT utility and displays the IMAGE dialog box shown in Figure 6.11.

2. Press Enter or click **Yes** IMAGE selection.

   This displays a summary of the selected disk's contents.

3. Press Enter or click **Yes** to acknowledge the contents summary message, and continue the UNFORMAT process.

   This initiates the UNFORMAT process. A complete message is displayed when the process is complete. ☐

150

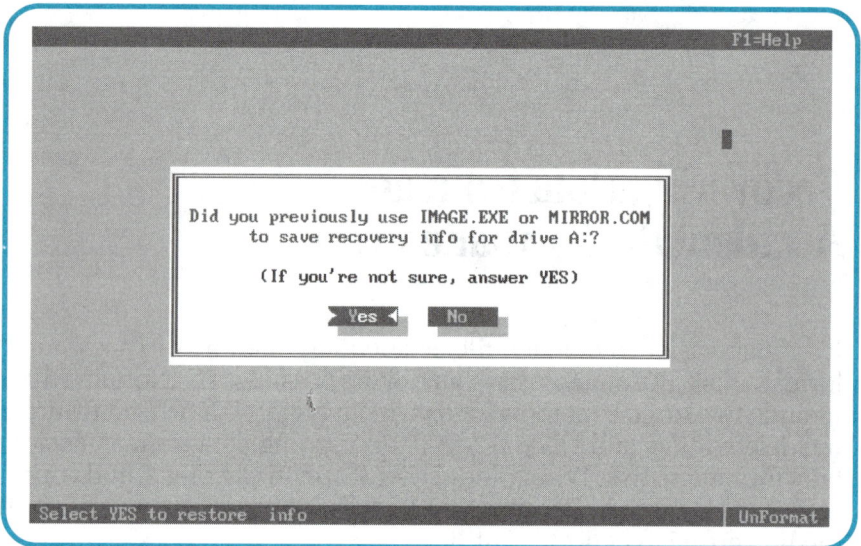

Figure 6.11 UNFORMAT will use an IMAGE file if one exists on the formatted disk.

If the disk you wish to UNFORMAT contains an up-to-date IMAGE.DAT file, the chances of a complete recovery are excellent. But don't worry if your formatted disk does not contain an

IMAGE.DAT file; it is still possible that UNFORMAT will recover everything that was on the disk. Unfortunately, some versions of DOS's FORMAT command will overwrite all the data on a disk during the format process. If you were unfortunate enough to have accidentally formatted a disk with this sort of destructive FORMAT, even UNFORMAT won't be able to recover your files. (Remember, SFORMAT's DOS mode performs a destructive format.)

Analyzing an UNFORMATted Disk

If you have the foresight to always use a nondestructive format such as the Quick or Safe modes of the Norton SFORMAT utility, you should have no trouble with a full recovery after an accidental format. It is also very important to make certain that all of your disks contain an up-to-date IMAGE.DAT file. (Refer to the SFORMAT and IMAGE utilities for IMAGE.DAT maintenance.)

151

Perhaps the most important rule to remember for data recovery is to employ the services of a recovery tool like UNERASE or UNFORMAT as soon as possible after the accidental deletion or format occurs. The longer you wait before using UNERASE or UNFORMAT, the greater the chances are of overwriting precious data clusters. If the disk you wish to UNFORMAT was nondestructively formatted and contains an up-to-date IMAGE.DAT file, UNFORMAT should be able to recover all your files with no additional intervention on your part. When the UNFORMAT process is complete, you should carefully inspect the contents of the disk and make certain the files and subdirectories are correct. If you determine that some files or subdirectories are missing after an UNFORMAT, you may need to use the UNERASE command to complete the recovery process.

If UNFORMAT is unable to locate an IMAGE.DAT file but is able to recover files and subdirectories, you'll have to do some additional housekeeping when UNFORMAT finishes. Without the IMAGE.DAT file, UNFORMAT does not know the names of a disk's subdirectories. Therefore, UNFORMAT names the subdirectories DIR.0, DIR.1, DIR.2, and so on. You'll need to use the NCD utility to rename these generically named subdirectories.

Without the IMAGE.DAT file, UNFORMAT also has no idea what was contained in the disk's system area (boot record, FAT, and root directory). This means that UNFORMAT cannot recover the files that previously existed in the accidentally formatted disk's root directory. You'll have to manually recover root directory files with the UNERASE utility (refer to the Manually UNERASEing Files section of Chapter 7).

> **Tip:** Refer to the DISKTOOL utility discussed in Chapter 7 if the UNFORMATted disk used to be bootable and you want to restore this feature.

Wiping Files from a Disk

In Chapter 3 you learned how to use the WIPEINFO utility to wipe a file from a disk so that its data cannot be recovered. WIPEINFO also lets you wipe an entire disk. Why would you want to wipe an entire disk? During the course of regular PC use, you are creating, copying, and deleting files that may contain sensitive data. As a result, some of this sensitive information may remain in unused clusters (because the DEL command doesn't remove a file's data from the disk). When the disk wipe feature is selected, WIPEINFO overwrites every part of the specified disk, including the unused clusters.

> **Caution:** Use the WIPEINFO utility with extreme caution because it overwrites a file's data clusters and makes recovery with UNERASE impossible.

Wiping a Disk with WIPEINFO

1. Type the command **WIPEINFO**, and press Enter.

This starts the WIPEINFO utility and displays the WIPEINFO screen shown in Figure 6.12.

2. Press the right arrow key and then press Enter, or click on the Drives command button.

This selects the Drives button in Figure 6.12 and displays the Wipe Drives screen shown in Figure 6.13.

152

3. Use the right and left arrow keys and press Space Bar or click with the mouse to select the drive(s) to wipe.

4. Press Enter, or click `Wipe`.

    A warning screen is displayed reminding you that you are about to destroy the contents of the disk in the specified drive.

5. Press **W** or click `Wipe` to continue the disk wipe process.

    WIPEINFO begins wiping the specified disk. A completion message is displayed when the wipe process is finished.

6. Press Enter or click `OK` to acknowledge the wipe completion message.

    The WIPEINFO screen in Figure 6.13 is redisplayed. □

153

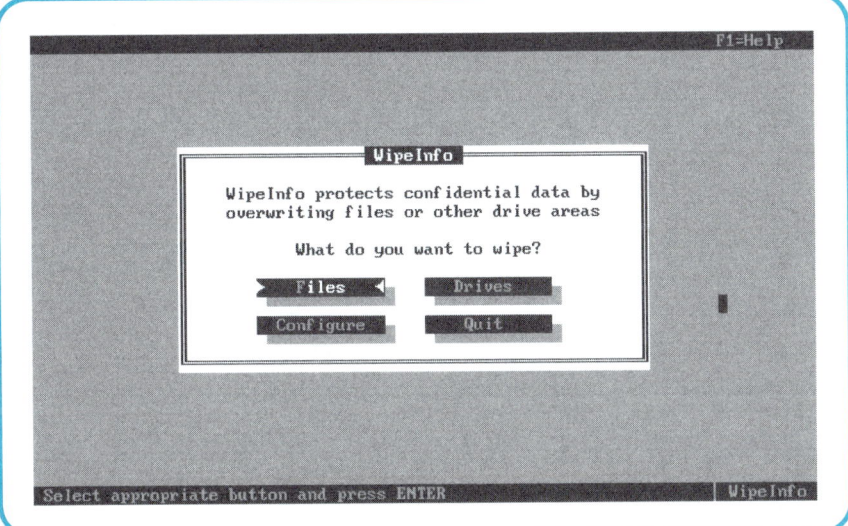

Figure 6.12   The WIPEINFO utility lets you wipe individual files or entire disks.

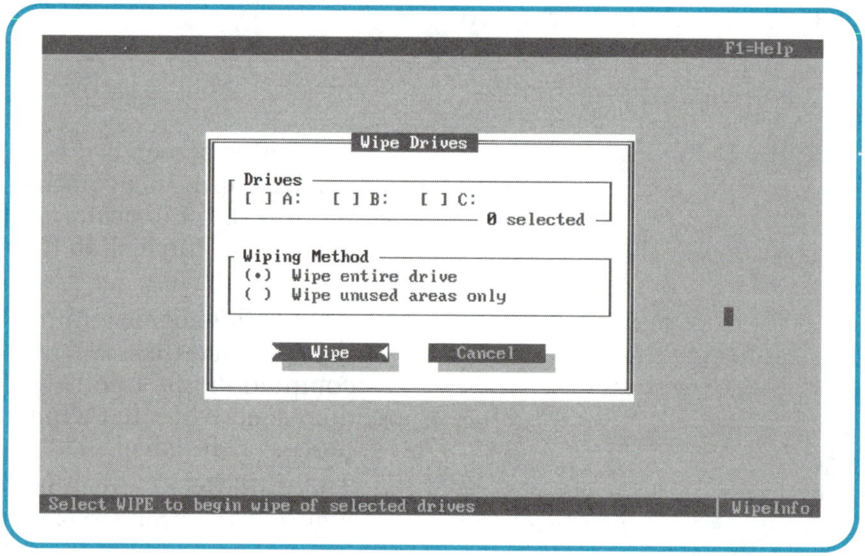

Figure 6.13   The Wipe Drives screen lets you select which drive(s) you wish to wipe.

Depending upon whether you reconfigured WIPEINFO in Chapter 3 or not, WIPEINFO overwrites each byte in every cluster of the disk one or more times. You can also specify what value WIPEINFO should use when overwriting data on a disk. Refer to the WIPEINFO Configuration section in Chapter 3 for a full discussion of wiping options.

Diagnosing and Correcting Disk Problems

As an experienced PC user, I've had a few encounters with unreliable hard/floppy disks. Unreliable disks can cause a variety of problems, including corrupt and disappearing files. Although the failure rate for disks is very low, even the slightest disk failure can cause great distress!

Consider this scenario: Let's say you've been working on a report for your boss for several days. The report is quite a few pages long and includes a slew of important tables and figures that have taken hours to create. Just as you are about to print the final copy of the report, your PC informs you that the file is "unreadable," or worse yet, it can't even find the file! One of the best steps you can take to avoid and correct disk problems like this is to use the Norton Disk Doctor (NDD) utility.

 Testing a Disk with Norton Disk Doctor (NDD)

1. Type the command **NDD**, and press Enter.

   This starts the NDD utility and displays the operation screen shown in Figure 6.14.

2. Press Enter or click on the Diagnose Disk option.

   This displays the Select Drives to Diagnose dialog box.

3. Use the up and down arrow keys or the mouse to highlight the drive you wish to diagnose, and press Enter or click Diagnose.

   NDD analyzes several areas of the specified disk; the Surface Test screen shown in Figure 6.15 is displayed when these tests are completed.

4. Press Enter or click Begin Test to accept the default settings shown in Figure 6.15 and begin the surface test.

   NDD tests every sector of the specified disk and displays the screen in Figure 6.16 when the test is complete.

5. Press Enter, or click Report.

   A report of the NDD session is created that can be viewed on the screen, printed out, or saved to a file. ☐

155

NDD performs a variety of tests in Step 3 of the preceding Quick Steps. During these tests, NDD examines the disk's partition table, boot record, file allocation table, directory structure, and file structure. When these tests are complete, NDD examines the disk's FAT in search of *lost clusters*. A lost cluster is a cluster that does not belong to any file but is shown as being in use in the FAT.

The surface test in Step 4 is the last test performed by the Norton Disk Doctor. Depending upon the options selected and the size of the disk being analyzed, the surface test can take anywhere from a few minutes to several hours to complete. When the default options are used, NDD tests each sector of the selected disk once and reports any problems it encounters.

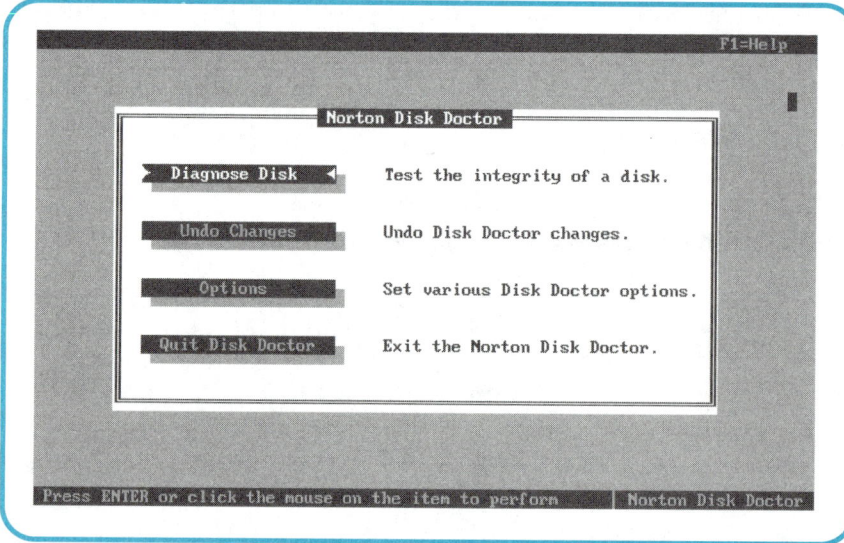

156

*Figure 6.14   Select the desired NDD operation from the Norton
Disk Doctor operation screen.*

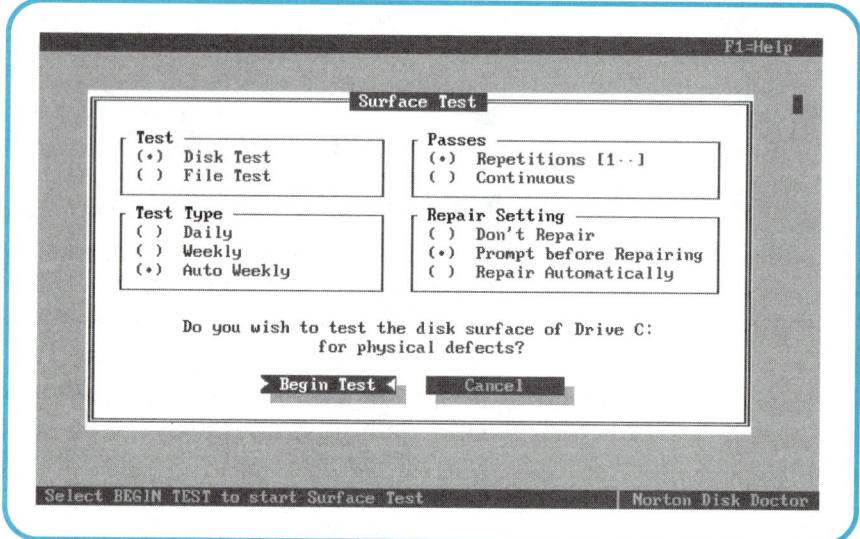

*Figure 6.15   The Surface Test screen offers several options for
additional NDD disk tests.*

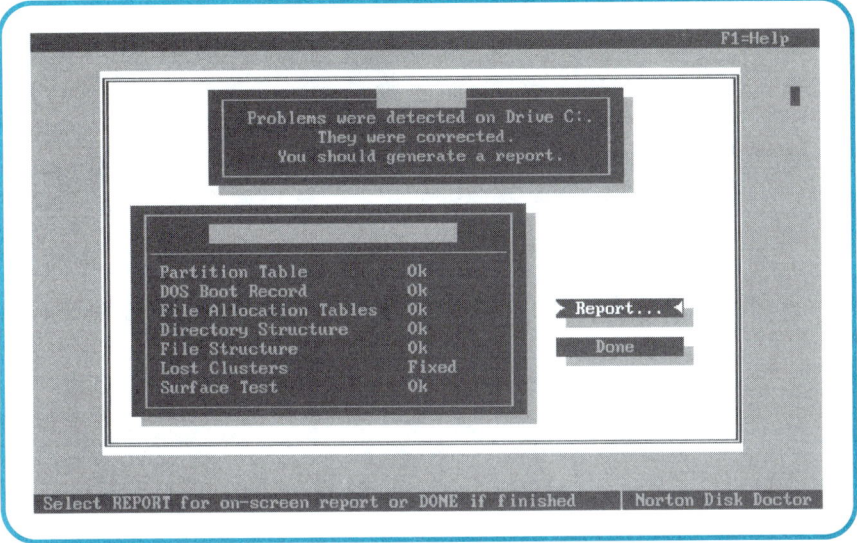

Figure 6.16   The NDD completion screen reports the results of all tests performed.

157

Surface Test Configuration

The screen in Figure 6.15 shows all the options available for the surface test operation. These options can be changed each time you run NDD or you can modify and save your settings using the Options button in Figure 6.14. The Disk Doctor Options screen shown in Figure 6.17 is displayed when you select the Options button. Press Enter or click to select the Surface Test button in Figure 6.17 and the Surface Test Options screen (Figure 6.18) is displayed.

The Surface Test Options screen in Figure 6.18 closely resembles the Surface Test screen in Figure 6.15. Both offer four surface test settings: Test, Passes, Test Type, and Repair Setting. Use the Tab key to jump quickly from one setting area to the next. Then use the up and down arrow keys and the Space Bar to select new surface test settings. Or, just click the mouse to make your selection.

The Test option in Figure 6.18 lets you choose between a Disk Test and a File Test. When you select the Disk Test option, NDD tests every sector of the selected disk, including those sectors not currently used by any files/directories (such as unused sectors). Select the File test option if you want NDD to skip unused sectors and test only those sectors currently used by a file/directory.

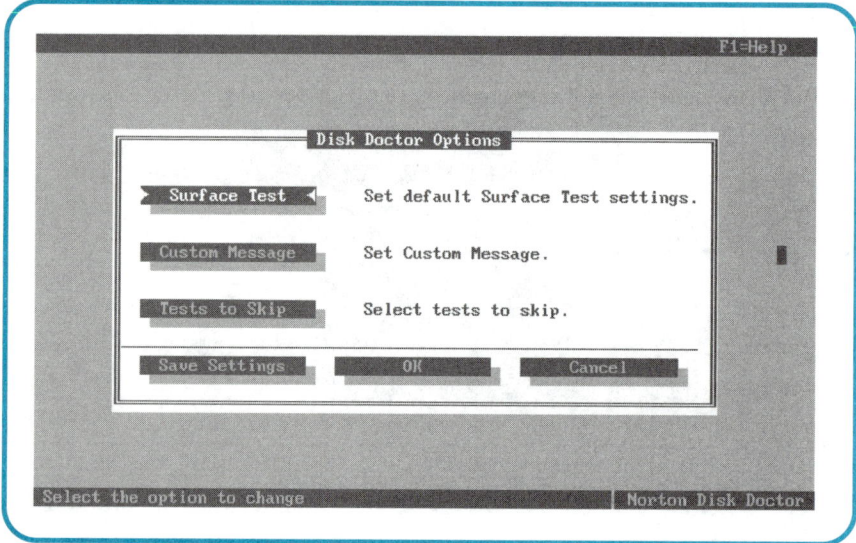

158

Figure 6.17   You can customize NDD with the Disk Doctor Options screen.

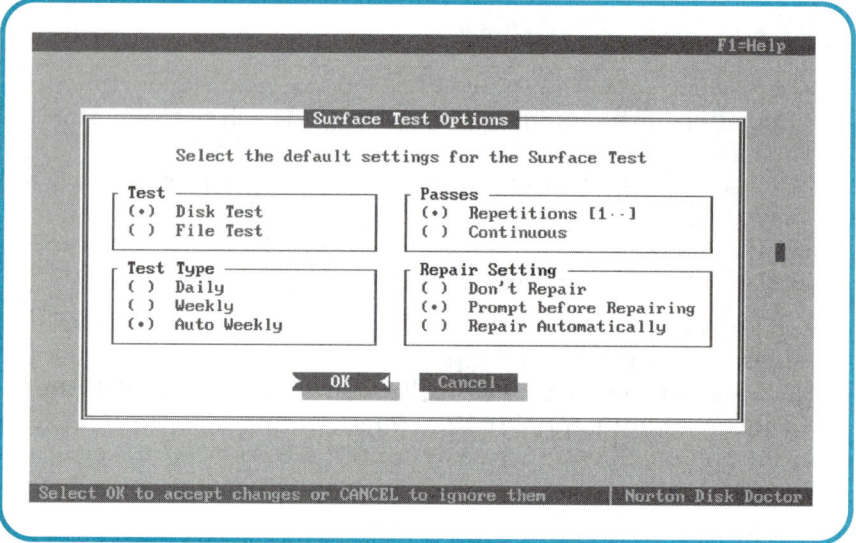

Figure 6.18   The Surface Test Options screen looks very similar to the Surface Test screen (Figure 6.15).

Use the Passes option to alter the number of times NDD runs the surface test. The default value is 1, but you can specify up to 999 repetitions. When you select the `Continuous` option, NDD performs the surface test over and over again until you abort it by pressing Esc or clicking on the left mouse button.

The Test Type option in Figure 6.18 lets you select either a Daily, Weekly, or Auto Weekly test setting. The Daily test is less sophisticated and time-consuming than the Weekly test, but the Weekly test can uncover certain disk problems that the Daily test may not detect. The Auto Weekly test is a combination of the Daily and Weekly tests. When you select Auto Weekly, NDD performs a Weekly test on Friday and a Daily test every other day of the week.

The last surface test configuration option lets you specify whether NDD should repair any disk problems it encounters. You may choose to

▶ Prevent NDD from making any repairs

▶ Have NDD prompt you before making repairs

▶ Let NDD automatically make all repairs without asking for your approval

159

NDD repairs disk problems by moving data from questionable clusters to more reliable locations on the disk. Further, NDD marks the questionable clusters as "bad" to prevent DOS from using them in the future.

Once you're satisfied with the surface test settings, press Enter or click `OK`, then select the `Save Settings` button on the Disk Doctor Options screen (Figure 6.17).

Other Disk Doctor Options

As you can see in the Disk Doctor Options screen (Figure 6.17), NDD offers two other configuration options: Custom Message and Tests to Skip. Use the Custom Message option if you want to display a special message when NDD encounters an error in its test process. The Set Custom Message screen shown in Figure 6.19 is displayed when you select the `Custom Message` button.

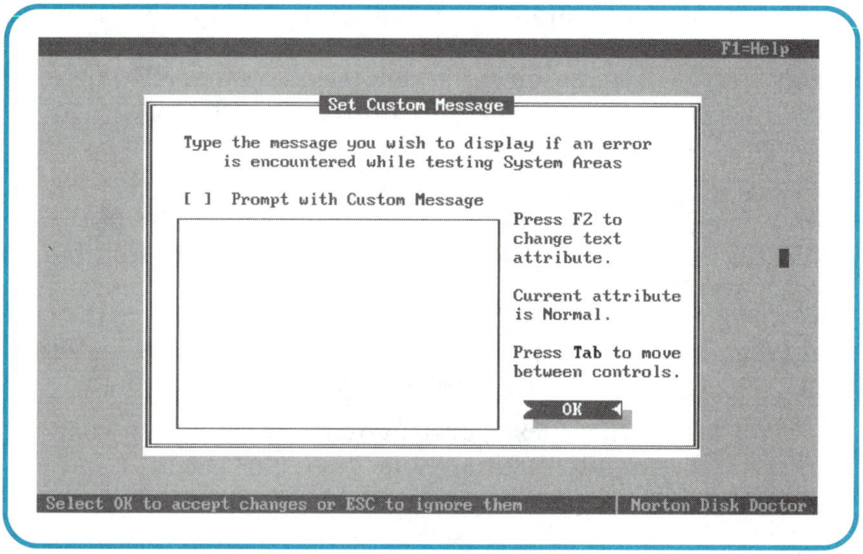

Figure 6.19   Use the Set Custom Message screen to create a special message that will be displayed when NDD encounters an error.

Press the Space Bar or click on the `Prompt with Custom Message` option in Figure 6.19, then press Tab or click in the message box to move the cursor to the message box. Type the desired custom error message in the message box (for example, `NDD has discovered a problem with your disk . . . please call 555-1234 to report this problem!`). Use F2 to select a special attribute for the error message text. Sample text attributes include underline, bold, and reverse video. When you are satisfied with your custom error message, press Tab or click to highlight the `OK` button and then press Enter to return to the Disk Doctor Options screen (Figure 6.17). Finally, select the `Save Settings` button to save your custom error message.

Select the `Tests to Skip` option shown in Figure 6.17 when you want to prevent NDD from running certain tests on your PC. The Tests to Skip screen shown in Figure 6.20 is displayed when you select this option.

NDD may run into problems during its test process if your computer is not a "true 100% IBM-compatible" PC. Certain compatibility problems may cause NDD to misbehave and lock up your PC. If your PC is having a problem running certain NDD tests, select the `Skip` option for the those tests and rerun NDD. Be sure to save your Tests to Skip settings by using the `Save Settings` button on the screen in Figure 6.17.

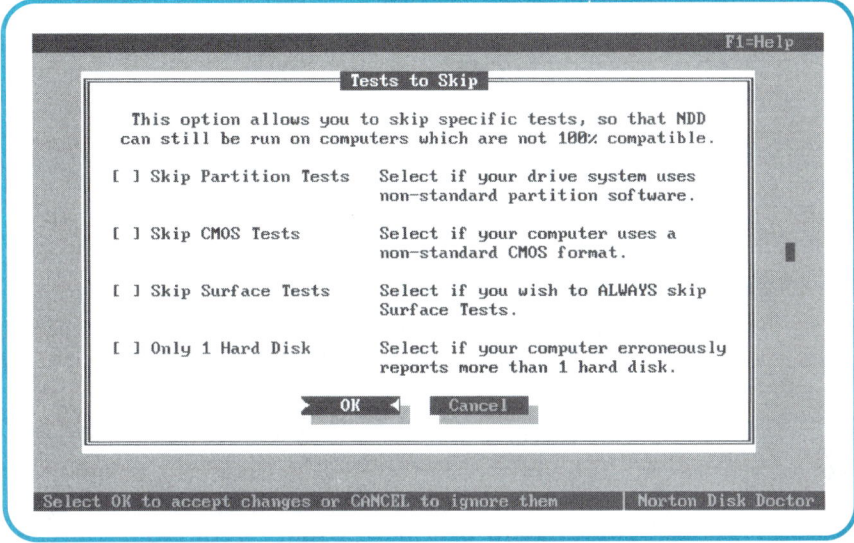

Figure 6.20   You can define which tests NDD should skip using the Tests to Skip screen.

161

Undoing NDD Repairs

Although NDD does a fine job of repairing most files, it is not infallible; that's why it's a good habit to always check its work. You should always create a report whenever you let NDD make repairs to a disk (refer to Step 5 in the NDD Quick Steps). Read through the NDD report to see what files or areas of the disk were repaired. Then check the repaired files to ensure that they truly have been "fixed."

For example, NDD recently repaired a file of mine called MEMO.DOC. I know that MEMO.DOC is a WordPerfect file so I used WordPerfect to load the MEMO.DOC file and check out the repairs. Fortunately, the repairs made by NDD appeared to fix the problems I had been having with MEMO.DOC. But what if my "fixed" file was in worse shape than it was in before NDD made its repairs? It occasionally happens; that's why NDD offers an undo feature.

It takes only a few moments to undo disk repairs made during the last NDD session. This is true because NDD saves disk repair information in a special file called NDDUNDO.DAT. NDD can use this undo data file to restore a disk to the same condition it was in before the disk repairs were made. Select the Undo Changes button on the Norton Disk Doctor operation screen (Figure 6.14), and follow the directions displayed to undo the disk repairs from the last NDD session.

What You Have Learned

In this chapter you learned about disk structures and several of the disk-related Norton utilities. More specifically, you learned:

▶ Eight bits constitute a byte, 512 bytes make up a sector, and a cluster contains one or more sectors (depending on the disk type).

▶ There are special regions or areas on a DOS disk where certain pieces of information must reside. These areas are known as the system area and the data area.

▶ The SFORMAT utility provides an easy-to-use alternative to DOS's unfriendly FORMAT command.

▶ The IMAGE utility saves a copy of a disk's system area (boot record, FAT, and root directory) in a hidden file called IMAGE.DAT. The UNERASE and UNFORMAT utilities use IMAGE.DAT to assist in quick and easy file recovery.

162

▶ The WIPEINFO utility can destroy the contents of an entire disk, including the data held in unused clusters.

▶ The Norton Disk Doctor utility can diagnose and correct many common disk problems.

Advanced Disk Management

In This Chapter

- ▶ *Viruses and disk protection*
- ▶ *Miscellaneous disk tools*
- ▶ *Protecting sensitive files*
- ▶ *Using the disk editor*
- ▶ *Manually UNERASEing files*
- ▶ *Optimizing disk performance*

This chapter explains the mysteries behind some of the more advanced disk-related tools in The Norton Utilities. The tools covered in this final chapter on the utilities offer a wide range of disk management power.

We first examine the DISKMON utility, which lets you monitor all disk activity on your system—a valuable tool for preventing computer viruses from wreaking havoc. We then cover several other utilities that let you do everything from encoding sensitive files to editing any segment of a disk. The last portion of Chapter 7 shows how to use The Norton Utilities to optimize your hard disk's performance.

Viruses and Disk Protection

A *computer virus* is a program that can cause irreversible damage to the data on your hard disk. Viruses are the computer equivalent of bacterial warfare; they are usually created by mischievous computer-whiz types. Viruses can find their way to your PC in a variety of ways. As a result, it's usually very difficult to determine exactly how and when a computer got "infected." To complicate matters, most viruses operate "behind the scenes" and can completely obliterate your hard disk before you know what's happened! To discover how to find and remove viruses that may have invaded your system, read Chapter 13—Protecting Your System with Norton AntiVirus.

164

Monitoring Disk Activity

Norton's DISKMON utility is a TSR utility that lets you monitor all disk activity on your system and can prevent computer viruses from destroying the contents of your hard disk. DISKMON also offers a disk park feature that protects your hard disk from damage when moving your PC from one location to another.

 Preventing Unauthorized Disk Write Activity

1. Type the command **DISKMON**, and press Enter.

   This runs the DISKMON utility and displays the Disk Monitor screen shown in Figure 7.1.

2. Press Enter, or click Disk Protect.

   This selects the Disk Protect button and displays the Disk Protect screen shown in Figure 7.2.

3. Select the Entire Disk option then the On button.

   This redisplays the Disk Monitor screen and shows the updated status of the Disk Protect feature.

4. Press Esc, or click Quit.   The DOS prompt returns,
                                        and DISKMON is activated
                                        as a TSR utility. ☐

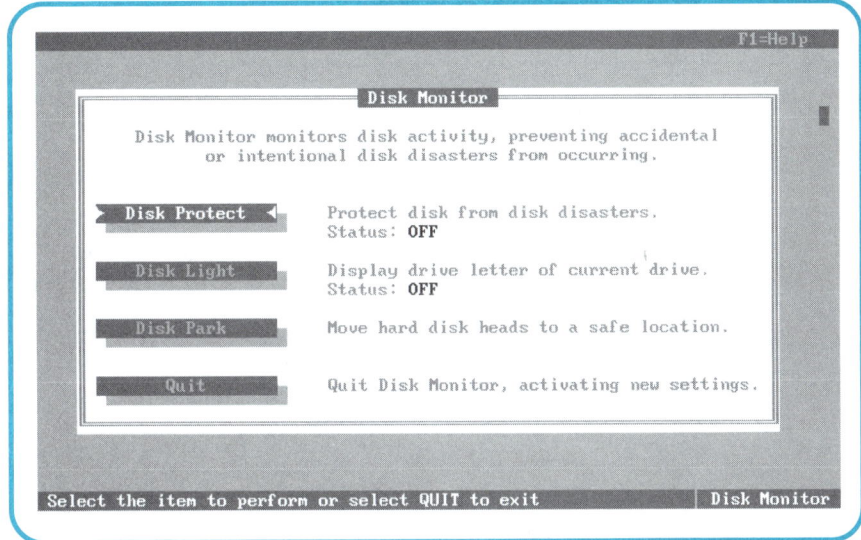

Figure 7.1   The Disk Monitor screen offers access to three useful disk utilities.

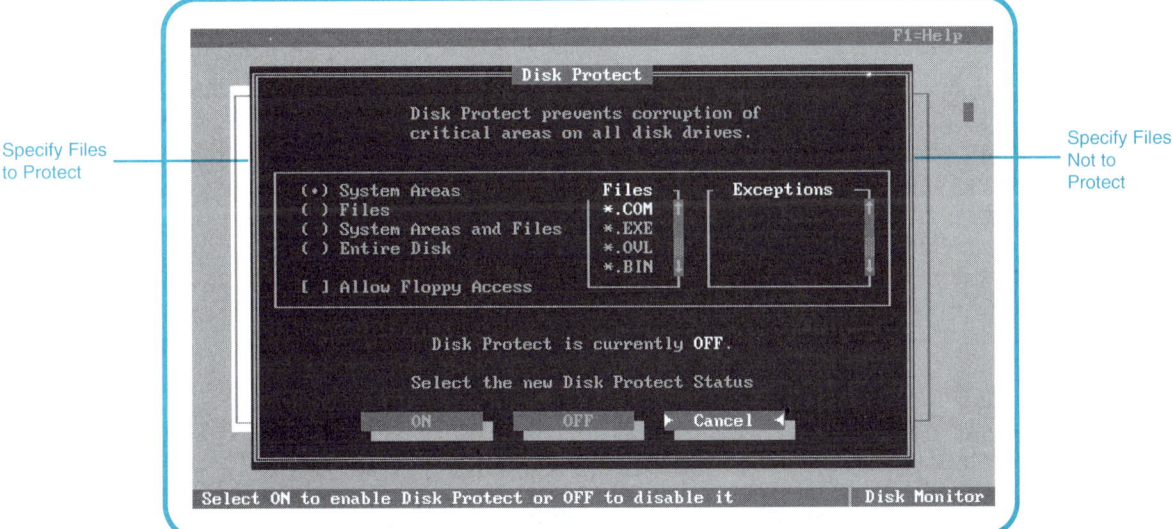

Figure 7.2   Use the Disk Protect feature to prevent unauthorized disk access.

When DISKMON is installed with the Entire Disk option, you will be notified before data is written to any disk on your PC (including both hard and floppy drives). The Disk Monitor dialog box shown in Figure 7.3 is displayed before each disk write operation.

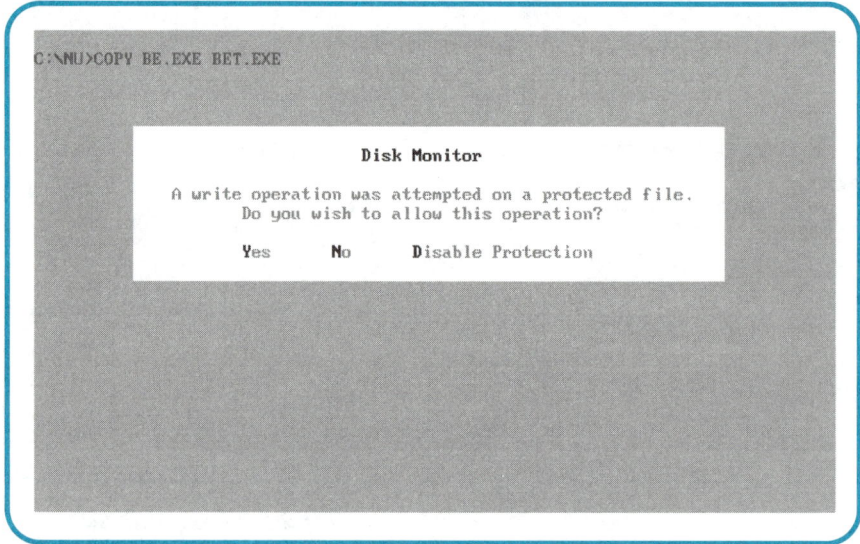

C:\NU>COPY BE.EXE BET.EXE

Disk Monitor

A write operation was attempted on a protected file.
Do you wish to allow this operation?

Yes   No   Disable Protection

Figure 7.3   The Disk Monitor dialog box pops up whenever an application tries to write to a protected disk.

Press **Y** to permit or **N** to prohibit the write operation when the dialog box in Figure 7.3 is displayed. The Disk Monitor dialog box may pop up several times during one file copy or save operation. Press **D** to temporarily disable the disk monitor feature when the Disk Monitor dialog box is displayed. You can also disable the disk monitor directly from the DOS prompt by executing the command **DISKMON /PROTECT-**. To reactivate the disk monitor execute the command **DISKMON /PROTECT+** at the DOS prompt.

Disk Monitor Options

The Disk Protect screen shown in Figure 7.2 offers several disk monitor options. If you're not concerned with entire disk protection, you can elect to protect just the system areas (boot record, FAT, and root directory) or files. In addition, you can use the Files and Exceptions selectors in Figure 7.2 to specify exactly which files you do and do not want protected. For example, let's say you want to monitor all Microsoft Excel spreadsheet data files except for those whose file names start with TEMP. You could specify `*.XLS` in the Files column and `TEMP*.XLS` in the Exceptions column of the Disk Protect screen.

Depending on the Disk Protect level selected, certain disk operations may cause the Disk Monitor dialog box (Figure 7.3) to pop up several times for write acknowledgment. The disk format process is a good example of an operation that can cause an enormous number of acknowledgment requests. The Allow Floppy Format option listed in the Disk Protect screen lets you format floppy disks without being bothered by the Disk Monitor dialog box. You should consider activating this option if you need to format floppy disks fairly often.

Disk Light

167

In addition to the Disk Protect feature already discussed, the DISKMON utility lets you monitor all disk activity (disk reads and writes) more simply. When DISKMON's Disk Light feature is activated, the TSR program displays the ID of the drive where disk read/write activity is occurring. The active disk drive ID (for example, C:) is displayed in the top right corner of the screen. Use the `/LIGHT+` and `/LIGHT-` options to turn the Disk Light feature on and off from the DOS command line (that is, `DISKMON /LIGHT- D` disables the Disk Light feature).

> **Note:** The Disk Protect and Disk Light features will display messages only while your monitor is in text mode. If you are running a graphics mode application (like Microsoft Windows), DISKMON cannot display Disk Protect/ Light messages.

Parking Your Hard Disk

Before you move your PC from one position or location to another, it is very important to prepare your hard disk for the relocation process. Hard disk drives are very sensitive devices and can easily be damaged while in transit. Use DISKMON's Disk Park feature to ensure your hard disk's safety before moving your PC. When you select the `Disk Park` button on the Disk Monitor screen (Figure 7.1), the Disk Park dialog box shown in Figure 7.4 is displayed.

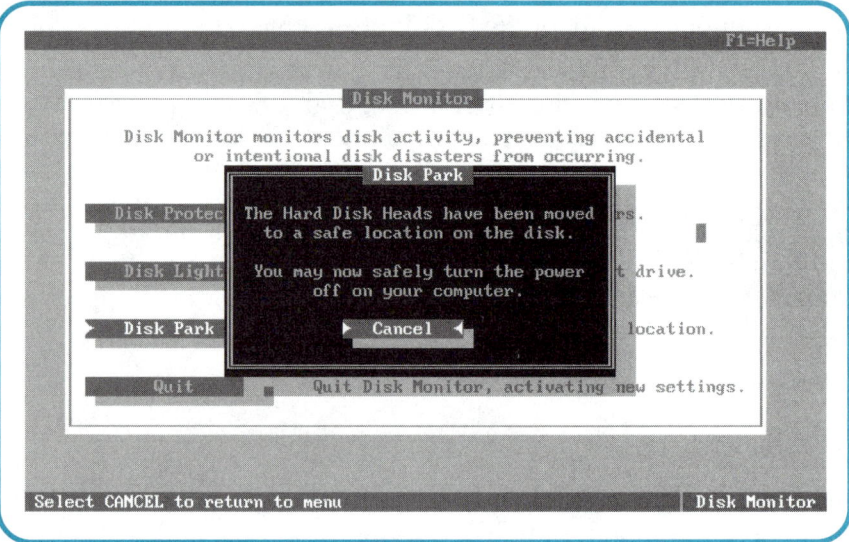

168

Figure 7.4   Park your hard drive to prevent damage during transportation of your PC.

As the dialog box in Figure 7.4 notes, DISKMON has parked your hard disk, and you should immediately power down your PC. I suggest using DISKMON to park your hard disk every day before you turn off your PC; you never know when you may need to move your system. You can also use DISKMON's /PARK option to park your disk directly from the DOS prompt (for example, **DISKMON /PARK**).

Miscellaneous Disk Tools

In earlier versions of The Norton Utilities (before release 5.0), the Norton Disk Doctor included a feature called Common Solutions. The Common

Solutions available through NDD let you perform three useful disk operations: make a disk bootable, recover from DOS's RECOVER command, and revive a defective diskette.

In version 6.0 of The Norton Utilities, the three operations that used to be part of NDD's Common Solutions are now available in a separate utility called DISKTOOL. The DISKTOOL utility also offers a couple of other valuable disk tools that let you mark bad clusters and save/restore important hard disk configuration information.

Using DISKTOOL to Make a Disk Bootable

The DISKTOOL utility can make a formatted disk bootable regardless of whether space was allocated for system files when the disk was originally formatted. (Refer to the SFORMAT Options section of Chapter 6 for a discussion of placing system files on a disk during the format process.)

169

 Making a Disk Bootable

1. Type the command **DISKTOOL**, and press Enter or click **Continue**.

   This runs the DISKTOOL utility and displays the Disk Tools information screen.

2. Read the information presented on the Disk Tools screen, then press Enter.

   The Disk Tools selection screen shown in Figure 7.5 is displayed.

3. Highlight the Make a Disk Bootable selection in the Procedures box, and press Enter or click Proceed.

   This displays a disk drive selection dialog box.

4. Highlight the drive ID of the disk you wish to make bootable (for example, A:), and press Enter.

   If you select a floppy disk drive in this step, DISKTOOL will ask you to insert a disk in the drive and press Enter. DISKTOOL then begins the process of making the selected disk bootable. ☐

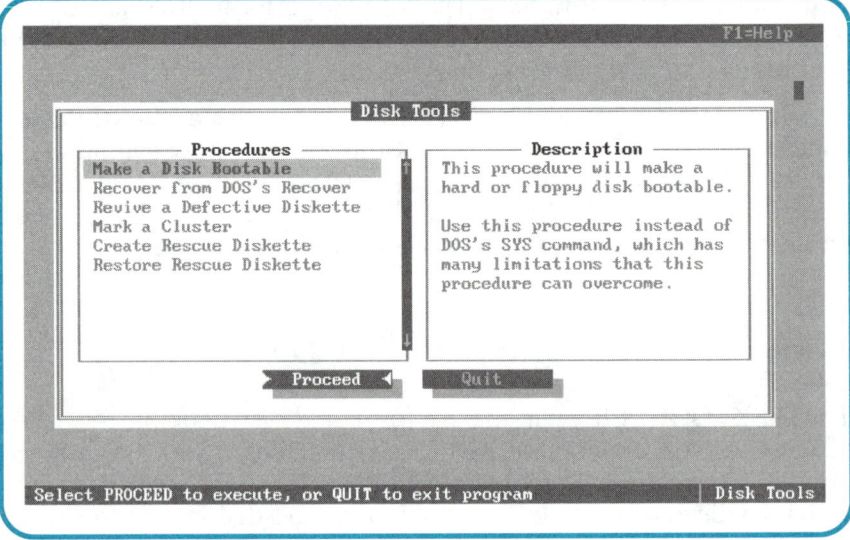

Figure 7.5   The DISKTOOL utility offers several selections for disk operations.

In order for a disk to be considered bootable, it must contain a couple of special hidden system files and DOS's command interpreter, COMMAND.COM. The Quick Steps outlined here place COMMAND.COM and the hidden system files on the specified disk. The DOS SYS command is also capable of copying the system files to a formatted disk. However, the SYS command for some older versions of DOS copies only the hidden files and does not copy COMMAND.COM. You have to manually copy COMMAND.COM after running SYS to make a disk bootable. It's very easy to forget to copy COMMAND.COM to a disk after running SYS, so if you have an older version of DOS, use DISKTOOL instead of SYS whenever you need to make a disk bootable.

Backtracking after a Disk RECOVERy

If you've ever used the DOS RECOVER command to rescue files from a defective disk, you're probably familiar with the mess it can create. When you ask RECOVER to recover a disk (for example, **RECOVER A:**) it gathers all the files and directories on the disk, places them in the root directory, and gives them meaningless names like file0001.rec, file0002.rec, and so on. When RECOVER is finished, it's up to you to inspect each of the filexxxx.rec files and determine its real name and whether it represents a file or a directory! Use the DISKTOOL utility instead of RECOVER, or use it to undo the mess created by RECOVER and return a disk to a more acceptable condition.

 Undoing a Disk RECOVERy

1. Type the command **DISKTOOL**, and press Enter.

   This runs the DISKTOOL utility and displays the Disk Tools information screen.

2. Read the information presented on the Disk Tools screen, then press Enter or click `Continue`.

   The Disk Tools selection screen shown in Figure 7.5 is displayed.

3. Highlight the `Recover from DOS's Recover` selection in the Procedures box, and press Enter or click `Proceed`.

   This displays a RECOVERy information screen.

171

4. Read the information presented in the RECOVERy information screen, and press Enter or click `OK`.

   This displays a disk drive selection dialog box.

5. Highlight the drive ID of the disk you wish to unRECOVER (for example, `A:`), and press Enter or click `OK`.

   If you select a floppy disk drive in this step, DISKTOOL will ask you to insert a disk in the drive and select `OK`. DISKTOOL then displays a couple of warnings before actually performing the unRECOVER; highlight the `Yes` button for each message, and press Enter to continue the unRECOVER operation. □

DISKTOOL does the best it can to return a disk to its preRECOVER condition, but it cannot recreate the names of the files and directories in the root directory—RECOVER zaps them permanently. Therefore, DISKTOOL is forced to use generic names for root directory entries when it undoes the RECOVER operation. When you inspect the contents of a disk after undoing a RECOVER, you'll notice that DISKTOOL uses generic names for root directory entries. For example, the files in the root directory are named file0001, file0002, and so on, and the directories are named DIR0000, DIR0001, and so on. You must rename these root directory entries to reflect their original names. The non-root directory entries (subdirectories and files in directories/subdirectories) on an unRECOVERed disk should appear as they did before the RECOVER operation.

Reviving a Defective Diskette

The third item in the Procedures box of the Disk Tools selection screen (Figure 7.5), Revive a Defective Diskette, lets you reformat a questionable disk without destroying the disk's contents. You should use this selection if you cannot read files from a disk and you want to preserve the data it contains. To revive data from a defective diskette, select the `Revive a Defective Diskette` option, and follow the simple directions provided by the DISKTOOL utility.

172

Marking Clusters

In Chapter 6 you learned that the Norton Disk Doctor (NDD) can diagnose and correct many common disk problems. When NDD finds a questionable cluster, it can move that cluster's data to a new location and mark the bad cluster so DOS doesn't try to use it in the future. The DISKTOOL utility also lets you mark bad clusters so DOS doesn't try to use them for data storage. As with DISKTOOL, to mark a bad cluster, select the `Mark a Cluster` option from the Procedures box of the Disk Tools selection screen (Figure 7.5), and follow the directions that are displayed.

It's usually best to let an intelligent utility like NDD take care of marking bad clusters. DISKTOOL lets you randomly designate certain clusters as "bad" without performing any test on them. Marking "good" clusters as "bad" is not dangerous because DISKTOOL, like NDD, moves the data in the bad cluster to a different location. However, DISKTOOL also lets you mark "bad" clusters as "good," which can be very dangerous! There's usually a good reason why "bad" clusters have been marked as such, and you should probably avoid re-marking a bad cluster as good.

Using a Rescue Diskette

You can use the last two features in the DISKTOOL utility to preserve and restore valuable system information. The DISKTOOL utility lets you create a "rescue diskette" containing the following system parameters: partition tables, boot records, and CMOS values. If your PC ever loses track of any of this system information, you can use the DISKTOOL utility to restore the values from the rescue diskette.

Q **Creating a Rescue Diskette**

1. Type the command **DISKTOOL**, and press Enter.

   This runs the DISKTOOL utility and displays the Disk Tools information screen.

2. Read the information presented on the Disk Tools screen, then press Enter or click Continue.

   The Disk Tools selection screen shown in Figure 7.5 is displayed.

3. Highlight the Create Rescue Diskette selection in the Procedures box, and press Enter or double-click on Create Rescue Diskette.

   This displays the Create Rescue Diskette information screen.

4. Press Enter, or click OK.

   This displays a disk drive selection dialog box.

5. Highlight the drive ID of the rescue diskette location (for example, A:), and press Enter or click OK.

   The DISKTOOL utility saves your PC's system information on the rescue diskette.

   □

Use the last DISKTOOL selection, Restore Rescue Diskette, as a last resort when you cannot access partitions on your hard disk and the Norton Disk Doctor utility cannot revive the disk.

Protecting Sensitive Files

The DOS ATTRIB command and Norton's FILEFIND utility can both be used to turn on the hidden file attribute for any personal/sensitive files

173

you want to protect on your PC. This is a good way to keep confidential files private since hidden files do not appear in directory listings. However, if someone is clever enough, they can use ATTRIB or The Norton Utilities to unhide your hidden files and expose your secrets.

Encrypting Files

To more effectively protect your private files, you should use Norton's DISKREET utility, which encrypts, or encodes, files so nobody else can interpret them.

 Encrypting a File with DISKREET

174

1. Type the command **DISKREET**, and press Enter.

    This runs the DISKREET utility and displays the Diskreet screen shown in Figure 7.6.

2. Select the **Files** button.

    The Files menu is displayed.

3. Press Enter to select the **Encrypt...** option in the Files menu.

    This displays the encryption file selection screen shown in Figure 7.7.

4. Use the arrow keys to change the selected directory/drive and highlight the file you wish to encrypt. Then press Enter or double-click with the mouse to select the drive, directory, and file you want to encrypt.

    This displays the File Encryption Output screen.

5. Press Enter or click **OK** to accept the default encrypted file name.

    The encryption password request screen is displayed.

6. Enter a secret password for the encrypted file (minimum of six characters), and press Enter.

    The password re-entry screen is displayed.

7. Type the secret password again for verification and press Enter.

DISKREET encrypts the selected file and displays a message when the process is complete. □

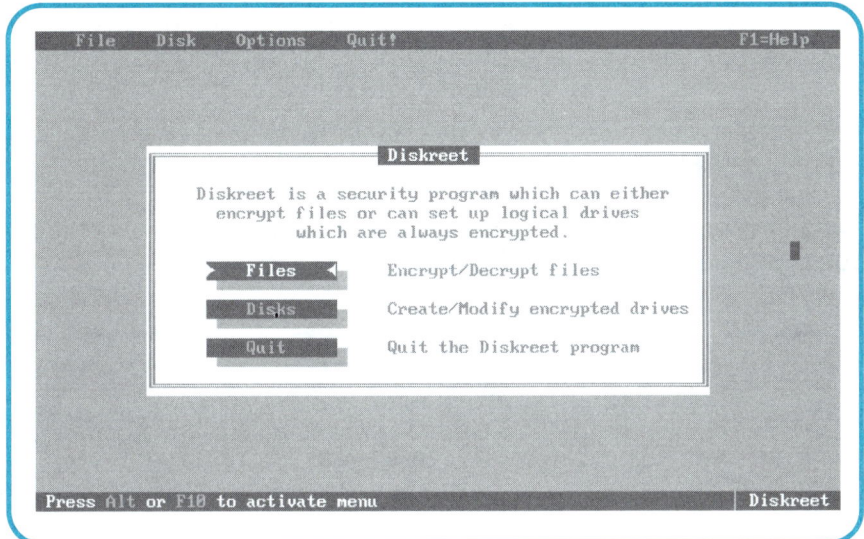

Figure 7.6   Use DISKREET to protect personal files.

175

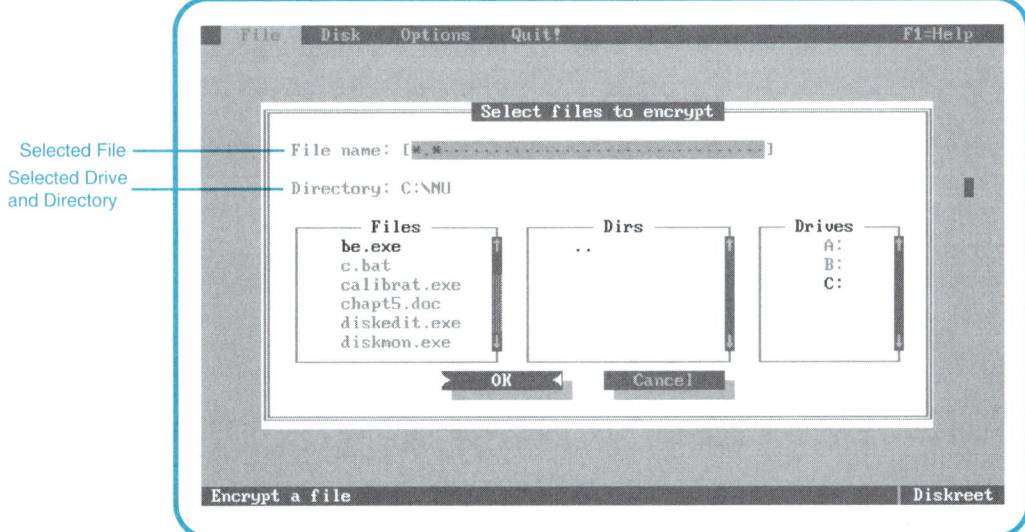

Selected File

Selected Drive and Directory

Figure 7.7   Use the encryption file selection screen to specify which file(s) you wish to encrypt.

Be careful when selecting an encryption password for Step 6. You'll need to specify this password later when you try to decode, or decrypt, the file. Don't use simple passwords like your name, address, or phone number, because they are obvious choices for others who may try to decrypt your files. On the other hand, don't use passwords that you might easily forget, because there's no way to reveal an encrypted file's password. If you forget the password, you may never be able to decrypt the file.

Encryption Options

Select the File options... entry in the Files menu to display the File Encryption Options screen shown in Figure 7.8.

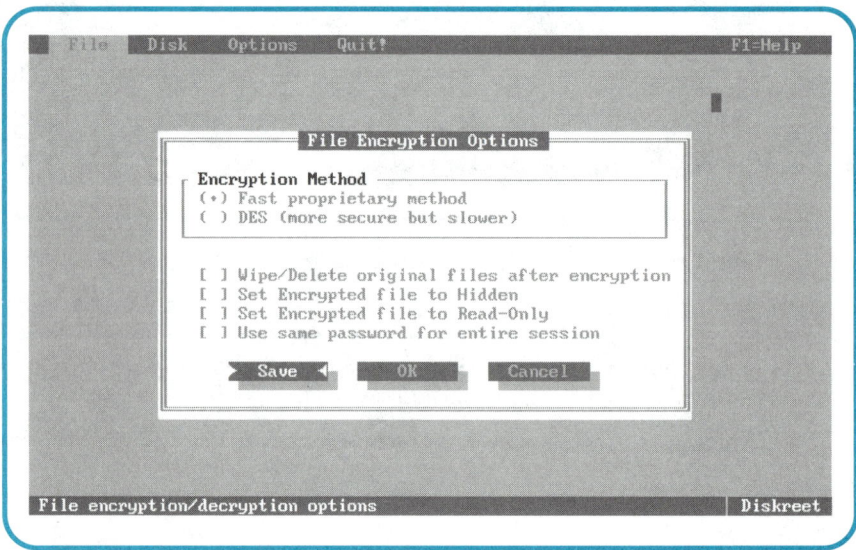

Figure 7.8   DISKREET offers several encryption options.

The DISKREET utility offers two methods of file encryption. The default DISKREET encryption method uses a proprietary encoding technique, and the other method uses the Data Encryption Standard (DES) technique, which has been approved by the U.S. Government as a highly secure encryption standard. Use the arrow keys and Space Bar or click to select the desired encryption method.

The other four options shown in Figure 7.8 let you specify whether

▶ The original file should be deleted after encryption

▶ The encrypted file's read-only and hidden attributes should be set

▶ The same password should be used for encryption throughout the DISKREET session

The password retention option is a handy feature if you want to encrypt several files with the same password. When this option is turned on, you have to enter the encryption password only once during the DISKREET session. Use the up and down arrow keys and the Space Bar or click with the mouse to select the desired DISKREET options, then select the Save button to preserve the settings.

Decrypting Files

177

The DISKREET file decryption process is very similar to the encryption process. Pull down the Files menu and select the Decrypt... option to display the Decryption File Selection screen shown in Figure 7.9.

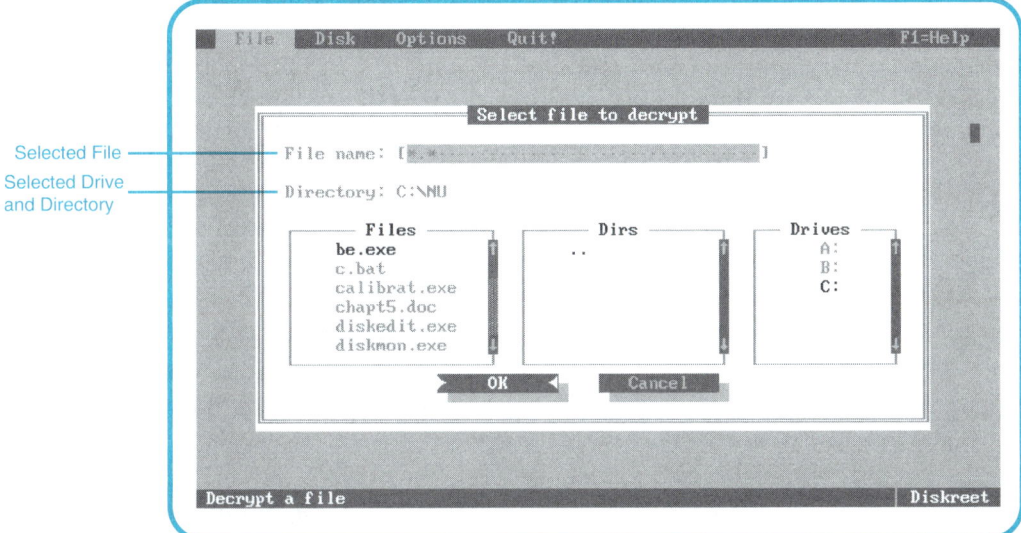

Figure 7.9 Use the Decryption File Selection screen to specify which files you wish to decrypt.

Use the arrow keys or double-click the mouse to change the selected directory/drive and highlight the file you wish to decrypt. Then press Enter, and the password request screen will be displayed. Enter the password you used to encrypt the file, and press Enter. If you enter the correct password, DISKREET will decrypt the specified file and display a message when the process is complete.

Using the Disk Editor

You can use many tools to view the contents of files on your disks. The DOS TYPE command offers one of the easiest ways to view, or dump, a file. To display the contents of a file called LETTER.DOC, use the command **TYPE LETTER.DOC**. TYPE does a pretty good job as long as the file you specify consists solely of displayable ASCII characters (like AUTOEXEC.BAT and CONFIG.SYS). If you try to use TYPE to view the contents of an executable file (for example, **TYPE NORTON.EXE**), however, you'll wind up with a bunch of gobbledygook on your screen, and your PC may even beep a few times!

As you can see, we need something more powerful than TYPE if our goal is to view the contents of any file on a disk. To complicate matters further, what if you want to browse through other nonfile areas of a disk such as the boot record, FAT, or unused clusters? Better yet, what if you're interested not only in viewing but also in modifying or editing the contents of any area of a disk? The Norton Utilities include a disk editor (DISKEDIT), which lets you perform a wide variety of tasks including viewing/editing virtually any byte on a disk.

 Browsing Through Files with DISKEDIT

1. Type the command **DISKEDIT**, and press Enter.

   This runs the DISKEDIT utility and displays the DISKEDIT screen shown in Figure 7.10.

2. Use the Object menu to change the active drive/ directory if necessary.

3. Highlight the desired file, and press Enter.

   Displays a hexadecimal/ ASCII view of the selected file (Figure 7.11). □

178

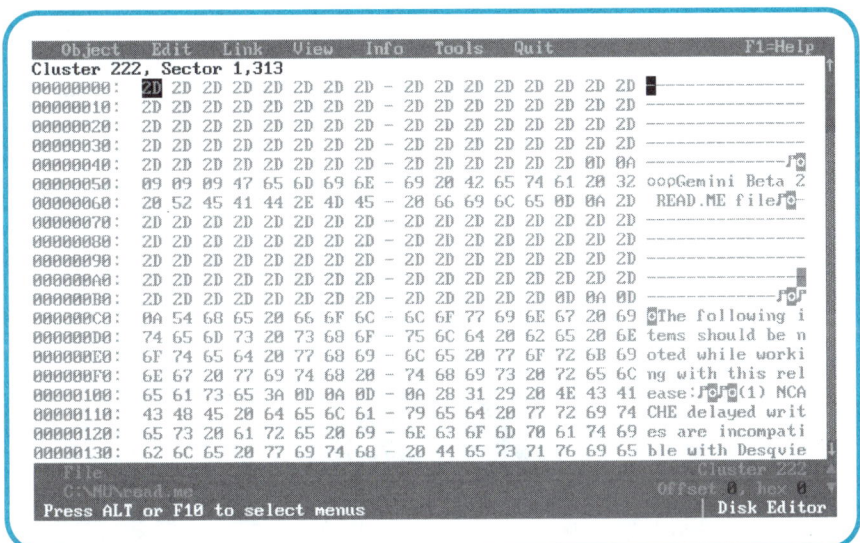

Object	Edit	Link	View	Info	Tools	Quit					F1=Help

```
Name      .Ext    Size    Date       Time      Cluster Arc R/O Sys Hid Dir Vol
Cluster 221, Sector 1,309
█████████           0      5-31-91    9:16 am    221                     Dir
..                  0      5-31-91    9:16 am      0                     Dir
FOUR      BAT      201      6-08-91    1:00 pm   10283  Arc
LISA      BAT      206      6-08-91    1:01 pm   10284  Arc
MENU      BAT     1959      6-08-91    4:17 pm   10285  Arc
MENU2     BAT     1387      6-08-91    4:51 pm   10286  Arc
ONE       BAT      179      6-08-91   12:23 pm   10287  Arc
C         BAT      307      6-08-91    1:07 pm   10282  Arc
TWO       BAT      206      6-08-91    1:01 pm   10289  Arc
THREE     BAT      359      6-08-91    1:02 pm   10288  Arc
NORTON    CMD     8124      5-31-91    9:35 am    4088  Arc
NDOS      COM    10603      4-29-91    6:00 am     355  Arc
DS        EXE    56600      4-29-91    6:00 am    3691  Arc
DISKREET  EXE    96696      4-29-91    6:00 am     223  Arc
NCC       EXE    66720      4-29-91    6:00 am    3590  Arc
FS        EXE     8600      4-29-91    6:00 am    3973  Arc
Cluster 221, Sector 1,310
NCACHE    EXE    54104      4-29-91    6:00 am    3664  Arc
NDD       EXE   120120      4-29-91    6:00 am    3190  Arc
```

Sub-Directory	Cluster 221
C:\NU	Offset 0, hex 0

Press ALT or F10 to select menus | Disk Editor

Archive Drive and Directory

Figure 7.10   *This DISKEDIT listing screen shows a listing of the active directory.*

Object	Edit	Link	View	Info	Tools	Quit	F1=Help

```
Cluster 222, Sector 1,313
00000000:  2D 2D 2D 2D 2D 2D 2D 2D - 2D 2D 2D 2D 2D 2D 2D 2D  ████----------
00000010:  2D 2D 2D 2D 2D 2D 2D 2D - 2D 2D 2D 2D 2D 2D 2D 2D  ----------------
00000020:  2D 2D 2D 2D 2D 2D 2D 2D - 2D 2D 2D 2D 2D 2D 2D 2D  ----------------
00000030:  2D 2D 2D 2D 2D 2D 2D 2D - 2D 2D 2D 2D 2D 2D 2D 2D  ----------------
00000040:  2D 2D 2D 2D 2D 2D 2D 2D - 2D 2D 2D 2D 2D 0D 0A     -----------
00000050:  09 09 09 47 65 6D 69 6E - 69 20 42 65 74 61 20 32  oopGemini Beta 2
00000060:  20 52 45 41 44 2E 4D 45 - 20 66 69 6C 65 0D 0A 2D   READ.ME file♪♬-
00000070:  2D 2D 2D 2D 2D 2D 2D 2D - 2D 2D 2D 2D 2D 2D 2D 2D  ----------------
00000080:  2D 2D 2D 2D 2D 2D 2D 2D - 2D 2D 2D 2D 2D 2D 2D 2D  ----------------
00000090:  2D 2D 2D 2D 2D 2D 2D 2D - 2D 2D 2D 2D 2D 2D 2D 2D  ----------------
000000A0:  2D 2D 2D 2D 2D 2D 2D 2D - 2D 2D 2D 2D 2D 2D 2D 2D  ----------------
000000B0:  2D 2D 2D 2D 2D 2D 2D 2D - 2D 2D 2D 2D 0D 0A 0D     ----------♪♬♪
000000C0:  0A 54 68 65 20 66 6F 6C - 6C 6F 77 69 6E 67 20 69  ♂The following i
000000D0:  74 65 6D 73 20 73 68 6F - 75 6C 64 20 62 65 20 6E  tems should be n
000000E0:  6F 74 65 64 20 77 68 69 - 6C 65 20 77 6F 72 6B 69  oted while worki
000000F0:  6E 67 20 77 69 74 68 20 - 74 68 69 73 20 72 65 6C  ng with this rel
00000100:  65 61 73 65 3A 0D 0A 0D - 0A 28 31 29 20 4E 43 41  ease:♪♬♪(1) NCA
00000110:  43 48 45 20 64 65 6C 61 - 79 65 64 20 77 72 69 74  CHE delayed writ
00000120:  65 73 20 61 72 65 20 69 - 6E 63 6F 6D 70 61 74 69  es are incompati
00000130:  62 6C 65 20 77 69 74 68 - 20 44 65 73 71 76 69 65  ble with Desqvie
```

File	Cluster 222
C:\NU\read.me	Offset 0, hex 0

Press ALT or F10 to select menus | Disk Editor

Figure 7.11   *Here, DISKEDIT shows a hexadecimal/ASCII view of a file.*

A Note on Hexadecimal Notation

Most of the information shown in Figure 7.11 may not be meaningful to you if you're unfamiliar with *hexadecimal notation*. The hexadecimal or, hex, numbering system is very similar to the decimal number system we use every day. In the decimal number system, values are written using some combination of the ten digits 0 through 9 (for example 1, 490, and 27662). These same ten digits are also used by the hex number system along with six additional values, A through F. Valid hex numbers include 4A, 11, and 3FC. It is customary to prefix a hex number with a dollar sign ($) to avoid ambiguity with decimal numbers. So our list of valid hex numbers may also be written as $4A, $11, and $3FC.

You don't have to understand hex to use DISKEDIT! In fact, you don't even have to know how to convert between hex and decimal—DISKEDIT includes a built-in hex-to-decimal conversion utility. Select the Hex converter... option from the DISKEDIT Tools menu, and the Converter dialog box is displayed. The Converter can convert from hex to decimal or vice versa, and it shows the ASCII character value of the number specified. In Figure 7.12, the Converter shows that the hex value $4D is equal to the decimal value 77, which is the ASCII value of the M character.

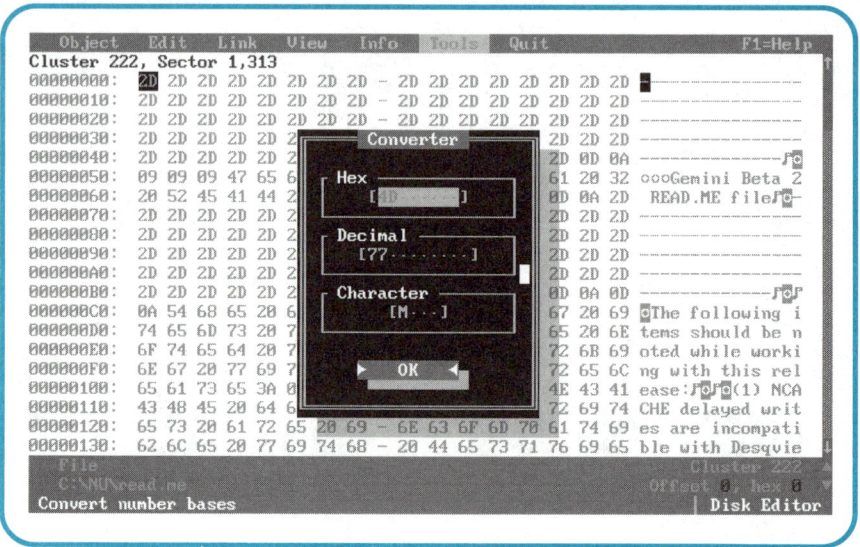

Figure 7.12   The hex converter shows decimal and ASCII translations of hex values.

Working With the Hexadecimal/ASCII View

Each row of information in Figure 7.11 shows the hexadecimal and ASCII values of 16 bytes in the selected file. The column of numbers along the left side of Figure 7.11 shows the *offset* (in hex) of the first byte in each row. The offset is a position indicator that is relative to the beginning of the selected file. For example, the first byte in the file is at offset 0, the second byte is at offset 1, the third byte is at offset 2, and so on.

The row of hex values starting at offset 00000060 is

```
20 52 45 41 44 2E 4D 45 - 20 66 69 6C 65 0D 0A 2D
```

(NOTE: The dash between 45 and 20 shows the midpoint of the line of 16 bytes and is not part of the data itself.) If you use the Converter to translate each of these values, you will learn that a hex 20 is a space, hex 52 is R, hex 45 is E, hex 4 is A, hex 44 is D, and so on. This same information is shown on the right side of the row in Figure 7.11; the ASCII translation for the 16 bytes in offset row 00000060 is READ.ME file:

181

```
20 52 45 41 44 2E 4D 45 - 20 66 69 6C 65 0D 0A 2D
   R  E  A  D  .  M  E       f  i  l  e
```

You can use any of the arrow keys to move the cursor from one row or byte to another. When you're viewing a file with DISKEDIT, two highlight blocks are used in conjunction with the blinking cursor. The highlight blocks work together to easily show the selected byte's location in both the hex and ASCII portions of the line. You can move the blinking cursor from the hex highlight box to the ASCII highlight box, or vice versa, by pressing Tab.

You can modify any of the values in the selected file if DISKEDIT is not restricted to read-only mode. (NOTE: Read-only mode may be turned on or off by using the Configuration... selection in the Tools menu. You should probably leave DISKEDIT in read-only mode until you become more familiar with how the utility works.) DISKEDIT accepts byte modifications in either hex or ASCII depending on the location of the blinking cursor; simply type the new hex/ASCII value(s) over the existing value(s). Press Enter when you are finished entering changes, and DISKEDIT will display a dialog box indicating which cluster was modified. You then have the opportunity to write or discard your changes and return to the DISKEDIT Directory Listing screen (Figure 7.10).

Selecting Other Views and Objects

The hex/ASCII view shown in Figure 7.11 is useful when you're looking for a detailed view of the selected file. DISKEDIT offers several other views depending on the type of data you're working with. The READ.ME file we viewed earlier is a text file that is somewhat difficult to read using the hex/ASCII view. READ.ME is shown in a more readable format if you select the As Text option in the View menu (Figure 7.13).

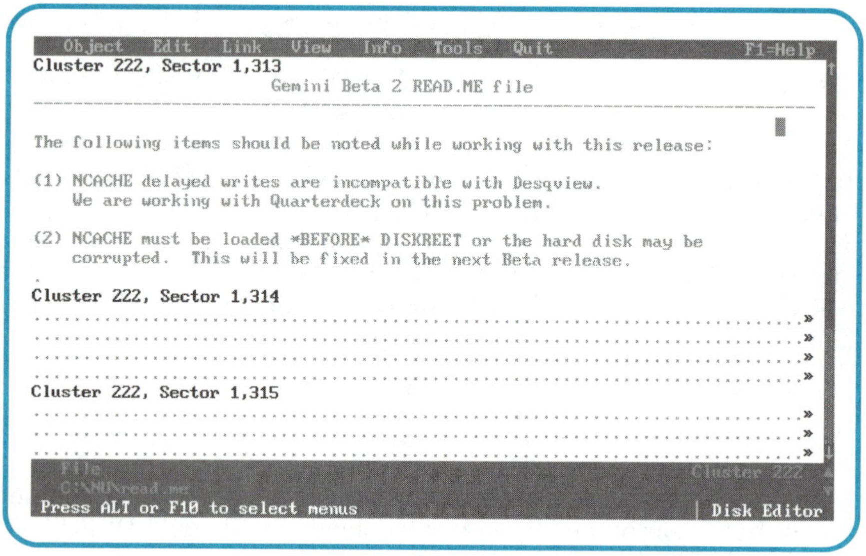

```
 Object   Edit   Link   View   Info   Tools   Quit                  F1=Help
Cluster 222, Sector 1,313
                        Gemini Beta 2 READ.ME file

The following items should be noted while working with this release:

(1) NCACHE delayed writes are incompatible with Desqview.
    We are working with Quarterdeck on this problem.

(2) NCACHE must be loaded *BEFORE* DISKREET or the hard disk may be
    corrupted.  This will be fixed in the next Beta release.

Cluster 222, Sector 1,314
..........................................................................»
..........................................................................»
..........................................................................»
Cluster 222, Sector 1,315
..........................................................................»
..........................................................................»
..........................................................................»
  File                                                         Cluster 222
  C:\NU\read.me
Press ALT or F10 to select menus                            | Disk Editor
```

Figure 7.13   The Text View selection shows READ.ME in a much more readable format.

DISKEDIT has enough intelligence to select the appropriate view depending on the type of object being displayed. For example, the As Directory option is used to display the directory listing in Figure 7.10.

As we saw earlier, DISKEDIT's Object menu lets you change the active drive/directory. The Object menu also provides several other selections including an option to display either the primary or secondary copy of the active drive's FAT. The screen in Figure 7.14 is displayed when you select the 1st Copy of FAT option from the Object menu.

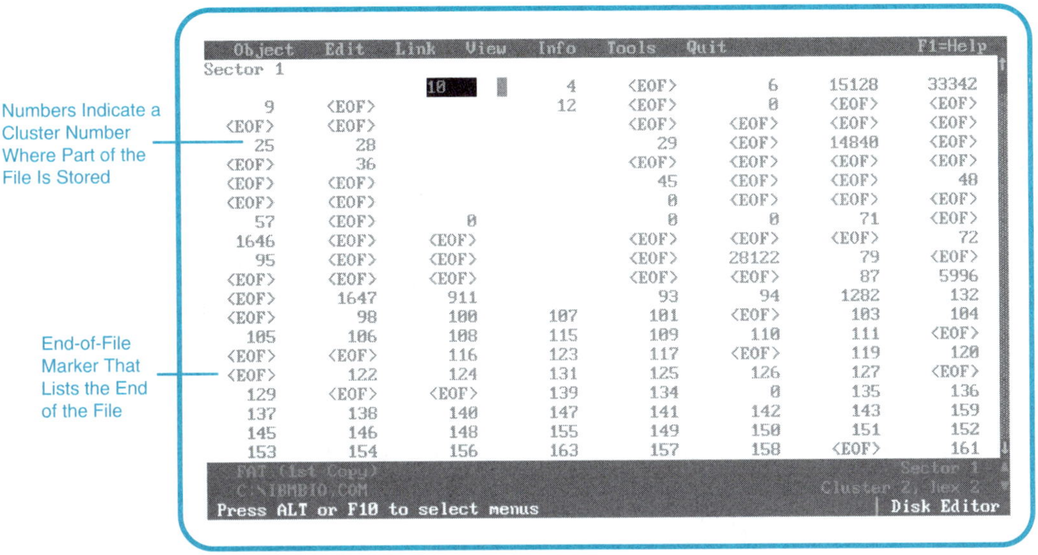

```
 Object   Edit   Link   View   Info   Tools   Quit              F1=Help
Sector 1
                    10      █       4    <EOF>       6    15128    33342
        9   <EOF>                  12    <EOF>       0    <EOF>    <EOF>
    <EOF>   <EOF>                       <EOF>    <EOF>   <EOF>    <EOF>
       25      28                       29    <EOF>   14840    <EOF>
    <EOF>      36                    <EOF>    <EOF>   <EOF>       48
    <EOF>   <EOF>                       45    <EOF>   <EOF>    <EOF>
       57   <EOF>           0            0       0      71    <EOF>
     1646   <EOF>  <EOF>           <EOF>    <EOF>   <EOF>       72
       95   <EOF>  <EOF>           <EOF>   28122      79    <EOF>
    <EOF>   <EOF>           <EOF>   <EOF>      87    5996
    <EOF>    1647    911             93      94    1282      132
    <EOF>      98     100    107     101    <EOF>     103      104
      105     106     108    115     109     110     111    <EOF>
    <EOF>   <EOF>     116    123     117    <EOF>     119      120
    <EOF>     122     124    131     125     126     127    <EOF>
      129   <EOF>  <EOF>     139     134       0     135      136
      137     138     140    147     141     142     143      159
      145     146     148    155     149     150     151      152
      153     154     156    163     157     158    <EOF>     161
 FAT (1st Copy)                                          Sector 1
 C:\IBMBIO.COM                                         Cluster 2, Hex 2
 Press ALT or F10 to select menus              |  Disk Editor
```

Numbers Indicate a Cluster Number Where Part of the File Is Stored

End-of-File Marker That Lists the End of the File

Figure 7.14   *You can browse through the FAT with DISKEDIT.*

183

When DISKEDIT displays a FAT, it shows the information in a FAT-view format. You can use the arrow keys to highlight different clusters in the FAT-view. Each value shown in the FAT-view screen indicates the status of a particular cluster. It's very easy to trace through the chain of clusters used in a file, especially since DISKEDIT highlights the chain in a special color (or places double greater-than signs [>>] next to each cluster in the chain on a monochrome monitor). If you're curious to find out what file the highlighted chain of clusters represents, press Enter, and the directory screen is displayed. The file represented by the chain of clusters on the FAT screen is automatically highlighted on the directory screen. As you saw earlier, you can press Enter again to view the contents of that file.

Select Memory Dump from the Object menu (or press Alt-M) to display a dump of your system's memory to the screen. When you select this command, the Memory Dump dialog box appears, asking you to specify starting and ending addresses of the memory to dump. Do so, then press Enter or click OK. The screen shown in Figure 7.15 appears, displaying the hex and ASCII contents of your system's memory.

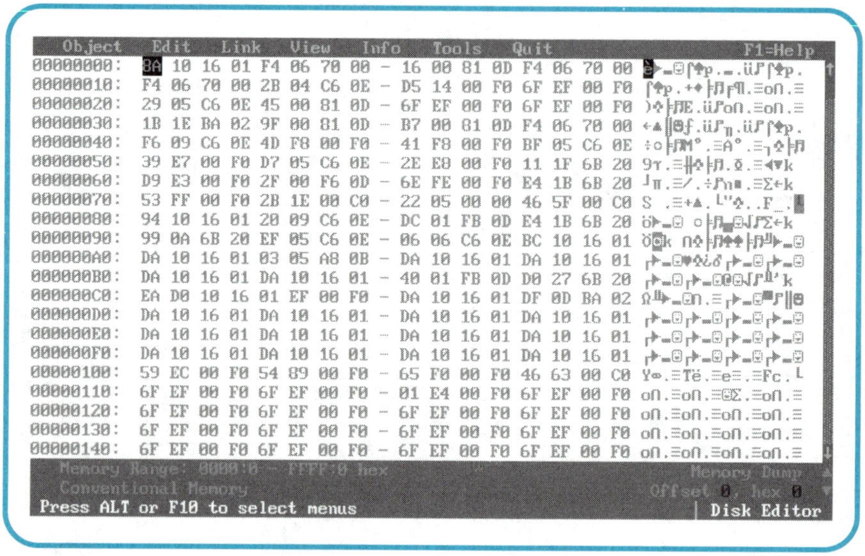

Figure 7.15   An example memory dump.

DISKEDIT is perhaps the most powerful and flexible Norton utility. It's so powerful, in fact, that in the hands of a novice user it can be quite lethal! Accidental modification of the wrong byte in a file, FAT, directory, and so on may cause major headaches for you and anyone else who uses your PC. So be careful when using DISKEDIT. As a precaution, you may want to consider leaving the DISKEDIT utility in read-only mode (see the Configuration . . . selection in the Tools menu).

Printing Your Selection

When you view an object on-screen, you have the option to print the object's contents. To do so, select Print as from the Tools menu or press Ctrl-P. The Print As dialog box appears, as shown in Figure 7.16. As you can see, you can either print the object to your printer or to disk. And, just as you can select several different on-screen views for objects, you can print several views. After you've made your dialog box selections, choose OK to print.

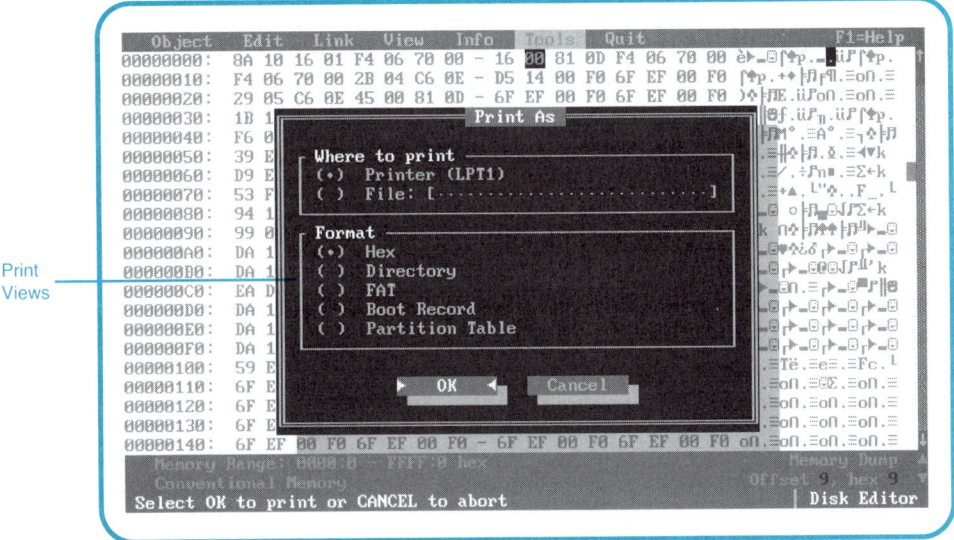

Print
Views

Figure 7.16   DISKEDIT's Print As dialog box.

185

Now let's see how to use the advanced features of UNERASE to manually recover accidentally deleted files.

Manually UNERASEing Files

In Chapter 3 you learned how to use Norton's UNERASE utility to resurrect accidentally deleted files. The unerase process can be very quick and simple if there has been little disk activity since the accidental deletion. Every time you COPY a file, save a file from a word processor, or perform a similar operation, you run the risk of overwriting the unprotected data of a deleted file. Therefore, the chances of recovering an accidentally deleted file are best if you run UNERASE immediately after the deletion.

The UNERASE utility reports a recovery prognosis for each deleted file it finds on your disk (Figure 7.17).

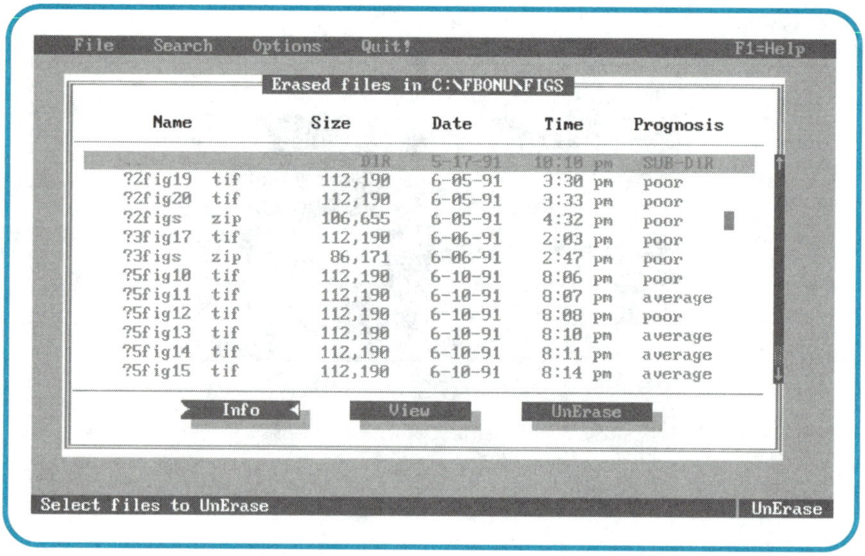

Figure 7.17   The UNERASE screen shown here reports a poor recovery prognosis for the ?2FIG19.TIF file.

UNERASE usually has no problem automatically recovering deleted files with an "excellent" or "good" prognosis. If you're trying to recover a file with an "average" or "poor" prognosis, however, you'll probably need to help UNERASE with the recovery process. Regardless of the prognosis listed, you should first try the automatic method to recover the deleted file. If UNERASE displays a message similar to the one shown in Figure 7.18, you'll have to try to manually recover any of the file's data that may still reside on the disk.

Select the Manual unerase... option from the UNERASE File menu to begin the manual recovery process. UNERASE then asks you to supply the first character of the name of the file to be recovered. After you type the file name's first character, the Manual UnErase screen in Figure 7.19 is displayed.

The panel on the left side of the Manual UnErase screen shows the file information UNERASE was able to locate including the file's name, attributes, time/date stamps, and size. The File Information panel also reports cluster information as you manually rebuild the deleted file.

The right side of the Manual UnErase screen contains several operation buttons you can select during the manual recovery process. Select the Add cluster... button to start rebuilding the file, and the screen in Figure 7.20 will be displayed.

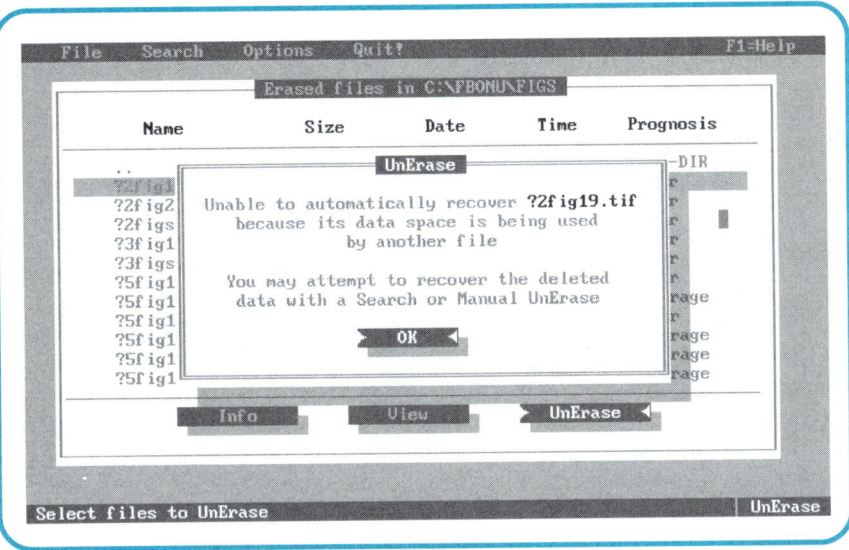

Figure 7.18 *UNERASE displays a failure message if automatic recovery is unsuccessful.*

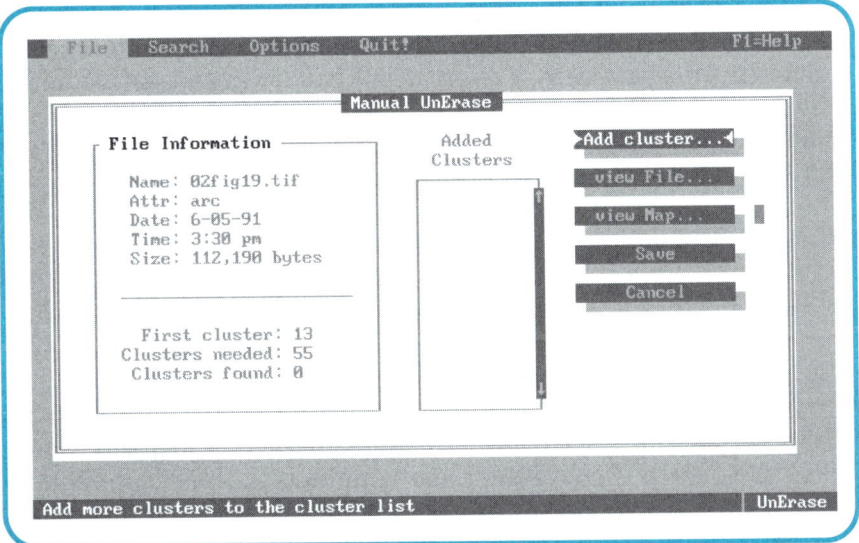

Figure 7.19 *Use the Manual UnErase feature to recover files that cannot be unerased automatically.*

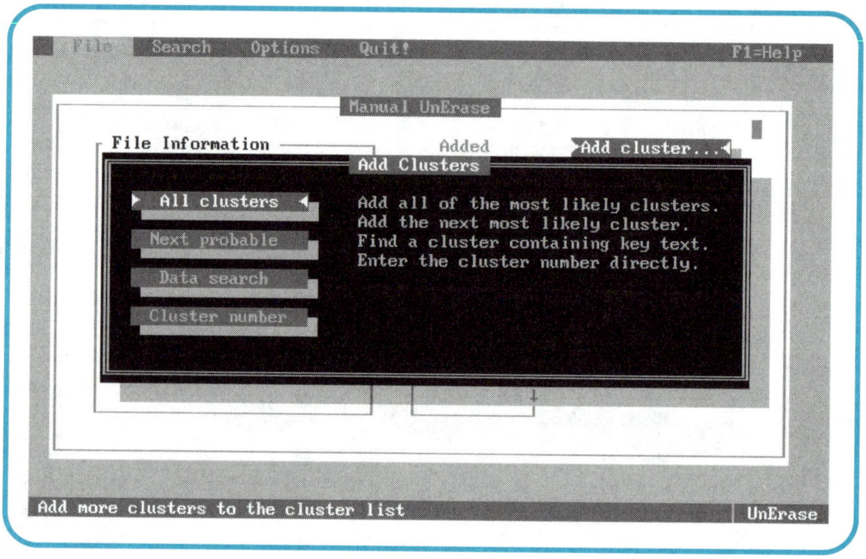

Figure 7.20   UNERASE offers several ways to add clusters to a file as you recover it.

188

Even though UNERASE may not be able to recover a deleted file automatically, it can still offer some useful information about which clusters the file occupied. The first time you try to manually unerase a file, you should select the All clusters button in Figure 7.20. When you select this button, UNERASE uses all available information to try to piece together the clusters from the deleted file. The Manual UnErase screen (Figure 7.19) is redisplayed after UNERASE gathers all the likely clusters for the file. Select the view File... button in Figure 7.19 to have a look at the clusters UNERASE has gathered.

Depending on what the view File . . . selection displays, you may want to either save the file with the recommended clusters or try another manual recovery approach. If you want to save the recovered file, press Esc to return to the Manual UnErase screen, and select the Save button. If the data contained in the recommended clusters doesn't even resemble the previous contents of the deleted file, you can try another, less automated mode of manual recovery. Press Esc a couple of times to return to the initial UnErase screen (Figure 7.17), then follow the directions provided earlier to reach the Add Clusters screen (Figure 7.20). Rather than letting UNERASE guess at the entire chain of clusters for the deleted file, you can select the Next probable or Data search buttons to build the cluster chain manually. The Data search feature is particularly useful when trying to recover text files because you can search the entire disk for a specific string of characters. As you manually add each cluster to the chain, be sure to use the `view File...` button to monitor the contents of the rebuilt file.

UNERASE is a powerful tool, but it's not without limitations. If some of the clusters from a deleted file have been overwritten, you cannot completely recover the file with UNERASE; however, you can still use UNERASE to recover manually as many clusters as possible. Now let's take a look at three important utilities that can improve the efficiency and speed of your hard disk.

Optimizing Disk Performance

189

You can use several tricks to make your PC operate at its peak performance level. I use the Norton Control Center utility (discussed in Chapter 2) to set my keyboard rate at the fastest setting. This step alone can create the illusion of a much faster PC! The Norton Utilities include three other tools that you can use to optimize your hard disk's performance. When used properly, these disk optimization tools can significantly increase the performance of even the slowest hard disk.

Using SPEEDISK

A badly fragmented disk is one of the most common causes of sluggish PC performance. The fragmentation that results from the everyday process of copying and deleting files can cause even the fastest hard disk to appear to be as slow as molasses! Use the Norton SPEEDISK utility regularly to keep your hard disk defragmented and efficient.

 Defragmenting Your Disk

1. Type the command **SPEEDISK**, and press Enter.

This runs the SPEEDISK utility and displays a drive selection dialog box.

2. Use the up and down arrow keys or the mouse to highlight the drive you wish to optimize. Press Enter, or click OK.

SPEEDISK analyzes the selected disk and displays the recommended optimization method (Figure 7.21).

3. Press Enter or click Optimize to accept the recommended method and begin disk optimization.

SPEEDISK optimizes the specified disk and displays a message when the process is complete. □

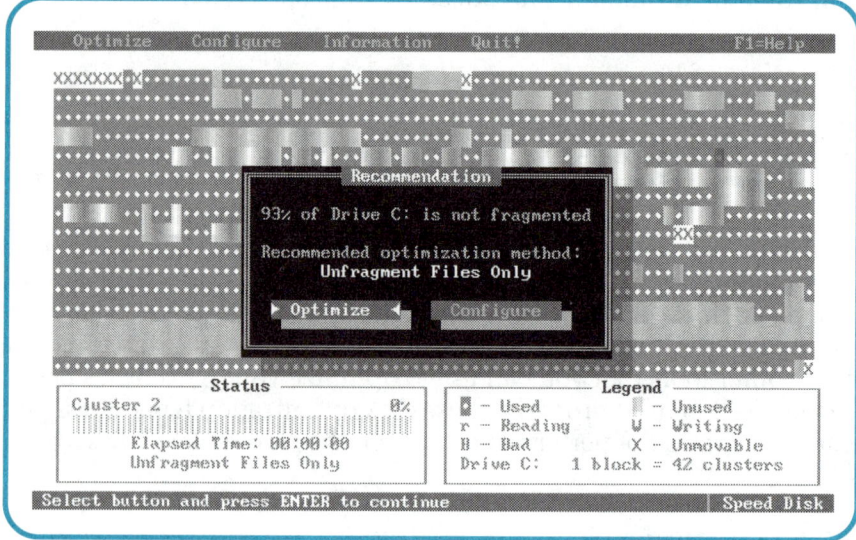

Figure 7.21   SPEEDISK recommends an "Unfragment Files Only" optimization method.

SPEEDISK offers five different methods of optimization, ranging from a full optimization to a file sort, which simply rearranges the order of files on the disk. After you specify which disk to optimize, SPEEDISK analyzes the disk and determines which optimization method should be used. You can accept SPEEDISK's recommended optimization method, or you can select a different method. Select the Optimization Method... option from the Optimize menu to see the list of optimization methods offered (Figure 7.22).

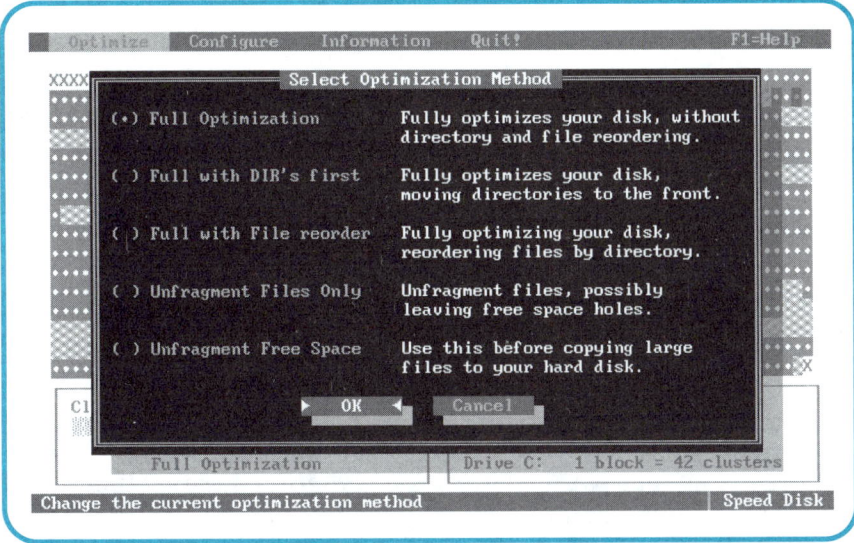

Figure 7.22   SPEEDISK offers several optimization methods.

191

Of the five optimization methods offered, the Full Optimization and Unfragment Files Only methods are perhaps the most valuable. SPEEDISK defragments files and moves all unused clusters to one contiguous area on the disk when the Full Optimization method is used. Full Optimization is the most time-consuming method offered by SPEEDISK, but it also organizes the disk in the most efficient manner possible.

In contrast, the Unfragment Files Only method is less time-consuming than Full Optimization, but it doesn't create the most efficient disk possible. As its name implies, the Unfragment Files Only method concentrates on unfragmenting files on the specified disk. However, there's no guarantee that every single file will be unfragmented when the optimization process is complete. Further, a disk optimized with the Unfragment Files Only method will probably still contain "holes" of noncontiguous unused clusters.

Use the Full Optimization method monthly and the Unfragment Files Only method weekly to maintain a highly efficient and organized disk.

Using a Disk Cache

Disk read/write operations are very slow compared to the time required to manipulate data in RAM. A disk cache utility maintains frequently accessed disk data in a RAM buffer to help expedite disk read/write operations.

Before a time-consuming disk read operation is performed, the disk cache checks its RAM buffer to see if it contains the requested data. If the requested data is found in the RAM buffer, the cache can provide it to DOS without having to perform a timely disk read operation. Similarly, the cache utility may buffer several disk write operations and perform them together in a more efficient manner.

192

> **Note:** The Norton Utilities Installation program includes an option to automatically install the cache utility. You can use the NVCONFIG program as follows to install the cache utility if you skipped this step in the installation process.

To utilize the NCACHE caching programs, you must use NVCONFIG to install it. Type `NVCONFIG` at the DOS prompt. Select the `Norton Cache` option. In the dialog box that appears, select either `Load from CONFIG.SYS` or `Load from AUTOEXEC.BAT` from the Loading section of the screen. You can then exit NVCONFIG.

After you add the NCACHE statement to your CONFIG.SYS file, you must reboot to activate the cache utility.

NCACHE is compatible with the memory usage of Windows 3.X. When you run Windows 3.X in enhanced mode, it can (and does) use some of the memory held by NCACHE. To specify a minimum amount of expanded or extended memory for NCACHE when you're running Windows 3.X in enhanced mode on your system, you can use NUCONFIG to load NCACHE from your CONFIG.SYS file. Then you can edit the DEVICE line for NCACHE to add the EXT and EXP commands with parameters. (Or, you can start NCACHE from the DOS prompt with the desired parameters and memory specifications.) For more on the EXT and EXP command parameters, see The Norton Utilities User Guide.

Using CALIBRAT

The CALIBRAT utility is perhaps the most powerful disk optimization tool included in The Norton Utilities. CALIBRAT (short for Calibrate) performs several tests to determine many important characteristics, including your hard disk's *interleave factor*. The interleave factor indicates how sectors are laid out within each track on a disk. The disk in Figure 7.23 has a 1:1 (pronounced "one to one") interleave factor, which means that each sector is adjacent to the next consecutive sector.

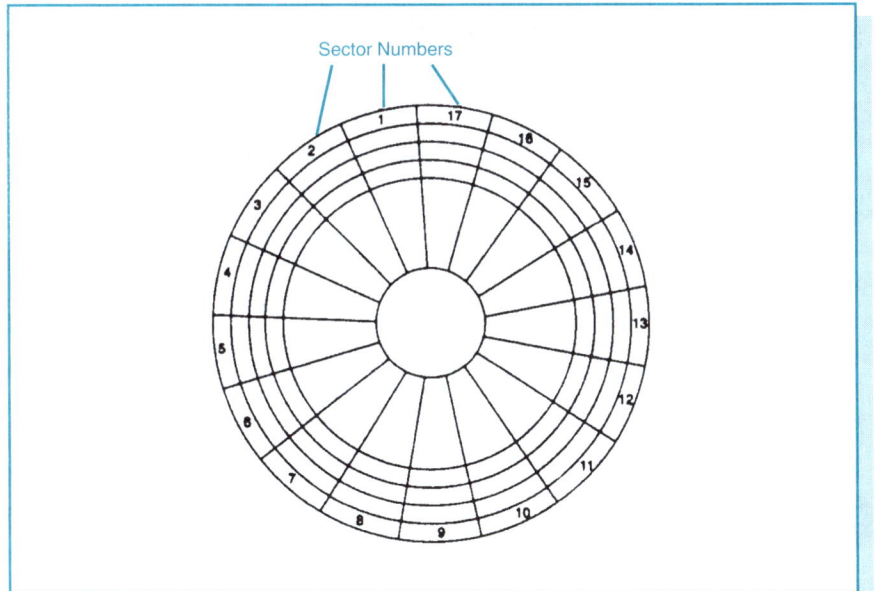

Figure 7.23   CALIBRAT shows that this disk has a 1:1 interleave factor.

193

The disk in Figure 7.24 has a 2:1 interleave factor, which means that you must skip a sector to get to the next consecutive one.

Similarly, a 3:1 interleave factor means that you must skip two sectors to get to the next consecutive one.

Your hard disk's interleave factor was probably set by the disk's manufacturer or your PC dealer when the disk was installed. Regardless of how your disk's interleave factor was set, a different interleave factor may produce a faster, more efficient hard disk. Use the CALIBRAT utility to determine and/or modify your hard disk's interleave factor.

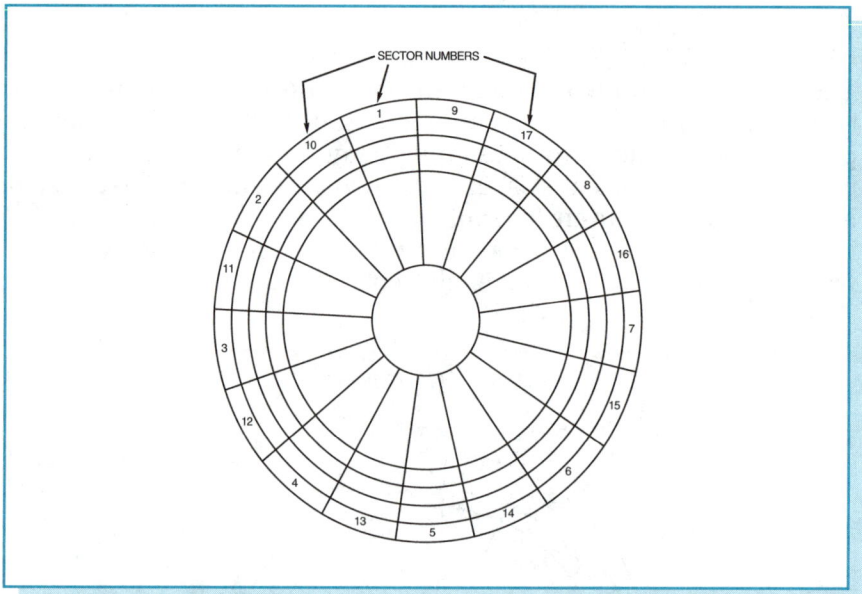

Figure 7.24 *This disk has a 2:1 interleave factor.*

194

 Caution: Always back up your hard disk before modifying the interleave factor with CALIBRAT. (See the Norton Backup program discussed in Chapter 12.)

Q **Modifying Your Hard Disk's Interleave Factor**

1. Type the command **CALIBRAT**, and press Enter.

   This runs the CALIBRAT utility, and displays a Calibrate information dialog box.

2. Press Enter or click Continue to acknowledge the Calibrate information dialog box.

   If it's the first time you've run CALIBRAT, you see a box advising you to back up your screen.

3. Press Enter, or click Continue.

   This displays an information dialog box that explains each of the tests that will be run on the specified disk.

4. Press Enter, or click Continue twice.

CALIBRAT performs a series of integrity and performance tests on your hard disk.

5. Keep pressing Enter or click Continue until the screen in Figure 7.25 is displayed.

This screen indicates the Current and Optimal interleave factors for the specified disk.

6 Press Enter if the Current and Optimal interleave factors are not identical.

This displays another test information dialog box.

7. Press Enter.

CALIBRAT performs a nondestructive format, and changes the disk interleave factor to the recommended optimal value. When the format process is complete, the report shown in Figure 7.25 appears. Follow the on-screen instructions to create a CALIBRAT report and/or exit the utility. ☐

195

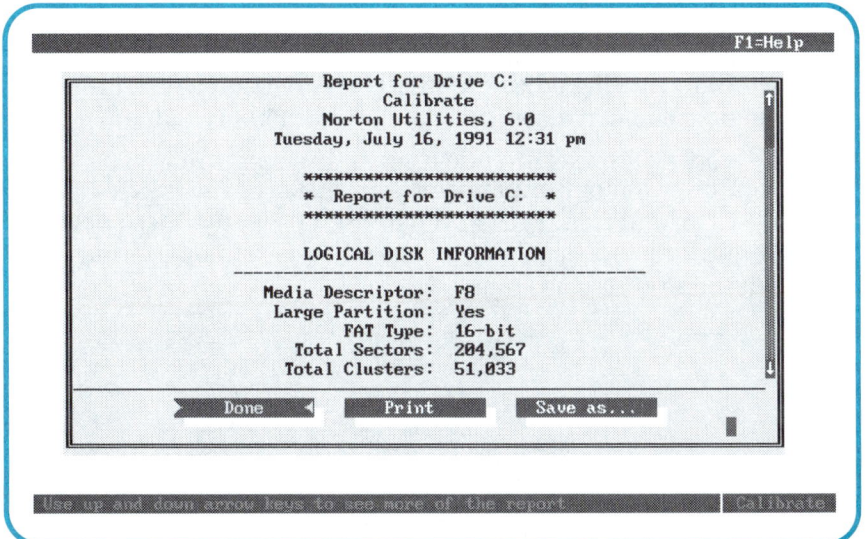

Figure 7.25   CALIBRAT reports on its tests of your hard disks.

As indicated in Step 7 of the preceding Quick Steps, CALIBRAT performs a nondestructive format of the specified hard disk when it alters the interleave factor. In other words, none of your disk's data should be lost during this format process. However, YOU SHOULD ALWAYS back up your disk before changing the interleave factor with CALIBRAT.

What You Have Learned

In this final chapter on The Norton Utilities, you learned how to use several advanced disk management tools to protect your valuable data and optimize your disk's performance. Specifically, you learned:

196

▶ DISKMON is a TSR utility that lets you monitor all disk activity on your system and can prevent computer viruses from destroying the contents of your hard disk.

▶ The DISKTOOL utility also offers a couple of other valuable disk tools that let you mark bad clusters and save/restore important hard disk configuration information.

▶ The DISKREET utility encrypts, or encodes, files so nobody else can interpret them.

▶ The DISKEDIT utility lets you perform a wide variety of tasks including viewing/editing virtually any byte on a disk or in memory. You can also print the disk or memory contents.

▶ The Norton Utilities include a set of three tools that you can use to optimize the performance of your disks: SPEEDISK, NCACHE, and CALIBRAT. When used properly, these disk optimization tools can significantly increase the performance of even the slowest hard disk.

Introducing NDOS

In This Chapter

▶ *DOS shells and NDOS*
▶ *Starting NDOS and getting help*
▶ *Using NDOS commands*

You'll learn in some later chapters of this book about The Norton Commander, another Norton program that functions as a "DOS shell." Shell programs give the user an easier way to run internal DOS programs. Unlike earlier versions of The Norton Utilities, version 6.0 offers the added capability of its own set of DOS-like commands, NDOS, which is compatible with DOS versions 2.1 and later. This chapter introduces you to NDOS and teaches you how to use its flexible features.

About NDOS

Often, shell programs (including the shells that come with more recent versions of DOS) offer interface to DOS through a user-friendly menu screen. NDOS works from the command prompt just like DOS does. The advantage is that NDOS users don't have to learn to navigate a new screen environment to use its commands.

Another critical advantage to using NDOS is that it increases the power of DOS. NDOS enhances the flexibility of many DOS programs by adding new capabilities and command switch options. For example, with NDOS, you can COPY more than one file at a time, as in `COPY TEST.DOC MEMO.TXT B:`. NDOS includes more than 40 commands DOS doesn't have, such as the ALIAS command, which lets you assign a special name to an often-used command or set of commands.

Starting and Unloading NDOS

The DOS COMMAND.COM file processes the commands you input to run the DOS programs. NDOS's command processor is NDOS.COM. To use NDOS, you need to install it using The Norton Utilities Installation program. (See Appendix A for more information about installation.)

198

> **Tip:** You may have already installed NDOS. Check your directory containing The Norton Utilities files to see if it contains NDOS's program files: NDOS.COM, NHELP.EXE, and NDOS.OVL.

```
C:\NU>ndos

NDOS XMS swapping initialized (24K)

DOS version 5.0
NDOS, Norton Utilities 6.0p02, Copyright 1991 by Symantec Corporation


C:\NU>
```

Figure 8.1   NDOS is loaded.

To start NDOS, change to the directory where you installed The Norton Utilities, for example by typing `C:\NU` and pressing Enter. At the prompt, type `NDOS,` and press Enter. NDOS is loaded, and the screen shown in Figure 8.1 appears.

You can return control of your system to COMMAND.COM at any time. Simply type `EXIT` at the prompt, and press Enter.

Getting Help

NDOS comes with a help facility that gives information about each command available. To get help once NDOS is loaded, press F1 at the prompt or type `NHELP,` and press Enter. The NDOS Help screen appears, as shown in Figure 8.2.

199

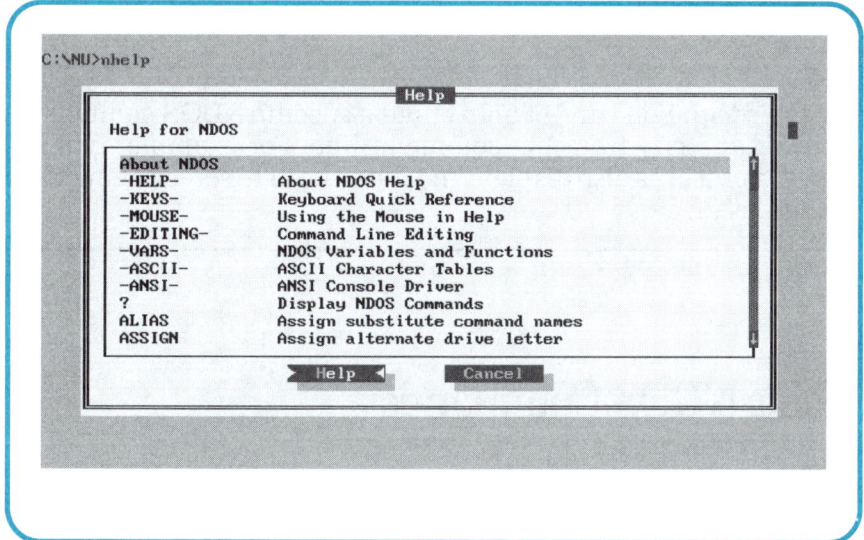

Figure 8.2   The opening NDOS Help screen.

Use the up and down arrow keys or click on a topic with the mouse to move the highlight among the Help screen topics. When the command you want information about is highlighted, press Enter or click on Help to display its Help screen. For example, Figure 8.3 shows the screen that appears when you select DESCRIBE from the main Help screen.

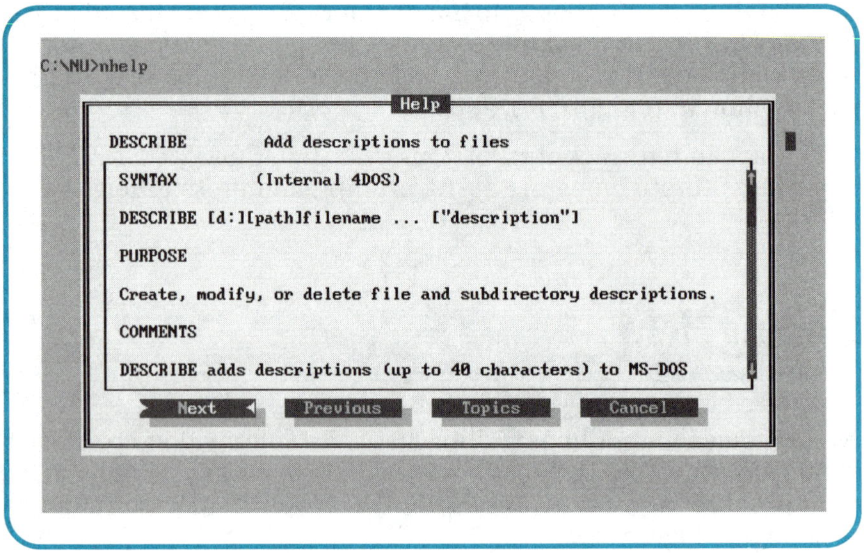

```
C:\NU>nhelp
```

```
┌───────────────────────── Help ─────────────────────────┐
│  DESCRIBE         Add descriptions to files            │
│ ┌──────────────────────────────────────────────────┐  │
│ │ SYNTAX        (Internal 4DOS)                      │↑ │
│ │ DESCRIBE [d:][path]filename ... ["description"]    │  │
│ │ PURPOSE                                            │  │
│ │ Create, modify, or delete file and subdirectory descriptions. │
│ │ COMMENTS                                           │  │
│ │ DESCRIBE adds descriptions (up to 40 characters) to MS-DOS │↓ │
│ └──────────────────────────────────────────────────┘  │
│   ► Next ◄      Previous       Topics        Cancel    │
└────────────────────────────────────────────────────────┘
```

200

Figure 8.3   The Describe help screen.

Tip: You can get help about a specific NDOS command directly from the command line. For example, typing **NHELP DESCRIBE** also displays the Describe help screen shown in Figure 8.3.

Using NDOS Commands

As you do for DOS commands, enter NDOS commands (with the necessary parameters and switches), and press Enter to execute them. (You've done this already to start NDOS and get help.) You must enter each command with the appropriate *syntax*. That is, you must follow certain rules in entering the *parameters* (additional information) and *switches* (control options) that go with the command.

For example, you can use the /C switch to temporarily load NDOS from DOS, execute an NDOS command, then return to DOS. Try the following steps using the NDOS BEEP command, which isn't offered by DOS:

1. If NDOS is loaded, type `EXIT`, and press Enter to return to DOS.
2. Type `NDOS /C BEEP`, and press Enter. Your computer should beep and return to the prompt (and DOS).
3. Type `BEEP`, and press Enter again. Your system displays the message "Bad command or file name," because DOS cannot execute the BEEP command.

The next few sections describe some special options you have for entering NDOS commands and describe a few of the most useful new NDOS commands.

Entering More Than One Command

In NDOS, you may enter more than one command on the command line before pressing Enter. To do so, simply separate each program command with the caret (^) character. For example, if I typed `DIR C:\MEMOS^BEEP` and pressed Enter, my system would display a list of all the files in the MEMO directory then beep.

201

Repeating Commands

As you execute NDOS commands, NDOS keeps a log of each command you type. You can search through NDOS's list of commands if you would like to reuse one, or modify and then reuse it. At the prompt, simply press the up arrow key to move back through the commands you executed. Pressing the down arrow will move you back to a more recent command. When the command you want to reissue appears at the prompt, simply press Enter to execute it.

Wild Cards

With DOS commands, you can generally use only two wild-card characters per full file name: one in the file name and one in the file name extension. (For example, you could type `DIR C:\MEMO\A*.*` to display a list of all the files in the MEMO directory that have a file name *starting with* A.) NDOS allows you to use an additional wild card in both the primary file name and the extension. (For example, you could type `DIR C:\NU\*A*.*X*` to find all the files in the NU directory with an A in the file name and an X in the file name extension.)

Specifying Multiple Files

Just as NDOS can execute multiple program commands by typing one command line, it can execute the specified command(s) on multiple files with dissimilar names. For example, the opening paragraph explained how you can COPY more than one file at a time, as in `COPY TEST.DOC MEMO.TXT B:`.

Hot NDOS Commands

Although there's not room in this book to review every NDOS command and its syntax, Table 8.1 lists the NDOS commands that beginning users are likely to get the most mileage from. After you become comfortable using the commands in Table 8.1 and are ready to move on to NDOS's more advanced features, or if you would like more information about the switches and parameters you can use with the commands in Table 8.1, consult your NDOS Manual that came with The Norton Utilities software.

Table 8.1   Hot NDOS COMMANDS

Command	Example	Description
ALIAS/ UNALIAS	`ALIAS LOOK DIR C:\MEMO`	Use to specify a new name for a command or group of commands you use frequently. (UNALIAS removes the new name assignment.) The example renames the command line DIR C:\MEMO to LOOK.
DESCRIBE	`DESCRIBE FUN.TXT "Company picnic details"`	Adds a description of up to 40 characters to files and subdirectories.
FREE	`FREE C:`	Tells you how much disk space, bytes used, and free bytes are on the specified disk. (FREE is much faster than DOS's CHKDSK.)

Command	Example	Description
LIST	LIST CHAP5.DOC	Displays the file contents on-screen, much like DOS's TYPE command. However, LIST you move forward and backward through the file's pages.
MOVE	MOVE FUN.TXT	Moves the specified file C:\MEMOS\FUN from the current directory to the specified destination directory.
SELECT	SELECT COPY	Displays a list of the files (C:\MEMOS*.TXT) A: matching the parameters in the parentheses, so you can choose files on which the specified command will operate. The example displays a list of the files with the .TXT extension in C:\MEMOS; select which of the files in the displayed list to copy to drive A:.

203

> **Caution:** Be careful when you use the ALIAS command not to specify an existing NDOS command name as the alias. This would cause NDOS confusion.

What You Have Learned

In this chapter, you learned about shell programs and The Norton Utilities' shell, NDOS. Specifically, you learned:

▶ NDOS interprets commands you enter at the prompt to execute system programs, just like DOS. NDOS offers enhancements to existing DOS commands as well as providing over 40 additional commands.

► Starting NDOS, getting help about NDOS commands, and returning to the DOS system are relatively simple procedures.

► NDOS offers some flexibility in the ways to enter commands and provides some useful commands.

204

Introducing the Commander

In This Chapter

▶ *What the Commander provides*

▶ *Installing, starting, and using the Commander*

▶ *Configuring the Commander for your use*

▶ *Getting on-screen help*

The Commander is a program that fulfills two important functions. Its major function is to act as a DOS shell—that is, it provides you with a visual interface for DOS. Instead of typing path names, file names, and long command lines at the DOS prompt, you simply select what you want from a list or pull-down menu, using your keyboard or mouse. In a sense, it "hides" the complicated workings of DOS behind a simple graphical interface, giving you more control over your directories and files. Its second function is to help transfer information between computers and facilitate the exchange of MCI mail. In this chapter, we'll look at some of the basic features of the Commander, how to install it, and how to run it. Once you get this program up and running, you may never want to return to your DOS prompt again!

What the Commander Provides

On a daily basis, you probably perform some sort of disk management activities. You might copy or delete files, rename them, or sort the files in a particular directory. To perform any of these tasks at the DOS prompt, you must remember the structure of your directory tree and enter a path name that leads to the directory that holds your files. Then, you must remember the syntax of the command and the names of the files you want the command to affect. Although that doesn't take a mastermind, it can get cumbersome, especially if you're in a hurry. With the Commander, you use *visual display panels* to help you view and select directories and files, and you select the commands you want to enter from menus.

206

Figure 9.1 shows how the visual display panels can simplify your disk management activities. The panels in Figure 9.1 have been set up to display a split screen. On the left is a picture of the directory tree for the C drive. On the right are all the files contained in the chosen directory. If you wanted to view this same list of files in DOS, you would have to change drives, enter a path to the NC directory (`cd\NC`), and then enter a directory command to list the files (including some switch to keep the directory from scrolling by too quickly). With the Commander, you simply enter the letter of the drive you want to view and then select the directory with the arrow keys. You can scroll through the list as quickly as you like and stop at any file. Selecting files is as simple as pressing the Enter key or clicking a mouse button.

Another advantage of the Commander is that you can view the contents of a file without having to load the file into an application. Using the Commander's file view interpreters, you can view (without changing) the data stored in files created with a variety of word processing, spreadsheet, database, and graphics programs. Table 9.1 provides a list of the formats you can view through the Commander.

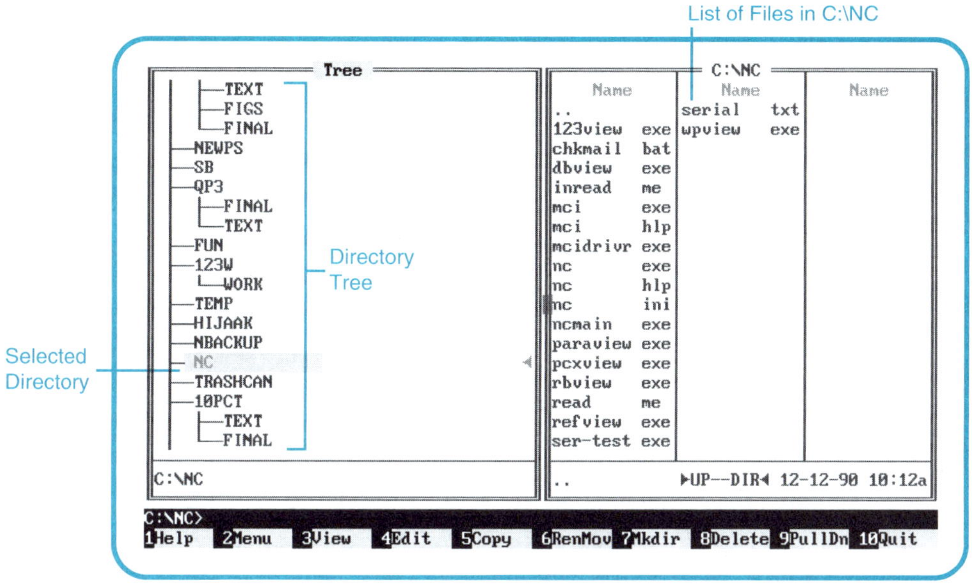

List of Files in C:\NC

Figure 9.1   The Commander's simplified interface makes it easy to find and manipulate files.

> **Tip:** If you don't see one of your application file formats listed in Table 9.1, don't panic. You can often convert your files to an acceptable format before using the Commander to view them. For example, you can save most word processing files in the ASCII format and some spreadsheet programs using the Lotus 1-2-3 format.

Although most of your disk management will deal with data files, the Commander helps you with your program files as well. If you want to run a program, you no longer have to enter a command at the DOS prompt. You simply highlight the program file that launches the program and press the Enter key, or point and click with your mouse. (To use the mouse, you must be using a DOS version later than 3.3 or have the required mouse driver—the software that came with your mouse.) In addition, you can use the Commander's "point-and-shoot" feature to load data files automatically into their applications. Just click on the file name for the data file, and the Commander will run the application and then load the file.

Table 9.1 File Formats Available for Viewing

Application	Format
Word Processing	WordPerfect (4.2, 5.0)
	Microsoft Word (4.0, 5.0)
	MultiMate (all versions)
	WordStar Pro (all versions)
	WordStar 2000 (all versions)
	Windows Write (all versions)
	Microsoft Works (all versions)
	XyWrite (all versions)
	ASCII text files
Spreadsheets	Lotus 1-2-3 (1.x-3.x)
	Symphony (1.0-2.0)
	Microsoft Excel (1.0-2.2)
	Multiplan (4.0)
	Microsoft Works (all versions)
	Quattro (all versions)
	VP-Planner Plus (all versions)
	Mosaic Twin (all versions)
	Words & Figures (all versions)
Databases	dBASE II, III, III+, IV
	Clipper (all versions)
Application	Format
	FoxBASE (all versions)
	Paradox (all versions)
	R:BASE (all versions)
	Microsoft Works (all versions)
	dBXL (all versions)
	Reflex (all versions)
Graphics	Any file with the .pcx format, such as PC Paintbrush files

208

The Commander provides several additional features that you may find useful as well. For example, the Commander Mail feature lets you send and receive documents via MCI Mail, an electronic mail service that's available through MCI Telecommunications Corporation. If you use a laptop computer and need to transfer data between it and your desktop computer, you'll find the Commander Link feature especially useful.

Installing the Commander

To get the most out of the Commander, you should have a hard disk. For purposes of this discussion, I'll assume that you do. Installing the Commander is easy. Before you begin, make a backup copy of all the diskettes of the size appropriate for your computer. (The software package includes two 5¼" diskettes and one 3½" diskette.) Put the original diskettes in a safe place, and use the backup copies for the installation.

209

The Commander diskettes include an Installation program. To ensure proper installation, you should use this program to copy the program files to your hard disk. As shown in Figure 9.2, the installation process is menu-driven. The following Quick steps summarize the procedure.

 Installing the Commander

1. Turn on your computer, and take any steps needed to reach the DOS prompt. For example, C:> or a similar prompt must appear on screen.

2. Type the letter of the floppy disk drive you're going to use followed by a colon, and press Enter. For example,

if you're going to use the A drive, type **a:** and press Enter. The drive letter appears on-screen.

3. Insert Disk 1 of the two 5¹/₄" diskettes (or the 3¹/₂" diskette) into the selected drive. For example, if you selected the A: drive in step 2, and A:> appears on the screen, insert the diskette in the A: drive.

4. Type **install**, and press Enter.

This starts the Installation program. Soon you will see the first of a series of questions.

5. Answer each question as it pertains to your system.

When asked if you want to put the Commander in your AUTOEXEC.BAT file, answer Yes, unless you have some reason for doing otherwise. If you answer Yes, you'll be able to run the Commander from any drive or directory by typing the required command at the DOS prompt.

210

6. When you are finished with the installation program, press Ctrl-Alt-Del to reboot your system.

This updates any changes to your AUTOEXEC.BAT file to ensure that the program runs correctly.

□

Tip: You can find out about last-minute updates or corrections to the program by viewing the READ.ME file located on one of the Commander diskettes. This information is probably not contained in the documentation that's included with the package. Print or view this file as soon as possible after installing the Commander. To view the file, start the Commander, select READ.ME from the Commander file directory panel, and press F3.

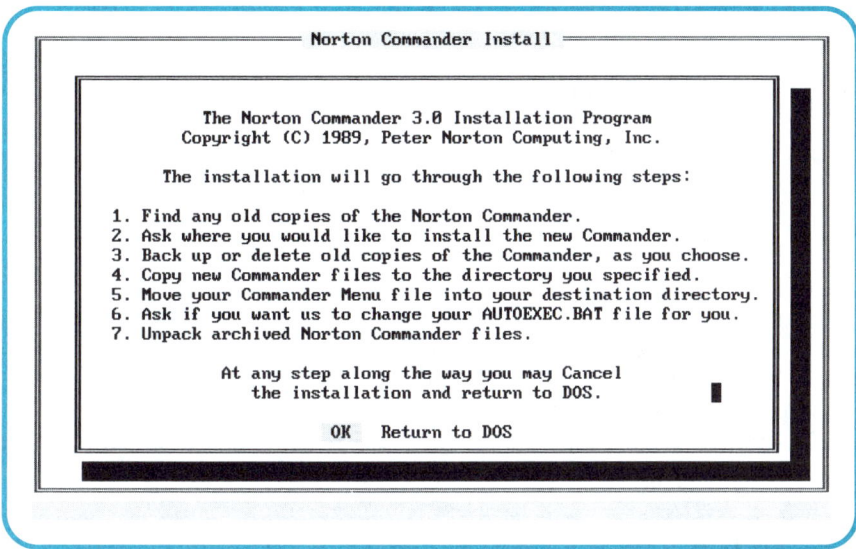

Figure 9.2   The Norton Commander Install menu takes you step by step through the installation process.

211

Starting the Commander

You can run the Commander in either of two ways, depending on whether you installed the program on your hard disk or are limited to using only floppy disks.

▶ If you installed the program on a hard disk, run the Commander as a stand-alone program. The Commander will exit RAM when you run another application and reload itself when you quit that application. This keeps the Commander from taking up valuable RAM.

▶ If you have only a floppy disk system, run the Commander as a memory-resident program. The Commander stays in RAM, freeing up your floppy disk drives for other work.

> **Note:** Although you can run the Commander in memory-resident mode with a hard drive, you're better off keeping it out of RAM. Run the Commander in memory-resident mode only if you have more RAM than you need or if you have to keep a floppy drive open. Besides, it doesn't take long for the Commander to quit and reload itself—you gain little by keeping it in RAM.

If you choose to modify your AUTOEXEC.BAT file, you can load the Commander as a stand-alone program by typing `nc` at any DOS prompt and pressing Enter. (If you did not choose to modify AUTOEXEC.BAT, you need to change to the directory that holds your Commander files before typing the command.)

If you want to run the Commander as a memory-resident program (one that stays in RAM), type

212

```
ncmain
```

at the DOS prompt and press Enter. (Again, if you choose not to modify the AUTOEXEC.BAT file, change to the Commander directory before entering the command.) Since this option keeps the Commander in RAM, less RAM is available for other programs. So why do it? If you have no hard drive, and you don't want to swap disks whenever you need to access the Commander directory files, this option keeps the Commander readily available.

The Commander Interface

Once you've loaded the Commander, you're greeted with the Commander interface, as shown in Figure 9.3. This screen consists of four parts: a panel on the right, a mini status box, a DOS prompt, and a function key bar. There's no left panel like the one in Figure 9.1 right now, but you'll learn how to display the second panel a little later.

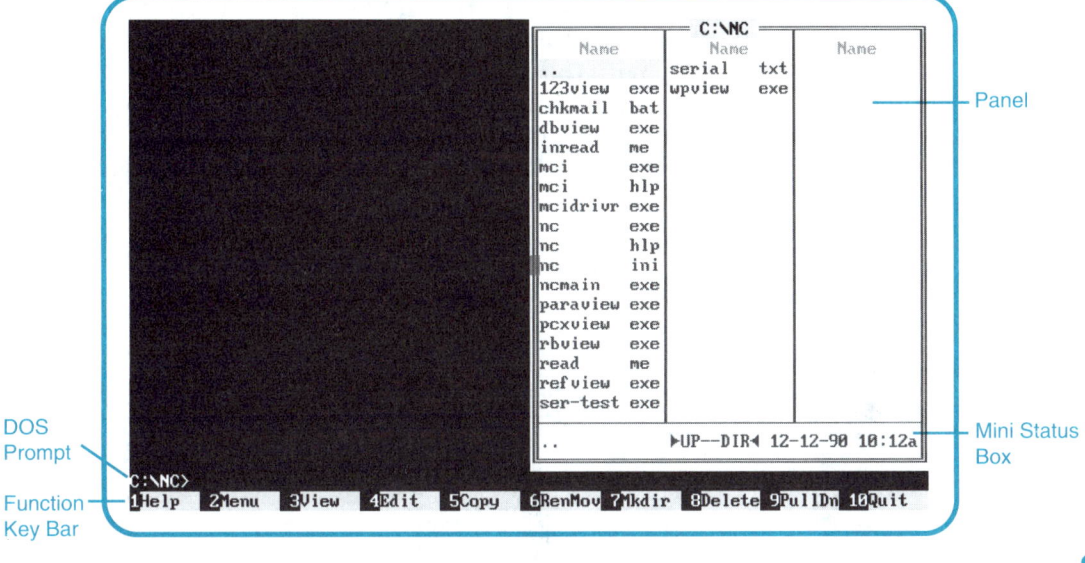

DOS Prompt

Function Key Bar

Panel

Mini Status Box

Figure 9.3 The Commander interface screen is the "main menu" or starting point for all operations.

213

The **panel on the right** initially displays the contents of the root directory of the current drive and any subdirectories within it. The names of the subdirectories (if any) are displayed in all uppercase letters. The names of the individual files appear in all lowercase letters. You'll see later how to configure the panel to display other information, such as a directory tree or the dates and times the files were created.

Just below the right panel is the **mini status box**. This box is handy for determining the size of the selected file and the date and time it was created. For example, when you first start the Commander, the mini status box shows this information for the highlighted file in the current directory.

You will also notice that the familiar **DOS prompt** still appears on screen in the lower left corner. You can use the DOS prompt to enter and execute any valid DOS command. You can use the DOS prompt and the Commander in tandem to gain even more control over your files. For example, you can change drives at the DOS prompt by typing the letter of the drive (for example, **a:**, **b:**, or **c:**) and pressing Enter. The files and directories for that drive then appear in the active display panel.

At the bottom of the screen is the **function key bar**. This bar lets you access many of the Commander operations by pressing the function key associated with that operation or by clicking on it with the mouse. As shown in Figure 9.4, you can activate a pull-down menu bar at the top of the screen by choosing the PullDn option on the function key bar. Either click on this option with the mouse or press F9. To pull down one of the menus, either click on it with the mouse, type the first letter of the menu name, or highlight the menu name with the left or right arrow key and press Enter.

214

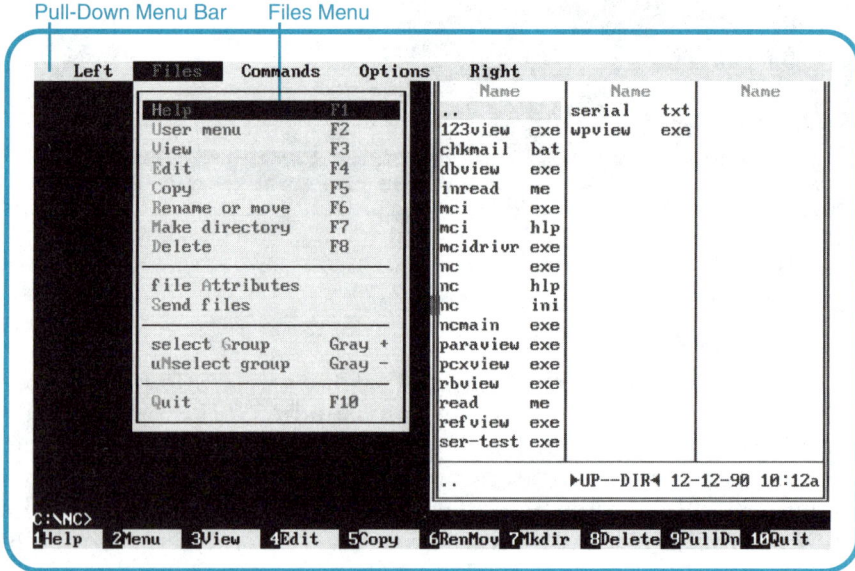

Figure 9.4   *The pull-down menu bar is shown here with the Files menu open.*

Selecting Items

The Commander makes it easy to move through a list of files and directories using either the mouse or the keyboard. Since all the file and directory names of the current directory are displayed in a panel, you can simply use the cursor keys or the mouse to scroll through the contents of that directory. Keep in mind that the panel remains visible even if you execute a DOS or Commander operation.

To change directories, simply select any of the directory names (the names in all uppercase letters) using the keyboard or mouse. If you're using the keyboard, press the cursor control keys (up, down, left, and right arrow keys, PgUp, PgDn, Home, and End) to highlight the name of the directory, and then press Enter to activate it. To return to the parent directory, select the [. .] symbol. If you're using a mouse, move the mouse pointer to the directory you want to activate and double-click the mouse button.

Once you activate a directory, the contents of the directory are displayed in a panel and are ready for further Commander operations. By selecting files in this way, you reduce the chances that you'll mistype a directory or file name.

Using the Keyboard

You've already seen that you can use the keyboard to perform any Commander operation. You can enter commands by pressing the appropriate function key, activate the pull-down menu bar, and use the cursor movement and Enter keys to select directories and files. For additional operations, the Commander offers several special keys you can press in combination with the function keys, as shown in Table 9.2.

215

Table 9.2   Special Keys and Operations

Key	Operation
Alt	The Alt key in combination with a function key executes several commands that are listed in the pull-down menus.
	Instead of having to work your way through a list of menus, you can enter one of these hot-key combinations.
Ctrl	The Ctrl key in combination with other keys serves as a toggle. For example, Ctrl-O turns both panels on and off.
Esc	The Esc key is generally used to quit several operations in progress. For example, pressing Esc quits the Edit and View operations, clears the command line at the DOS prompt, and cancels and closes any dialog and alert boxes.
Shift	Pressing Shift in combination with a function key produces a more general version of the same operation without the shifted command.

Using a Mouse

If you have a mouse, choosing items on the Commander screen is even easier. However, you need to keep a few rules in mind. To use your mouse more effectively, refer to Table 9.3 for some basic rules.

Table 9.3   Mouse Rules

Location	Operation
In panels	*Point*—Click left button to move highlight bar.
	Scroll—Hold down left button and move mouse up or down.
	Load Program—Double-click left button.
	Change Directories—Double-click left button.
	Select or Unselect—Click right button.
	Select or Unselect Group of Files—Hold down right button and drag cursor to highlight group.
In menus	*Show Menu Bar*—Click either button on top line or click left button on PullDn option.
	Select Menu Item—Click either button.
In dialog boxes	*Select Item*—Click left button.
	Select Item and Exit Dialog Box—Click right button.
	Accept Highlighted Action—Click right button outside dialog box.
	Cancel Dialog Box Action—Click left button outside dialog box.
Escaping	*Escape from Alert or Dialog Box*—Click left and right buttons.
	Escape from Dialog Box Only—Click left button.

216

> **Note:** Throughout our discussion of the Commander, we assume that you're using a two-button mouse that's configured for right-hand use. To configure the mouse for your left hand, refer to the section on configuring the Commander later in this chapter. If you configure your mouse for your left hand, use the left button when we say to use the right button.

Configuring the Commander for Your System

Now that you know how to move around the screen, you're ready to start setting up the Commander for your own personal use. First, you'll set up the overall appearance and operation of the Commander:

1. Press F9 (or click on the PullDn command in the Function key bar) to display the menu bar at the top of the screen.

2. Choose Options from the menu bar, opening the Options menu.

3. Press Enter or click on Configuration to choose the Configuration command. This opens the Configuration dialog box, as shown in Figure 9.5.

4. Use the up and down arrow keys to move between options or click on the option, and use the Space Bar to select a given option. The following list explains the various options:

217

> **Screen colors**. You can configure your system for a black-and-white, color, or laptop display, depending on your system.

> **Screen blank delay**. If you don't touch your keyboard or mouse for a certain amount of time, your screen will go blank and display star bursts. This protects your screen against damage caused by burn-in. Choose the desired delay time, or turn it off altogether.

> **File panel options**. If you don't want hidden files to be displayed (for security reasons), unselect the first option. If you want the cursor to move to the next file when you select a file with the Ins key, select the second option.

> **Tree panel options**. If you select the Auto Change Directory option, whenever you highlight a directory in the tree panel, its files are listed in the opposite panel.

> **Other options**. This option box lets you set other useful options. You can choose to display the menu bar at all times, automatically save your configuration changes, reverse your mouse buttons, and reset your mouse more quickly after entering a command (for the mouse port on a COMPAQ or PS/2).

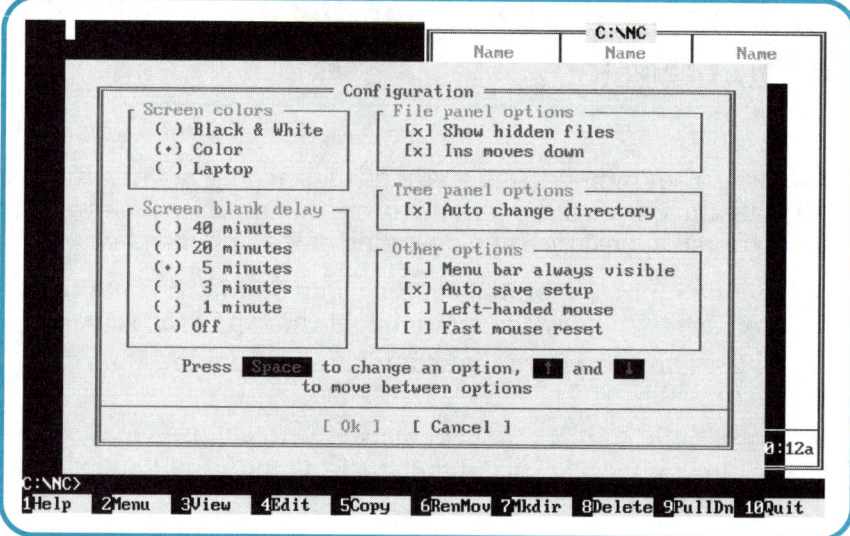

Figure 9.5 *The Configuration dialog box allows you to customize the Commander to your specifications.*

218

Using the Panels

Now that you have the overall configuration set, you can begin setting up your panels. The setup is easy to perform and easy to change whenever you like, so feel free to stop reading and play with different setups along the way.

If the pull-down menu is not displayed at the top of the screen, choose the F9 PullDn command from the function key bar. As you can see, the pull-down menu bar contains five menu options, two of which control the panels: Left and Right. The menus are identical except for the fact the one controls the left panel and the other controls the right one. If you want to turn the left panel on, open the Left menu and press Enter. Only one panel is active at a time. To switch from one to the other, press Tab. The title of the active panel appears in reverse video, and the highlight bar appears in its directory listing.

Now, open either the Left or Right menu to see how you can manipulate these panels. The first option on the menu is Brief. Select that option now, and the panel you've just selected will look something like the one on the left in Figure 9.6. This option displays a list of the subdirectories and file names for the chosen directory—nothing else. Now, reopen the Left or Right menu, and choose the Full option. Your panel should now look something like the panel on the right. This display gives you a little more information about your file, telling you not only the name of the file but also its size and the date and time it was created.

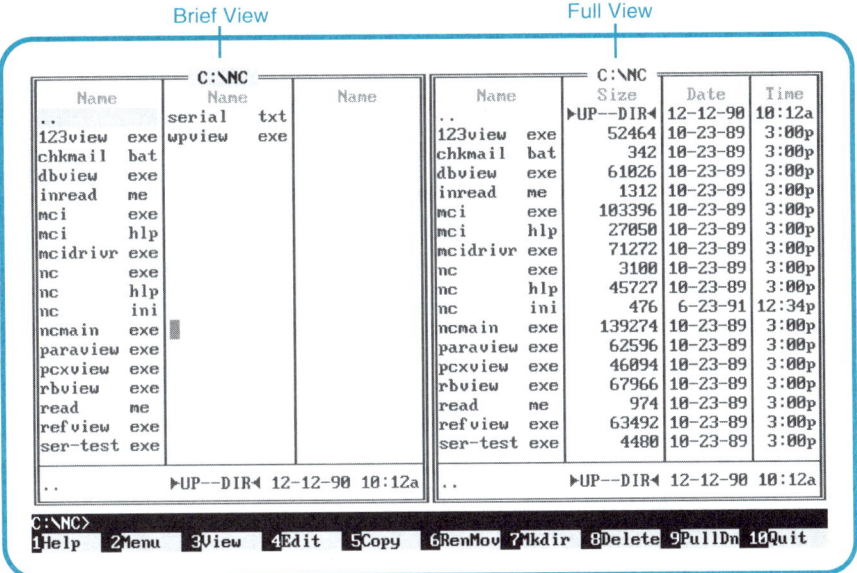

Figure 9.6 *You can choose between two display options: brief and full.*

If you want to know some information about your system and your current drive and directory, choose the Info command from the Left or Right menu or press Ctrl-L. This opens a dialog box that tells you how much RAM is installed in your system, how much is available, the capacity of your drive, how much storage space you have left, and how much storage space your files are taking up. To return to the previous display of the panel, press Ctrl-L.

The next option on the Left or Right menu is Tree. By choosing this option or pressing Ctrl-T, you can display a directory tree of the current drive. One of the most common ways to use the two panels is to set up the left panel to display a directory tree and the right panel to display a brief or full list of files. (You saw such a setup in

Figure 9.1.) That way, you can choose a directory in the left panel and then switch to the right panel (with the Tab key) to work with the files in that directory.

The next option, quick View, lets you view (but not alter) the contents of a selected file. Just highlight the file in question (make sure it's one the Commander can handle), and choose the quick View option or press Ctrl-Q. The contents of the file appear in the opposite window, helping you decide whether that's really the file you want to work with.

The last option we will deal with in this section is the On/Off option. This option simply lets you turn either of the panels on or off. Choose this option or press one of the following hot-key combinations:

Hot Key	Action
Ctrl-P	Turns inactive panel on or off.
Ctrl-O	Turns both panels on or off.
Ctrl-U	Flips panels (left to right and vice versa).
Ctrl-F1	Turns left panel on or off.
Ctrl-F2	Turns right panel on or off.

Changing Drives

You can change the drive that either panel represents at any time. The procedure is simple. Press Alt-F2 or choose the Drive command from the Left or Right menu, depending on which panel you want the change to affect. A dialog box appears, presenting you with a list of available drives. Select the drive you want to activate.

> **Tip:** Don't forget that you will have your DOS prompt at the bottom of the screen. The easiest way to change drives is to type the drive letter followed by a colon next to this prompt and press Enter.

220

Sorting Your Files

After you activate the drive you want to work in, you may want to change the way the files are sorted in the panel display. Press F9 to activate the pull-down menu bar, and open either the Left or Right menu. The second set of options on this menu lets you select various sorting schemes for your files. Choose Name, and the Commander will sort files and subdirectories alphabetically by name first then by extension. If you choose eXtension, files will be sorted by extension first and then name.

The files in the left panel in Figure 9.7 are sorted by extension. Notice that all files with the .bat extension precede files with the .exe extension. The files in the right panel have been sorted by size, largest to smallest. You can also sort according to the date and time the files were created, or you can leave the files unsorted.

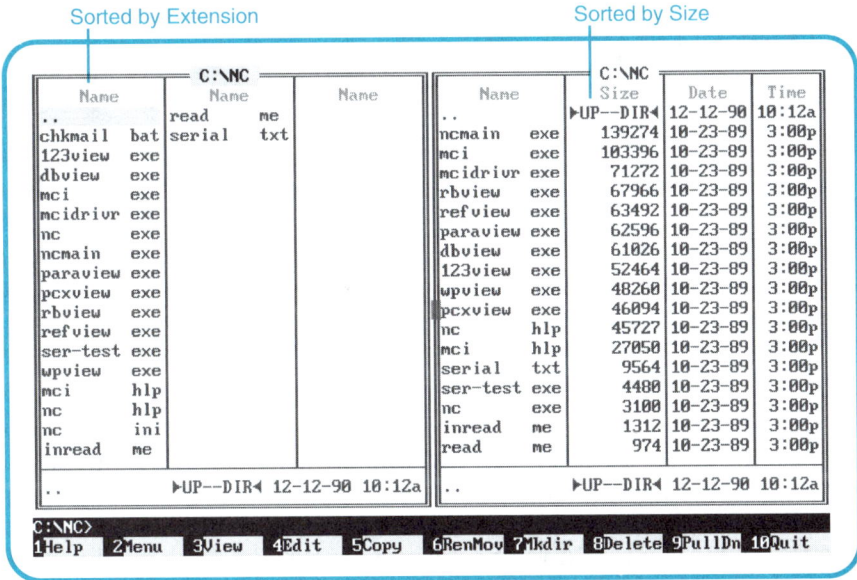

Figure 9.7   You can choose to sort your files by name, extension, time, or size.

Narrowing the List

If your panel is cluttered with a bunch of files you don't want to work with, choose the fiLter option from the Left or Right menu. This command lets you display only the range of files you want to work with. For example, you can display only those files with the .doc extension and filter out superfluous .bak files.

When you choose this option, the Commander presents a dialog box, giving you three choices. The ALL option lets you view all the files in the directory. The Executable files option lets you view only program files. This is useful if you want to run applications from the Commander and you don't want to wade through a bunch of data files. The last choice lets you customize the filter with wild-card entries of your own.

222 Getting Help

If you ever need help when you're performing an operation in the Commander, press F1 or choose the Help command from the Files menu. This displays a window, as shown in Figure 9.8, that gives you helpful information about whatever task you're performing at this time. You can scroll up or down in the window to read all the information available, or you can choose Previous or Next to view the next item in the window. Choose Cancel to close the Help window and return to the task you were performing.

If the Help window doesn't pertain to what you're trying to do, choose the Index option at the bottom of the screen. This opens the Help index, shown in Figure 9.9. This index provides a comprehensive list of topics that the Commander can help you with. Highlight the item you need help with and press Enter, or double-click on it with the mouse.

In addition to Help windows and the Help index, the Commander displays dialog and alert boxes to help guide you in your tasks. The dialog boxes ask you to enter additional information or to confirm your choice. The alert boxes warn you that you may be getting yourself into trouble.

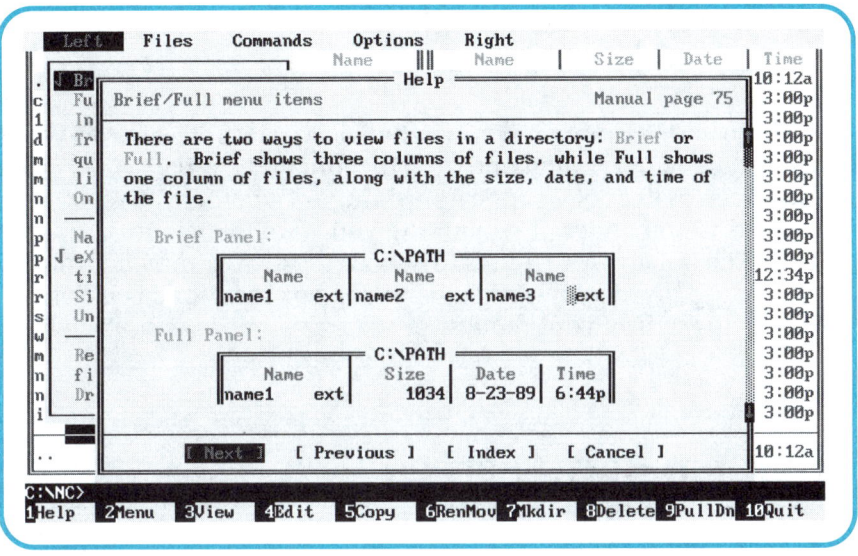

*Figure 9.8   A Help window is available at any time by
pressing F1.*

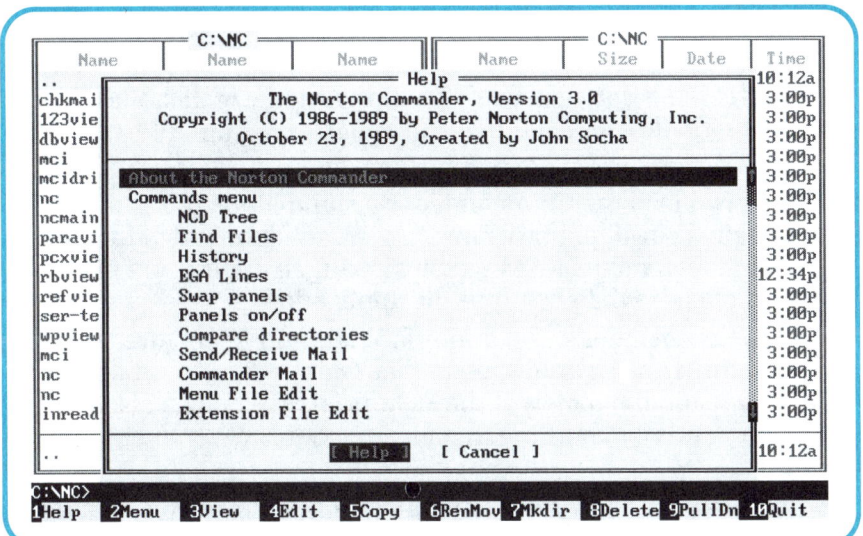

*Figure 9.9   The Help index allows you to locate Help screens
for any topic quickly.*

Leaving the Commander

You can leave the Commander in either of two ways. The fastest way is to select the F10 Quit command from the function key bar at the bottom of the screen. A dialog box appears, asking you whether you really want to quit the Commander. If you're sure you want to exit, press Y; if not, press N. The other way to quit is to choose the Quit command from the Files menu. This displays the same dialog box mentioned earlier, and you have to confirm your request.

What You Have Learned

224

In this chapter you learned about the Norton Commander and how to set it up to perform disk management activities. You also learned:

▶ The Commander serves two functions. First, it acts as a visual interface for DOS, giving you more control over your disks, directories, and files. Second, it helps you transfer information between two computers.

▶ The Commander lets you view the contents of data files, run program files, and automatically load a program into an application.

▶ You can load the Commander as a stand-alone program or as a memory-resident program. As a stand-alone program, the Commander exits RAM when you run an application program and reloads when you quit the application.

▶ The Commander's visual interface lets you select directories and file names by pointing at them rather than by typing path names and file names at the DOS prompt. You can also enter commands by choosing them from menus rather than typing them.

▶ You can configure the Commander for however you intend to use it, and you can manipulate the panels to display various views of your directories and files.

Managing Files and Disks with the Commander

In This Chapter

225

▶ *Finding, selecting, and copying files*
▶ *Renaming, moving, and deleting files*
▶ *Viewing and editing files*
▶ *Maintaining your directories*
▶ *Using the DOS command line*
▶ *Running applications from the Commander*

You can see just from looking at the Commander's opening screen that disk management is going to be much easier from now on. Everything you need is right on screen—all you need to do is make your selections. In this chapter, you'll start using the Commander to perform common disk maintenance tasks, such as copying, deleting, and moving files. You'll also learn how to use advanced features that let you view and edit files without leaving the Commander, as well as other features that let you automatically load application programs from within the Commander. You'll also learn to use the Commander for building and manipulating your directory structure.

> **Tip:** You'll notice that several of the heads in this chapter include the name of a function key or keystroke. These *hot keys* give you a shortcut to performing the task. Instead of working your way through a series of menus, just press the specified hot key. Of course, if you can't remember a particular hot key, the menus are always there to help.

Managing Your Files

226

Most of your work in the Commander will center around file management. You can use the Commander's shell structure to take control of your files—you'll no longer be a slave to the syntax of DOS commands or to the jumbled lists of files that scroll by faster than you can read.

Finding Files (Alt-F7)

Before you can perform any operation on a file or a group of files, you need to find the files you want to work with. In DOS, you have to rely on your memory. If you forget where you put the file or what you named it, you're in for a long search. If you mistype the file name, DOS tells you the file does not exist. Type the right name at the wrong prompt, and you get the same blank stare.

The Commander gives you much more help in finding your files. You simply activate one of the drives where you think your file is located and enter a file name, which may include wild cards. The Commander searches all the directories in that drive and displays a list of all the files that match your entry. You can then switch to the directory that contains that file and proceed with whatever task you wish to perform.

The first step in searching for a file is to activate the drive where you think the file is located. You can do this in either of two ways. The quickest way is to type the letter of the drive next to the DOS prompt and press Enter. You can also change drives by choosing the `Drive` command from either the Left or Right menu and supplying the necessary information. Once you've selected the drive you want to search, perform the following quick steps to find your file.

Q Finding Files

1. Press Tab to activate the panel you want to search.

   The title of the active panel appears in reverse video, and the highlight bar appears within the panel.

2. Select the `Find file` command from the Commands menu, or press Alt-F7.

   The Commander displays the Find File dialog box, shown in Figure 10.1.

3. Type the name of the file you want to search for (wild-card characters are permitted). For example, if you want to find all files with the .DOC extension, type ***.doc**. Type something like **ch?.doc** to find a list of files such as CH1.DOC and CH3.DOC.

4. Press Enter.

   The Commander begins its search and displays all the files that match your entry. Figure 10.2 shows such a listing.

5. Move the highlight bar over the file you want.

6. Press Enter to activate the directory that holds the file.

   The Commander automatically activates the panel for that directory and moves the highlight bar to the file you selected. □

227

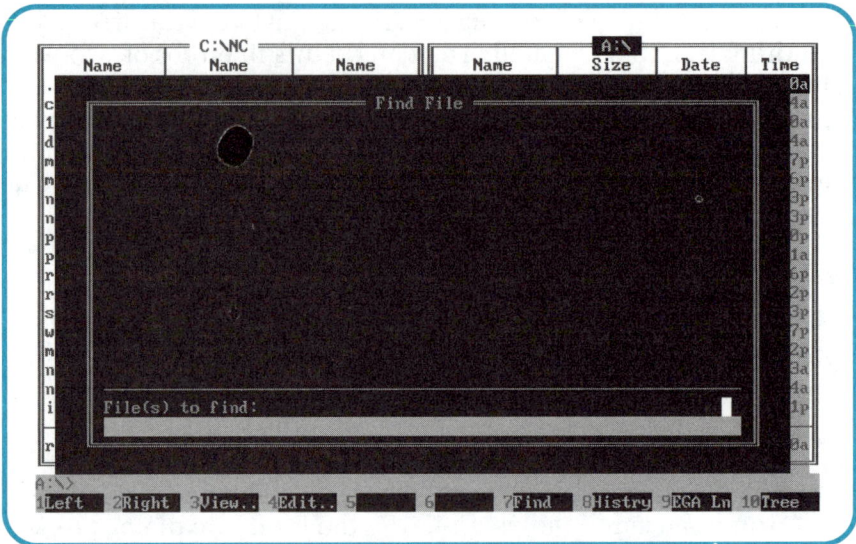

Figure 10.1 *The Find File dialog box lets you search for a file by name.*

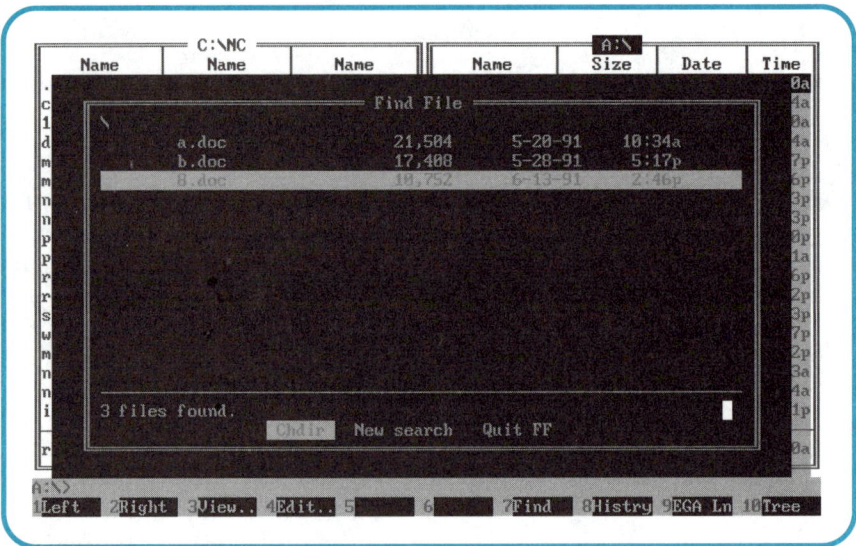

Figure 10.2 *The Commander displays a list of files that match the search entry.*

Selecting and Unselecting Files

One of the most complicated aspects of working with files in DOS is selecting the files you want to work with. Working with an individual file is usually no problem, but when you want a command to affect several files at once, DOS is inflexible. For example, if you want to copy three files—CASH.WK1, CH8.DOC, and FIG0801.PIX—from one directory to another, you have to enter three separate copy commands. With the Commander, however, selecting files is as simple as pressing a single keystroke or clicking with your mouse.

Individual Files (Ins)

To select an individual file with the keyboard, move the highlight bar over the name of the file you wish to select and press Ins. The selected file name turns yellow on a color monitor or appears brighter on a monochrome monitor. You can select as many files as you like. To unselect a file, highlight it again and press Ins. Selecting individual files with the mouse is even easier. Point to the file you wish to select, and press the right mouse button.

229

Groups of Files (Gray +/–)

To be fair to DOS, we must admit that the wild-card entries that DOS permits do help in handling files. What would we do without the *.* entry? The Commander offers this same flexibility, allowing you to select a range of files. But the Commander doesn't stop there. It also offers an Unselect feature. You can select all the files within a given directory, then use the Unselect feature to unselect the group of files you don't want to work with. The following quick steps lead you through the file selection process.

 Selecting or Unselecting a Group of Files

1. Press Tab to activate the panel you want to work with.

   The title of the panel appears in reverse video, and the highlight bar appears.

2. Press the gray + key (the + key on the numeric keypad) to select a group of files, or press the gray – key to unselect a group.

   A dialog box appears as in Figure 10.3, asking you to type an entry for the files you wish to select or unselect. *.* appears in the box, indicating that unless you type an entry, all the files in that directory will be affected.

3. Type your entry.

You can use the standard DOS wild-card characters. The * matches any group of characters. The ? matches any single character. For example `ch?.doc` will select CH1.DOC and CH2.DOC, but not CH10.DOC or CH2.WP5.

4. Press Enter.

If you selected files, those files turn yellow on a color monitor or appear brighter on a monochrome screen. If you unselected files, the file names return to their original appearance. □

230

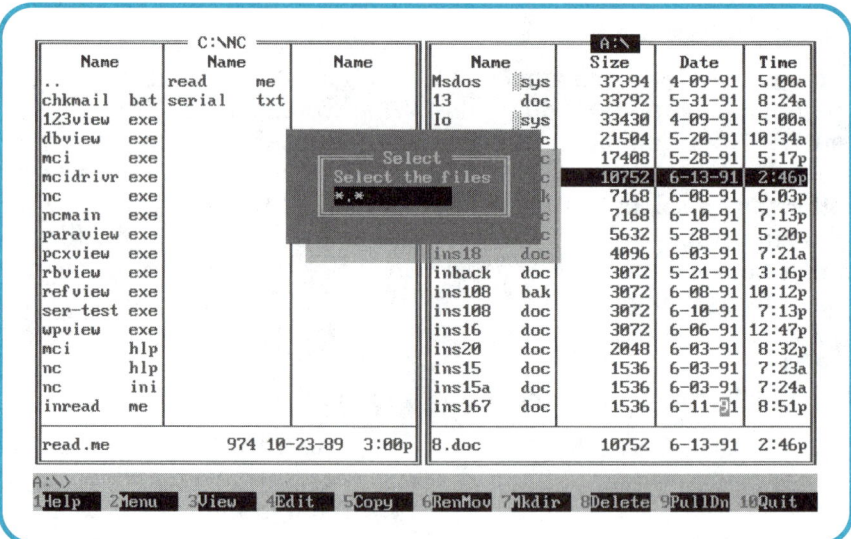

Figure 10.3   The Select dialog box lets you select or unselect groups of files.

> **Caution:** Review the group of files you selected to make sure those are the files you want to affect. If you select the wrong group of files and then enter a command such as Delete, you could get yourself into trouble. The Commander's dialog and alert boxes will force you to be careful, but take your own precautions anyway.

When you select a group of files, the mini status box (at the base of the panel) shows you how many files you selected and how many bytes those files occupy. This is helpful information if you're running out of room on your hard disk. If you're copying files to a floppy disk, however, the Commander will let you start copying the files and will tell you if you need to insert an additional disk to hold the rest of the files. Just make sure you have enough blank, formatted disks on hand.

231

Copying Files (F5)

Once you've selected the file or group of files you want to copy, copying the files is easy. Choose the Copy command from the Files menu or press F5. The Copy Files dialog box appears, as shown in Figure 10.4. Choose this same command with the Shift key pressed down, and you'll see the dialog box in Figure 10.5. This dialog box lets you supply the source and destination for the files as well.

As you can see, the dialog box assumes that you wish to copy the files to the directory represented by the inactive panel. You can edit the entry by moving the cursor to the part you want to change, entering the correct information, and deleting the incorrect information. If you want to cancel the original entry altogether, type the name of the drive and directory to which you want to copy the files. For example, to copy the files to D:\SAMPLE\FILES, type `d:\sample\files`. As soon as you begin to type, the entry that was originally displayed disappears, and the characters you type appear in the box.

In the bottom of the Copy files dialog box are three options: Copy, Tree, and Cancel. To begin copying the selected files to the specified drive and directory, press Enter or click on Copy to choose the Copy option. Selecting the Tree option lets you choose the copy destination from a directory tree of the active directory. Selecting the Cancel option lets you change your mind about copying the files.

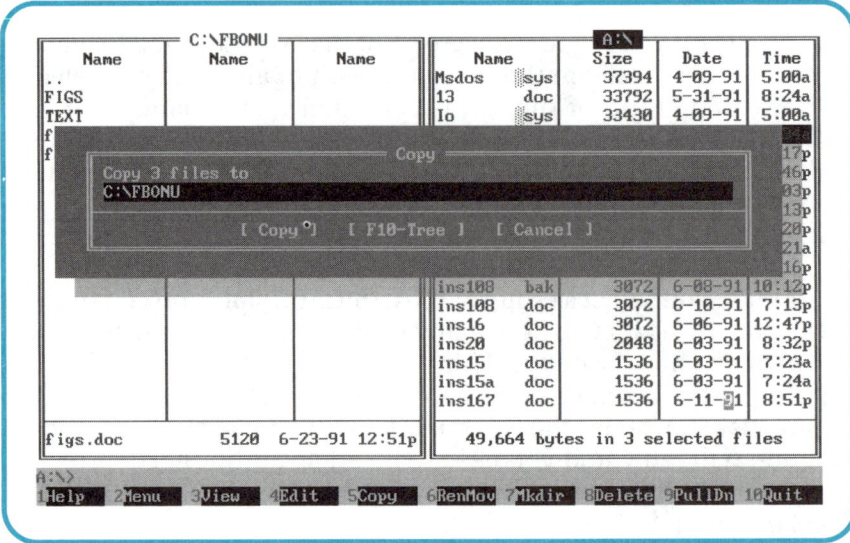

232 Figure 10.4 *The Copy dialog box lets you specify a destination for the selected file.*

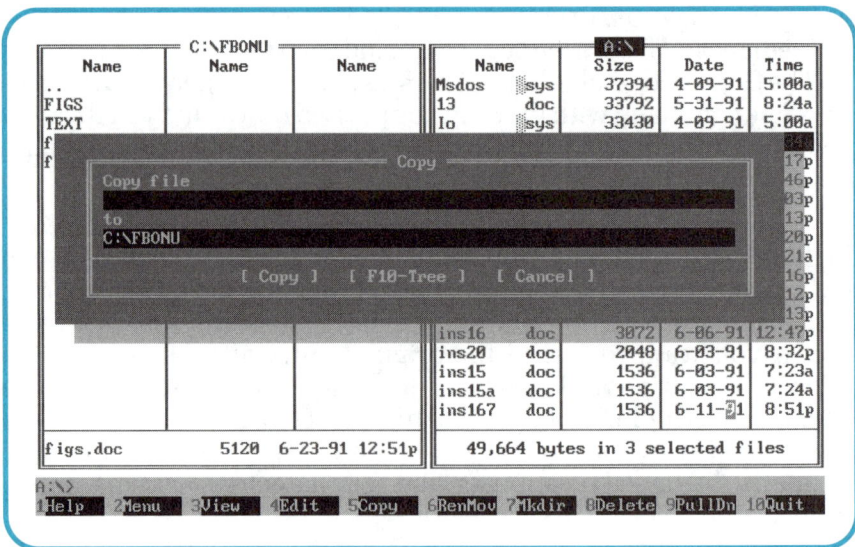

Figure 10.5 *The alternate Copy dialog box lets you supply both a source and a destination.*

If you choose the Copy option, the Commander begins copying the selected files from the source to the destination. A dialog box appears on screen, indicating which file is being copied and how the process is progressing. If you want to abort the copy process at any point, press Ctrl-Break or Esc. If you try to copy a file to a disk or directory that contains a file of the same name, you'll see the alert box shown in Figure 10.6. This box warns you that you are about to overwrite an existing file, giving you a chance to change your mind. If you want to overwrite the file, press Enter. If you want to skip the file and proceed to the next one, choose the Skip option. If you want the Commander to overwrite all files on the target that have the same file names as those in the source, choose All.

233

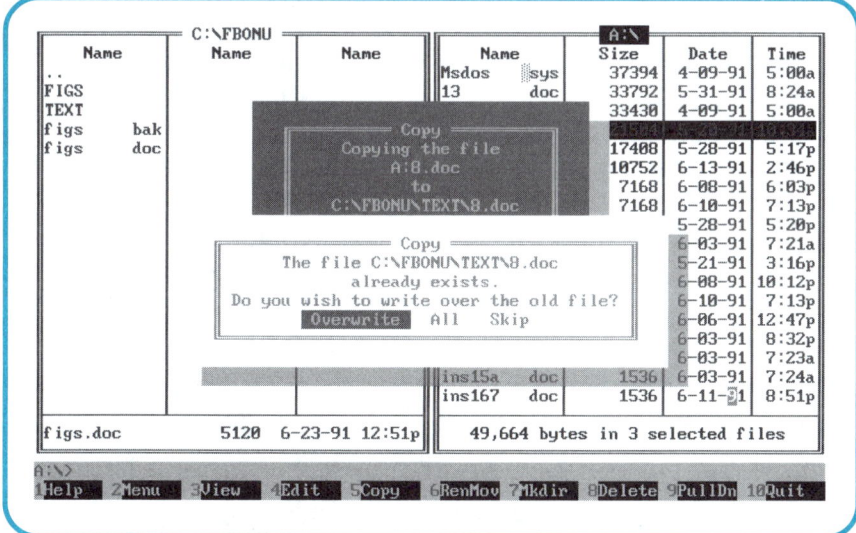

Figure 10.6   The overwrite warning alert box warns that you are about to replace an existing file.

Tip: You can use the Copy command to print a text file. When the dialog box asks you to name the target for the copy, type **prn**. This tells the Commander to copy the file to the printer.

Renaming Files (F6)

Occasionally, you may have to rename a file or a group of files either to give you a better idea of what those files contain or to allow you to use current names for other files. Whatever the reason, the Commander makes it easy to rename your files.

 Renaming Files

1. Highlight the file you want to rename.

2. Press F6 or choose the `Rename or move` command from the Files menu.

   The Rename dialog box appears, as in Figure 10.7, prompting you to enter a new name for the file.

3. Type a new name for the file, following the DOS file name restrictions.

   The file name can be no more than eight characters long. The extension can be up to three characters.

4. Press Enter.

   The dialog box disappears. The file is renamed but kept in the same directory.□

234

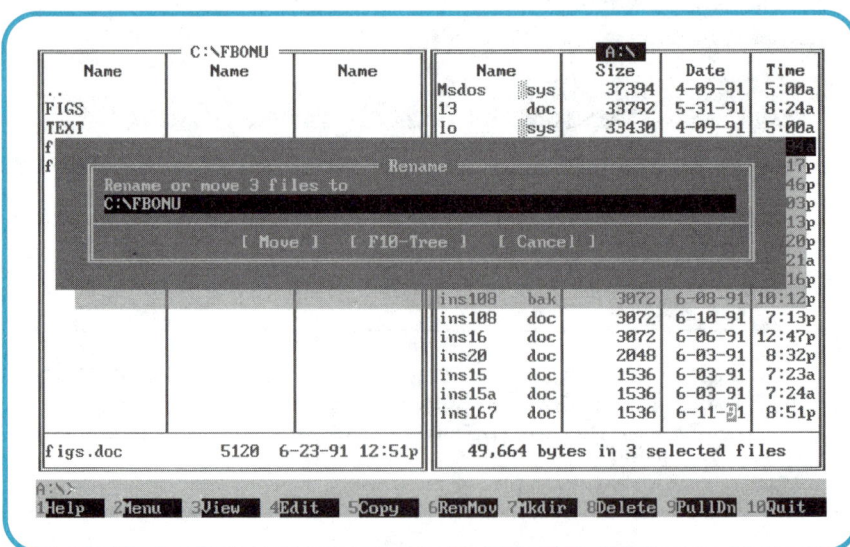

Figure 10.7 The Rename dialog box prompts you to enter a new name for the file.

> **Caution:** If you try to use a file name that's already in use in the current directory, the Commander will display an alert box telling you that the name is already being used. You cannot use the same name for two files in the same directory.

Moving Files (F6)

Move Files is one of the Commander's most useful features, simply because DOS has no comparable command. If you want to move files in DOS, you have to copy the files from the source to the target and then delete the files from the source. With the Commander, you move the files from the source to the target with a single command that operates much like the Copy command.

To begin, select the file or files you want to move. Then, press F6 or choose the `Rename or move` command from the Files menu. The Commander displays the same dialog box as in Figure 10.7. The Commander assumes that you want to move the file to the directory represented by the inactive panel. If that's not the case, type the path name of the directory you want to use for the target. For example, if you want to move the files to D:\SAMPLE\FILES, type `d:\sample\files`. You can also choose the target by selecting the `Tree` command at the bottom of the dialog box and choosing the directory from a tree display. After you've selected the target, press Enter to move the selected files.

235

> **Tip:** You can rename and move a file at the same time. When the Rename dialog box appears on screen, type the path name of the target directory, including the new file name for the file.

Deleting Files (F8)

Deleting files is easy. In fact, it may be too easy, so be careful, especially when using wild-card characters.

Deleting Files

1. Select the files you want to delete. Use the Ins key, the mouse, or the gray + or – keys as explained earlier.

2. Press F8 or choose `Delete` from the Files menu.

A dialog box appears, asking for your confirmation.

3. If you're absolutely sure you want to delete the files, press Enter or click on `Delete`. If you're not sure, select `Cancel`.

If you selected a single file and pressed Enter, the file is deleted. If you tried to delete a group of files, the Commander asks again for confirmation.

4. Press Enter or click on `OK` to confirm your request, or choose `Cancel` to cancel it.

If you press Enter, the Commander displays a dialog box that displays the name of each file it deletes. When the dialog box disappears, all the files have been deleted. □

236

By holding down the Shift key when choosing `Delete`, you can access the Delete dialog box as shown in Figure 10.8. You can enter a path name to activate any directory, and you can use wild cards to select a range of files. Although that's convenient, it makes this command almost as dangerous as the DOS DELETE command. In other words, if you attempt to delete a single file, the Commander won't ask for your confirmation. It will, however, ask you to confirm the deletion of several files. Be careful with wild cards, or you may need to make use of The Norton Utilities.

Setting File Attributes

If you share your computer with others, or if you're connected to a modem or network, you may wish to protect some of your files from accidental or intentional mangling. To do so, you can change your files' attributes. Begin by selecting the file or group of files whose archive bit you want to change. Then, choose the `file Attributes` command from the Files menu. (Sorry, there's no hot key for this one.) The Commander displays the Attributes dialog box, as shown in Figure 10.9.

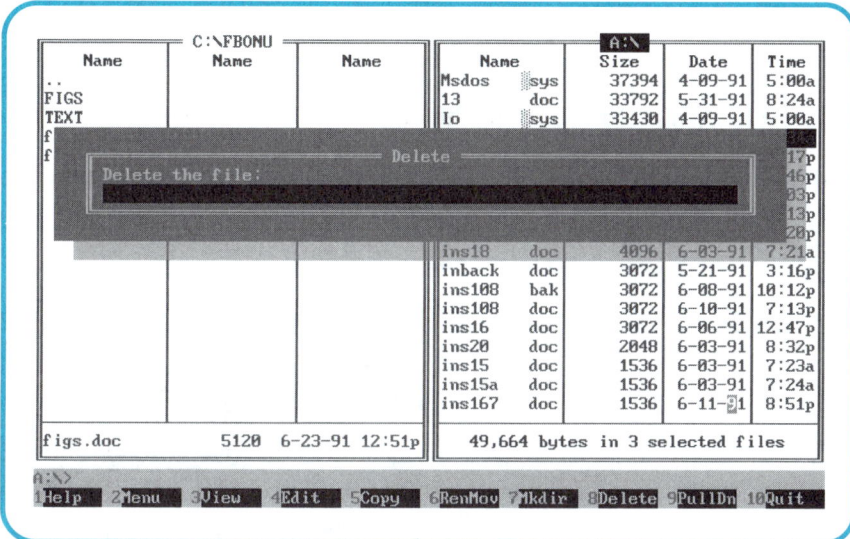

Figure 10.8   *The Delete dialog box lets you activate any directory and delete a group of files.*

To set an attribute, use the Space Bar or mouse to place an X in the box next to the attribute. When the attributes are set as desired, choose the Set command at the bottom of the box to set the attributes or the Clear command to clear them. Let's look at the attributes in turn:

Read only. The read-only attribute write-protects the file. You can read the file or execute it, but you can't change it.

Archive. The archive attribute shows whether or not the file has been modified since the last time it was backed up. Setting this attribute ensures that the file will be backed up.

Hidden. This attribute hides the files so that they don't appear in your directory. If you try to edit the file, the Commander won't let you. To exit the edit process, choose Don't Save.

System. This attribute hides and write-protects system files, giving you some protection against viruses and hackers. Don't set this attribute unless you know what you're doing.

Viewing a File's Contents (F3)

Many times, you'll need some information or a document, but you're just not sure which file contains the information you're looking for. You could load each file into its application to view its contents, but that would take a while. The Commander helps you solve this problem by letting you view the contents of any selected file that's compatible with the Commander. (Refer to Chapter 9 for a list of applications that the Commander supports.)

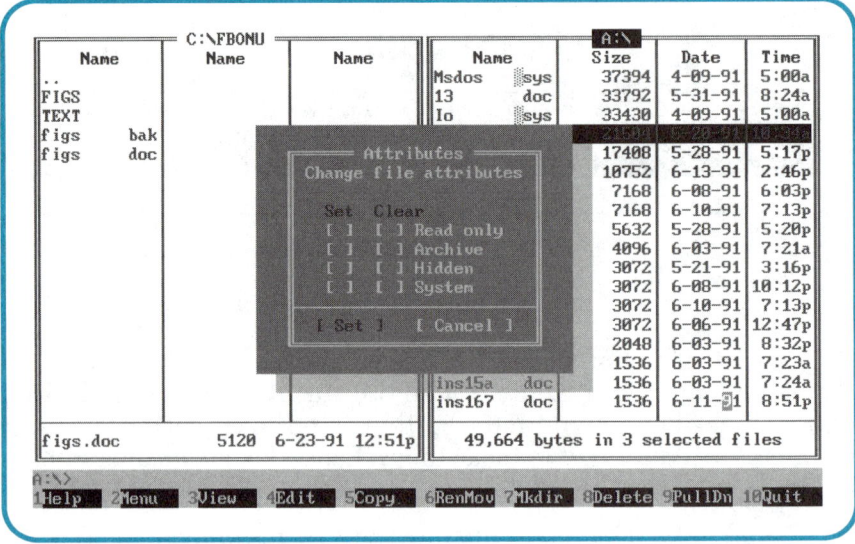

Figure 10.9   Use the Attributes dialog box to protect your files.

To view a file, first highlight the name of the file you want to view. Press F3 or choose the View command from the Files menu. The contents of the file appear on screen, as shown in Figure 10.10.

At the top of the screen is a title bar that displays the name of the application (in this case, Word) and the path and file name for the file that's displayed. This line includes additional information that varies depending on the type of file you're viewing. For a database file, the Commander shows you which record you're viewing. For a word processor document, you see the column number for the left margin, the size of the file, and the percent of the file that's above the top of the screen. At the bottom of the screen is function key bar. This, too, varies depending on the type of file. Refer to Table 10.1 for a list of the function keys and their uses.

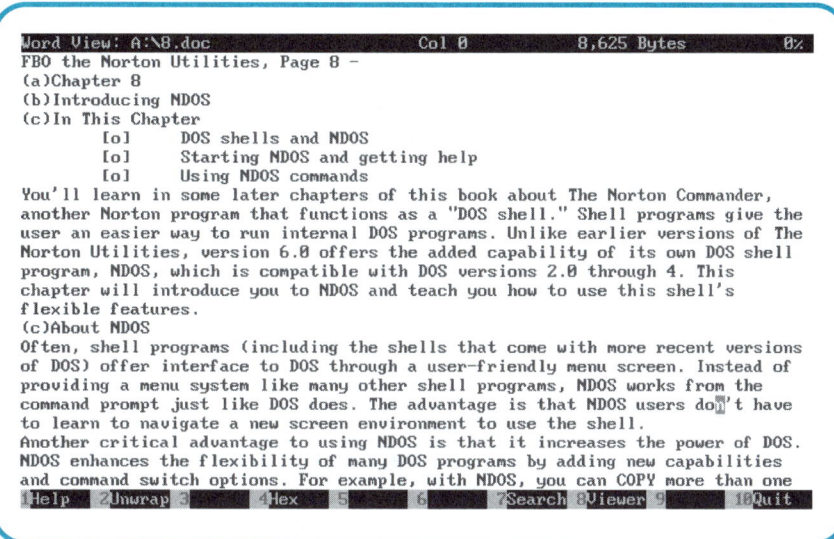

```
Word View: A:\8.doc                    Col 0         8,625 Bytes        0%
FB0 the Norton Utilities, Page 8 -
(a)Chapter 8
(b)Introducing NDOS
(c)In This Chapter
        [o]       DOS shells and NDOS
        [o]       Starting NDOS and getting help
        [o]       Using NDOS commands
You'll learn in some later chapters of this book about The Norton Commander,
another Norton program that functions as a "DOS shell." Shell programs give the
user an easier way to run internal DOS programs. Unlike earlier versions of The
Norton Utilities, version 6.0 offers the added capability of its own DOS shell
program, NDOS, which is compatible with DOS versions 2.0 through 4. This
chapter will introduce you to NDOS and teach you how to use this shell's
flexible features.
(c)About NDOS
Often, shell programs (including the shells that come with more recent versions
of DOS) offer interface to DOS through a user-friendly menu screen. Instead of
providing a menu system like many other shell programs, NDOS works from the
command prompt just like DOS does. The advantage is that NDOS users don't have
to learn to navigate a new screen environment to use the shell.
Another critical advantage to using NDOS is that it increases the power of DOS.
NDOS enhances the flexibility of many DOS programs by adding new capabilities
and command switch options. For example, with NDOS, you can COPY more than one
1Help  2Unwrap 3      4Hex   5      6      7Search 8Viewer 9      10Quit
```

Figure 10.10   A word processor view screen showing the contents of a Microsoft Word 5.0 document.

239

Editing Files (F4)

The Edit File feature lets you edit files that are smaller than 25K. To edit a file, first highlight the name of the file. Then, press F4 or choose the Edit command from the Files menu. The file is loaded into the Commander's File Editor and appears on screen, as shown in Figure 10.11.

> **Tip:** If you know the name of the file you want to edit and don't want to mess around highlighting it, or if you want to open a new file, press Shift-F4. A dialog box will appear, letting you enter a name for the file. Type a path name (if necessary) and a file name, and press Enter. If the file exists, it will appear on screen. If the file does not exist, the Commander will ask whether you want to create the file.

Table 10.1   The View Function Keys

Key	Text	Database	Spreadsheet
F1	None	Gives information about the file.	Gives help regarding spreadsheets.
F2	Toggles word wrap.	Reveals the name of each field or attribute.	None
F3	Toggles Unzoom if screen was originally a quick view.	Toggles Unzoom screen.	Toggles Unzoom screen.
F4	Switches view from hex to ASCII format.	Provides spreadsheet view of records. Press F4 again to view highlighted record.	None
F5	None	Lets you choose the number of the record you wish to view.	Lets you specify the cell number you wish to view.
F6	None	None	None
F7	Search for text string. Shift F7 repeats the search.	Search for text string. Shift-F7 repeats the search.	Search for label or text string. Shift F7 repeats the search.
F8	Displays a list of viewer options.	Displays an index of tables you've created.	None
F9	None	None	None
F10	Quit	Quit	Quit

Let's look at this screen. At the top of the screen is a status line that provides some information about the display. On the left is the title of the file editor (Edit), followed by the path name and file name of the file that's displayed. When you begin to edit, an asterisk appears in the middle of this line. To the right of the asterisk is the line number and column number, specifying the cursor location. The number on the far right indicates the amount of space available in the editor's buffer. To the right of that number is the ASCII code for the character that's under the cursor.

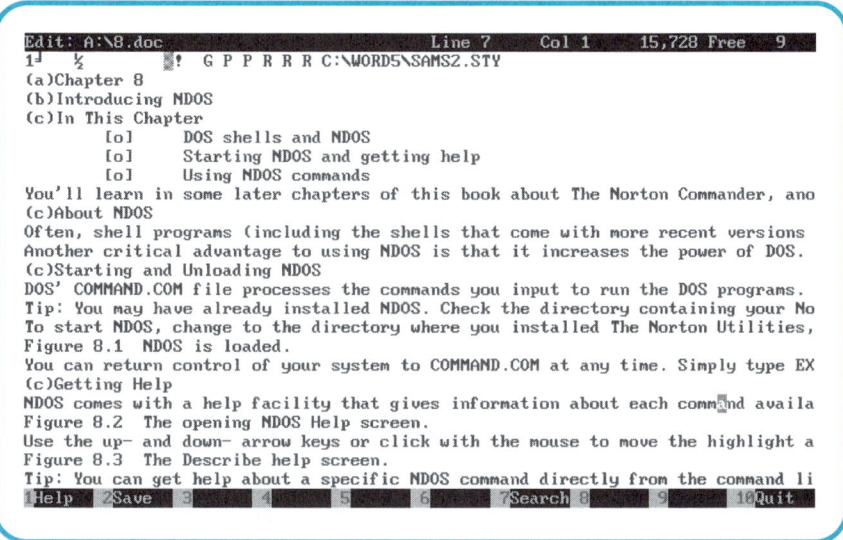

```
Edit: A:\8.doc                        Line 7     Col 1     15,728 Free   9
1⌐    ½     ▌!  G  P  P  R  R  R  C:\WORD5\SAMS2.STY
(a)Chapter 8
(b)Introducing NDOS
(c)In This Chapter
        [o]        DOS shells and NDOS
        [o]        Starting NDOS and getting help
        [o]        Using NDOS commands
You'll learn in some later chapters of this book about The Norton Commander, ano
(c)About NDOS
Often, shell programs (including the shells that come with more recent versions
Another critical advantage to using NDOS is that it increases the power of DOS.
(c)Starting and Unloading NDOS
DOS' COMMAND.COM file processes the commands you input to run the DOS programs.
Tip: You may have already installed NDOS. Check the directory containing your No
To start NDOS, change to the directory where you installed The Norton Utilities,
Figure 8.1  NDOS is loaded.
You can return control of your system to COMMAND.COM at any time. Simply type EX
(c)Getting Help
NDOS comes with a help facility that gives information about each command availa
Figure 8.2  The opening NDOS Help screen.
Use the up- and down- arrow keys or click with the mouse to move the highlight a
Figure 8.3  The Describe help screen.
Tip: You can get help about a specific NDOS command directly from the command li
1Help  2Save   3       4       5       6       7Search 8       9       10Quit
```

Figure 10.11   *A word processor document loaded into the Commander's File Editor*

241

At the bottom of the screen is the now-familiar function key bar. Notice that many of the function keys are similar to those that appeared in the View screen. The only difference is that now the F2 key is used for saving a file. You can press Shift-F2 to display a dialog box that lets you enter a new name for the file. To exit this screen, press F10 or choose Quit from the function key bar. By pressing Shift-F10, you can quit and save the changes to disk.

You can move the cursor around with the standard cursor control keys, as shown in Table 10.2, or use your mouse for even quicker movement. This table also lists some keys you can use to delete text. To insert text, simply type the text you wish to insert using the keyboard. If you prefer to work with a different file editor, choose the Editor command from the Options menu. Select the External option, and then enter the name of the external editor you wish to use. For example, if you have the Norton Editor and you want to use it instead, enter **ne**.

Table 10.2   The Edit Text Keys

Key	Combination Action
↑	Move cursor up one line
↓	Move cursor down one line
←	Move cursor left one character without deleting
→	Move cursor right one character without deleting
Ctrl-←	Move cursor left one word
Ctrl-→	Move cursor right one word
Home	Move cursor to beginning of line
End	Move cursor to end of line
PgUp	Move cursor one page up
PgDn	Move cursor one page down
Ctrl-Home	Move cursor to beginning of file
Ctrl-End	Move cursor to end of file
Backspace	Delete character to left of cursor
Del	Delete character under cursor
Ctrl-Backspace	Delete one word to left
Ctrl-T	Delete one word to right
Ctrl-Y	Delete line
Ctrl-K	Delete from cursor position to end of line
Ctrl-Q	Quote next character

Managing Your Disks and Directories

Gaining control over your files is an important first step in keeping your hard disk organized and uncluttered. But to do a complete job, you need to be able to manipulate your directory structure; that is, you need to be able to create new directories and remove directories that are no longer in use. The Commander gives you all the tools you need to perform these tasks quickly.

In addition, the Commander gives you much more freedom in how you structure your disk. For example, in the past, most books would tell you to make your directory tree very shallow. If you made the tree too deep, you ended up with path statements a mile long. Every time you wanted to access a file, you'd have to enter these ungodly path statements, without making a typo. Now that you can select a directory rather than type a path name, you can make your directory tree as deep as necessary, making it possible to work with smaller groups of files.

The Norton Commander
Directory (NCD) Tree

You've already seen that the Commander displays the structure of your disk in the form of a directory tree. Because of this simplified display, you can attach new directories and lop off empty ones by simply highlighting the directory and entering the appropriate command. You can do this in either the panel display or a special display called the NCD Tree, as shown in Figure 10.12. To see this display, press Alt-F10 or choose the NCD tree command from the Commands menu. The currently active directory is highlighted.

243

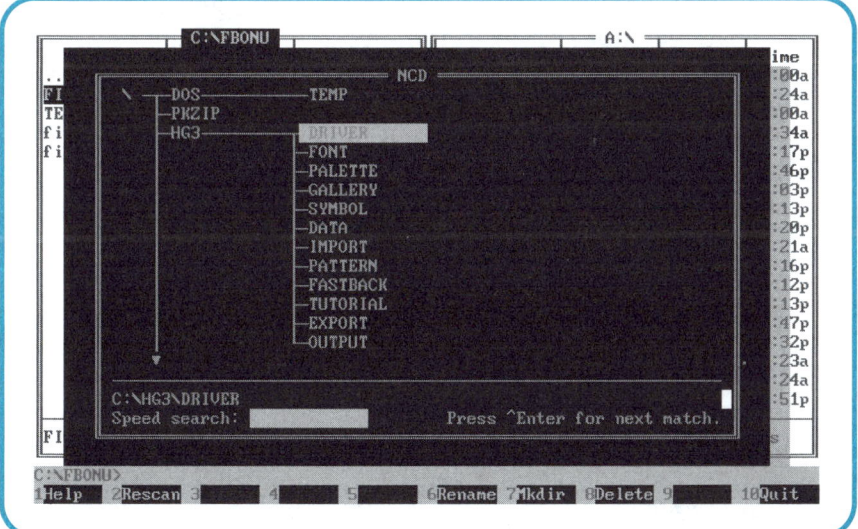

Figure 10.12 The NCD tree provides a graphic representation of your directory structure.

You can move the highlight bar to any directory by using the cursor keys or clicking on the directory with the mouse. If you press the Enter key, this display disappears, and the directory you highlighted becomes the active directory. You can even search for a directory on the directory tree.

 Searching for a Directory on the NCD Tree

1. Press Alt-F10 or choose NCD tree from the Commands menu.

   The currently active directory is highlighted.

2. Press the left arrow key or the mouse to move the cursor to the beginning of the tree.

   The root directory is highlighted.

3. Start typing the name of the directory.

   As you type, the highlight bar moves to the directory that matches the characters you typed so far until it reaches the directory that matches your latest entry. □

At the bottom of the screen is a function key bar that offers the following additional commands:

Rescan. Whenever you add or delete a directory, your change may not appear in the directory tree. Choose this command or press F2 to have the Commander update the directory structure to display the changes.

Rename. Choose this command or press F6 to rename a directory. A dialog box will appear asking you to enter the new name.

Mkdir. Move the highlight to the directory for which you want to create a subdirectory. Then, press F7 or choose this command. You'll be asked to enter a name for the subdirectory. Type the name, and press Enter. You now have a new subdirectory.

Delete. To delete a directory, make sure the directory you want to delete is not active and is empty; otherwise, the Commander will not delete it. Then, choose this command or press F8.

Quit. Press F10 or choose the Quit command to close this window and return to your panels.

Making Directories (F7)

You can create a new directory either in the tree view of the panel display or in the NCD Tree display. Move the highlight bar over the directory under which you want the new directory. Then choose the `Make directory` command from the Files menu, or press F7. In either case, a dialog box appears, asking you to enter a name for the directory. You can enter a name of up to eight characters plus a three character extension. Press Enter, and the new directory is created and highlighted.

Deleting Directories (F8)

Deleting directories is even easier than making them. Before you begin, however, make sure the directory you wish to delete is not active. That is, the title of the panel that represents the directory must not be displayed in reverse video. Also, make sure the directory is empty. You can't delete a directory, even in DOS, if the directory contains a file. When these conditions are met, highlight the directory you want to delete. Then choose the `Delete` command from the Files menu, or press F8. If you're deleting the directory from a panel, the Commander displays a dialog box asking you to confirm your choice. Press Enter to delete, or choose `Cancel` if you change your mind. If you're deleting the directory from the NCD Tree, the directory disappears without asking for confirmation.

245

> **Note:** If you selected the `Auto Change Directory` option in the Configuration dialog box, you cannot delete a directory using the panel tree display. As soon as you highlight the directory, it becomes active, and the Commander prevents you from deleting it. To delete the directory, open the menu for the panel with the tree display, and select `Full` or `Brief` to turn off the tree display. You can now delete the directory. Your other option is to turn off the `Auto Change Directory` option. Choose `Configuration` from the Options menu. Move the cursor to the Auto Change Directory option, and press the Space Bar or click the mouse button. Move the cursor to the Ok button, and press Enter or click `OK`. You can now delete a directory from the tree.

Running Applications from the Commander

If you're working in the Commander and you decide you want to exit and begin working in some other application, you can exit the Commander and load your other application with a single command. All you need to do is highlight the name of the file that executes your program, and press Enter. For example, if you wanted to run Microsoft Word, you would highlight the file WORD.EXE in the panel, and press Enter.

The Commander offers two additional features that let you load your applications. The first lets you set up a menu that lists all your applications. To run the application, you choose its name from the menu. The second lets you launch an application and load a file into it simply by selecting the data file you want to work with from the panel listing. The following sections tell you how to set up and use these more advanced features.

246

Creating a Menu for Running Your Applications

You may have noticed the F2 Menu command in the function key bar at the bottom of the screen. If you press that key now, you'll see a dialog box that tells you there's no file available for that command. Let's fix that problem by creating the file.

Press F9 to pull down the Commands menu. At the bottom of this menu are two choices: Menu file edit and eXtension file edit. Choose the Menu file edit option. The Commander displays the User Menu dialog box, asking you which menu you want to edit. The Main option lets you edit the Commander's main menu. This menu is accessible from anywhere in the Commander. The Local option lets you create a local menu that's accessible only from within a particular directory. Choose the Main option now to display a screen like the one in Figure 10.13. (Yours won't have text at the top.) At the bottom of the screen is a Help window that provides a brief explanation of the operation.

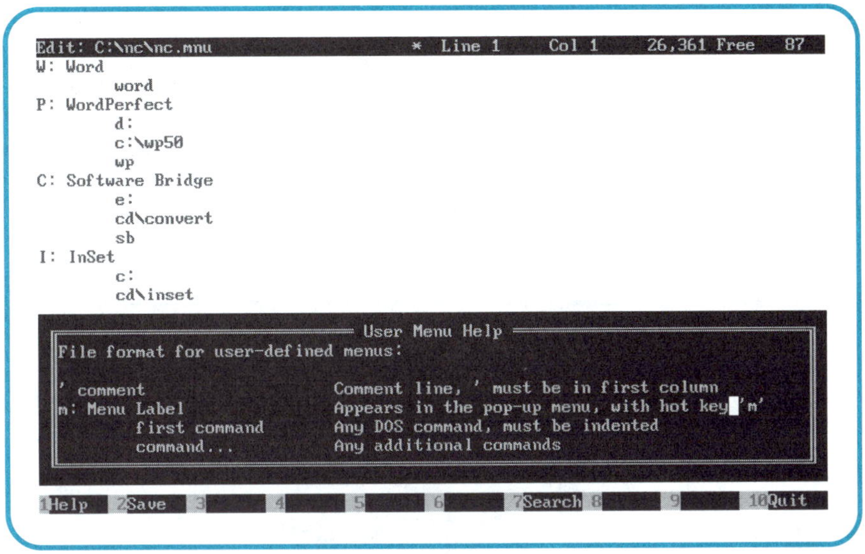

```
Edit: C:\nc\nc.mnu              *  Line 1    Col 1    26,361 Free   87
W: Word
        word
P: WordPerfect
        d:
        c:\wp50
        wp
C: Software Bridge
        e:
        cd\convert
        sb
I: InSet
        c:
        cd\inset
╔══════════════════════ User Menu Help ══════════════════════╗
║File format for user-defined menus:                         ║
║                                                            ║
║' comment              Comment line, ' must be in first column║
║m: Menu Label          Appears in the pop-up menu, with hot key 'm'║
║     first command     Any DOS command, must be indented    ║
║     command...        Any additional commands              ║
╚════════════════════════════════════════════════════════════╝
1Help 2Save  3     4      5      6      7Search 8      9      10Quit
```

Figure 10.13   The Edit Menu screen is shown here with a Help window.

247

Now you're ready to begin typing the commands that run your applications. Choose an application you want to run (for example, WordPerfect). Type a single letter to represent a quick-key command for running the application. For example, you may wish to type P for WordPerfect. Type a colon and a space followed by the name of the program you want to run. Your first line should look something like this:

```
P: WordPerfect
```

Press Enter, then press Tab to indent the second line. (Press Tab to indent all subsequent command lines as well.) Type the commands you would normally type at the DOS prompt to run your program. For example, you probably have to access the drive and directory that hold your program files and then type a command to load the program. If you were creating a menu item to run WordPerfect, and your program files were in D:\WP5, your command lines would look like the following:

```
P: WordPerfect
d:
cd\wp5
wp
```

Press Enter at the end of the last line. You can create as many of these entries as you need. When you're done typing your entries, press F2 or choose `Save` to save the file, and then press `F10 Quit` to exit the screen. Now, when you choose the `F2 Menu` command, you'll see a User menu like the one in Figure 10.14. Type the letter that corresponds to the application you want to run, or select the application with the highlight bar. The Commander automatically loads the application.

248

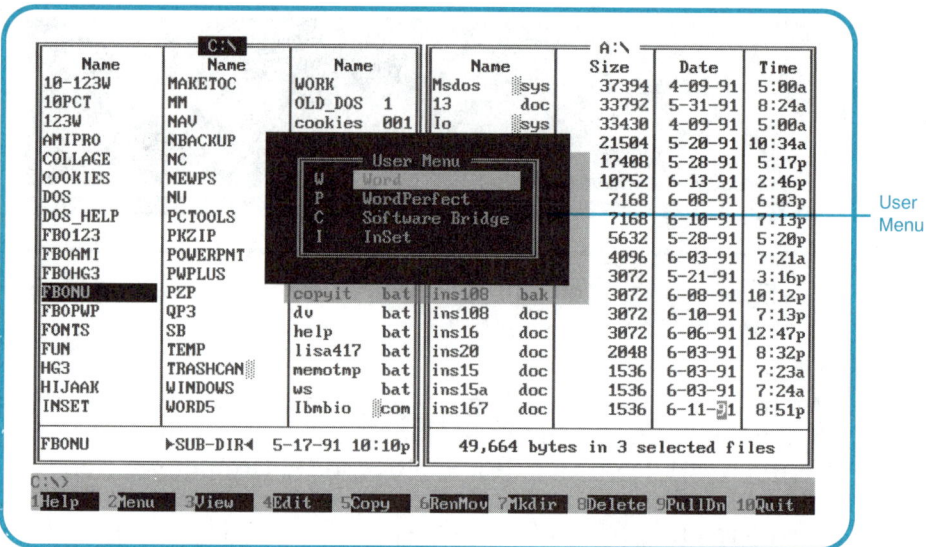

Figure 10.14   *The User Menu screen lets you select the application you want to run.*

The Point-and-Shoot Feature

The point-and-shoot feature lets you run an application and load a file into the application by selecting the file from the panel listing. To be able to do this, however, you must create an *extension file* (NC.EXT) similar to the menu file explained previously. To begin, choose the `eXtension file edit` command from the Commands menu. This opens an Edit screen similar to the one in Figure 10.13.

Type the file extension of the files you want to be able to automatically load into a given application. For example, if you want all files with the extension .DOC loaded into Word, type **doc** followed by a colon. Press Space Bar, and type the command required to run the application from any directory. That is, if you can run Word by typing `word` at any DOS prompt, then do so. If, however, you must supply a path to the Word files, then type the complete path followed by the command. For example, you could type

```
f:\word5\word !.!
```

The parameter !.! tells the Commander to enter the file name on the command line. The following list provides alternatives to what you can have entered on the command line:

!.!	Enter file name and extension
!	Enter file name without extension
!:	Enter current drive letter followed by colon
!\	Enter path statement
!!	Enter single exclamation point

249

After typing the command, press Enter. Repeat the process for as many extension files as desired. Press F2 to save the setup to disk. Then, whenever you want to run an application and load a file into that application, simply select the file you want to load from the panel listing. That is, either highlight the file name and press Enter or double-click on the file with the left mouse button. The Commander does the rest.

What You Have Learned

In this chapter you learned about the Norton Commander and how to use it to perform several operations more easily than you could using DOS. You also learned:

► The Find Files feature lets you search an entire disk drive for a file or group of files.

► The Ins key allows you to select individual files or groups of files using the gray + or gray – key.

► Once you've selected a file or group of files, you can enter any of several commands to copy, delete, rename, or move the files. You can even change file attributes for a file to protect it from external threats.

▶ The F3 View command lets you view the contents of a file without changing the contents.

▶ The Commander's File Editor lets you edit files without exiting the Commander.

▶ The NCD tree (Alt-F10) gives you an overall view of your directory tree. This tree offers several commands that simplify directory maintenance, making it easy to create new directories or delete empty ones.

▶ The Commander's User menu lets you run applications from the Commander by selecting the application from a menu.

▶ The point-and-shoot feature lets you run an application from the Commander and load a file into the application with a single command.

250

Communicating with the Commander

In This Chapter

▶ *Connecting two computers with Commander Link*

▶ *Copying files from another computer*

▶ *Configuring your system for Commander Mail*

▶ *Sending messages via Commander Mail*

▶ *Checking your mail*

The Commander offers two features that let your computer communicate with other computers. Commander Link creates a communication link between two computers so you can copy files from one computer to another—from laptop to desktop, for example. Instead of having to use floppy disks as an intermediary, you can copy files directly from hard disk to hard disk. Commander Mail allows you to send E-mail, FAXes, and telexes, via modem, using your MCI Mail account. In this chapter, you'll learn how to set up your system and configure the Commander to perform these two important tasks.

Using Commander Link

Like all of the Commander features, Commander Link is easy to run. Once the two computers are connected and are running Commander Link, you simply copy files from one to the other, just as you would copy files from one directory to another. Before you can do that, however, you must connect the two computers with the proper cable and have the Commander installed on both systems.

Connecting the Two Computers

The first step in establishing a link between the computers is to purchase the proper serial null-modem cable (RS-232) for the two computers you intend to connect. Make sure the cable is a null-modem cable (it should be marked). If it's not a null-modem cable, you'll need to purchase a null-modem adapter. You need a cable to connect the COM1 or COM2 port on one computer to the COM1 or COM2 port on the other. Check the back of your computer to see if the ports are marked. If they are, you're in luck; if not, refer to the documentation that came with your computer or call your dealer. Write down how many pins each has (9 or 25) and whether the port is male (has pins) or female (has receptacles for pins). (The serial ports are usually male, but don't bet on it.) When you know what you need, obtain the required cable and any necessary adapters from your local computer store.

> **Note**: Your printer is probably connected to the parallel port at the back of your computer. If you have a mouse or a modem, it is probably connected to your serial port. If you have only one COM port on your computer, you'll have to disconnect any device that's connected to it before you can proceed.

With both computers turned off (to protect them), connect the COM1 or COM2 ports using the cable. Then, boot each computer. Make sure the Commander is installed on both computers, and start the program on each.

Before you perform the next step, decide which computer you want to use to control the transfer of data. This computer will be your *master*. The other computer, will be the *slave*; it will do only what the master computer tells it to do. If you've connected a laptop to your desktop computer, use the desktop as the master and the laptop as the slave. Now, open the Left or Right menu on your master computer and choose the Link command. This opens the dialog box shown in Figure 11.1.

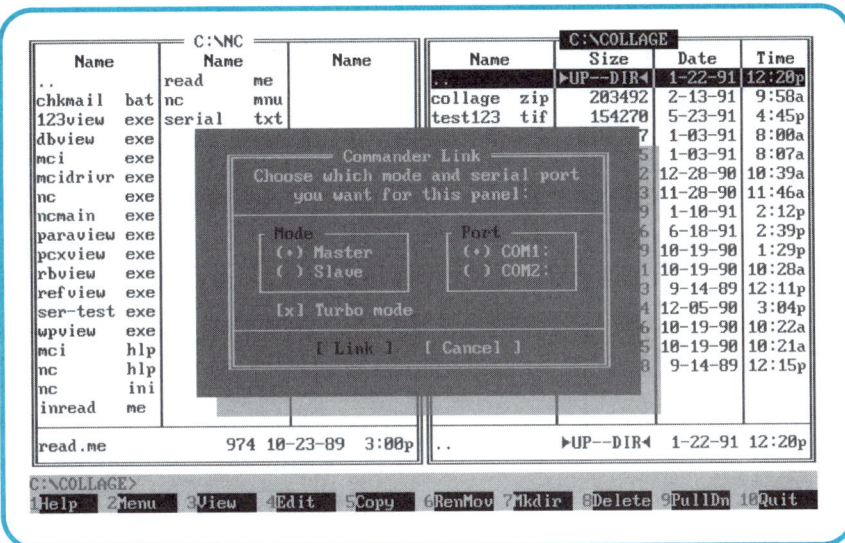

253

Figure 11.1   Use the Commander Link dialog box to set up the link.

Tip: If your slave computer is on the right, use the Left menu to establish the link. The Right menu will then show a list of files on the slave, organizing the panels to correspond to the location of the computers.

Choose the Master option by highlighting it and pressing the Space Bar or by clicking on it with the mouse. Choose COM1 or COM2 in the same way depending on which COM ports you connected. Select the Link button. A dialog box appears, telling you that Commander Link is waiting for you to set up Link on the slave.

Now, move to your slave computer. Open either the Left or Right menu, and select the `Link` command. Select `Slave` for this computer, and select the same COM port you specified for the master. Highlight the `Link` button, and press Enter. It takes a few seconds for the Commander to establish the link. A dialog box appears, telling you that your slave is now set up to process requests from the master. The right panel on the master computer shows a list of files on the current directory of the slave, as shown in Figure 11.2.

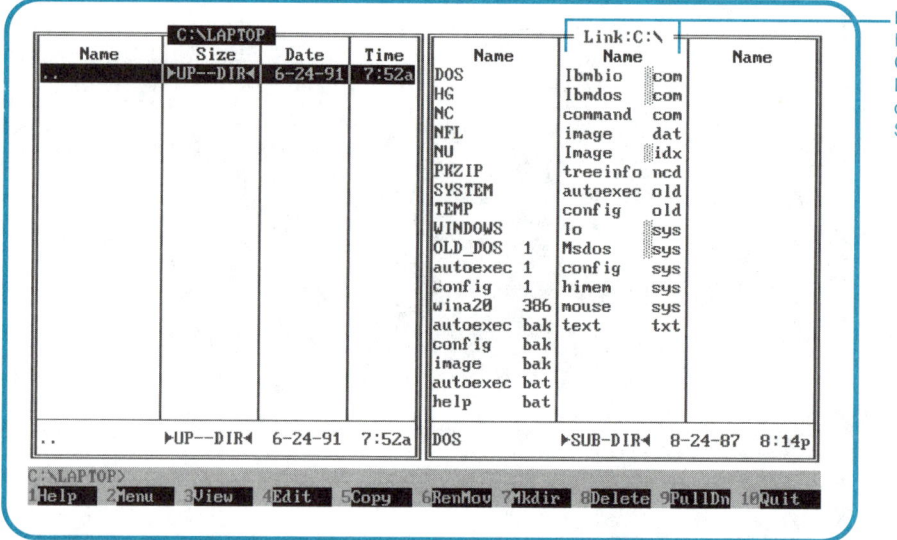

List of Files in the Current Directory of the Slave

254

Figure 11.2   The Link screen displayed on the master computer.

Note: If you get a message telling you to set up the other computer as the master, and you already did that, you may have a problem with the connection between the serial ports. Activate the directory C:\NC, highlight the file called `SERIAL.TXT`, and press F3. This file provides a list of possible causes for the problem and for problems you may face using MCI Mail.

Transferring Files

Now that the two computers are linked, the rest is easy. You can copy or move files between the two computers or rename or delete files on the slave by entering commands on the master. The following quick steps tell you how to copy files from slave to master. You'll be working on the keyboard of the master computer.

 Copying Files Using Commander Link

1. Press Tab to activate the panel for the slave.

   The highlight bar moves to the slave panel.

2. Change to the drive and directory you want to access.

   The panel display changes, listing all the files in the active directory.

3. Select the files you want to copy by pressing the gray + key, by pressing Ins, or by clicking with the mouse.

   The files are highlighted in the right panel.

4. Press F5 or select the Copy command from the Files menu.

   The Copy dialog box appears, telling you the destination of the copied files.

5. If the destination is correct, press Enter. If it's not correct, enter a new drive and directory, and press Enter.

   Link begins copying the selected files to the specified drive and directory on the master. □

255

Terminating the Link

When you're done performing your tasks with Link, open the Left menu on the master, and choose the Link command again. Power down both computers as you normally would, and with both computers off, disconnect the serial null-modem cable. (To protect your system, you should always turn off the power before connecting or disconnecting a cable.)

Using Commander Mail

The most difficult thing about Commander Mail is setting up your system to run it. Once you've established an MCI Mail account and have your system hooked up to a modem, the feature itself is very easy to use. The system lets you transfer data to and from others who are hooked into the same system. Commander Mail also lets you send letters, FAXes, and telexes (paper mail) to those who do not have MCI accounts, or messages to those who use CompuServe or Telemail X.4000.

Basic Requirements

If you don't have an MCI Mail account, call 1-800-444-6245 for information on what you must do. When this is taken care of, you are ready to begin. Make sure your model is properly connected. The model must be connected to a power supply and a phone line that works. Many offices have separate phone receptacles that are marked DATA for modem connections. If you have an external modem, connect the modem to the COM1 or COM2 port on the back of your computer. If the port is not marked, refer to the manual that came with your computer or call your dealer. If you have an internal modem, connect the phone line to the modem jack at the back of your computer. Once your computer is connected to the modem, you are ready to set up the Commander Mail feature.

Setting Up Commander Mail

The first time you select the `commander mail` command from the Command menu, you're greeted by the screen shown in Figure 11.3. Press Enter or click OK, and the Commander displays the screen shown in Figure 11.4, requesting information about your account.

Enter your first initial and last name, and press Enter. Type a password up to eight characters to prevent unauthorized access to your account. In the MCI ID field, type your seven-digit MCI ID number (this is optional). Move the cursor to the Receive box. If you want to be able to receive messages, highlight to Yes and press the Space Bar, or use the mouse. If you want to send messages only, select No. If necessary, use the Tab key to move around the dialog box and change any of the information.

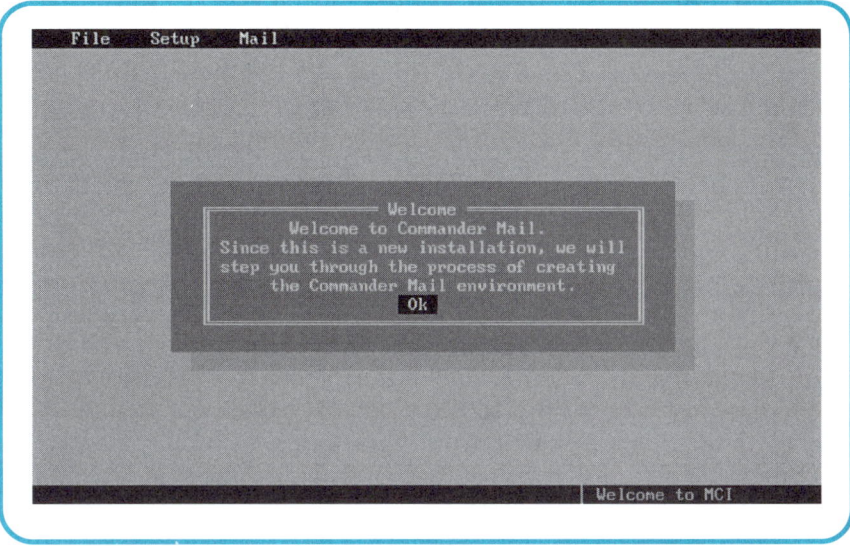

Figure 11.3   The opening Commander Mail screen greets you at startup.

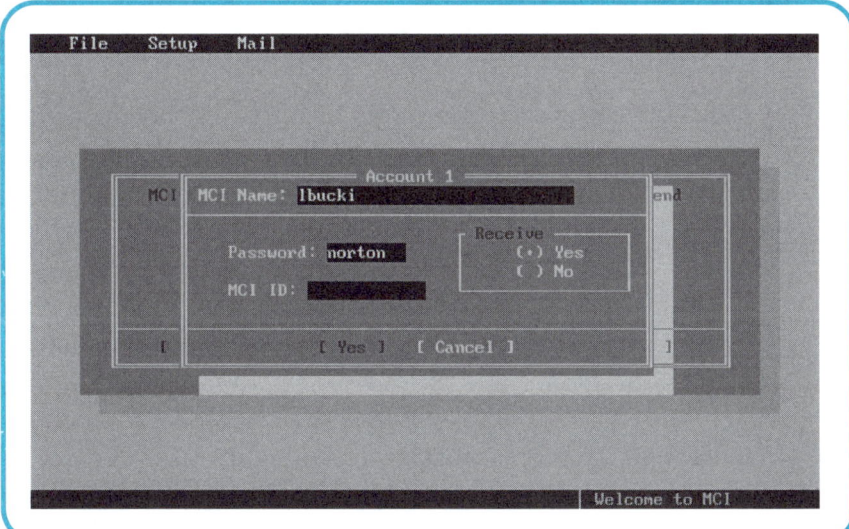

Figure 11.4   The Account 1 dialog box prompts you to enter account information.

When the information is correct, select the Yes button at the bottom of the box. Another dialog box appears, asking you whether you want to use the account you set up, add or modify an account, or delete an account altogether. If you're sharing your computer, you may set up Commander Mail for more than one account.

When you're finished setting up all your accounts, select the Ok button at the bottom of the box. Another dialog box appears, showing you the paths to your IN, OUT, and SENT directories. These directories act as mailboxes. Later, you'll put files in the OUT directory to send them, and you'll check your IN directory for incoming mail. If these defaults are acceptable, select Yes. If you want to change the defaults, move the cursor to the path you want to change and type a path to the directory you want to use. When you're done, select the Yes button. This opens the modem dialog box shown in Figure 11.5.

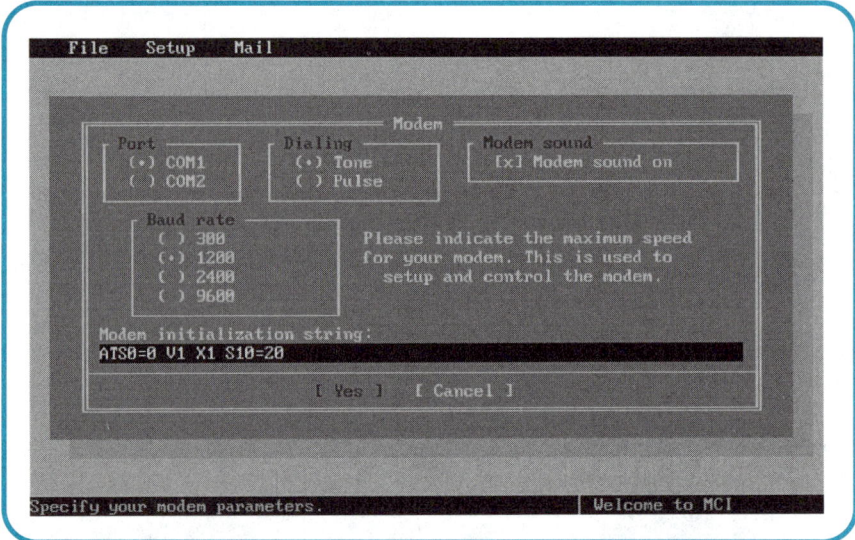

Figure 11.5   Use the Modem dialog box to configure the Commander Mail for your system.

In the Port box, select the COM port that your modem is connected to. Next, find out if you have tone or pulse telephone service. To do this, pick up your phone and dial a few numbers. If you hear tones of varying pitches, you have tone service. If you hear clicks of various lengths, you have rotary or pulse service. Press Tab to move the highlight to the Dialing box and select the correct setting. If you want to listen to the modem as it works, move the highlight to the Modem sound box, and press the Space Bar. Next, move the highlight to the Baud rate box, and select the baud rate for your modem. (Check the documentation that came with your modem to determine the baud rate.) At the bottom of the dialog box is a Modem initialization string. This information is supplied for you, and you should not have to edit it. If you have problems sending or receiving mail, check the documentation that came with your modem to determine whether you have to edit this string.

When you're done, select the Yes button at the bottom of the box. This opens the Phone Number dialog box. The Phone field contains the national 800 number you can dial to contact MCI. You can change this to a local number. In the Prefix field, enter any number you have to dial to get an outside line. In many offices, for example, you have to dial 9 before dialing your number. Type a comma after the prefix, telling the modem to pause for a dial tone. Select the Yes button to end the setup operation and display the Commander Mail screen.

259

A dialog box appears asking if you want to make a directory C:\NC\IN. Press Enter three times to create the IN, OUT, and SENT directories. Another dialog box appears, informing you that Commander Mail has created a parameter file. Press Enter, and your In Box appears on-screen. This is the box that contains any messages you may receive. Whenever you run Commander Mail, it displays this screen first, to inform you of any incoming mail.

The Commander Mail Screen

When you press Esc or select Ok, the In Box disappears from the screen, leaving the main Commander Mail screen, shown in Figure 11.6. At the top of the screen is a pull-down menu bar listing three available menus:

- ▶ File
- ▶ Setup
- ▶ Mail

Press F9 to activate the menu bar, then select the name of the menu you want to open.

The File menu offers three options. You can get on-line help by selecting the Help command or pressing F1. This menu also lets you access MCI customer support. To quit Commander Mail and return to the main Commander screen, select Quit.

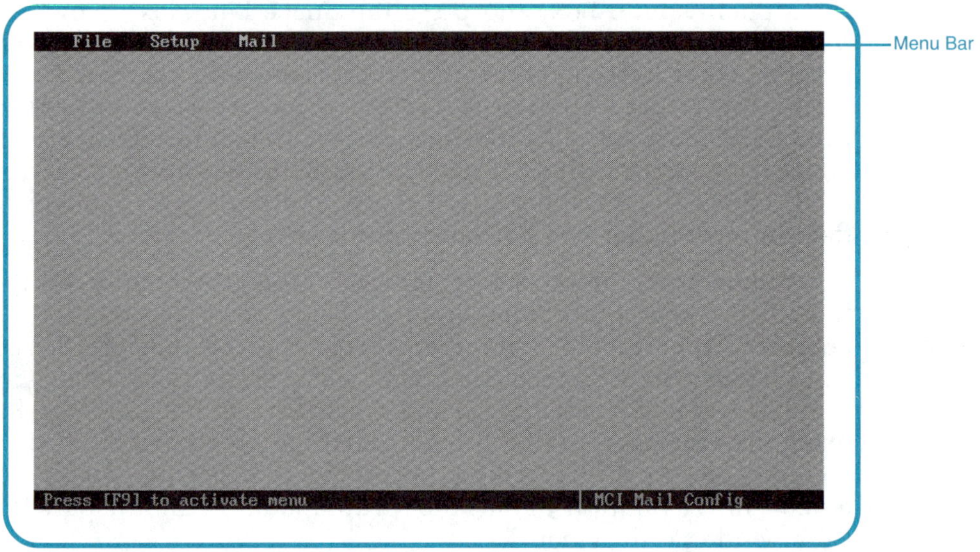

```
  File    Setup    Mail                                                      ──── Menu Bar




















 Press [F9] to activate menu                            MCI Mail Config
```

260

*Figure 11.6   Press F9 to activate the menu bar on the main
Commander Mail screen.*

The Setup menu offers several options that let you configure
the Commander Mail. The first option, Address book, is one of the
most useful options on this menu. It lets you create an address book
to store all the information you need to send messages and mail to
your most frequent contacts. If you choose Add, a dialog box appears,
asking you to choose the type of mail system you want to use. After
making your selection, the Mail Subscriber Address box appears, as
in Figure 11.7. This box lets you enter information about your
contacts. The remaining options on the Setup menu let you change
any of the information you entered to originally set up Commander
Mail.

The third menu, Mail, lists the options you'll use to send and
receive messages. You can check your In Box for incoming messages,
create new messages, send and receive messages, reply, and lots
more. You'll learn more about these options in the following sections.

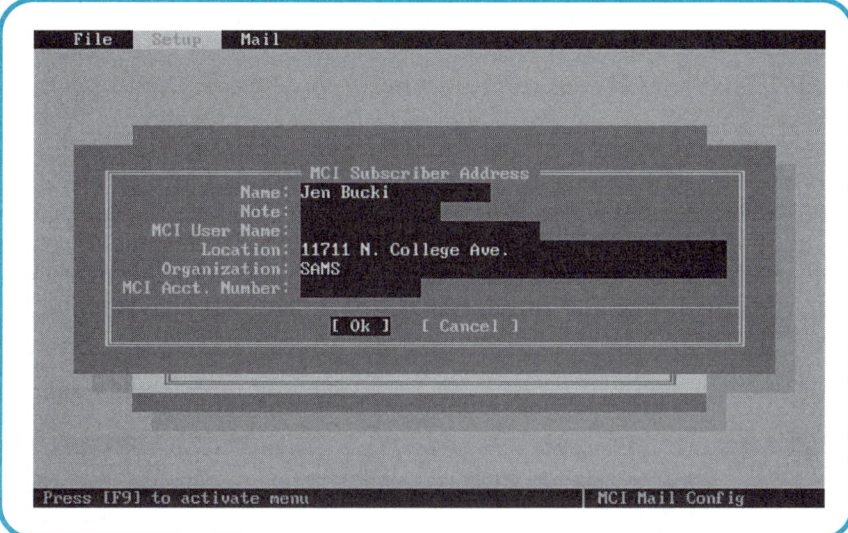

Figure 11.7   Creating an entry for the Address Book.

261

Creating a Message

Before you can send a message, you have to create one. Press Ctrl-N or select New Message from the Mail menu, displaying the screen shown in Figure 11.8.

With the highlight in the To: or CC: field, press Enter to display the Edit Send List dialog box. This box lets you enter information about the person you wish to contact. At the bottom of this box are the following five buttons:

List gives you access to your Address Book. Instead of typing in the required information, you can select a destination from the book.

New lets you bypass the Address Book and create a new entry.

Remove lets you delete a name on the list.

Handling gives you four options that let you specify how you want the mail handled. You can ask for confirmation of receipt or for priority status; you can specify a charging category; or you can alert your contact by phone that the mail has been received.

OK lets you accept the information entered in the box.

After you've entered the required information about the receiver, move the cursor to the space under the Handling field, and type your message. Press F10 or Esc to leave the screen and open a dialog box that asks if you want to save the message. Select the Save option. This returns you to the main Commander Mail screen. You can create additional messages or send the messages you just created.

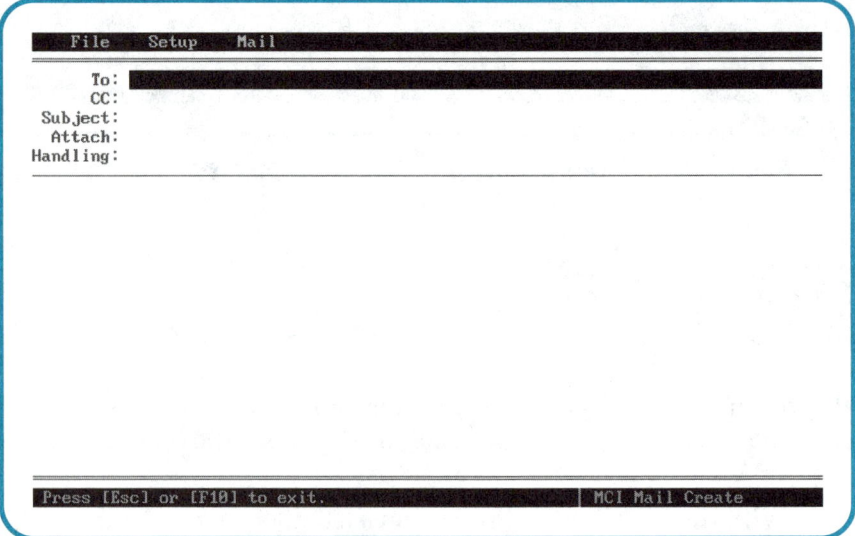

Figure 11.8   Press Ctrl-N to begin creating a message.

Sending and Receiving Messages

Whenever you want to send or receive information, you must tell Commander Mail to initiate contact between MCI mail and your computer. You send and receive messages at the same time, using a single command. When you're ready to send or receive a message, Press Ctrl-S or select the Send/receive command from the Mail menu. The Send/Receive dialog box appears, informing you of Commander Mail's progress. Commander Mail automatically establishes contact, sends your messages, receives incoming messages, and terminates the process.

Checking Your In Box

If anybody sent you a message before you established contact with MCI mail, that message should now be in your IN directory. Press Ctrl-B or select In box from the Mail menu to display the In Box screen, shown in Figure 11.9. This screen lists the messages that are stacking up in your In Box. Perform the following quick steps to check your In Box.

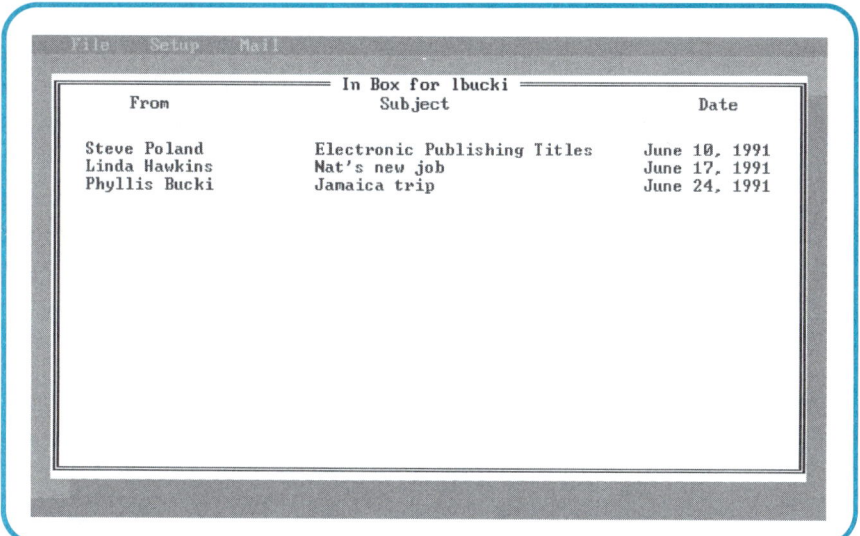

263

Figure 11.9   Press Ctrl-B to view a list of messages in your In Box.

 Checking Your In Box

1. Press Ctrl-B or select In box from the Mail menu.

    This opens the In Box screen, giving you a list messages that you have received.

2. Move the highlight bar to the message you want to read, and press Enter.

    The message appears on-screen.

3. Use the cursor keys or mouse to read the rest of the message.

4. Use the gray + and gray – keys to read the next message or the previous one.

5. Press Esc.
This takes you back to the list of messages in your In Box.

6. Press Esc.
This takes you back to the main Commander Mail screen. □

What You Have Learned

264

In this chapter you learned about Commander Link and Commander Mail, which gives you the ability to communicate directly with other systems near and far.

► Commander Link lets you transfer files directly from one computer to another.

► In order to run Commander Link, you must connect both computers with a serial null-modem cable and install the Commander on both computers.

► The Commander Mail feature lets you send E-mail, FAXes, and telexes, via modem, using your MCI mail account. Before you can use Commander Mail, your computer must be connected to a modem, and you must have an MCI Mail account.

► The Address Book lets you store information about several of your most frequent contacts, so you don't have to reenter the information every time you want to send a message.

Using the Norton Backup

In This Chapter

- ▶ *Setting up the Norton Backup*
- ▶ *How to back up your hard disk*
- ▶ *How to restore data from backup diskettes*
- ▶ *Basic and advanced level options*
- ▶ *How to create Setup files for PreSet backup and restore*

An Ounce of Prevention

The Norton Backup, which is a separate program from The Norton Utilities, provides a simple means of protecting your information and the time it took you to create it. The program "backs up" (copies) files from your hard disk onto floppy diskettes in a special compressed format. Should you lose your hard disk files, the Norton Backup lets you "decompress" and restore them from your backup diskettes onto your hard disk. Version 1.2 of the Norton Backup features increased reliability in the way it records data and faster data restoration. Version 1.2 also works with a wider range of IBM PC compatible systems.

How can you lose files from a hard disk? Let me count the ways. Your hard disk can "crash" due to power spikes, system failure, or physical damage. You can inadvertently erase files or directories. You can accidentally reformat your hard disk. You can even lose your hard disk contents to a computer virus.

Regular backup of your hard disk files prevents their total loss in the event of disaster. The frequency with which you back up your hard disk depends on how often you use it and how sensitive or difficult it is to recreate your files. With the Norton Backup, you can easily back up all files on a daily basis. Many users, however, find that a complete monthly backup, with weekly or daily backups of new or changed files only, is adequate for their needs.

The Norton Backup provides options that let you not only set your backup frequency but also select the files that you want to back up, the degree of compression (which determines whether a backup requires more diskettes or more time), whether you want the accuracy of copied data verified (which also affects speed), and more. The options available to you depend on which of the three Norton Backup levels you use:

266

Basic	Lets you select which files to back up, choose between five types of backup, and select from eight backup options.
Advanced	Lets you choose from more backup options and create custom setup files that let you use the Norton Backup at PreSet level.
PreSet	Lets you run a backup or restore operation with only a few keystrokes, with options previously set up in the Advanced Level.

This chapter explains the Basic level in detail. As a beginner, that is the level you will most likely use. It also explains Advanced options and the PreSet backup and restore, although it does so in less detail.

Getting Started

Before you can perform your first backup, you must install and configure the Norton Backup. Both procedures are easy and quick.

Screen prompts guide you through the process of copying files from the Norton Backup diskettes, answering a few questions, and starting tests that set up the program for your particular computer system. In the following sections, you will learn how to install, configure, start, and exit from the Norton Backup, as well as how to use the On-Line Help system.

Keyboard and Mouse Use

As you run the Norton Backup, dialog boxes both provide information and ask for input. You provide some of the input by selecting items on the screen. To select an item using the keyboard, highlight it by pressing Tab or the arrow keys, then press Enter. To turn a checkbox on or off, highlight it and then press the Space Bar. Use Backspace and Del to erase characters that you type.

To select an item using the mouse, position the cursor over the item, and click with either button. To select or deselect drives, directories, and files to back up or restore, right-click on your selection.

267

Installing the Norton Backup

To begin installation, you need the Norton Backup Diskettes (two 5¼" or one 3½"). Installation is an eight-step process, as shown on the initial Norton Backup Installation screen in Figure 12.1. The final step begins program configuration, which is explained in the next section. During installation you are asked to make certain decisions.

▶ Which floppy disk drive you are installing the Norton Backup from. This will be A: or B:.

▶ Where the Norton Backup will be installed. This will be your hard drive, usually C:, in a directory called NBACKUP that the program creates. If your hard disk contains more than one drive, you can specify a different drive (for example, D:). You can also give the directory a different name, as long as it is no more than eight characters long.

▶ Whether or not you want to save or write over an existing version of the Norton Backup, if you already have the program on your hard disk.

▶ Whether or not you want the Norton Backup to revise the
PATH command in your AUTOEXEC.BAT file so that you can
run the Norton Backup from any directory. This is a good idea,
because it saves you the trouble of changing to the NBACKUP
directory before running the program.

▶ Whether or not you want the program to change your
CONFIG.SYS file to set the BUFFERS parameter at 30. This
allows you to run the Norton Backup more efficiently.

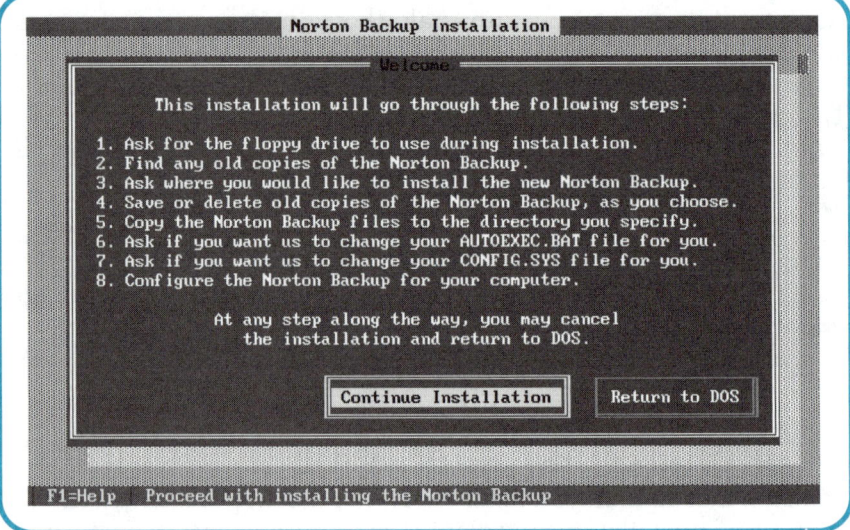

268

*Figure 12.1   The initial Norton Backup Installation screen
shows the eight steps you need to follow.*

At any time during installation, you can stop the process and
return to the DOS prompt by selecting Return to DOS on the
Installation screen. You can also skip certain steps, such as changing
the AUTOEXEC.BAT and CONFIG.SYS files or running the program
configuration. If you are installing from 5¼" diskettes, you will be
prompted to insert Diskette 2 during the file copy operation.

 The Norton Backup Installation

1. Insert the Norton Backup Disk-   The A> or B> prompt
   ette 1 in A: or B:. Change to   appears.
   that drive by typing
   A: or B: and pressing Enter.

2. Type **Install**, and press Enter.

   The copyright screen appears followed by the initial Norton Backup Installation screen in Figure 12.1.

3. Select Continue Installation.

   A dialog box asks you which drive contains the Norton Backup.

4. Select the drive that contains Backup Diskette 1 (A: or B:).

   The program searches for existing Norton Backup files, then asks for the drive and directory on which the program will be installed. C:\NBACKUP is the default.

5. Type in a new drive and/or directory name if you do not want the default. Skip this step if the default is okay.

   The new names replace the default.

6. Select Accept Directory.

   If the program already exists on disk, you may be asked if you want to save or write over the old program. Otherwise, the Copy Files dialog box appears.

269

7. Select Copy to begin copying program files. Repeat this step for Diskette 2 if prompted to do so.

   The AUTOEXEC.BAT dialog box appears when all files are copied.

8. Select OK on the AUTOEXEC.BAT and CONFIG.SYS dialog boxes.

   The Configuration dialog box appears.

9. Select Configure at the Configure Now prompt to proceed with program configuration (described in the next section).

□

Configuring the Norton Backup for Your System

The Norton Backup Configuration screen shown in Figure 12.2 appears automatically when you select OK at the Configure Now prompt at the end of installation. You can also reconfigure your system at any time by selecting Configure from the Norton Backup main menu, displayed when you start the program.

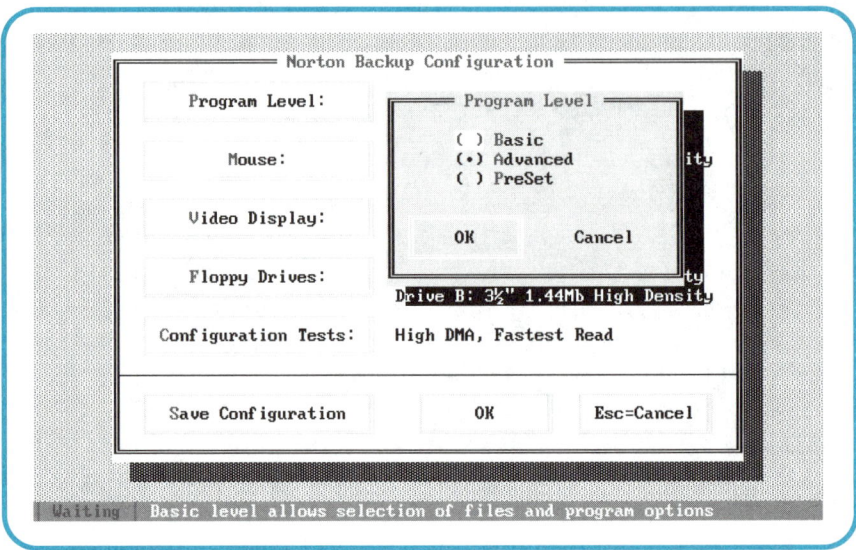

Figure 12.2   The Norton Backup Configuration screen shows setup options. The Program Level: dialog box is selected automatically.

The Norton Backup Configuration screen shows several setup parameters for which you will choose options. These include:

Program Level	Basic, Advanced, or PreSet
Mouse	Right- or left-handed and degree of sensitivity
Video Display	Type and resolution of your monitor
Floppy Drives	Drives available on your computer
Configuration Tests	Diagnostic tests of your computer and the program

Program Level Settings

The default program level is Advanced. Change the setting to Basic until you become more experienced with the Norton Backup. It is easy to change the setting later if you desire.

Mouse Settings

The Mouse settings let you configure the mouse for ease of use. The Mouse Button setting lets you choose between Left-Handed or Right-Handed operation. Instructions in this book are based on the Right-Handed option; the Left-Handed option reverses mouse instructions.

The Sensitivity setting determines the distance that the cursor moves across the screen when you move the mouse. It can be set to Low, Medium, or High, with Low producing the least amount of screen movement. Medium is the default.

The Double Click setting determines how rapidly one click must follow another to be recognized as a double-click. Slow allows a longer interval; the default is Medium. The Acceleration setting determines the acceleration of mouse movement and can be set to None, Medium, or Fast. The default is None.

Video Display Configuration Settings

271

The Video Display configuration settings are set automatically to match your monitor, but they can be changed if necessary. Accept the default settings unless you are sure that they are incorrect. Turn on the Reduced Display Speed option if you have an older CGA monitor that is subject to "snow." Turn off the Expanding Dialog Windows option if you want dialog boxes to pop on the screen rather than appear more gradually.

Floppy Drives Configuration Settings

The Floppy Drives configuration settings are set to match your floppy disk drives. Check the settings, and change them if necessary.

Configuration Tests

The Configuration Tests are conducted automatically and require only that you (1) approve their continuation at various points by selecting OK from a dialog box and (2) insert floppy diskettes when prompted by the Insert Diskette message within flashing brackets. The diskettes do not need to be formatted, but they do need to match the floppy disk drive configuration (size and density) set up earlier. When the tests are complete, you are shown the configuration settings; approve them by selecting Accept Settings.

Caution: The first Configuration Test, the Direct Memory Access (DMA) test, checks your computer's DMA chip to make sure the Norton Backup uses the chip's optimum speed. Some DMA chips may fail the test and cause the computer to "freeze," particularly if you are running a version of the Norton Backup prior to Version 1.1. If this occurs, simply turn your computer off and on again, then restart the program by typing **nbackup** at the DOS prompt. Select the following options in order on the next three screens: `Configure`, `Configuration Tests`, and `Confidence Test`. You can then complete configuration.

The Initial Norton Backup Configuration

272

1. From the initial Norton Backup Configuration screen, select the program level you want, then select `OK`.

   The Mouse Configuration dialog box appears.

2. Select Mouse Button, Sensitivity, Double Click, and Acceleration options. Then select `OK`.

   The Video Configuration dialog box appears.

3. Check the Color Palette and Screen Lines options and change if necessary. Turn checkboxes for Reduced Display Speed and Expanding Dialog Windows on or off as desired. Select `OK`.

   The Floppy Drive Configuration dialog box appears, with the Diskette Change Line Text box over it.

4. Follow the instructions and select `Start Test`.

5. Check that Floppy Drive settings match your floppy disk drive specifications, and change them if neccessary. Select `OK` when done.

   The first Configuration Test screen appears. The program can read your system configuration, so the Floppy Drive settings should normally not need to be changed.

6. Follow the screen prompts to complete all tests. Insert diskettes when flashing brackets and message prompts you to Insert diskette # 1 and Insert Disk # 2. You will need to insert the diskettes again during test verification.

The Configuration Tests dialog box appears showing the final system settings determined by the tests.

7. Select Accept Settings.

The Save Configuration dialog box appears.

8. Select Save.

A dialog box asks you to personalize your copy of the program.

9. Complete the registration by typing in your name and your company name (if appropraite). Then select OK.

The screen shows a dialog box stating that the Norton backup has been installed.

10. Select OK from the dialog box.

You are returned to the DOS prompt. □

273

Running the Norton Backup

If you allowed the program to alter your AUTOEXEC.BAT file during installation, you can start the Norton Backup from any directory on your hard disk. For example, you can start the program from any of the following prompts:

```
C:\>
C:\WORDS>
C:\NBACKUP>
```

To start the program, simply type

```
nbackup
```

This takes you to the Norton Backup main menu, shown in Figure 12.3. From this menu you can choose one of four boxes: Backup, Restore, Configure, or Quit. Backup and Restore begin immediately upon selecting them, at the level you selected during configuration. Choosing Configure takes you to the main Configuration screen, which allows you to reconfigure the program (to change the program level or any other system settings). Selecting Quit exits the Norton Backup and returns you to the DOS prompt.

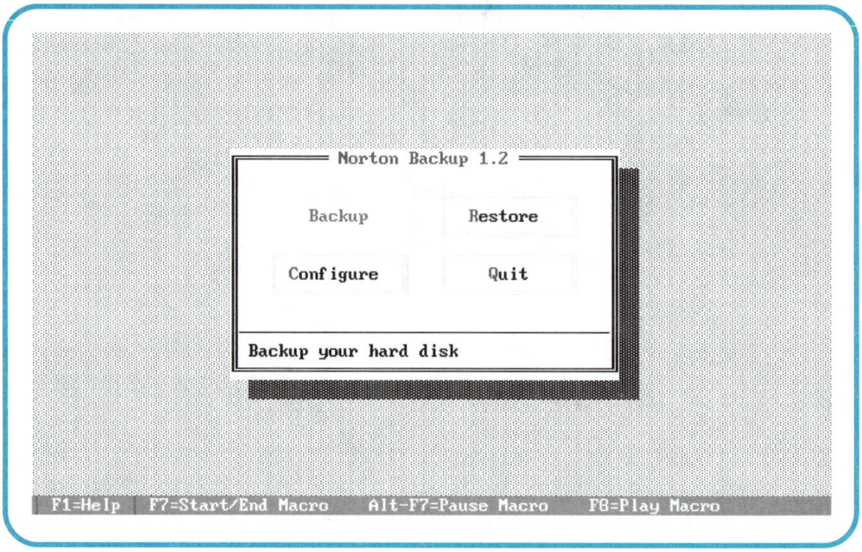

274

Figure 12.3   Use the Norton Backup main menu to start the backup or restore process, to change configuration options, or to exit the Norton Backup.

Getting Help When You Need It

Although the Norton Backup is easy to use, you may occasionally need help with a particular operation or desire more information on available options. This help is available at any time from within the program through the On-Line Help system. To enter this system, press F1 or click on the F1=Help command in the lower left corner of the screen. A screen similar to the one shown in Figure 12.4 appears.

The help screen shows information related to the operation that you were performing when you entered the Help system. You can scroll the screen to read additional information using the cursor control keys or the mouse scroll bar.

Some words or phrases on the screen may be highlighted or displayed in a different color. These phrases are linked to additional information on specific topics, which you can also select. Use Tab to highlight a linked phrase, then press Enter to display the information—or right-click on the phrase with the mouse.

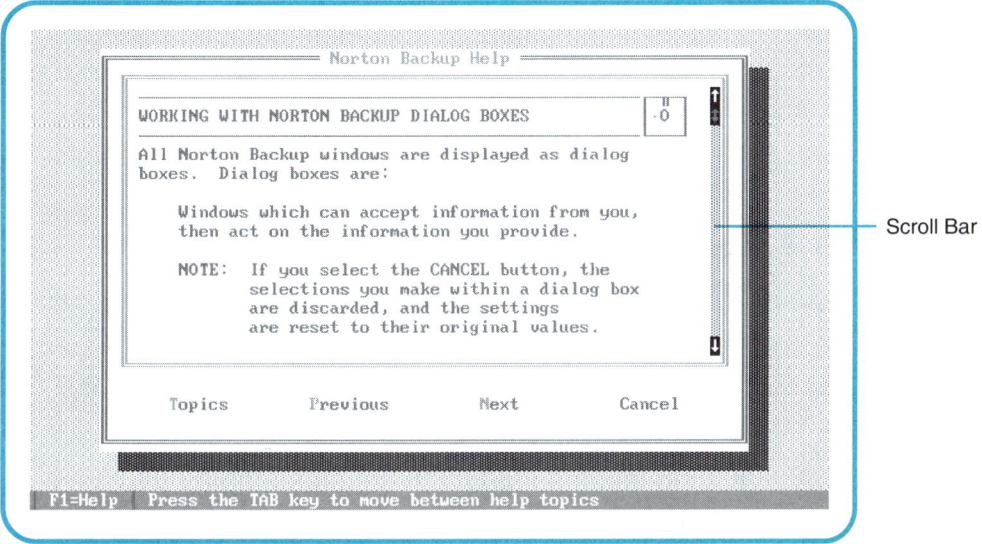

Scroll Bar

*Figure 12.4   The Norton Backup Help screen displays informa-
tion on the last operation you were performing.*

At the bottom of the screen is a menu of additional Help
options:

Topics displays an index of all Help topics. Select a topic
from the list to see more detailed information on it.

Previous shows the last help screen viewed. If you are at the
initial help screen, this option is not available.

Next shows the next available help screen on the topic
selected.

Cancel takes you out of the On-Line Help system and returns
you to the screen from which you left.

If an option is not available, the highlight will skip over it when you
attempt to select it.

Exiting the Program

When you are finished using the Norton Backup, exit the program by
selecting Quit from the main menu (Figure 12.3). This returns you to the
DOS prompt from which you started the program.

If you select the Quit After Backup (or Quit After Restore) option at the start of either operation, the program quits automatically when the operation is complete and returns you to the DOS prompt. These options are explained later in the chapter.

The Basic Backup

The Basic backup gives you considerable power and a number of options for protecting your hard disk files. Even though it is not as fully featured as the Advanced backup, it gives you as much control as you are likely to need in the beginning.

The following sections take you through the initial setup, options, and execution of a Basic backup. The steps described here are essentially the same for the Advanced backup, so they are not repeated in the Advanced backup section. The quick steps for the Basic backup take you through the process in an abbreviated form. More detail on each step is provided in the sections that follow.

 Running the Basic Backup

1. Select Backup from the main menu.

   The Norton Basic Backup screen appears, as shown in Figure 12.5.

2. If you want to back up a different drive than the one currently displayed, select the new drive(s) in the Backup From: box.

   ALL files appears next to the elected files.

3. If you want to change the floppy disk drive that the backup files will be copied to, select the Backup To: box. Choose the drive you want in the window that appears, then select OK.

   The Norton Basic Backup screen reappears with the new floppy disk drive shown.

4. If you want to specify a different type of backup than the one shown, select the Backup Type: box. Choose the desired type in the window that appears, then select OK.

The Norton Basic Backup screen reappears with the new backup type shown.

5. Select Options to check or change the Basic options.

The Backup Options window appears.

6. Select the desired options. An X in the checkbox indicates that the option is selected. is selected. When all desired options are checked, select OK.

This sets your options, and the Norton Basic Backup screen reappears.

7. If you want to check or change which files are set to be backed up, choose the Select Files box. Otherwise, skip to Step 9.

The Backup Files screen appears. If you are running Backup for the first time,all files in all directories in the selected drive are marked for backup. Otherwise, the files last selected for backup are marked.

277

8. Select (or deselect) the directories and files to be backed up. Select Display to check and change any file display options.When all files are selected, select OK.

The Norton Basic Backup screen reappears.

9. Select Start Backup.

The Norton Backup screen appears, and the backup begins.

10. Watch in the lower left Diskette Progress box, and replace and replace diskettes as prompted.

When the backup is complete, you are returned automaticallyto the DOS prompt (if the Quit after Backup option is set to On), or a Backup is complete prompt is displayed.

11. Select OK at the prompt to complete the backup.

You are returned to the main menu. ☐

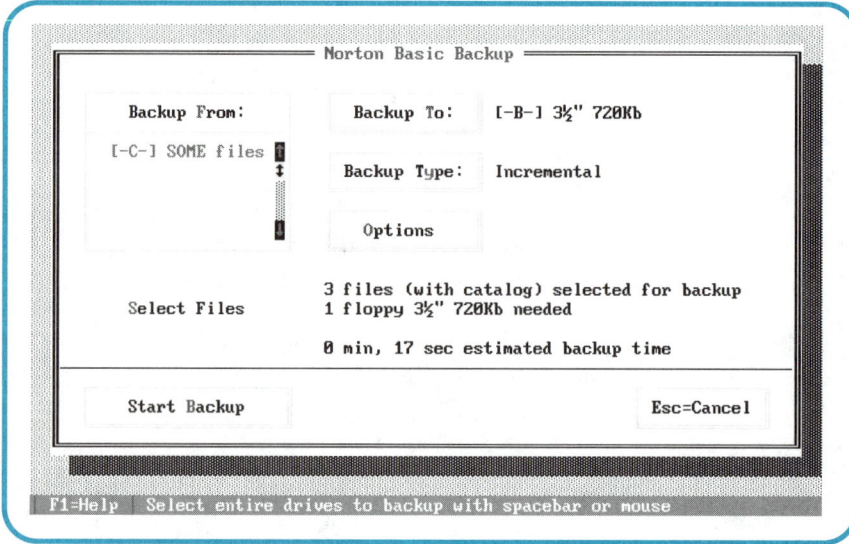

Figure 12.5   The Norton Basic Backup screen prompts you for backup information and options.

Selecting the Backup Drives

You may back up files from one or more hard drives, but the drives must contain files before you can select them. The Backup From: box on the Norton Basic Backup screen shows all drives available on your hard disk. The current drive (whether selected or not) is marked with an arrow. When you choose Select Files, the contents of the current drive are displayed.

The drive that you back up to is the target drive onto which you will save the backed up files. Next to the Backup To: box is the default floppy disk drive selected by the program. If you want to change this drive, select the `Backup To:` box, then select a different drive from the list displayed.

> **Caution**: Although you can specify a hard disk drive to back up to, your resulting backup files will do you little good in the event of a total hard disk disaster. It is better to back up your files onto floppy diskettes.

Selecting the Backup Type

There are five types of backups from which you can choose:

- ▶ Full backup
- ▶ Incremental backup
- ▶ Differential backup
- ▶ Full Copy
- ▶ Incremental Copy

To understand the differences among these types, you must know how files are marked, or *flagged*. When a file is created or changed (worked with in any way), it is marked with one type of flag. When a file is backed up, it is marked with another type of flag. In this way, the program is always able to tell which files have been backed up and which files have been changed since they were backed up.

279

Full Backup

A full backup backs up all files that you select and flags them as backed up. When you first back up your hard disk, you should perform a full backup. After that, you may need to do a full backup only once a week or once a month, depending on how often you use your computer.

Incremental Backup

An incremental backup backs up only selected files that are marked as created or changed since your last full backup. After it backs up these files, it updates their backup flags. In subsequent backups, if these files have not been changed, they are not backed up. However, the next time you work with the files, they are again marked as changed and included in your next backup. Use this type of backup if you work with many different files. Use different diskettes for each incremental backup, however, unless you don't mind losing the older versions of the backed up files.

Differential Backup

A differential backup backs up all selected files that you have worked with since your last full or incremental backup. Unlike an incremental backup, it does not flag the files as backed up. As a result, the files are backed up again on your next backup, even if they haven't been changed. Use this type of backup if you work with the same few files every day and want a continuously updated set of backup files.

Full Copy

This type of backup backs up all selected files, regardless of whether they have been changed or not. It does not flag the backed up files, so it does not affect full or incremental backups that you have regularly scheduled. Use this type of backup when you want to transfer files from one location to another.

> **Caution:** Do not confuse a Full Copy backup with the DOS COPY command. With COPY, files on the floppy are ready to use; with Norton Backup, Full Copy, you must restore the files before you can use them.

280

Incremental Copy

An incremental copy is similar to a full copy, but it backs up only selected files that have changed since the last backup of any type and does not change the backed up flag on any files copied.

Selecting Backup Options

The options that you select in a Basic level backup determine the speed of your backup operation, the number of backup diskettes required, the accuracy of the backup, and other factors, all of which are explained in the following sections. These options, shown in Figure 12.6, can be set to On or Off only. After all options are set to your satisfaction, select OK to return to the Basic Backup screen.

> **Note:** Although some of the options you set affect the backup time and number of backup diskettes, their effect may not be reflected in the estimated backup time and number of diskettes shown on the Basic Backup screen.

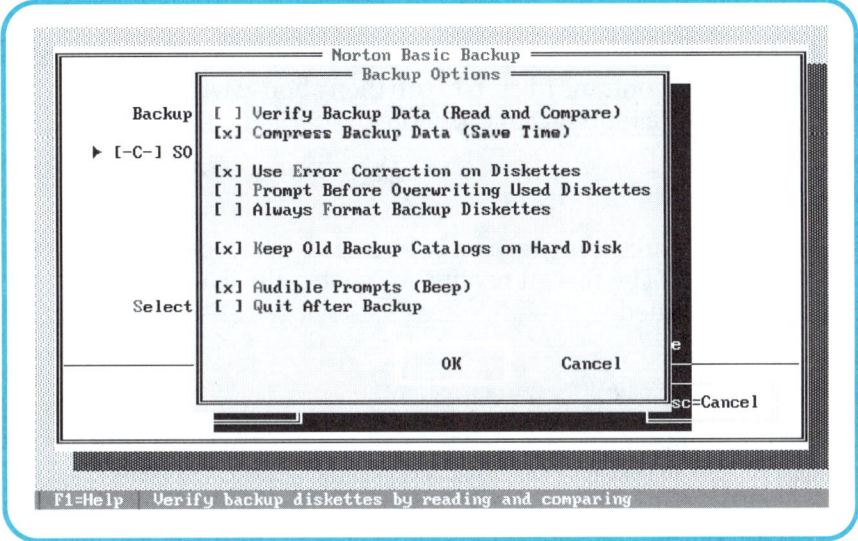

Figure 12.6   An X between the brackets indicates that an option is on.

Verify Backup Data (Read and Compare)

This option instructs the program to check the backed up data to make sure there are no errors in it and that it matches the original data. In a Basic backup, only the highest level of verification—Read and Compare—is available. This ensures an accurate data transfer; it also slows down the backup by as much as 50% when turned on.

Compress Backup Data (Save Time)

This option saves the data in a compressed format that requires fewer backup diskettes. There are higher levels of compression available in an Advanced backup, which save even more diskette space, but they slow down the backup process more.

Use Error Correction on Diskettes

The Norton Backup makes available a special error correction system that increases the possibility of recovering data from damaged diskettes. It is best to leave this option on.

Prompt Before Overwriting Used Diskettes

With this option on, the Norton Backup alerts you if your backup diskette already contains files. You can then choose whether or not you want to overwrite (and erase) those files.

Always Format Backup Diskettes

This option instructs the program to format all backup diskettes before writing to them. The format occurs automatically, even if the diskette is already formatted.

Keep Old Backup Catalogs on Hard Disk

A backup catalog provides an index of your backed up files and is necessary for the restore operation. Normally, when you perform a full backup, all interim catalogs since the prior full backup are deleted. With this option on, catalogs from previous backups are saved, so you can restore files from earlier backups. However, these catalogs do occupy space on your hard disk.

Audible Prompts (Beep)

This option adds a beep to prompts during the backup. This is a useful option if you don't want to sit and watch the screen during your entire backup.

Quit After Backup

With this option on, the program automatically returns you to the DOS prompt rather than the program main menu when the backup operation is finished.

Selecting Files To Back Up

You can back up all files in all directories on your hard disk, or you can back up only selected files in selected directories. The Select Backup Files screen, shown in Figure 12.7, is where you make your selections. The directories are listed on the left side of the screen; the files in the highlighted directory are listed on the right side of the screen. An arrow to the left of a directory means that all files in it are selected for backup. A smaller double arrow means that some files in the directory are selected for backup. A checkmark next to a file name means that the file is selected for backup.

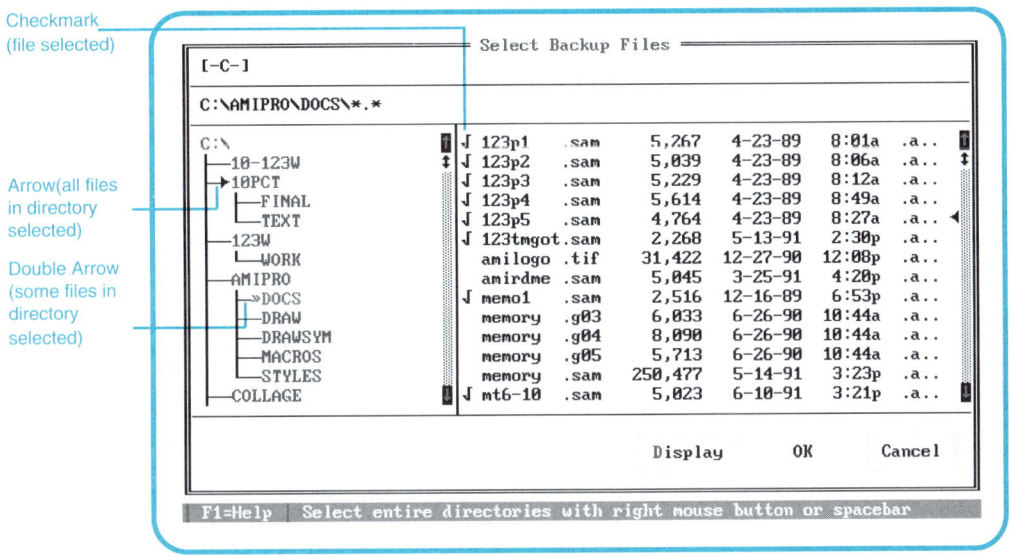

Checkmark (file selected)

Arrow(all files in directory selected)

Double Arrow (some files in directory selected)

√	123p1	.sam	5,267	4-23-89	8:01a	.a..
√	123p2	.sam	5,039	4-23-89	8:06a	.a..
√	123p3	.sam	5,229	4-23-89	8:12a	.a..
√	123p4	.sam	5,614	4-23-89	8:49a	.a..
√	123p5	.sam	4,764	4-23-89	8:27a	.a..
√	123tmgot	.sam	2,268	5-13-91	2:30p	.a..
	amilogo	.tif	31,422	12-27-90	12:08p	.a..
	amirdme	.sam	5,045	3-25-91	4:20p	.a..
√	memo1	.sam	2,516	12-16-89	6:53p	.a..
	memory	.g03	6,033	6-26-90	10:44a	.a..
	memory	.g04	8,090	6-26-90	10:44a	.a..
	memory	.g05	5,713	6-26-90	10:44a	.a..
	memory	.sam	250,477	5-14-91	3:23p	.a..
√	mt6-10	.sam	5,023	6-10-91	3:21p	.a..

Select Backup Files

[-C-]

C:\AMIPRO\DOCS*.*

C:\
├─10-123W
├▶10PCT
│ ├─FINAL
│ └─TEXT
├─123W
│ └─WORK
├─AMIPRO
│ ├▶DOCS
│ ├─DRAW
│ ├─DRAWSYM
│ ├─MACROS
│ └─STYLES
└─COLLAGE

Display   OK   Cancel

F1=Help   Select entire directories with right mouse button or spacebar

Figure 12.7   The Select Backup Files screen shows the selection status of all directories and of the files in the highlighted directory.

283

When you have selected all the files to include in the backup, select OK from the options menu. If you change your mind about your file selections, select Cancel to return to the Norton Basic Backup screen without changing your original file selections.

The Display Option

This option lets you choose the way in which files are sorted and displayed on the Select Backup Files screen. It also lets you display information about the size and number of selected files. Choosing this option brings up the Display dialog box, shown in Figure 12.8.

The first display option, Sort Files By:, lets you arrange the displayed files by file name, file extension, size, date, or attribute (hidden, archived, and so on). For example, if you arrange files by name, they are sorted alphabetically. If you arrange them by size, they are sorted with the largest files first. Arranging by date sorts files with the most recently created files first.

The File Filter: option lets you limit the range of files that are shown in the file list. The default shown in Figure 12.8 is *.*, which means that all files in the directory are displayed. If I changed this default to *.COM, then only files with the COM extension would be displayed. If I changed it to ANSI.*, then only files with the file name ANSI and any extension would be displayed.

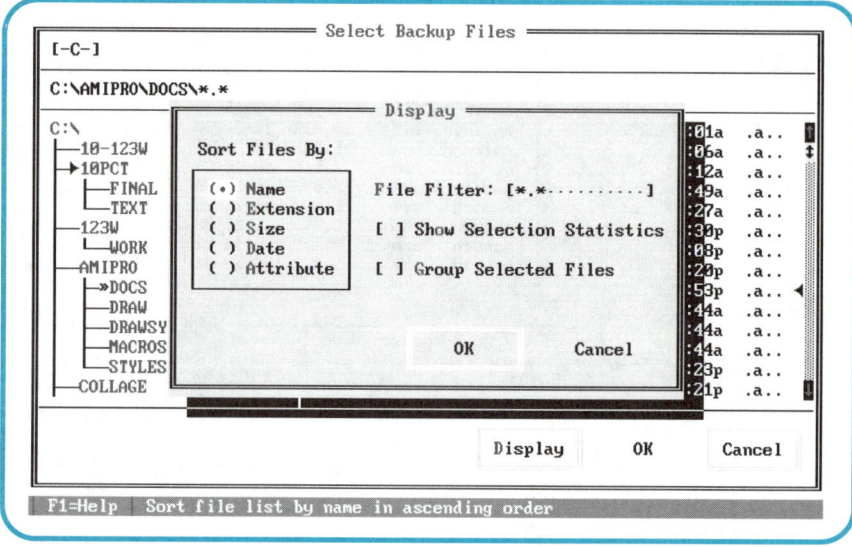

Figure 12.8 *The Display dialog box lets you arrange selected files for easier viewing.*

 **Note**: Any files selected before you set a file filter remain selected, even though they are not displayed on the file list.

The Show Selection Statistics option, when on, displays information on the total size of all files on your hard disk, total number of files on your hard disk, total size of all selected files, and total number of selected files.

Turning the Group Selected Files option on causes all selected files in a directory to be grouped together at the start of the file list, followed by unselected files.

> **Note:** All of the backup selections you make are stored automatically in a *setup file*. In a Basic backup, this file is named DEFAULT.SET. This file loads automatically and sets the default settings for all backups and restores until you change the settings again. In Advanced backups, you can save setup files under other names.

Starting the Basic Backup

When you are ready to begin the backup operation, select Start Backup from the Norton Basic Backup screen (Figure 12.5). The backup progress screen shown in Figure 12.9 appears.

Once the backup begins, you simply insert floppy diskettes when prompted in the Diskette Progress block. If the Always Format Backup Diskettes option is on, the diskettes do not have to be formatted. An estimate of the number of diskettes you will need is shown in the lower right window of the screen. This estimate is based on the last backup you performed. If you have changed the compression option since your last backup, you may need more or fewer diskettes than the estimate shows.

After you insert each diskette, a bar moves across the bracketed area next to the drive letter in the Diskette Progress area, tracking the actual transfer of data until the diskette is full. If the diskettes you insert are not blank and the Prompt Before Overwrite option is on, you will be asked if you want to overwrite the files on the diskette. Select Overwrite if you want to continue the backup with that diskette. Otherwise, insert a different diskette, and select Retry.

285

> **Note:** During backup, the disk drive light on your computer always remains on, even while you are removing and inserting diskettes. This is normal and not a cause for alarm.

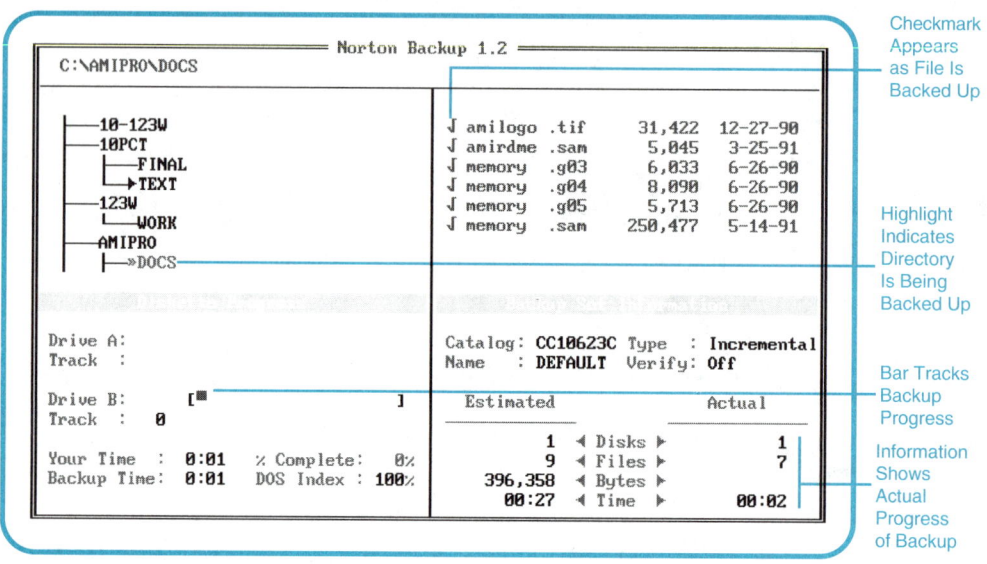

Checkmark Appears as File Is Backed Up

Highlight Indicates Directory Is Being Backed Up

Bar Tracks Backup Progress

Information Shows Actual Progress of Backup

286

Figure 12.9   The backup progress screen shows the status of your backup operation.

Other information shown on the screen during backup includes:

Your Time	The time it takes you to swap diskettes
Backup Time	The computer's time backing up files
% Complete	How much of the backup is complete (useful for estimating how many more diskettes you may need)
DOS Index	An indicator of the program's efficiency
Catalog	The name under which the backup catalog (index) will be stored (include this name on each backup diskette label)
Type	The backup type you selected
Name	The setup file name (DEFAULT.SET in a Basic backup)
Verify	Data Verification option selected (on or off)
Disks	Estimated versus actual number of diskettes used
Files	Estimated versus actual number of files backed up

Bytes	Estimated versus actual bytes of data backed up
Time	Estimated versus actual total backup time

After you remove each full backup diskette, label it with the date, backup diskette number, and catalog name shown on the screen. You can cancel the backup operation at any time by pressing Esc. When backup is complete, a dialog box informs you. Select OK from this box to exit the backup progress screen and return to the main menu.

Advanced Backup

An Advanced backup is performed in essentially the same way as a Basic backup. The difference between the two is in the options available. One of these options, Setup File, is discussed later in this chapter because it relates specifically to the PreSet level backup and restore.

287

To perform an Advanced backup, you must first set the level on the Configuration screen. Select Configure from the main menu. From the Configuration screen, select Program Level then Advanced. When the Configuration screen reappears, select Save Configuration then Save. When you return to the main menu, select Backup. The Norton Advanced Backup screen shown in Figure 12.10 appears.

Select the drive to backup from, the drive to backup to, and the backup type as described in the Basic backup. The Advanced Backup Options and Select Backup Files screens are described in the following sections.

Advanced Backup Options

Many of the Advanced backup options are similar to the Basic options. However, instead of being limited to turning the option on or off, you have a number of choices for each option. The advanced Backup Options screen, shown in Figure 12.11, contains five options that you can set and five options that you can turn on or off. Four of the five on/off options are the same as the corresponding Basic backup options.

They are

- ▶ Always Format Diskettes
- ▶ Use Error Correction
- ▶ Keep Old Backup Catalogs
- ▶ Quit After Backup

The remaining on/off option, Proprietary Diskette Format, sets up the program to use a special diskette format that lets the backup run faster and store more data on each diskette.

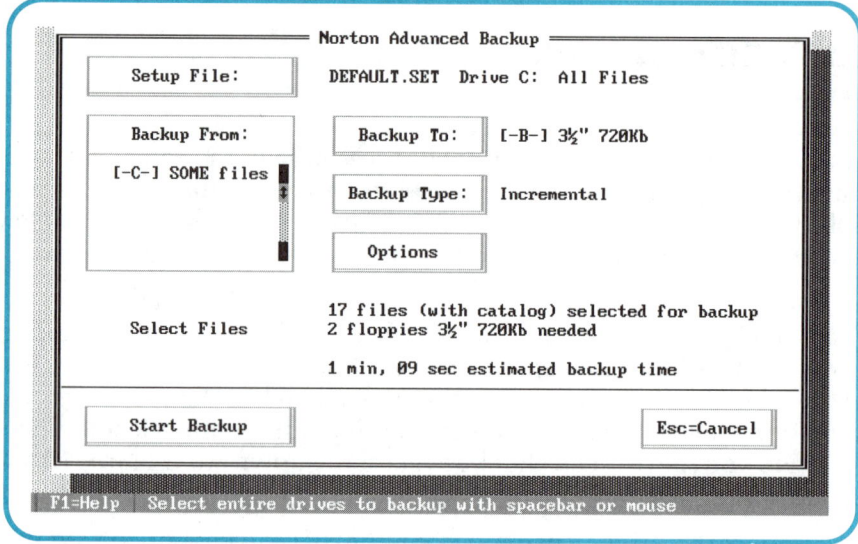

Figure 12.10 The Norton Advanced Backup screen is similar to the Norton Basic Backup screen, but offers the Setup File: box.

Data Verification Option

Selecting this option brings up the Data Verification dialog box, containing four choices. Off results in the fastest backup, but there is no guarantee that the backup data will match the original data. Read Only reads the data on the backup diskette to make sure there were no recording errors. Sample Only reads every eighth track on the backup diskette, checks it for recording errors, and compares it to the original data. Read and Compare reads all data on the backup diskette, checks it for recording errors, and compares it to the original data. This slows down the backup process by the greatest amount but ensures that your backup is completely accurate.

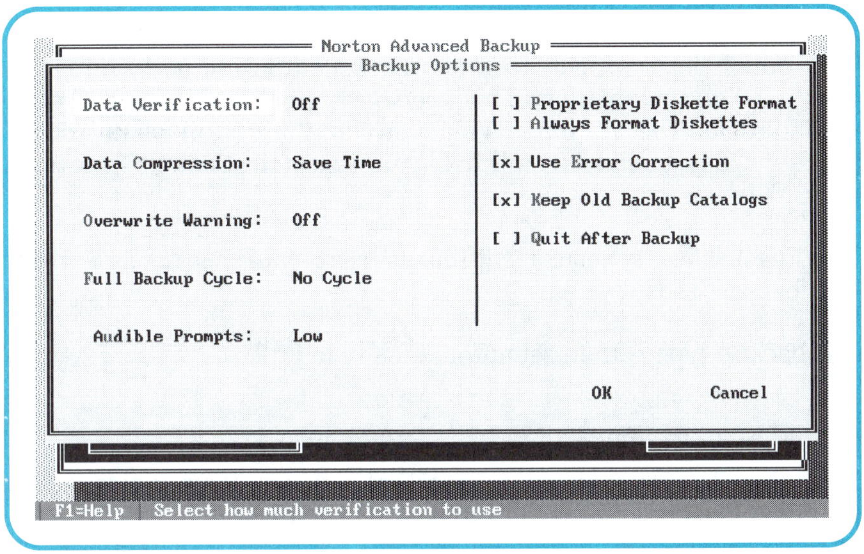

```
┌─────────────────── Norton Advanced Backup ───────────────────┐
│                      Backup Options                          │
│                                                              │
│  Data Verification:   Off          [ ] Proprietary Diskette Format │
│                                    [ ] Always Format Diskettes     │
│                                                              │
│  Data Compression:    Save Time    [x] Use Error Correction  │
│                                                              │
│                                    [x] Keep Old Backup Catalogs │
│  Overwrite Warning:   Off                                    │
│                                    [ ] Quit After Backup     │
│                                                              │
│  Full Backup Cycle:   No Cycle                               │
│                                                              │
│  Audible Prompts:     Low                                    │
│                                                              │
│                                        OK          Cancel    │
│                                                              │
└──────────────────────────────────────────────────────────────┘
 F1=Help   Select how much verification to use
```

Figure 12.11   The advanced Backup Options screen offers additional backup options.

Data Compression Option

There are four Data Compression choices. The choice you make affects both the speed of the backup (and restore) and the number of backup diskettes required. Off gives you the fastest backup speed, but it uses the greatest number of diskettes. Save Time gives some degree of compression and slows down the backup process a little. Save Disks (Low) sets the program for a higher degree of compression; consequently, it uses fewer diskettes and takes more time. Save Disks (High) gives maximum compression, uses the fewest diskettes, and takes the most time.

Overwrite Warning Option

This option lets you choose whether you want the program to prompt you before overwriting (and erasing) existing files on used backup diskettes. Your choices are Off (no prompt), Regular DOS Diskettes (prompts before overwriting any DOS-formatted diskette containing data), Norton Backup Diskettes (prompts only if diskettes contain previous backup data), and Any Used Diskette (prompts before overwriting any diskette containing any data). If you regularly reuse backup diskettes, you may want to choose Off, as the prompts slow down the backup process.

Full Backup Cycle Option

This option lets you set up a regular schedule for performing full backups. You set the interval between backups to any number of days, with the default set at 7 days. When you start the Norton Backup on the scheduled day, you see the following message if the Backup Type is not set to Full:

```
The backup schedule indicates that you should do a full
backup today.
```

The backup type is then set automatically to Full.

Audible Prompts Option

This option lets you set the volume of the beep that accompanies backup prompts. The choices are Off (no beep), Low, and High.

Advanced File Selection

File selection in an Advanced level backup is the same as in the Basic level backup, with the addition of three options, shown in Figure 12.12.

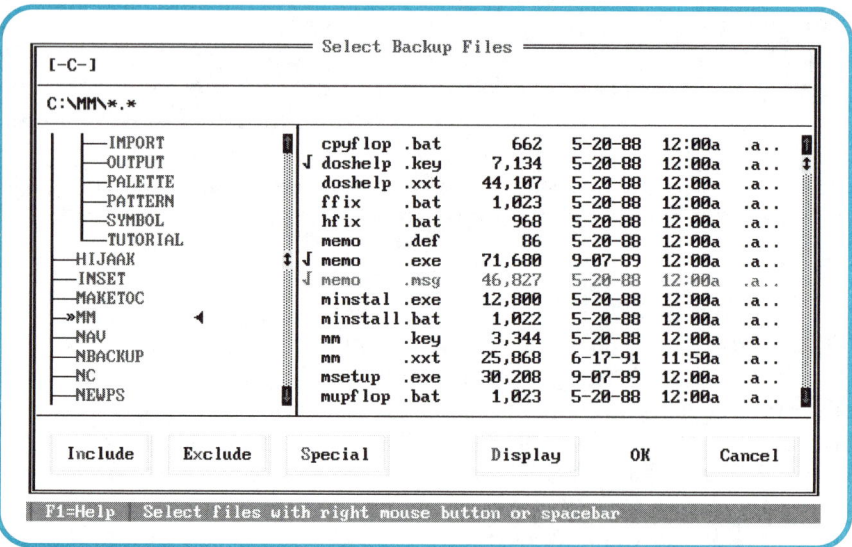

Figure 12.12 The Advanced level Select Backup Files screen offers additional selection options.

The Include, Exclude, and Special options give you alternate ways of selecting files to back up, other than marking them individually on the file list. Include lets you specify files to include in the backup. Exclude lets you specify files to exclude from the backup. And Special lets you further specify files to exclude by date, type, or name. Files excluded on the Special screen are marked on the File Selection screen with a dot instead of a checkmark and cannot be selected for backup.

For example, assume that you store all files for a particular client in a directory called \CLIENT on your C: drive. Some files are created in Word and have a DOC or BAK extension. Other files are spreadsheet files with a .WK1 extension. You want to back up all files in this directory except the BAK files and two highly sensitive budget files (call them BUDGET1.WK1 and BUDGET2.WK1). The following steps show how you would make this file selection.

1. From the File Selection screen, select Include.
2. In the Path box type C:\CLIENT. In the File box, type *.*, then select OK.
3. From the Select Files screen, select Exclude.
4. Type C:\CLIENT in the Path box and *.BAK in the File box. Select OK again.
5. From the Select Files screen, select Special.
6. In the Special Selections box, select Copy Protected Files. In the next dialog box, type in the two file names that you want to exclude: (C:\CLIENT\BUDGET1.WK1 and C:\CLIENT\BUDGET2.WK1).
7. Finally, select OK twice.

291

If you have more than one directory to include or exclude, you can select the Include or Exclude box, then Edit Include\Exclude List, then Edit, and type in the drives, directories, and file names on the resulting screen.

The Basic Restore

The Restore operation is the means by which you can retrieve any or all of the files you back up. Hopefully, you will never experience the sort of hard disk disaster that requires restoration of all backed up files. A more likely scenario is that you will accidentally overwrite an important file with a newer version, then discover that you need information from the older file. With Restore, you can easily retrieve that one important file.

The following quick steps give you an overview of the Restore operation. Each step, option, and concept is then explained in greater detail in the sections that follow.

 Running the Basic Level Restore

1. Select **Restore** from the main menu.

The Norton Basic Restore screen appears, as shown in Figure 12.13.

2. Select the drive to **Restore From**. The default is the floppy disk drive to which you copied your files during your last backup.

3. Select the **Catalog:** box from the Norton Basic Restore screen.

The Catalog screen appears.

4. Select the catalog name that matches the backup you wish to restore. Select any other catalog options, and then select **Load**.

The Norton Basic Restore screen returns (Figure 12.13).

5. Select **O**ptions to check or change the Basic Restore options.

The Basic Restore Options screen appears, with a check-box beside each option.

6. Turn options on or off, then select **OK**.

The Norton Basic Restore screen returns.

7. Select the **Select Files** box.

The Select Restore Files screen appears.

8. Select the directories and files to restore. Select **Display** to check or change file display options. Select **Show** Versions to display multiple versions of a file if you have selected a master catalog to restore. When you have marked all files to be restored, select **OK**.

The Norton Basic Restore screen returns, showing the total number of files selected for the Restore operation.

9. Select Start Restore.

The Alert screen appears. A prompt indicates which backup diskette to insert.

10. Insert the diskette(s) when prompted.

The program automatically restores your selected backup files and prompts you when the restore process is complete.

11. Select OK.

The program returns you either to the main menu or to the DOS prompt, depending on the setup option you chose. ☐

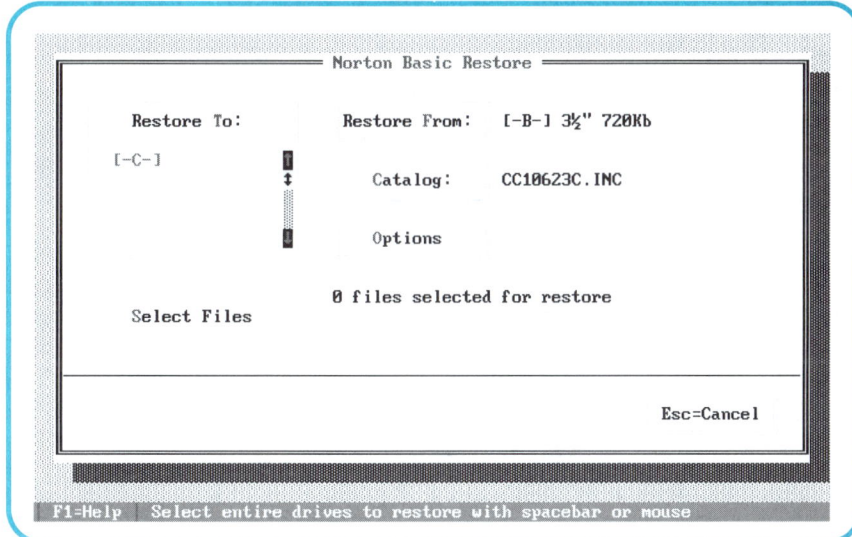

Figure 12.13   The Norton Basic Restore screen assumes that you want to restore files to the drive from which they were backed up.

Selecting the Drives to Restore To and From

You do not have to choose a drive to restore to; the program knows which drive you last backed up from and automatically restores to that drive. (If you want to restore to a different drive than the one you backed up from, you must perform an Advanced restore.)

Likewise, the program sets the Restore From drive as the drive you last backed up to. You can change the Restore From drive—if, for example, you wish to restore an earlier backup that was made on a different drive than your most recent backup. Select Restore From: on the Basic Restore screen. This gives you a list of all drives on your system. Select the desired drive, then select OK.

What Is a Catalog?

A catalog is a list of the files that are included in a particular backup, with information about each file's location on the backup diskette(s). The information contained in a backup catalog is critical to the successful restoration of backed up files. For this reason, a catalog file is created automatically during each backup and stored in two locations: on the hard disk (in the directory containing the Norton Backup) and on the last backup diskette. Thus, if your hard disk is ever erased completely, the backup catalog can still be retrieved from the backup diskettes themselves.

There are two types of catalogs: the *individual catalog* for a particular backup and a *master catalog*. As a rule, you use an individual catalog to restore backup files.

Catalogs for individual backups each have distinctive names, but the names follow a format. Once you learn to read this format, you can tell much about a backup from its catalog name alone. Table 12.1 shows the elements in the sample catalog name CC10315A.INC.

Table 12.1   Elements in the Sample Catalog Name CC10315A.INC

Element	Description
C	First drive backed up
C	Last drive backed up
1	Last digit of backup year
03	Backup month
15	Backup day
A	Sequence of backup (A-Z). Indicates first backup of day, B would indicate second backup of day, and so on.
INC	Type of backup (.FUL = Full; .INC = Incremental; DIF = Differential; .CPY = Full or Incremental Copy)

The second type of catalog, the master catalog, contains all of the catalogs created with the same setup file since the last full backup. A master catalog name is the same as the name of the setup file used to create it, but it has a .CAT extension. So if you use the DEFAULT.SET setup file when you back up, the master catalog created has the name DEFAULT.CAT. If you perform many backups using the same file, the master catalog lets you see all of the individual catalogs for the different backups (and view the files they contain) to determine which catalog you need to use.

Selecting Catalog Files

When you choose the Restore operation, the program checks its own directory for catalog files and selects the most recently created catalog. You can choose a different catalog file by selecting Catalog on the Basic Restore screen. This brings up the Select Catalog dialog box shown in Figure 12.14.

295

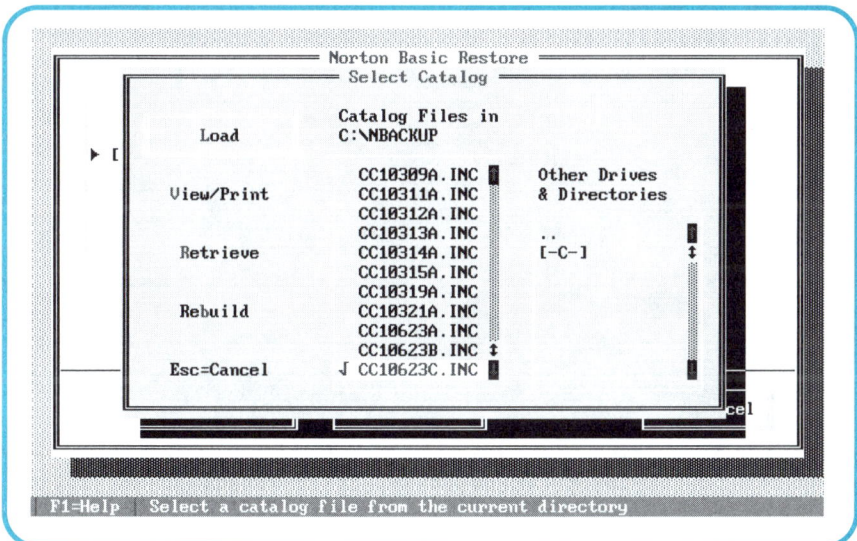

Figure 12.14   The Select Catalog dialog box includes several options.

On the right side of the screen is a list of available drives with the current drive highlighted. In the center of the screen is a list of catalogs available on the highlighted drive. Select a different drive or catalog by highlighting your choice and pressing Enter (or click on your choice with the right mouse button).

The screen also makes available four options. Two of them—Retrieve and Rebuild—are explained in the next section. Load does what its name implies: loads the selected catalog and returns you to the Norton Basic Restore screen. If you change the catalog selection, you must load it before you can proceed with the Restore operation.

ViewPrint lets you preview the selected catalog, so you can see if it contains the file(s) you want to restore. It also lets you print the contents of a catalog, for a hard copy "index" of your backup. Selecting this option takes you to a screen similar to the Select Backup Files screen. The View Catalog screen, shown in Figure 12.15, shows all directories on the selected drive and all files backed up in the highlighted directory.

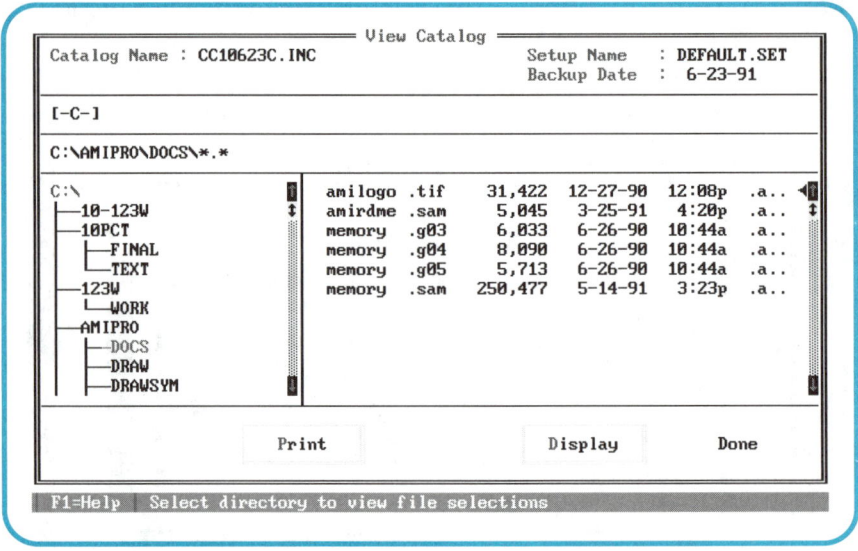

Figure 12.15   The View Catalog screen shows a list, or catalog, of directories on the drive.

The Display box at the bottom of the screen is identical in function to the Display box on the Select Files screen. Selecting the Print option takes you to the Printer dialog box. Here you select your printer port (LPT1 is the default), continuous feed or single sheet paper, the number of lines to print per page (60 is the default for $8^1/_2'' \times 11''$ paper), and if you want to print to a text file on disk instead of to your printer (enter a name for the text file in the brackets). When you have completed your printer setup, select Start Printing. When printing is complete, the program returns to the View Catalog screen.

The Show Versions option lets you display all versions of your files since your last full backup, if there are different versions of the files and if you have selected a master catalog for viewing. Each version of the file is differentiated by the date or time of its creation. On the Versions List, which appears when you select this feature, you can select which version of the file you want to restore.

Retrieving and Rebuilding a Catalog

If the program does not find the catalog file on your hard drive (if, for example, your entire hard disk has been erased), you can retrieve it from its second location—on the last of your backup diskettes. Select Retrieve from the Select Catalog dialog box. In the Retrieve Catalog dialog box, select the floppy disk drive for the backup diskettes, then insert the last backup diskette when prompted.

297

You can also use this option to select a different drive and directory on your hard disk from which to load a catalog. This is useful if your hard disk is undamaged but you have stored your catalog files in a separate directory.

If disaster has truly struck (your hard disk has been erased and the last backup diskette has been damaged), all is not lost. As long as some of your backup diskettes are readable, the program can rebuild at least a partial catalog file from special files that are stored on each backup diskette. Select Rebuild from the Select Catalog dialog box. On the Rebuild Catalog dialog box, select the floppy disk drive for your backup diskettes, and insert the backup diskettes when prompted.

If your last backup was to your hard disk and the hard disk itself is undamaged but the catalog file is gone, specify the drive and path containing the backup files on the Rebuild Catalog dialog box.

When a catalog has been retrieved or rebuilt, remember to Basic Restore screen.

Selecting Restore Options

When you select Options on the Norton Basic Restore screen, the Restore Options dialog box appears, as shown in Figure 12.16. This box contains seven options, which you can turn on or off.

▶ Verify Restore Data (Read and Compare) verifies that the data restored to your hard disk matches the data on the backup diskettes. As in the backup operation, verification slows down the restore process somewhat.

▶ Prompt Before Creating Directories informs you during the restore operation if the drive to which you are restoring does not contain a directory that you've selected to restore. You may then choose to Create Directory or Skip Directory.

▶ Prompt Before Creating Files similarly informs you if the drive to which you are restoring does not contain a file that you've selected to restore. You can choose whether you want to Restore the file anyway, Skip that file, or Cancel Restore.

▶ Prompt Before Overwriting Existing Files warns you when an existing file on your hard disk is about to be overwritten (erased) by a file that you've selected to restore. You can choose from Overwrite, Do Not Restore (keep the existing file), or Cancel Restore.

298

▶ Restore Empty Directories lets you restore directories that contain no files—for example, a \TEMP directory that is used for temporary files.

▶ Audible Prompts (Beep) accompanies each prompt during restore with a beep.

▶ Quit After Restore returns you to the DOS prompt, rather than to the Norton Backup main menu, when the restore is complete.

Selecting Files to Restore

You can select all files that have been backed up in the current drive by right clicking on the drive (or pressing the Space Bar) in the Restore To: box. You must do this after making any catalog selections, because exiting the Select Catalog dialog box erases any file selections.

> **Caution:** If you select ALL files to restore, you run a greater risk of overwriting a newer version of a file with an older version. Unless you are restoring all files to a completely erased hard disk, it is better to take the time to select the files you want to restore, or perform an Advanced level restore where you can select from more overwrite options.

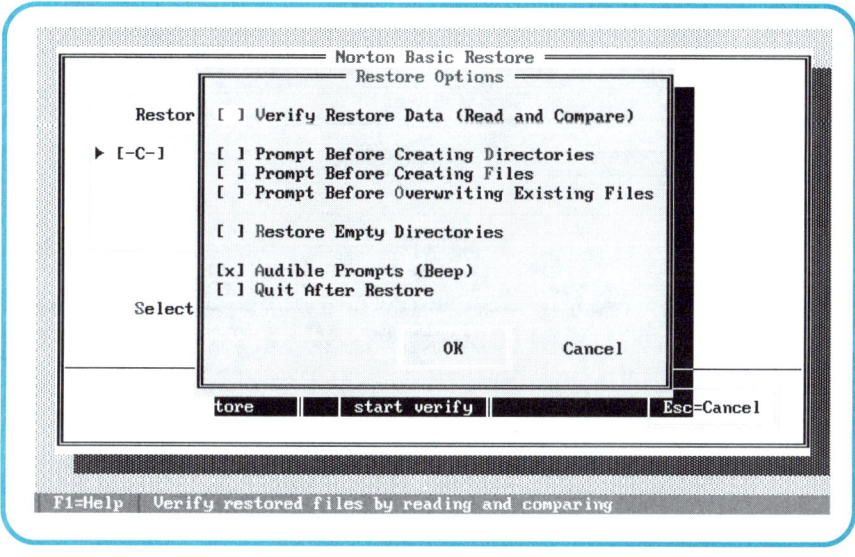

Figure 12.16   The Restore Options dialog box lets you customize the way Norton Basic Restore operates.

If you do not want to restore all files, the Select Files box takes you to the Select Restore Files screen, shown in Figure 12.17. This is nearly identical to the Select Backup Files screen, except for the Show Versions option at the bottom of the screen. This option works the same on the Select Restore Files screen as it does on the View Catalog screen.

The directories and files shown on the screen are those listed in the backup catalog file selected. You select directories and files to be restored from this list exactly as you selected directories and files to be backed up. The Display option also works the same as on the Select Backup Files screen.

Starting the Basic Restore

After you have selected files to be restored and have returned to the Basic Restore screen, you start the restore operation by selecting the Start Restore box. This box is not available until you load a catalog file and select files to restore.

After you start the restore, a message prompts you to insert the first backup diskette (if you backed up to a floppy disk drive). After inserting the disk, select Continue, and the progress screen shown in Figure 12.18 appears.

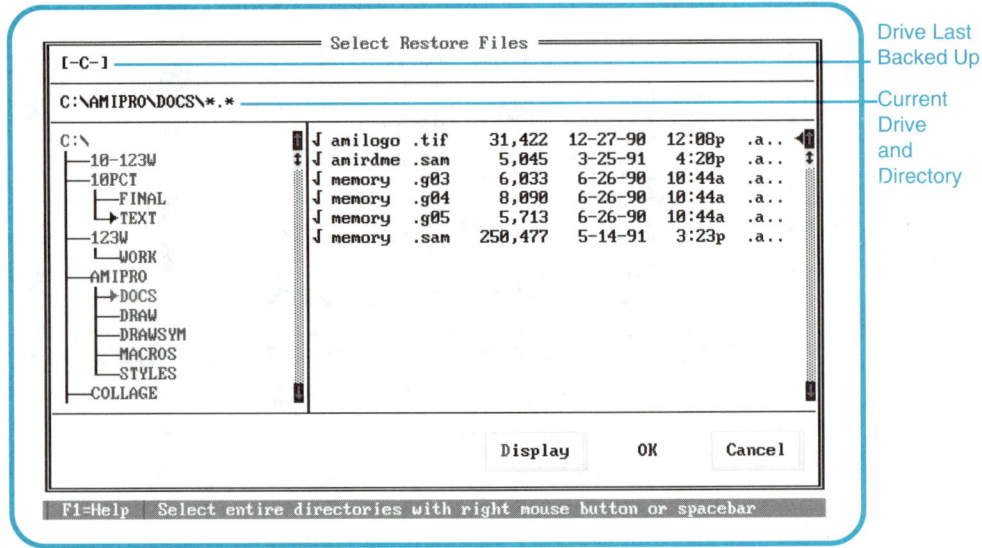

Figure 12.17   The Select Restore Files screen is similar to the Select Backup Files screen.

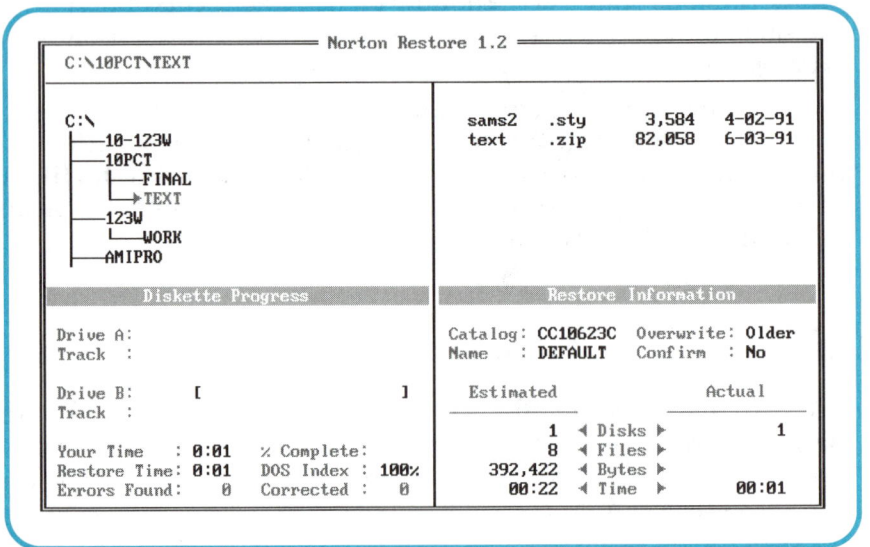

Figure 12.18   The basic restore progress screen provides prompts and statistical information about the restore.

During the restore process, screen prompts let you know when to insert diskettes and when you need to make restore decisions (based on the restore options you set). Files change color as they are restored, and a moving bar in the lower left window of the screen tracks the progress of the restore operation. A prompt informs you when the restore is complete. Select OK at the prompt to return to the Norton Backup main menu or the DOS prompt (depending on whether you selected the Quit After Restore option).

The Start Verify Option

Although Start Verify appears as a feature on the Restore screen, it may also be thought of as part of the backup process. Start Verify compares the backup files to be restored with the corresponding files on your hard disk. It performs essentially the same function as the Read and Compare Data Verification option and can be used as such if you perform a backup or restore without this option set.

301

If you want to use Start Verify for data verification after a backup or restore operation, you need to do so before writing to your hard disk again; otherwise, the files may not match. Also, you cannot use this feature if you have selected either the Restore To Other Drive or Restore To Other Dir(ectories) option in an Advanced restore. These options make it impossible to compare the original backup files with the restored files because they are on different drives or directories.

When you select Start Verify, a screen message prompts you to insert the backup diskettes. Another prompt tells you when verification is complete. Select OK at this prompt to end the process and return to the main menu.

Advanced Restore

An Advanced restore offers additional control that makes it considerably more powerful than the Basic restore. Like the Advanced backup, it offers additional data verification options, file selection criteria, the

Setup File: option, plus overwrite control and the capability of restoring to a drive or directory other than the one last backed up.

Select an Advanced restore from the Configuration screen. When you return to the main menu, select Restore. The Norton Advanced Restore screen appears, as shown in Figure 12.19.

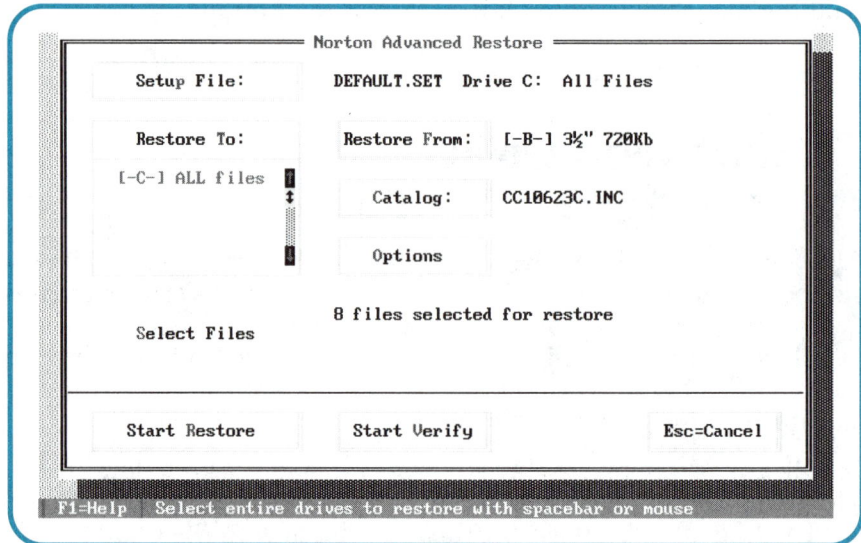

```
═══════════════ Norton Advanced Restore ═══════════════

   Setup File:        DEFAULT.SET  Drive C:  All Files

   Restore To:        Restore From:    [-B-] 3½" 720Kb

   [-C-] ALL files

                         Catalog:      CC10623C.INC

                         Options

                      8 files selected for restore

   Select Files


   Start Restore      Start Verify                Esc=Cancel

 F1=Help   Select entire drives to restore with spacebar or mouse
```

Figure 12.19 The Norton Advanced Restore screen is similar to the Norton Basic Restore screen but offers the Setup File: option.

As in the Basic restore, the Restore To: drive is the drive last backed up. Select the Restore From: drive and the catalog as described previously in the section entitled "The Basic Restore." Advanced options and file selection are described in the next two sections.

Advanced Restore Options

There are nine advanced restore options, as shown on the Restore Options screen in Figure 12.20. Of these nine, three options are exactly the same as in the Basic restore: Data Verification:, Restore Empty Dirs, and Quit After Restore. The remaining six advanced options offer choices that greatly increase your control over the restore procedure.

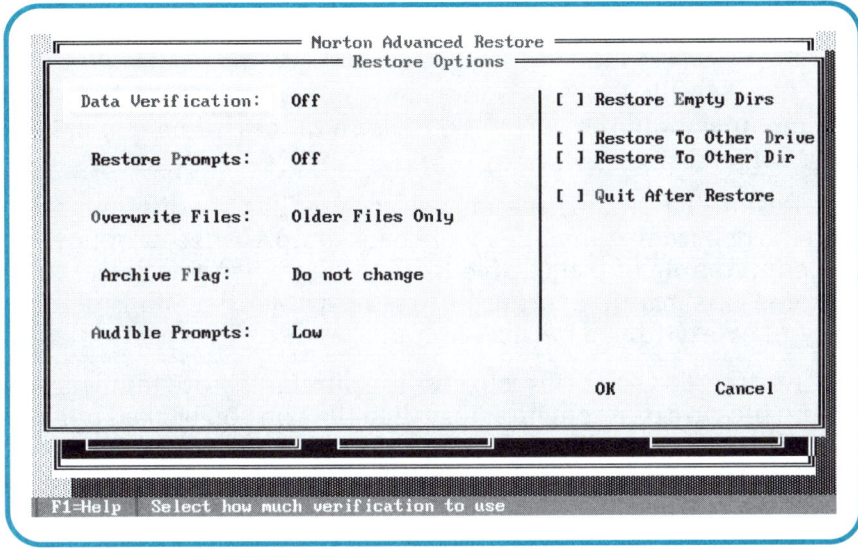

Figure 12.20   The advanced Restore Options screen offers powerful choices not available in a Basic restore.

Restore Prompts lets you choose the situations in which you are informed of a restore activity and gives you the option to continue that activity or skip it. The two options are Prompt Before Creating Directories (if a directory to be restored does not exist on your hard disk) and Prompt Before Creating Files (if a file to be restored does not exist on your hard disk).

Overwrite Files lets you avoid accidentally overwriting a new version of an existing file with an older backed up version. Your choices are Never Overwrite Files (files with the same name as an existing file are not restored), Always Overwrite Files (backed up files overwrite and erase any existing version of the files on your hard disk), and Overwrite Older Files Only (only overwrites files prior to the last backup). A fourth option—Prompt Before Overwriting Files—can be selected in combination with either Always Overwrite Files or Overwrite Older Files Only. This option informs you during restore that you are about to overwrite an existing file and gives you the option to Overwrite, Do Not Restore, or Cancel Restore.

The Archive Flag option lets you choose how a restored file is flagged. When a file's archive flag is on, the Norton Backup sees the file as not backed up. When the archive flag is off, the program sees a file as backed up. Leave Alone—Do not change leaves the archive flag as it was before the restore. Clear—Mark as backed up turns the archive flag off. Set—Mark as NOT backed up turns the archive flag on.

The Audible Prompts option sets the volume of the beep that accompanies prompts during the restore process. The choices are Low, Off, and High.

Restore To Other Drive lets you restore files to a different drive than the one from which they were backed up. With this option on, you are prompted for the drive to restore to when you select Start Restore. This feature is useful for restoring older versions of a file without overwriting a newer version.

Restore To Other Dir(ectories) is a similar feature that lets you restore files to a different directory than the one you backed up. You actually select the directory to restore to after you select Start Restore. A prompt asks you for the new directory name.

304 *Advanced File Selection*

File selection is the same in Advanced level as in Basic level, except for the Special feature. When selected from the Select Restore Files screen, this feature gives you additional criteria for including or excluding files to restore. Date Range lets you include all files within a range of dates. Copy Protected Files lets you select up to five files to mark as copy protected and exclude from the restore. Exclude Read Only Files, Exclude System Files, and Exclude Hidden Files let you exclude all files with Read Only, System, or Hidden attributes.

Preparing Setup Files for PreSet Backup or Restore

You can create your own setup files for each type of backup or restore you want to run, name the files, save them, use them to run quick and easy PreSet backups or restores, and even copy them for others to use. The process is very easy, but it must be done from the Advanced Backup or Restore screen.

Creating a Setup File

To create a setup file for a PreSet backup or restore, you must first go to the Advanced Backup or the Advanced Restore screen. Select the drives, options, files, or catalog (for a restore) that you want, then select `Setup File` at the top of the screen. This takes you to the Setup File dialog box, shown in Figure 12.21.

Existing Setup Files

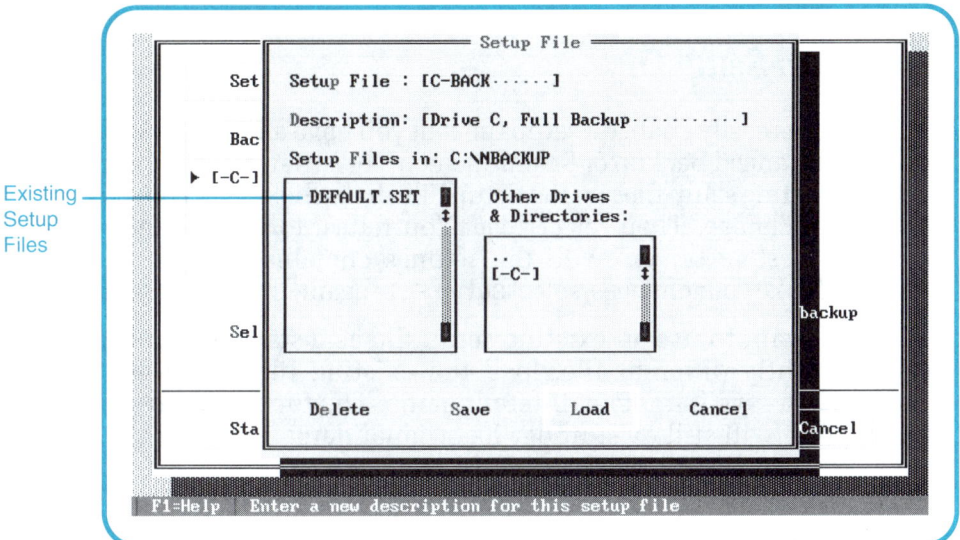

Figure 12.21   The Setup File dialog box is accessed from the Advanced Backup or Restore screen.

305

From this dialog box, you can name and save a setup file that contains all the backup or restore information you just set. Highlight the bracketed name next to Setup File and type in a new setup file name. The name can be up to eight characters long—for example, C-BACK. An extension of .SET is attached automatically to the name when you save the file.

Next, highlight the bracketed text to the right of Description:. Type in a brief description of the setup file you are creating, up to 24 characters—for example, `Drive C, Full Backup`. If you press Enter at this point, a prompt warns you that the setup file is about to be created and asks if you want to Create or Cancel the setup file.

The Setup File dialog box stores your setup file in C:\NBACKUP unless you select a different drive and directory. To do so, select a drive from the Other Drives & Directories list. The list will change to display the directories in that drive. Select the directory you want from that list. The new drive and directory will replace C:\NBACKUP next to Setup Files in:.

Finally, select Save. That's all there is to it. You return to the Advanced Backup or Restore screen, where you can create another setup file under another name if you wish.

Changing a Setup File

You can just as easily change a setup file that you have already created. From the Advanced Backup or Restore screen, select Setup File. From the list of existing setup files on the Setup File dialog box, select the file you want to change. Then select Load. You return to the Advanced Backup or Restore screen, with the settings contained in that file displayed. Make your changes, select Setup File again, then select Save.

If you want to use an existing setup file as a starting point to create a slightly different file, load the existing file, make your changes, then save it under a different name. The file you used as a starting point will still exist under its original name.

Installing a Setup File for Others

If you want to share a setup file with other, less experienced users, you can transfer it to the other person's NBACKUP directory using a floppy diskette. You must transfer two files for the setup file to work: the file you created with the .SET file name extension and another file that the program creates automatically with the same file name and an .SLT extension. Use the DOS COPY command to copy both files onto a floppy diskette.

Say you want to transfer setup file C-BACK, which is stored on your hard disk in C:\NBACKUP, to another user's \NBACKUP directory on the D: drive. Your floppy disk drive is A:. First, make sure you are on the C: drive, then use the following commands to copy the files to a blank floppy diskette:

```
copy \nbackup\c-back.set a:
copy \nbackup\c-back.slt a:
```

Insert the diskette containing the copied files into the other user's floppy disk drive and type

```
copy a:*.* d:\nbackup
```

This copies both files on A: to D: in the \NBACKUP directory.

PreSet Level Backup and Restore

Once you have a setup file, you can perform backups and restores in the PreSet level. This involves fewer keystrokes and less time, because your drives, options, catalog (for restore), and files (for backup) are already set.

The quick steps in the next two sections take you step by step through the PreSet backup and restore. First, select the PreSet level from the Configuration screen. When you return to the main menu, select either Backup or Restore.

307

> **Tip:** If you want to start the Norton Backup with a particular setup file already loaded, type the name of the setup file after NBACKUP; for example,
>
> **NBACKUP C-BACK**

The PreSet Backup

When you select a PreSet backup, the screen shown in Figure 12.22 appears. In a PreSet backup, you do not have to select the drive to back up from, the backup options, the files to be backed up, or the backup type (in fact, you don't even have the option). This information is all stored in the setup file.

You do have to select a setup file from the list in the PreSet Backups box. You can (but don't have to) select a drive to back up to. The default drive is part of the setup file, but you can change it if you wish.

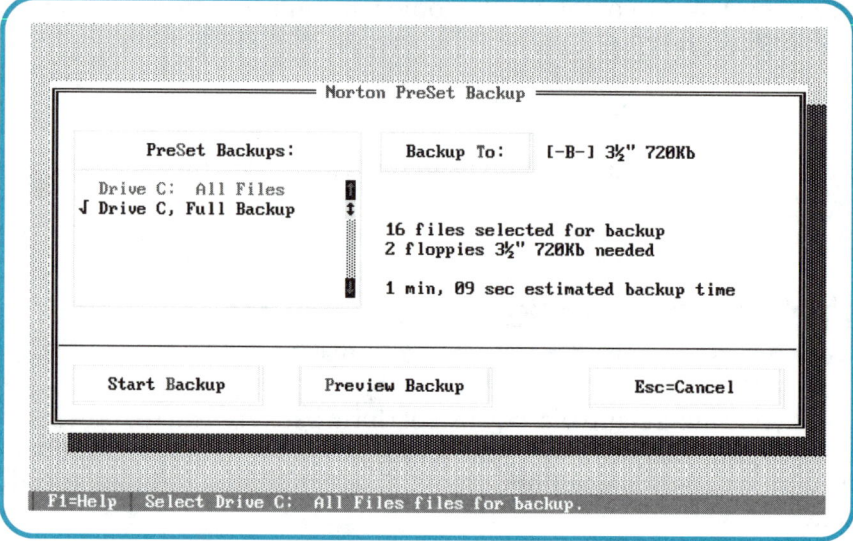

```
═══════════════ Norton PreSet Backup ═══════════════

      PreSet Backups:          Backup To:     [-B-] 3½" 720Kb

    Drive C:  All Files
  √ Drive C, Full Backup        16 files selected for backup
                                2 floppies 3½" 720Kb needed

                                1 min, 09 sec estimated backup time


    ┌─────────────┐    ┌─────────────────┐    ┌─────────────┐
    │ Start Backup│    │ Preview Backup  │    │  Esc=Cancel │
    └─────────────┘    └─────────────────┘    └─────────────┘

 F1=Help │ Select Drive C:  All Files files for backup.
```

308

Figure 12.22   The Norton PreSet Backup screen asks you for the name of the setup file.

 Running a PreSet Backup

1. Select Backup from the main menu.

   The Norton PreSet Backup screen appears.

2. Select a setup file from the PreSet Backups: list.

   A checkmark appears next to the selected file.

3. Select Backup To: if you want to back up files to a different drive than the default shown. Select a new drive from the list in the resulting dialog box, then select OK.

   The new drive appears on the PreSet Backup screen.

4. Select Preview Backup if you want to see which files have been selected for backup. Select Done to return to the Norton PreSet Backup screen.

   The Preview Backup screen appears, containing the same information shown in the Select Files screen in a Basic or Advanced backup. You cannot make changes to this screen.

5. Select Start Backup.	The Backup screen prompts you to insert diskettes and tracks the progress of the backup. A message informs you when the backup is complete.
6. Select OK.	You return to the main menu or to the DOS prompt. ☐

The PreSet Restore

The PreSet Restore screen is similar to the PreSet Backup screen with the addition of a Select Files box. Unlike a PreSet backup, you must select the files to restore, because this information is likely to have changed since the setup file was created.

In a PreSet restore, you do not need to select restore options. These are contained in the setup file. You can (but don't need to) set a drive to restore files from. This information is also contained in the setup file. The setup file for a PreSet restore is the setup file used for the last PreSet backup.

309

Running a PreSet Restore

1. Select Restore from the main menu.	The Norton PreSet Restore screen appears.
2. Select a setup file from the Restore Type (catalog) list.	A checkmark appears next to the selected file.
3. Select Restore From if you want to restore files from a different drive than the default shown. Select a new drive from the list in the resulting dialog box, then select OK.	The new drive appears on the Norton PreSet Restore screen.
4. Select the Select Files box.	The Select Restore Files screen appears. This is the same as the Basic Select Restore Files screen (refer to Figure 12.17).
5. Select the files to restore, then select OK.	The number of files selected appears on the Norton PreSet Restore screen.

6. Select `Preview Restore` if you want to see which files have been selected to restore. Select `Done` to return to the Norton PreSet Restore screen.

The Preview Restore screen appears, with the same information shown in the Select Files screen. Youcannot make changes to this screen.

7. Select `Start Restore`.

The Restore screen prompts you to insert diskettes and tracks the progress of the retore procedure. A message informs you when the restore is complete.

8. Select `OK`.

You return to the main menu or to the DOS prompt. □

310 Using Macros with the Norton Backup

A macro is a mini program that automates a process. The Norton Backup allows you to create such a program by recording the keystrokes you use to complete a process. Then when you run the macro (with a keystroke or two), it "replays" all of the keystrokes you recorded. The result is a significant savings in time.

The setup file that allows you to run a PreSet level backup can itself be thought of as a macro. Once you create and save the setup file, you "replay" your original selections when you choose a PreSet backup. In fact, when you create a macro, you store it in a setup file. You can create as many macros as you wish, but you can store only one macro in a given file.

Recording a Macro

Before you record a macro, it is a good idea to map out the process that you want to automate, keystroke by keystroke (you cannot use a mouse when recording a macro). Note that special keystrokes must be substituted for keystrokes that make certain types of selections. This prevents you from actually running a backup or restore operation when all you want to do is set up a macro to run a backup or restore. These special keystrokes and other keys used in macros are listed in Table 12.2.

Table 12.2   *Macro Keystrokes*

Keystroke	Description
Ctrl + Enter	Use instead of Enter when you don't want the recorded keystroke to activate a process during recording
Ins	Use instead of Space Bar to turn an option on when recording
Del	Use instead of Space Bar to turn an option off when recording
F7	Start\stop recording a macro
Alt + F7	Pause during recording (inserts a pause to allow input when the macro is replayed)
F8	Replay a macro

To record a macro, you must first load the setup file where you will store the macro. After loading the setup file, return to the main menu. All macros must start from here. Follow the following quick steps to record the macro.

311

 Recording a Macro

1. From the main menu, press F7.

   The word Recording replaces the F1=Help message in the lower left corner of the screen.

2. Perform the keystrokes needed to complete the process you want to automate. (Refer to Table 12.2 for substitute keystrokes for Enter and the Space Bar.)

   You see the action resulting from each keystroke, as if you were actually completing the process, unless you use substitute keys.

3. Press Alt + F7 to insert a pause in the macro, whenever you want the user to make a menu selection or enter information.Select OK from the menu or press F7 to resume recording.

   The word Waiting replaces Recording during the pause.

4. When you are finished recording, press F7.

   The macro is saved automatically in the setup file currently loaded. ☐

Playing a Macro

When you want to replay a macro, first load the setup file containing it, then press F8. The message Working appears in the lower left corner of the screen, unless the macro is pausing for input. Then the message is Waiting. Even though the Working message is visible, you cannot use either the keyboard or mouse because the macro is in control of the program.

What You Have Learned

In this chapter you learned to back up and restore your files using the Norton Backup. You also learned:

312

▶ You can choose from three levels of backup and restore: Basic, Advanced, and PreSet. You choose the program level from the Configuration screen.

▶ Five different types of backups are possible: full, incremental, differential, full copy, and incremental copy. Copy backups do not use the DOS COPY command and must be restored using the Norton Backup.

▶ The data verification option affects the speed and accuracy of a backup. The greater the degree of verification, the slower the backup.

▶ The data compression option affects the speed and number of diskettes used in a backup. The greater the degree of compression, the fewer diskettes are used and the slower the backup becomes.

▶ Overwrite options let you choose whether the program prompts you before overwriting (and erasing) previous files on a diskette or on your hard disk.

▶ The Start Verify option is offered on the Restore screen, but it can be used immediately after a backup to verify that the backup data matches the original data.

▶ A catalog contains an index of the files backed up in a particular backup session. Each catalog has a unique name and is stored both on the hard disk and on the last diskette of the backup set.

▶ The catalog for a particular backup is necessary to restore those backed up files. If a catalog is lost from your hard disk, it can be retrieved or rebuilt from the backup diskettes.

▶ The settings for a backup or restore are saved in a setup file named DEFAULT.SET. In the Advanced level, you can create your own setup files, to save backup or restore settings for use by yourself or others in PreSet level.

313

Protecting Your System with The Norton AntiVirus

In This Chapter

- ▶ *Understanding viruses*
- ▶ *Introducing The Norton AntiVirus*
- ▶ *Installing The Norton AntiVirus*
- ▶ *Intercepting viruses*
- ▶ *Scanning for and removing viruses*

Chapter 7's explanation of Norton's DISKMON utility gave you a brief glimpse of computer viruses and how you can monitor your hard disk for unauthorized activity. This chapter examines a new method of protecting your system—The Norton AntiVirus.

What Are Viruses?

A *virus* is software that enters your system by attaching itself to another file. The virus will attach to the boot sectors of a hard or floppy disk, any program on your disk, or a system file such as COMMAND.COM. You can get viruses from floppy disks or in files you download to your system with a modem.

Once the virus is on your system, it copies itself over and over until it is triggered to do what it's programmed to do. Often, a certain date or time or starting a certain program will trigger a virus. Once triggered, a virus may destroy data or prevent a particular program from operating correctly. Or, a virus may simply display a message. But beware! Even seemingly harmless viruses can cause system crashes.

Hundreds of viruses now have been identified. Once a virus is discovered, programmers can analyze it for "signature" characteristics that can be identified on disk. Virus identification programs like The Norton AntiVirus can scan your disks for the signatures of known viruses. (Norton calls the virus signatures *virus definitions*.)

316

Introducing The Norton AntiVirus

The Norton AntiVirus program offers two forms of protection against viruses. The *Virus Intercept* component of The Norton AntiVirus checks any file you run or copy for viruses and alerts you when it detects a virus. The *Virus Clinic* component of The Norton AntiVirus lets you scan a disk for viruses and repair or delete infected files. You can customize how both Virus Clinic and Virus Intercept operate to best meet your needs. In addition, Virus Clinic offers the security of password protection so unauthorized users can't alter how it's configured.

To run The Norton AntiVirus, you must have an IBM PC or compatible system with two disk drives or a hard drive, and 384K of RAM. You can use the Install program to set up AntiVirus to run from your hard drive (described next), or you can manually install The Norton AntiVirus to work on a system with two disk drives. (Installation on a system with two disks is described later in this chapter.)

> **Tip:** Before you install The Norton AntiVirus, check the READ.ME file on the program disk for specific information about how to use The Norton AntiVirus with your system.

Hard Drive Installation

Installing The Norton AntiVirus on your hard disk system is basically a three-step procedure. First, you must scan your hard drive for viruses that may already be on your system and repair or delete the infected files. Next, you should create a backup copy of The Norton AntiVirus disks. Then you can run the Install program.

Scan Your System

Scanning your hard disk with the Virus Clinic before you install The Norton AntiVirus program is essential to ensure that AntiVirus program files aren't corrupted by a virus when they're copied to the hard disk. You should also back up your entire hard disk before scanning, because repairing virus-infected files can cause irreversible damage to files. If you make a backup, at least you'll have one copy (albeit virus-infected) of the file you need.

317

> **Tip:** If you have any compressed files on your hard disk, decompress them before scanning for viruses. Virus Clinic cannot scan compressed files for viruses.

Ideally, to start the scan procedure you should boot your system from your original, write-protected DOS disk, if you have it. If you don't have one now, copy your DOS files to a disk and write-protect the disk. (Because you can't copy files to a write-protected disk, it is virus free.) Likewise, use your original, write-protected Norton AntiVirus Program Disk for the scan procedure. The following steps walk you through the scan procedure.

1. Insert your original copy of The Norton AntiVirus Program Disk in drive A:. Type **A:**, and press Enter to display the A:\> or A> prompt.

2. Type **NAV**, and press Enter. A screen appears and asks you to enter Your Name: and your Company Name:. You must enter at least one space in each line, even though the information won't be saved to disk because the disk is write-protected. Press Enter after each entry, then press Enter again to OK what you typed.

3. The Virus Clinic opening screen appears, as shown in Figure 13.1. The Scan drive dialog box appears in the center of the screen. This box opens automatically each time you start the Virus Clinic. At the left side of the dialog box is a list of the drives on your system, with the first choice highlighted. Use the arrow keys or click with the mouse to highlight the drive letter for your hard disk (or the first drive letter if your hard disk has more than one drive partition).

318

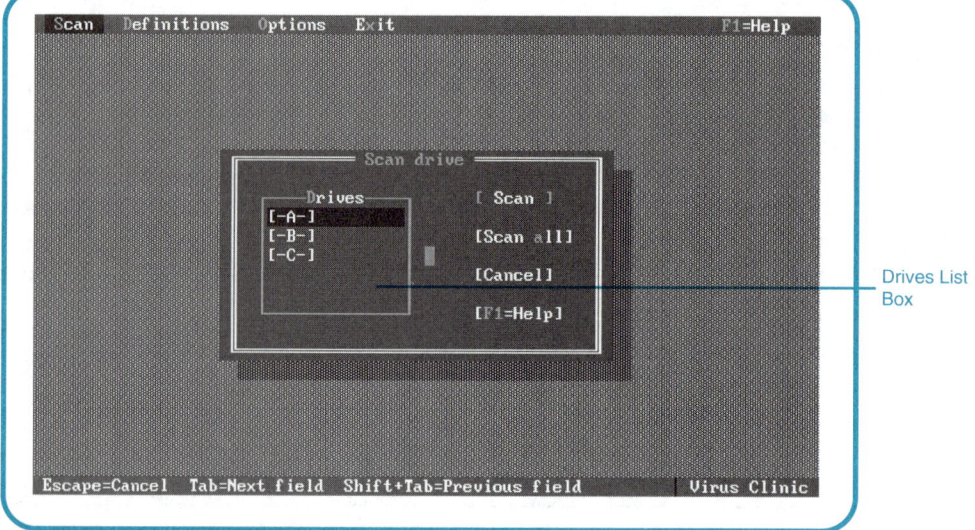

Drives List Box

Figure 13.1   *The Virus Clinic opening screen.*

4. Press Enter to begin the scan. (You can press Esc at any time to cancel the scan.)

5. The Scan Results screen appears and shows each drive, directory, and file name as the scan progresses. At the end of the scan, the Scan Results screen lists any infected files, the type of virus infecting each, and a summary of the scan results. Figure 13.2 shows the Scan Results screen. If the scan detects no viruses, you can simply press Esc to progress to Step 8 of this procedure.

6. If the Scan Results screen does list infected files, you'll need to repair them. Press **A** or click to select the `Repair all` command button from the list of command buttons at the left side of the screen. (Make sure you've made backup copies of all your hard drive files before you choose Repair

all.) Virus Clinic repairs each file and displays a message below each file it successfully repairs.

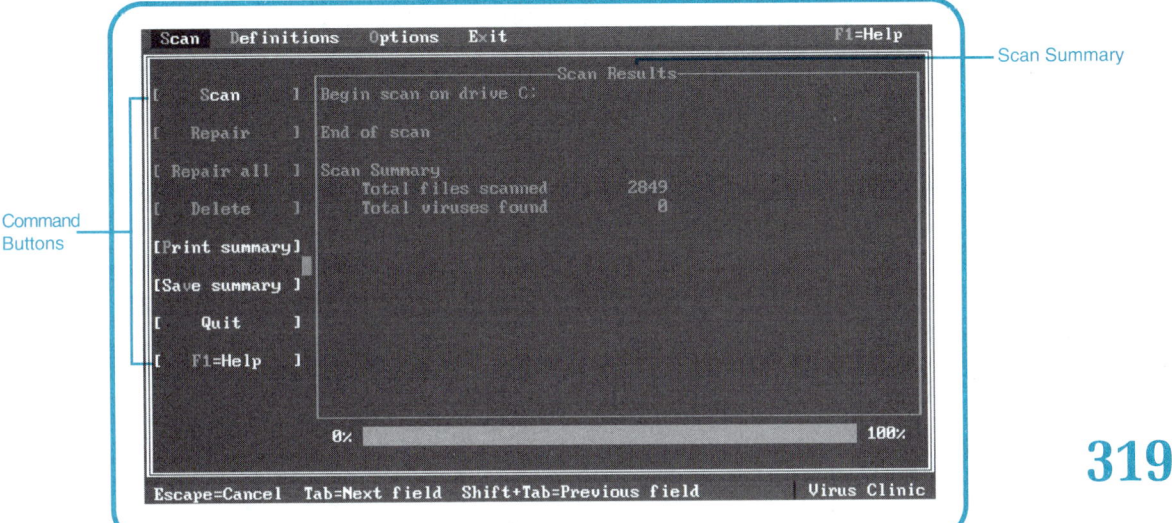

Figure 13.2 The Scan Results screen.

7. Press **s** or click the Scan command button to rescan the repaired hard drive.

8. Press Esc or click on the Quit command button to close the Scan Results screen and return to the main Virus Clinic screen.

9. If you have another drive on the hard disk to scan, press Alt-S or click on Scan in the menu bar to open the Scan menu. Press **D** or click on Drive to redisplay the Scan drive dialog box.

10. Repeat Steps 3 through 9 to scan additional drives partitioned on the hard disk.

11. When you're finished, press F10 to exit the Virus Clinic and return to the DOS prompt.

Now that you've scanned your hard drive, you're ready to proceed with the next step in installing The Norton AntiVirus on your hard disk system: creating a working copy of the original Norton AntiVirus Program Disk.

319

Copying Your Program Disk

As when you install other software, you should make a copy of the original Norton AntiVirus Program Disk and work from the copy rather than the original. Store the original in a safe place. You'll need a blank 5¹/₄" 360K or 3¹/₂" 720K disk. (Use the same size disk as the program disk you're using.) To copy the disk,

1. Place the original disk in drive A: (or B:). Type the DOS command **DISKCOPY A: A:** (or **DISKCOPY B: B:**). Press Enter.
2. Follow the screen prompts to swap disks in and out of the drive.
3. When the copy process is complete, a prompt asks whether you would like to copy another disk. Press **N**, then press Enter to return to the prompt.

320 Running Install

The Install program on The Norton AntiVirus Program Disk streamlines the hard disk installation procedure. It copies the program files to the specified drive and directory and modifies (or creates) your CONFIG.SYS file so Virus Intercept will automatically load when you start your system. Use the following steps to run the Install program.

1. Put your copy of the Program Disk into drive A:. Type **A:**, and press Enter to move to the A:\>.
2. Type **INSTALL**, and press Enter.
3. The first screen of The Norton AntiVirus Install program appears, asking you to specify the type of monitor your system uses: Color or Black & White. Choose the appropriate monitor type. Here or at any time during the installation procedure, choose Quit to leave the Install program.
4. An explanation screen about the Install program appears. Choose Continue.
5. A screen prompts you to enter the drive you're installing from. Press Enter to verify drive A:.
6. Another screen prompts you to specify a drive and PATH (directory) on your hard disk for The Norton AntiVirus files. (It suggests a directory named \NAV.) Choose Continue to accept Norton's suggestion, or type a new drive and directory and then choose Continue.

7. Install creates the specified directory and tells you as it copies program files to the hard disk. Then it asks whether you would like The Norton AntiVirus program added to the PATH statement of your AUTOEXEC.BAT file. Choose Add to do so or Skip to bypass this step.

8. Install displays its next screen. Press Enter to select CONFIG.SYS to have Install automatically modify your CONFIG.SYS file so that Virus Intercept loads automatically each time you start your system. (I strongly recommend you choose this option.) Otherwise, choose Reboot to complete the installation procedure or Quit to exit Install.

9. When you choose CONFIG.SYS, Install displays the screen shown in Figure 13.3. The screen lists the contents of your CONFIG.SYS file, including the new line DEVICE=C:\NAV\NAV_.SYS, which is the line that loads the Virus Intercept program. Make sure this is the first line in CONFIG.SYS. To move the line to the top, use the down arrow key to highlight it. Then select the Move command button. Press the up arrow key to move the line to the top of the list, then press Enter to accept your change.

321

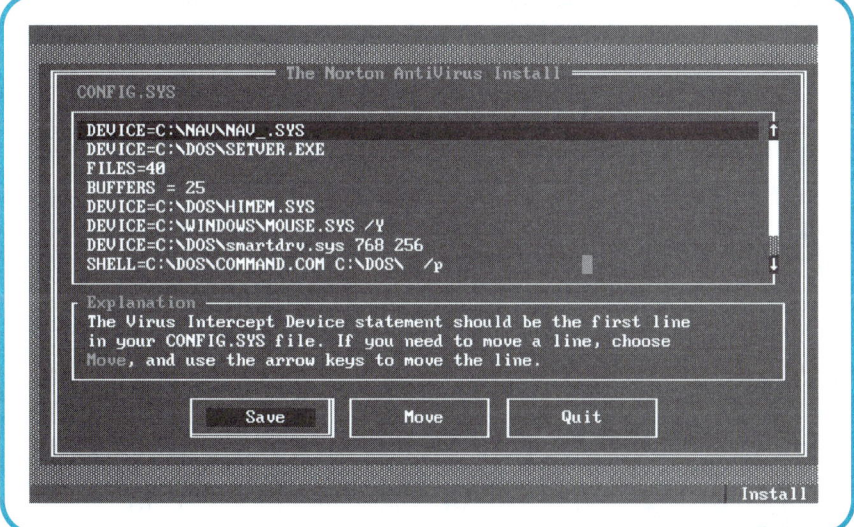

Figure 13.3   Modifying your CONFIG.SYS file.

10. Choose Save to write the changes to CONFIG.SYS.

11. Choose `Reboot` from the final screen to restart your computer so Virus Intercept will be active. Install reminds you to remove The Norton AntiVirus Program Disk from Drive A:. Do so, then choose `OK`.

 Tip: If you want to start your system without loading Virus Intercept, hold down both Shift keys while the system boots.

Now, Virus Intercept is loaded, and you can run Virus Clinic. But before you start to use The Norton AntiVirus program, you probably will want to customize the program. To do so, see the section entitled Configuring The Norton AntiVirus later in this chapter.

322

Setting Up The Norton AntiVirus to Run with Windows

If you choose, you can run The Norton AntiVirus program from Microsoft Windows version 3.0. The Norton AntiVirus Install program copies the files you'll need to work with Windows to the same directory as the rest of the AntiVirus program files. The following Quick Steps describe how to use Windows' Program Manager to set up The Norton AntiVirus to run with Windows.

Q Setting The Norton AntiVirus Up to Do Windows

1. At the Program Manager, press Ctrl-F6 repeatedly or click to activate the icon for the program group where you want to place The Norton AntiVirus icon.

   The icon's name should highlight.

2. Choose `File` by clicking or pressing Alt-F.

   The File menu appears.

3. Choose `New` by clicking or pressing Enter.

   The New Program Object dialog box appears.

4. Press `I` or click to select the Program Item button. Press Enter, or click `OK`.

   The Program Item Properties dialog box, shown in Figure 13.4, appears.

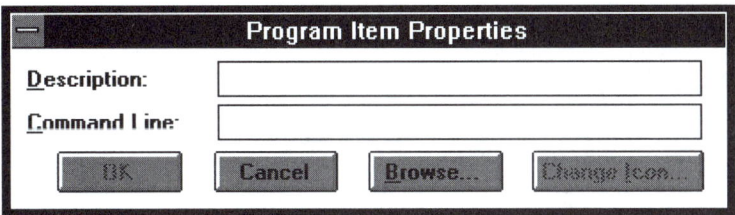

Figure 13.4 The Program Item Properties dialog box.

323

5. Type **NAV** or another short name in the Description: text box, and press Tab.

The cursor moves to the Command line: text box.

6. Type the drive and directory where The Norton AntiVirus program files are, followed by the file name NAV.PIF. For example, type **C:\NAV\NAV.PIF**.

7. Press Alt-I or click the Change Icon... button.

The Select Icon dialog box appears, with the default icon name in the File Name: text box.

8. Type the drive and directory where your AntiVirus program files are, followed by the file name NAV.ICO. For example, type **C:\NAV\NAV.ICO**. Press Enter.

The Select Icon dialog box closes.

9. Press Enter, or click OK.

The Program Item Properties dialog box closes. The Norton AntiVirus program is set up to run with Windows and has an icon in the window for the program group icon you specified. Figure 13.5 shows The Norton AntiVirus icon installed in a window. □

To run The Norton AntiVirus from Windows, simply move to the window containing the NAV icon, and double-click on the icon.

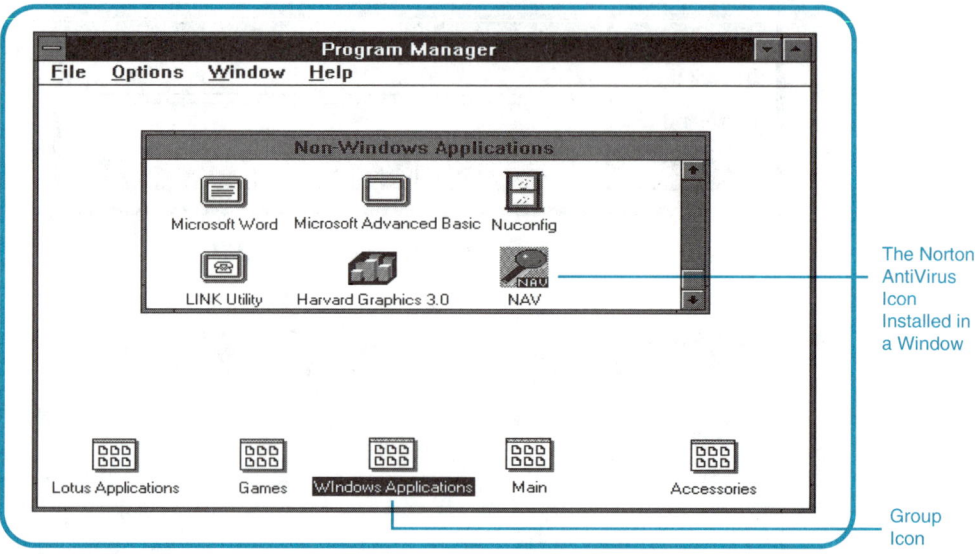

The Norton
AntiVirus
Icon
Installed in
a Window

Group
Icon

324

Figure 13.5   *The Norton AntiVirus icon in Windows.*

Two-Disk Installation

If you have a system with two floppy disk drives and no hard drive, you can use The Norton AntiVirus by copying its program files to your system (startup) disk. The Norton AntiVirus requires 140K of disk space. As for hard disk installation, first use your original copy of The Norton AntiVirus Program Disk to scan your system (in this case, the startup disk), then create a working copy of the original program disk and store your original in a safe place.

The rest of the two-disk installation procedure is simple. First, you must copy The Norton AntiVirus files to your startup disk, then modify your CONFIG.SYS file so Virus Intercept will load when you start your system. (If you don't have a CONFIG.SYS file on your system disk, refer to The Norton AntiVirus User Manual for instructions on creating one that will load Virus Intercept.) The procedure for two-disk installation follows:

1. Place your startup disk in drive A:, and turn on your computer.

2. Put your copy of The Norton AntiVirus program in drive B:.
   Type `B:`, and press Enter to log on to drive B:.

3. Type `COPY *.* A:`. Your system copies The Norton AntiVirus
   files to your startup disk in Drive A.

4. Type `A:`, and press Enter to return to the A>. Remove the
   Norton AntiVirus Program Disk from drive B: and store it in
   a safe place.

5. Make sure DOS's EDLIN program is on your startup disk. If
   not, copy it there from your original DOS disk.

6. Type `EDLIN CONFIG.SYS` and press Enter. DOS displays `End of`
   `input file` and an *.

7. Type `1I` and press Enter to insert a new first line in
   CONFIG.SYS. Then type `1I DEVICE=\NAV_.SYS`, and press
   Enter.

8. Press Ctrl-C to end editing. An * appears. Press `E`, then press
   Enter to return to the prompt.

9. Type `TYPE CONFIG.SYS` to list the file on-screen so you can
   check your changes.

10. Reboot your computer so the changes you made to
    CONFIG.SYS take effect. Virus Intercept will load automati-
    cally. Then you can run Virus Clinic as instructed later in
    this chapter.

325

 Note: You also can use any other ASCII text to make your
changes to CONFIG.SYS.

Running Virus Intercept

As you've already learned, the installation procedure sets up Virus
Intercept to run each time you start your system. It stays in your
computer's memory and constantly checks for signs of viruses as you
work. Because Virus Intercept stays in memory, it is known as a TSR
program. When you start your system, a small message box appears to
let you know that Virus Intercept is loaded, as shown in Figure 13.6.

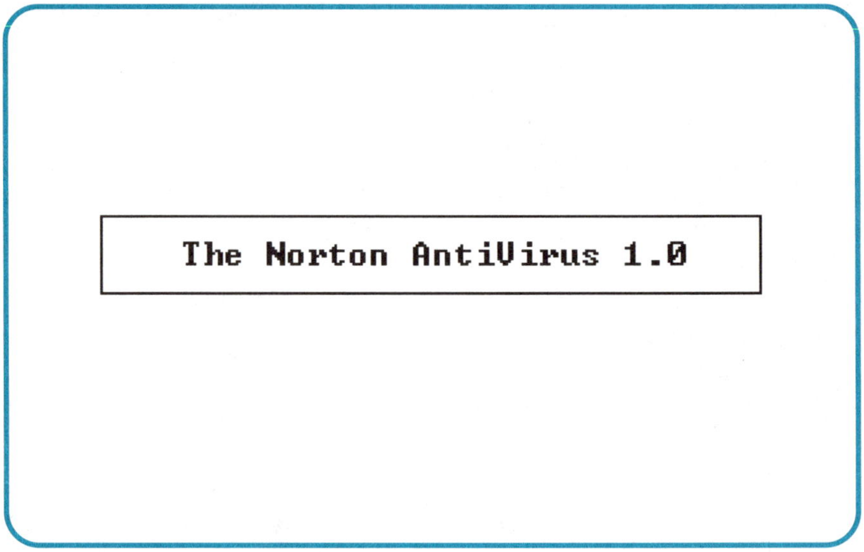

The Norton AntiVirus 1.0

326

Figure 13.6   *Virus Intercept loads when you start your system.*

Virus Intercept checks for known viruses each time you run a program file or copy a file of any type. When it detects a virus, it sounds a siren-like alert and flashes an alert box that shows the full path and name of the infected file and the type of virus. At this point, you should select the **Stop** button to cancel running the program or copying the file. Because Virus Intercept detects only the first virus it encounters, you need to stop and scan your entire drive with Virus Clinic, as described later in this chapter.

You can customize some of the basic Virus Intercept options through Virus Clinic. You can enable or disable the alert siren sound and the alert boxes. You can have Virus Intercept remove the alert box by specifying the number of seconds the box should appear on screen. By default, Virus Intercept keeps an *audit trail* file that records all your responses to alert messages. You can turn the audit trail off or assign a new name to the audit trail file. And, you can enter a customized message for the alert box. See the section entitled Configuring The Norton AntiVirus later in this chapter to learn how to choose configuration options.

Tip: You will have better results running The Norton AntiVirus from Windows if you disable the alert boxes and set the alert box to be removed from the screen after at least one second.

Your audit trail file may become quite large. From time to time, print out the audit trail file or copy it to another disk and rename the working version with the Norton Commander. (See Chapter 10.) Then you won't have to examine as much material if you need to look at the audit trail file.

Running Virus Clinic

As described earlier, Virus Clinic enables you to scan your disks for viruses, repair infected files, add new virus definitions, and configure The Norton AntiVirus program, including Virus Intercept.

To start Virus Clinic on a hard drive system, type **NAV** at the prompt, and press Enter. (You'll have to change to the drive and directory containing The Norton AntiVirus program before typing the startup command if you did not add The Norton AntiVirus to your AUTOEXEC.BAT PATH statement.) On a system with two floppy disks, put the disk where you installed The Norton AntiVirus in drive A: or B:. Move to the appropriate prompt, if necessary, by typing **A:** or **B:**. Type **NAV**, and press Enter. Or, you can double-click on the NAV icon if you want to start Virus Clinic from Windows. In any case, the main Virus Clinic screen appears with the Scan drive dialog box on top, as shown in Figure 13.7. You can press Esc to close the dialog box now or press Enter to scan the drive highlighted in the drives box.

Moving Around

Getting around in the Virus Clinic environment is easy. To select a pull-down menu from the menu bar, press Alt plus the highlighted letter in the menu name. Figure 13.8 shows the Scan pull-down menu. When the menu is visible, select a command by pressing the highlighted letter in the command name. You also can select a menu command by pointing to the menu name and holding the left mouse button, pulling the highlight down to the command you want, and releasing the mouse button.

The Norton AntiVirus also has dialog boxes with check boxes, radio buttons, text boxes, and command buttons. Figure 13.9 shows the Configuration dialog box.

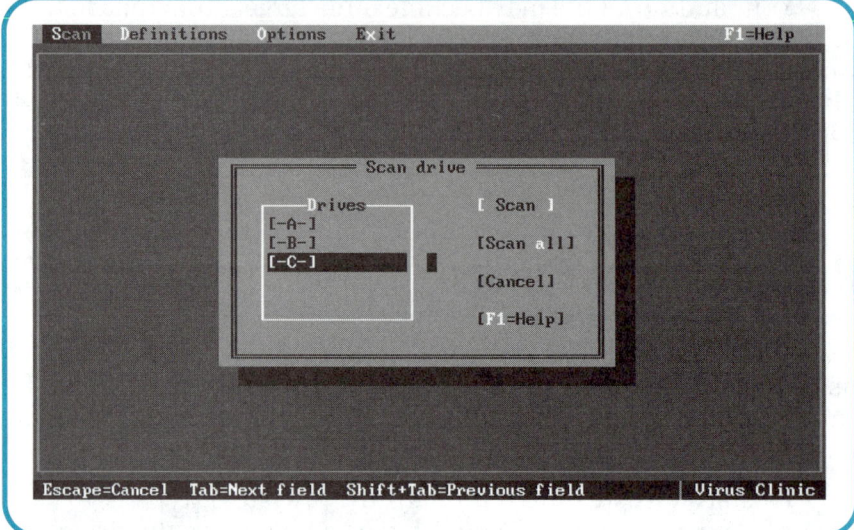

Figure 13.7   The main Virus Clinic screen, with the Scan drive dialog box on top.

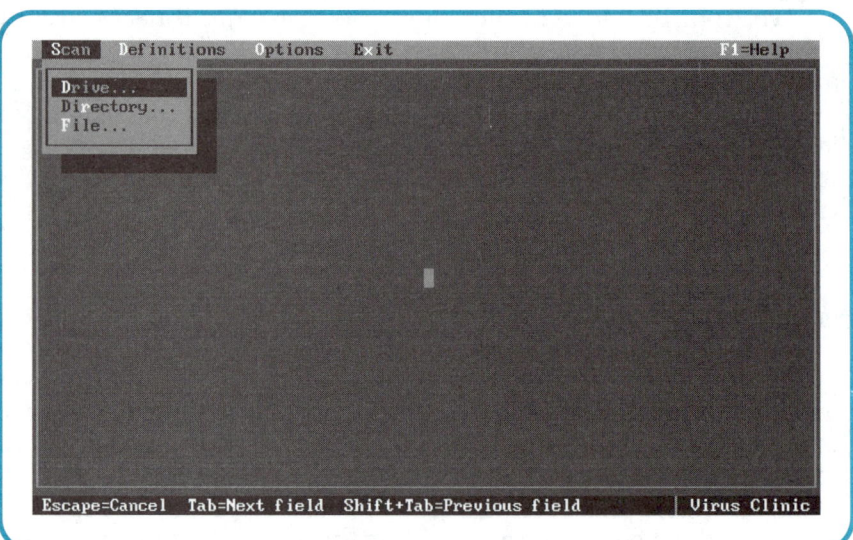

Figure 13.8   The Scan pull-down menu.

▶ You can select an option by pressing the highlighted letter in its name or by clicking with the mouse.

▶ Alternatively, you can use Tab to move the cursor among the options, then perform a second step to select the option.

When the cursor is in a check box, press Space Bar to select that option.

Move to a text box, and type your entry.

Move to a command button, and press Enter to perform the command.

Only one option button can be selected at a time.

▶ Press Esc at any time to close a menu or dialog box.

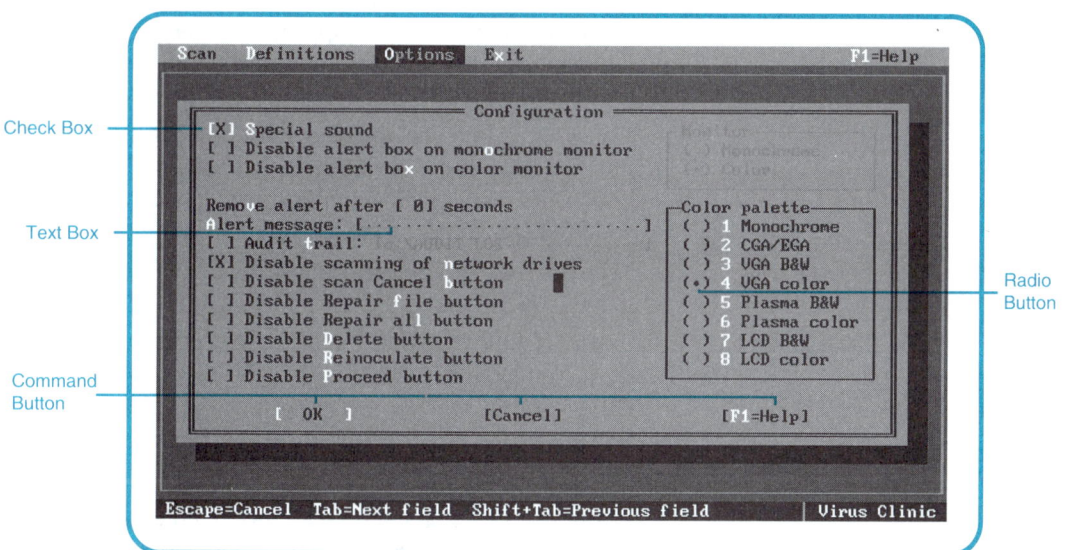

329

Figure 13.9   The Configuration dialog box.

Configuring The Norton AntiVirus

Look again at Figure 13.9, the Configuration dialog box. Use this dialog box to customize how both Virus Intercept and Virus Clinic operate. When you've specified all the options you want, select OK to save the configuration options you requested. You display this box from the main AntiVirus screen by opening the Options menu, then selecting Configure. Use the techniques for working with dialog boxes described in the previous section to select the options you want. Table 13.1 describes the options in the Configuration dialog box.

Table 13.1   The Configuration Dialog Box

Option	Effect When Selected
Special sound	Sounds an alert siren when Virus Intercept detects a virus
Disable alert box on monochrome monitor	Turns off the Virus Intercept alert box on monochrome monitors
Disable alert box on color monitor	Turns off the Virus Intercept alert box on color monitors
Remove alert after [ ] seconds	Enables you to enter a time, in seconds, that the Virus Intercept alert box will remain on screen
Alert message	Enter a custom message to appear in the Virus Intercept alert box, such as a message to call the network administrator
Audit trail	Makes Virus Intercept create and keep an audit trail file that records your responses to alert boxes; also enables you to enter a new PATH and file name for the audit trail file
Disable scanning of network drives	Keeps unauthorized users from scanning the network drives and tying up the server
Disable scan Cancel button	In Virus Clinic, prevents the user from canceling a scan by pressing Esc or choosing the Cancel button
Disable Repair file button	Turns off the option to repair an infected file at the Scan Results screen in Virus Clinic
Disable Repair all button	Turns off the option to repair all infected files at the Scan Results screen in Virus Clinic
Disable Delete button	Turns off the option to delete infected files at the Scan Results screen in Virus Clinic
Disable Reinoculate button	Turns off the Reinoculate button in the reinoculate alert box, if you have chosen advanced scanning from the dialog box that appears when you select Scan options from the Options pull-down menu
Disable Proceed button	Turns off the Proceed button in both the Virus Intercept alert box and the inoculate alert box for advanced scanning; the Proceed button is used to ignore the alerts

330

Option	Effect When Selected
Monitor	Selects the type that matches the adapter card connected to your system
Color palette	Specifies the screen appearance that works best with your system

You can password-protect your configuration settings so they can't be changed by unauthorized users. Preventing unauthorized configuration changes is particularly useful if you're using Norton AntiVirus on a network.

To assign a password to your configuration settings, pull down the Options menu and select Set password. Enter a password of 34 to 15 characters in the Enter new password: field and press Enter, then retype the password in the Verify password: field and press Enter.

To change the password later, use the Change password choice on the Options menu. Type the old password and the new password, pressing Enter after each. Verify the password, then press Enter again to activate the new password. To specify no new password, simply press Enter at the new password and verification fields.

331

Scanning

The scan procedure is similar to the one you used to scan your hard disk when you installed The Norton AntiVirus. Begin by pulling down the Scan menu. It offers you the choice to scan by Drive, Directory, or File. At the end of each type of scan, the Scan Results screen summarizes the findings of the scan. See the section entitled Working with the Scan Results Screen to find out how to proceed. The following sets of Quick Steps summarize each of the scan procedures.

 Scanning a Drive

1. Select the Scan menu.   The Scan pull-down menu appears (see Figure 13.8).

2. Select Drive.   The Scan Drive dialog box appears, as shown in Figure 13.7.

3. Use the up and down arrow keys or click with the mouse to highlight the name of the drive you want to scan in the Drives box.

4. Press Tab to highlight the Scan button then press Enter, or click on Scan.

Virus Clinic begins the scan and displays the Scan Results screen. When the scan is complete, a summary appears. See Figure 13.2 for an example. ☐

Scanning a Directory

1. Select the Scan menu.

The Scan pull-down menu appears (see Figure 13.8).

2. Select Directory.

The Scan Directory dialog box appears, as shown in Figure 13.10.

3. Type the drive and name of the directory you want to scan in the Subdirectories: text box and press Enter. Or, move to the Directories box by pressing Alt-D, then use the arrow keys and press Enter to select the directory. You can also double-click on a directory with the mouse.

4. Press Alt-B, or click on the Begin button.

Virus Clinic begins the scan and displays the Scan Results screen. When the scan is complete, a summary appears. See Figure 13.2 for an example. ☐

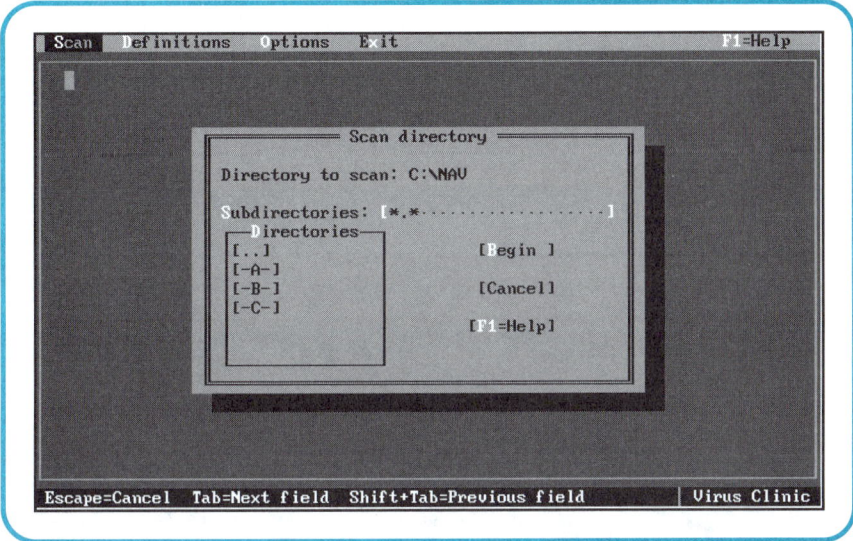

Figure 13.10   The Scan directory dialog box.

 Scanning a File

1. Select the Scan menu.

   The Scan pull-down menu appears (see Figure 13.8).

2. Select `File`.

   The Scan File dialog box appears, as shown in Figure 13.11.

3. Simply type the full drive, directory, and file name in the Name: text box to specify the file you want to scan. Alternatively, move to the Files box by pressing Alt-F, move among the files and directories with the up and down arrow keys, then press Space Bar to make a selection. You can select drives, directories, and file names in the Files box by double-clicking with the mouse.

4. Select the OK button.

Virus Clinic begins the scan and displays the Scan Results screen. When the scan is complete, a summary appears. See Figure 13.2 for an example. □

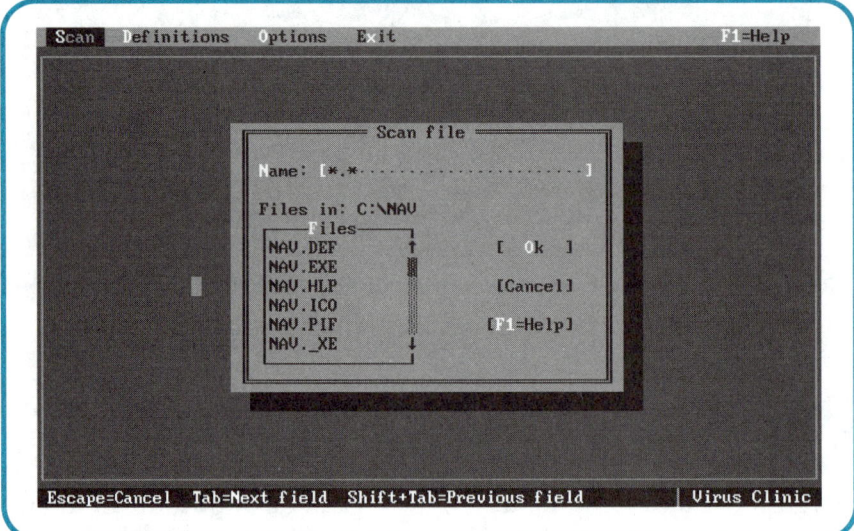

Figure 13.11 The Scan file dialog box.

Working with the Scan Results Screen

Whether you scan a drive, directory, or file, you have several options at the Scan Results screen when the scan is complete.

If the scan finds no viruses, you can

▶ Select the Print summary and/or the Save summary button to print or save the scan results.

▶ Select the Quit button to return to the main Virus Clinic screen.

If the scan finds viruses, you should

1. Exit Virus Clinic and back up your system. Repairing files can damage them, so you'll want up-to-date backup copies of

your files, even if infected. (If you can't completely repair the file, you may be able to retrieve the needed data from a backup in another way.)

2. Print or save the scan summary, if you choose.

3. Repair or delete the infected files by selecting the `Repair`, `Repair all`, or `Delete` button.

4. Select `Scan` to double check your system.

5. If your system is now clean, select `Quit`.

Virus Definitions

As new viruses are identified, you can get the definitions for the viruses and add them to The Norton AntiVirus program so you can scan for the new viruses on your system. Symantec Corporation, the makers of The Norton AntiVirus, will keep registered users informed about new viruses and provide new virus definitions. You can also get new definitions by calling the 24-hour Virus Newsline or through their bulletin board system.

335

For information about getting and adding virus definitions, see your User Manual. To see what virus definitions are currently on your system, you can print a list. The following Quick Steps explain how.

 Printing the List of Virus Definitions

1. Pull down the Definitions menu.

2. Select `List virus names`.

   The List virus names dialog box appears, as shown in Figure 13.12.

3. Press Alt-P or click on the `Print` command button.

   The list prints.   □

Leaving the Virus Clinic

After you've completed working with the Virus Clinic, you'll want to leave the program. Start by returning to the main screen. Press Esc, then press Enter to exit. With the mouse, click and hold to pull down the Exit menu, pull the highlight down to Yes, and release the mouse button.

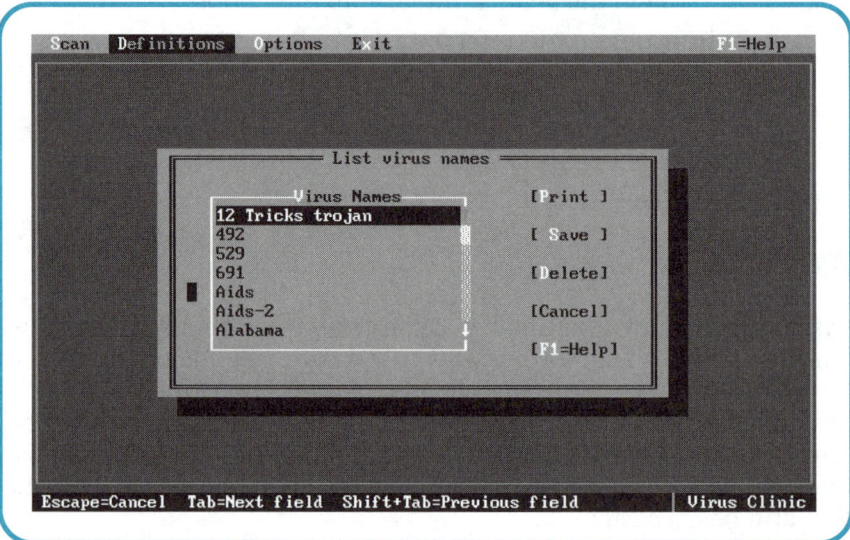

Figure 13.12   The List virus names dialog box.

What You Have Learned

In this chapter you learned about The Norton AntiVirus and protecting your disks from viruses. Specifically, you learned:

▶ Viruses are programs that attach themselves to files on your system and replicate until they're triggered by an event such as a certain date or running a certain program. When triggered, viruses can do anything from displaying a crazy message to erasing your data.

▶ The Norton AntiVirus program protects your system in two ways. Virus Intercept checks for viruses on files you copy or run and alerts you when one is present. The Virus Clinic enables you to scan your disks for viruses and repair infected files.

► You can run The Norton AntiVirus program on a hard disk system or on a system with two floppy disk drives. When you have a hard disk, you can also run The Norton AntiVirus from Windows.

► Virus Intercept loads automatically when you start your system and flashes an alert when it encounters a virus. Stop the current operation and scan your entire disk with Virus Clinic to find and remove the viruses present.

► Virus Clinic scans drives, directories, and files. After the scan, you have the option to repair or delete files. You can also configure The Norton AntiVirus from the main Virus Clinic screen.

► You can get new virus definitions from the makers of The Norton AntiVirus and add the definitions to your copy of the program.

337

Appendix A

Installation and Configuration

The Norton Utilities come with an Installation program that automatically lets you specify which Norton utilities to install. It then decompresses the program files and places them in the disk drive and directory you specify. During or after the installation procedure, you can use the NUCONFIG program to configure The Norton Utilities to run most effectively with your system.

Using the Emergency Disks

If you accidentally erase files on your hard drive or format your hard drive, *do not install The Norton Utilities*. Installing The Norton Utilities could overwrite the data you want to retrieve. You can perform three rescue operations with the Emergency Disk(s) that came with The Norton Utilities: unformat a hard drive, recover erased files, and diagnose a disk with Norton Disk Doctor.

▶ To unformat your hard drive, reboot the computer with a DOS system diskette (see Floppy Disk Installation later in this appendix to learn how to create a system disk), insert Emergency Disk 1 (5 ¼") or the Emergency Disk (3 ½") in drive A. Type A:UNFORMAT and press Enter to start the unformat operation, then follow the on-screen prompts.

▶ Insert Emergency Disk 2 (5¹/₄") or the Emergency Disk (3¹/₂") in drive A to recover erased files. Type `A:UNERASE` and press Enter to activate the UnErase utility, then follow the on-screen prompts.

▶ If you have disk problems, use Emergency Disk 1 (5¹/₄") or the Emergency Disk (3¹/₂"). Put the disk in drive A, type `A:NDD`, and press Enter. Select Diagnose Disk, then follow the on-screen prompts.

Hard Disk Installation

340

In earlier versions of The Norton Utilities (before version 5.0), you could use DOS's COPY command to place the utilities on your hard disk. Many of the utilities in version 6.0 are in a special compressed format on the distribution disks, so you must use the Installation program to decompress them on your hard disk. The Installation program also performs several extra useful operations such as creating a directory for The Norton Utilities and tailoring the utilities for your system. A typical installation using the Installation program takes about 10 minutes.

The Installation program is very easy to use, because it provides helpful explanations throughout the process. The program displays a series of screens and dialog boxes with many options and command buttons. To select an option or command button, use the arrow keys or Tab to highlight the option you want, then press Enter. You can also click on your choice with the mouse. To exit the Installation program at any time, point to the icon that looks like a minus sign in the upper left corner of the dialog box, and click with both mouse buttons. Following are the general steps for installing The Norton Utilities on your hard disk.

1. The Norton Utilities distribution diskettes are labeled for identification. Make a backup copy of your distribution disks using DOS's DISKCOPY command, and store the originals in a safe place. (Note: If you're copying the 5¹/₄" Norton disks, you'll need to copy the Installation and Utilities disks to 1.2 Mb, high-intensity disks and the two Emergency disks to 360K, double-density disks.) Run the Installation program from the backup copies.

2. Find the Installation Disk, insert it in drive A: (or B:), type
   A:INSTALL (or **B:INSTALL**), and press Enter. This command
   starts the Installation program and displays the opening
   screen, as shown in Figure A.1.

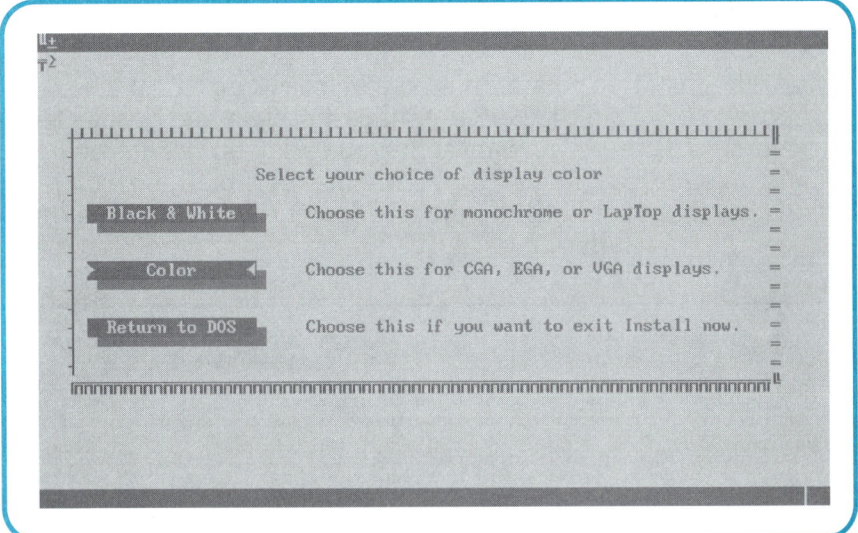

*Figure A.1   The Initial Norton Utilities Installation screen
program to install The Norton Utilities on your computer.*

3. Select the display color you want (or choose Return to DOS
   to exit the Installation program).

4. The Installation program displays an information screen that
   warns you that installation may overwrite erased files on
   your hard drive. Choose Return to DOS if you want to retrieve erased files. Otherwise, choose OK to continue installation.

5. Another information screen appears. Read it, then choose
   Continue.

6. The next screen lets you specify the drive and directory
   where the Installation program should place the utility files.
   The program tells you if you have an earlier version on your
   system and suggests the drive and directory where it's
   located as the drive and directory for version 6.0. If you don't
   have another version on your system, the Installation program suggests you install The Norton Utilities in C:\NU.

Press Enter or click the `Continue` button to accept Norton's suggestion, or type another drive and directory name and press Enter.

7. If you do not have enough room on your drive for all the Norton files, Installation displays a screen telling you it has selected as many files as possible for installation. Choose `OK` to continue.

8. At the Install Program Files screen (see Figure A.2), use the arrow keys then Space Bar or click to select and deselect The Norton Utilities you want to install. Click on the scroll arrows at the right side of the file names box to move through the list with the mouse. Select the `Install` button to continue installation.

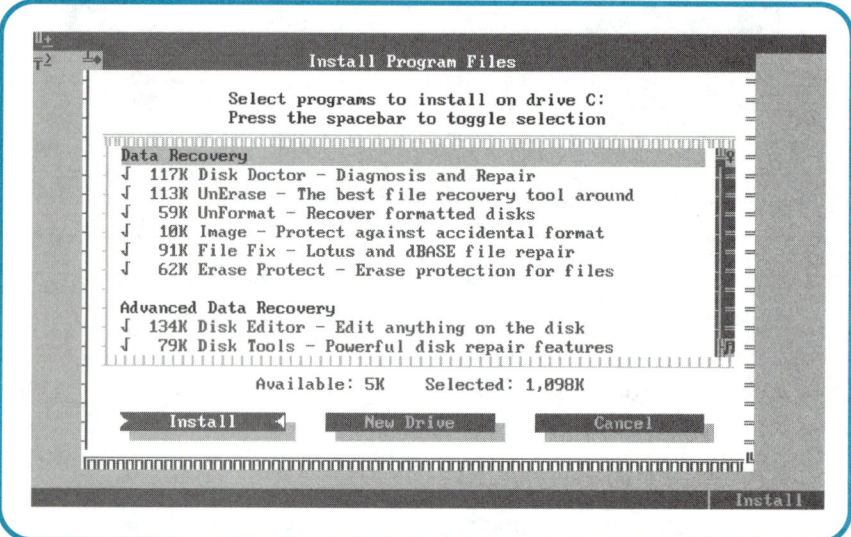

Figure A.2   **The Install Program Files screen lets you choose which utilities to install.**

9. The Installation program delete files from the old version of the Norton Utilities (if any) and prompts you to put the Installation disk in the appropriate drive. (It should already be there. If not, place it in the drive.) Press Enter.

10. The Installation program begins copying files to your hard drive. Follow the prompts to insert disks as the installation continues.

11. Next, if you're using DOS 5.0 on your system, the Installation program gives you the option of adding help for The Norton Utilities to the DOS 5.0 help file. Choose Add Help or Don't Add Help, as you desire.

12. Next, you must enter your name at the Installation program prompt so you can complete the installation procedure. Type your name, then press Enter or Tab. Also enter your company name, then press Enter twice or select OK to continue installation.

13. The Installation program next displays a screen for The Norton Utilities Configuration program, shown in Figure A.3. Choose Easy to add The Norton Utilities to the PATH statement of, set the Norton Utilities variable in, and add Image (a utility that automatically creates a hidden backup copy of your files) to your system's AUTOEXEC.BAT file, then return to the Installation program. Choose Advanced to use the Configuration program. Choose Quit to return to the Installation program. You can reconfigure The Norton Utilities any time later. For more about the Configuration program, see the section later in this appendix entitled Configuration.

343

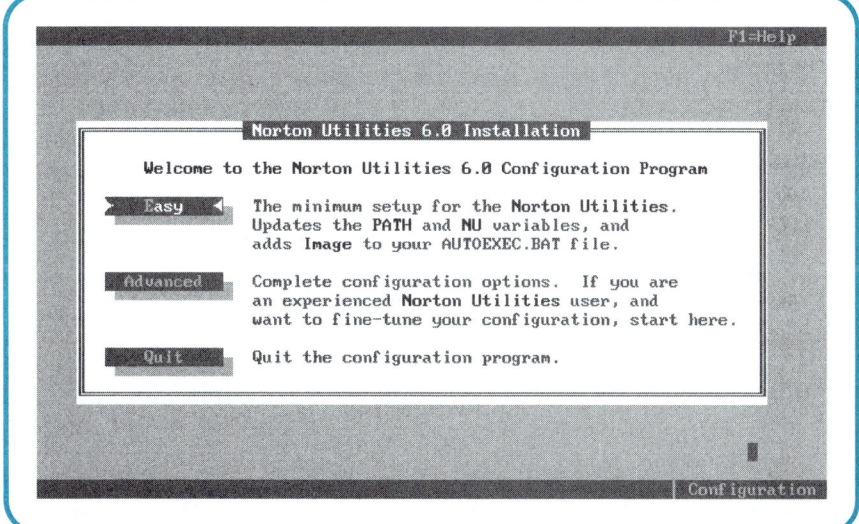

Figure A.3   The Installation program asks whether you want to configure The Norton Utilities.

14. When you return to the Installation program, you have the option to Reboot your system, Go to Program, or Return to DOS. Choose the appropriate option to complete the Installation program.

After you've installed The Norton Utilities, be sure to read the READ.ME file in the utilities directory. The READ.ME file contains important information that doesn't appear in The Norton Utilities documentation. Use DOS's TYPE command to list the READ.ME file and pause for each screenful of information (that is, enter `TYPE READ.ME ¦MORE`). If you have a printer connected to your PC, you can use the command `COPY READ.ME PRN:` to print a copy of READ.ME.

Floppy Disk Installation

If your PC has no hard disk, you might still be able to use the Installation program to place The Norton Utilities on a floppy disk. You will probably want to install them on a bootable floppy disk so you don't have to swap disks to access them. (A *bootable* disk contains special system files that your PC needs to start up, or "pull itself up by the bootstraps." Create a bootable disk by changing to the drive and directory that contains your DOS files, putting a blank formatted floppy disk in drive A:, and typing `A:SYS` or `A:/S` for DOS 4.1. You can also insert the disk in Drive B: and type `B:SYS` or `B:/S`.) But how much space is available on a bootable floppy? The answer to this question depends on a few other questions:

1. What version of DOS is on the bootable floppy?
2. What size floppy disk are you using (360K, 720K, 1.2 Mb, or 1.44 Mb)?
3. Besides DOS, how many other programs or utilities are already on the bootable floppy disk?

Use DOS's DIR command to determine how much space is available on your bootable floppy before trying to use the Installation program. (DIR displays the total number of bytes free at the bottom of a directory listing.) Then run the Installation program as described for hard disk installation. Put the Installation Disk in drive A and the bootable floppy in drive B:. Type `A:INSTALL`.

> **Note:** An important exception in the installation proce-
> dure is that when you are asked where the Installation
> program should place the Norton program files, type `B:`. (Or, if
> you've inserted the Installation Disk in drive B: and type
> `B:INSTALL`, specify A: as the drive for The Norton Utilities
> program files.)

When you reach the Install Program Files screen (see Figure
A.2), select or deselect the files you wish to install, and note the total
size of the selected files at the bottom of the screen. You can select
and deselect different files to determine exactly which utilities will
fit on your bootable disk. After you've selected all the utilities that
will fit on your bootable disk, choose the `Install` button to continue
the installation process.

If you can't fit all the utilities you need on one bootable disk,
you can use the same steps to create another floppy disk containing
the remaining utilities.

345

Configuration

You can control many aspects of how The Norton Utilities work with
your system. Specifying these options is called *configuring* The Norton
Utilities. You can start the Configuration program using one of the
following methods:

▶ Select the `Advanced` option from the Configuration screen that
appears during installation.

▶ At the DOS prompt, move to the drive and directory that
contains The Norton Utilities, type `NUCONFIG`, and press Enter.

▶ Select the NUCONFIG command from the list at the left side of
The Norton Utilities Integration (main) screen, by highlighting
it with the down arrow key then pressing Enter or clicking with
the mouse.

When you start the Configuration program, the main Configuration screen appears, as shown in Figure A.4. The screen has
buttons with the names of the features you can alter, along with a
brief description of each option.

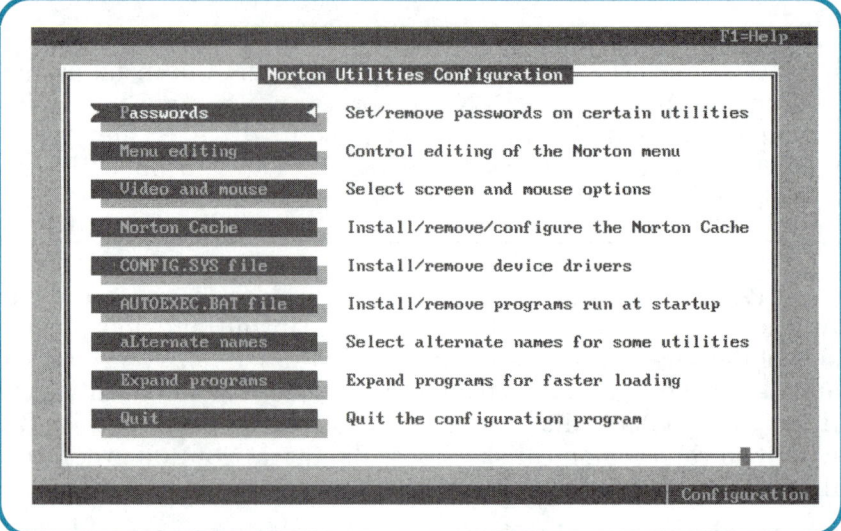

Figure A.4   The Norton Utilities Configuration screen, with buttons for the aspects of the program you can configure.

Tip: You can choose options quickly at the main Configuration screen by pressing the highlighted letter in the button name.

Choosing an option button displays a dialog box with the choices for the option. Use the arrow keys or the mouse to move among the *check boxes* (they look like brackets with a space between, [ ]) for the dialog box choices. Press Space Bar or click with the mouse to select a choice; an X appears beside it.

Following are the options available in The Norton Utilities Configuration program and a description of each:

▶ The *Passwords* button displays the Password Protection screen shown in Figure A.5, which lists the utilities to which you can assign a password. Configuration assigns the same password to all utilities you select. Press Enter or click on Set Passwords when you've selected the utilities you want to protect. Configuration displays the Set Password box. Enter a password of up to 15 letters, then press Enter or click the OK button. Configuration will ask you to verify the password.

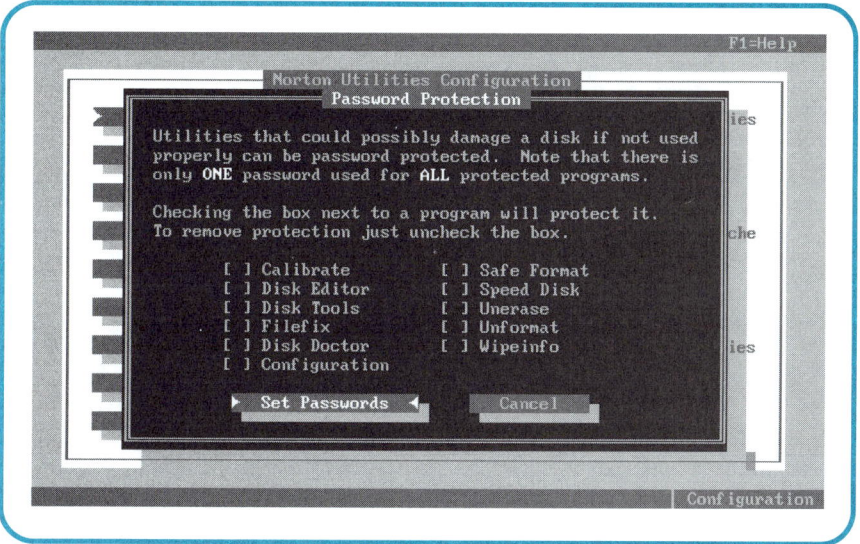

Figure A.5   The Password Protection screen.

> ✏️ **Tip:** To be able to access a utility without a password again, deselect it at the Password Protection screen, then press Enter or select `Set Password`.

▶ The *Menu editing* button displays a dialog box that lets you enable or disable the ability to add or delete programs from the menu in The Norton Utilities Integration (main screen) program. Click or use Space Bar to enable or disable menu editing, then select `OK`.

▶ The *Video and mouse* button displays the dialog box shown in Figure A.6, which lets you specify screen colors and set graphical, mouse, and screen options. Choose the `Save` button after you've specified all the options you wish.

   If you select `Custom Colors` from the *Screen Colors* area, you can then choose the `Customize Colors` button at the bottom of the dialog box to specify the custom colors in the Color Setup dialog box that appears. Choose a screen area in the box at the left, then select the `Change` button to display a Select New Color palette, from which you can choose a color scheme. When you have customized the screen colors, you can save them as the custom colors or set them as the default colors.

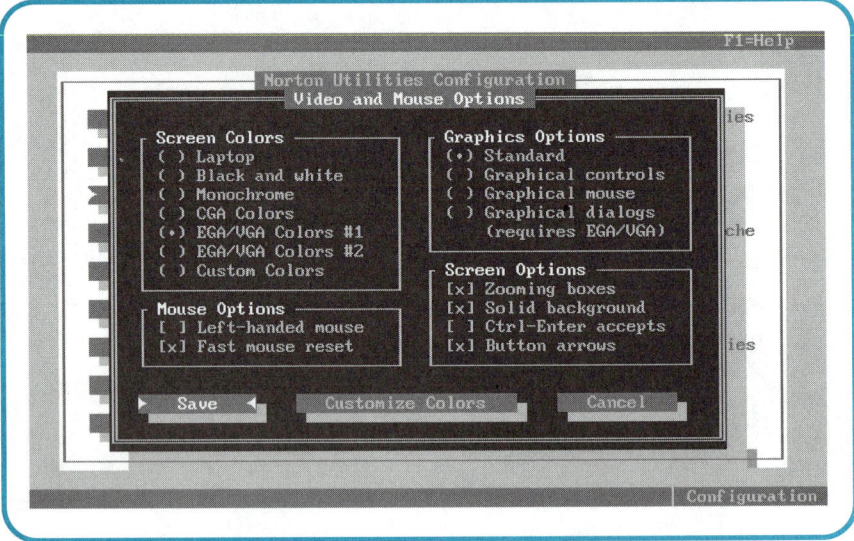

Figure A.6 *The Video and Mouse Options dialog box.*

348

The *Graphics options* area lets you specify whether to display the Norton screens with standard (text) or graphical characters. The graphical options are only supported if you system has an EGA (Enhanced Graphics Adapter) or VGA (Video Graphics Array) adapter.

The *Mouse options* area lets you set the mouse for left-handed use. Users with serial and Compaq mouse ports or an IBM PS/2 should use the Fast mouse reset option.

There are several *Screen Options*. You can set dialog boxes to zoom when they open, choose a solid screen background, and display arrows on command buttons. Also, the Ctrl-Enter accepts option changes the way you work with dialog boxes. Selecting this option means you will use Enter to move between dialog box options instead of Tab and use Ctrl-Enter to accept your choices instead of Enter.

▶ The *Norton Cache* button displays the dialog box shown in Figure A.7, which lets you activate the Norton Cache utility if you did not do so during installation. You can deactivate Cache if you've been using it by choosing the Do not load the Norton Cache option. Otherwise, you can specify whether to load Cache from your system's CONFIG.SYS or AUTOEXEC.BAT file when you boot the computer. The Configuration program will add the appropriate lines in either file. In addition, the dialog box lets you specify whether Cache loads in high or conventional memory, enable IntelliWrites and SmartReads, and set memory usage when running Cache from DOS or Windows. The Advanced button displays another dialog box with more options for using IntelliWrites and SmartReads, setting Cache Block size, and optimizing Cache performance. Once you've set your options for Cache, you must reboot your computer for the options to take effect.

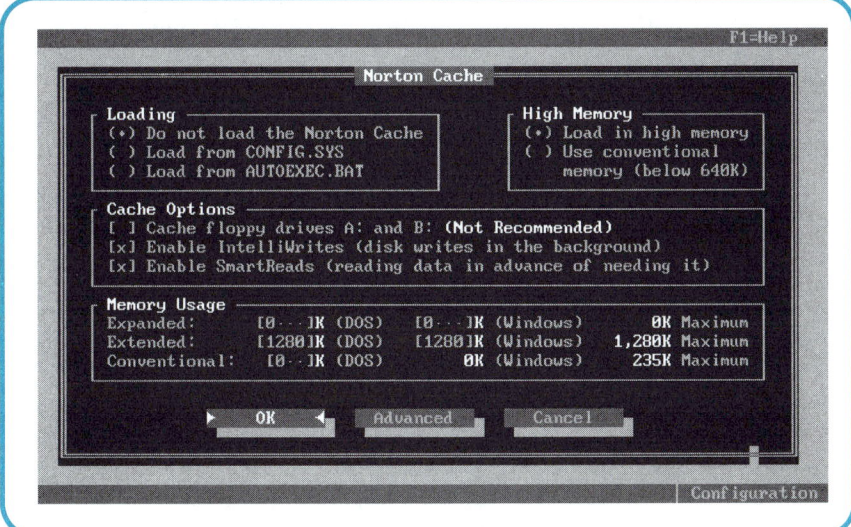

349

Figure A.7   ***Specifying how the Norton Cache runs with your system.***

▶   Choose CONFIG.SYS file from the Configuration screen to insert command statements in your system's CONFIG.SYS file for device drivers for DISKREET.SYS, PCSHADOW.SYS, NDOS.COM, and KEYSTACK.SYS. (For more on DISKREET.SYS, see Chapter 7. For more on NDOS.COM, see Chapter 8.) After you make your selections and choose OK, reboot your computer for the changes to take effect.

▶ The *AUTOEXEC.BAT file* button on the Configuration screen lets you set up your AUTOEXEC.BAT file to run certain utilities automatically when you start your system. In addition to adding The Norton Utilities directory to the PATH statement in AUTOEXEC.BAT and setting The Norton Utilities environment variable, you can choose to run the DISKMON, ERASE PROTECT, IMAGE, and NDD utilities automatically. When you make your selections and choose OK, Configuration adds the necessary lines to your AUTOEXEC.BAT file automatically. Reboot your system to make your changes take effect.

> **Caution:** Be selective in choosing utilities to run automatically. The utilities use memory your system could need to run other applications.

350

▶ The aLternate names button displays the screen shown in Figure A.8. As you can see, you can select abbreviated, two-letter names for several of the utilities. If you select the shortened version of the utility name, then you can type the two-letter name at the DOS prompt to start the utility rather than the full name. You can also rename the Safe Format (SFORMAT.EXE) program to FORMAT (in place of DOS's FORMAT.EXE, which will be renamed XXFORMAT.EXE). I highly recommend that you make this replacement, because SFORMAT is an excellent utility and much more user-friendly than FORMAT. (See Chapter 6 for a complete explanation of SFORMAT.) Choose the OK button after you've made your selections. You can also pick the All Short Names button to give all the Utilities short names.

▶ Normally, The Norton Utilities programs are stored in compressed form on disk to save space. They expand automatically when you run them. This may cause a delay in running the utilities on slower systems. The *Expand programs* button at the Configuration screen gives you the option to expand one or more utilities to their full size to start more quickly. Select the OK button from the Expand Program Files screen to display the Expand Program Files dialog box, shown in Figure A.9. Use the arrow keys and Space Bar or simply click with the mouse to select the commands you want to expand. After you've made your selections, choose the Expand button.

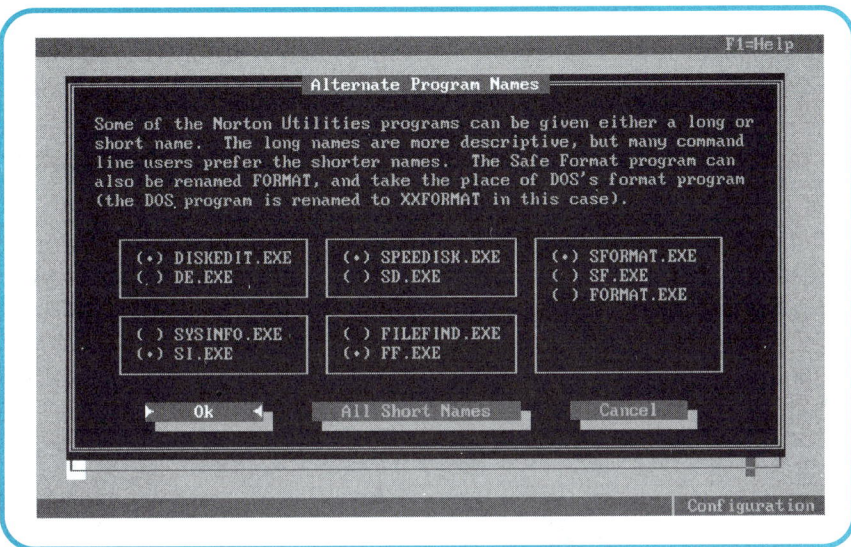

Figure A.8 **Alternate Program Names dialog box.**

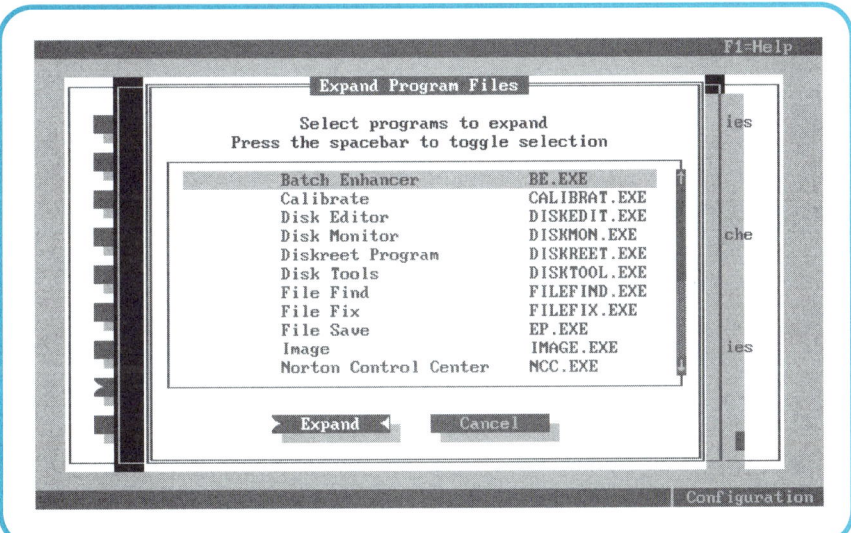

Figure A.9 **The Expand Program Files dialog box.**

> **Caution:** You can't recompress files after you've ex-
> panded them. You can, however, delete the expanded
> file and reinstall the compressed version.

▶ The final button on the Configuration screen, Quit, lets you
leave the Configuration program and return to the Installation
program, the DOS prompt, or The Norton Utilities Integration
(main) screen.

After you've installed and configured The Norton Utilities,
you're ready to begin using its handy programs.

352

Command Line Utilities

You can start all the programs that come with The Norton Utilities either through the main Norton menu program or by typing a command at the DOS prompt. Several of the utilities, in particular, are especially easy to use from DOS. These are known as the *command line utilities*.

Using the command line utilities from the DOS prompt rather than the main Norton screen offers the convenience of bypassing menu selections. You can also include command line utilities in the batch files you create. You start each of the command line utilities by typing its two-character name at the DOS prompt. (If you did not add The Norton Utilities to your PATH statement when you installed the program, you need to return to the directory containing The Norton Utilities program files first.) Specify special conditions for an operation, called *parameters*, by typing *startup switches* (special codes) along with the command that starts the utility.

This appendix describes Norton's seven command line utilities and explains the parameters and switches you can use with each.

Directory Sort (DS.EXE)

Organizing files in a more coherent order makes it easier for you to find and retrieve the files you need. As described in Chapter 5, the Directory Sort utility places one or more directories in order according to date, extension, name, size, or time. If the directory you sort contains subdirectories, they are grouped first, followed by files. Directory Sort does not move hidden files or those with system attributes so as not to disturb any write-protection methods you may be using. By default, files are sorted in ascending alphabetical order when sorting by name or extension, smallest to largest when sorting by size, or least recent to most recent when sorting by date or time.

Chapter 5 describes how to use Directory Sort in its full-screen version. To use Directory Sort from the command line, type *sort-keys* along with the command name when you start the utility. Table B.1 lists the sort-keys and other parameters you can specify when using Directory Sort.

354

Table B.1   Directory Sort Command Line Sort-Keys

Use	By Entering	To Sort
D	DS D	By file creation date
E	DS E	By extension
N	DS N	By file name
S	DS S	By file size
T	DS T	By file creation time
–	DS *(sort-key)*–	In reverse order
drive:\directory	DS *(sort-keys)* *drive:\directory*	A drive or directory other than the current drive and directory
/S	DS /S	Files in subdirectories of the current directory

You can enter more than one sort-key per operation by typing all sort-keys you wish after the command. Directory Sort first orders the files according to the first sort-key you enter (the *primary sort*), then by the second sort-key, and so on. For example, typing **DS ND** at the DOS prompt would sort the files in the current directory by file name, then by creation date.

File Attributes (FA.EXE)

As explained in Chapter 3, DOS tracks specific *attributes* for each file stored on disk: archive, hidden, read-only, and system. (See Table 3.1 for an explanation of each attribute.)

Attributes protect a file from being accidentally overwritten and remind you to back up certain files. However, on occasion you may need to change a file's attributes to update it or to change a file to read-only to protect it. In addition to using the FILEFIND utility (see Chapter 3) or the Norton Commander (see Chapter 10) to change a file's attributes, you can use the File Attributes command line utility.

Type **FA** at the DOS prompt to list all the current directory's files and their attributes. Including + with an attribute switch turns that attribute on, while including – with an attribute switch turns that attribute off. Table B.2 summarizes the switches you can use with the FA command.

Table B.2   File Attributes Command Line Switches

Switch	Function
/A	Sets the archive attribute
/CLEAR	Removes all file attributes
/DIR (+ or –)	Assigns or removes the hidden attribute to a directory
/H	Sets the hidden attribute
/P	Pauses after each screenful of files displayed
/R	Sets the read-only attribute
/S	Makes the command line act on subdirectories of the current directory
/SYS	Sets the system attribute
/T	Displays the file and directory totals
/U	Lists any files with an attribute set

355

You may also specify a specific drive, directory, and file name (including the wild-card characters * and ?) with the File Attributes command. For example, typing **FA D:\WORD5*.DOC /R+** would assign read-only status to all the files with the .DOC extension in the WORD5 directory of drive D:.

File Date (FD.EXE)

The File Date command line utility does just what you'd expect. It enables you to assign a different date and/or time to a file or group of files. Simply type `FD` at the DOS prompt to assign the current system date and time to all the files in the current directory. You may also specify a file or group of files in the command line, as in typing `FD A:\JOEB\TEST1.TIF`. Table B.3 summarizes the switches you can enter with the FD command.

Table B.3   *File Date Command Line Switches*

Use	To
/D:*month-day-year*	Assign the given date to the specified file(s)
/P	Pause after displaying each screenful of files
/S	Assign the new date/time to files in the current directory's subdirectories
/T:*hour:minute:second*	Assigns the given time to the specified file(s)

File Locate (FL.EXE)

If you've ever forgotten an exact file name or where you've stored a particular file, you know that searching disks and directories can be a frustrating and time-consuming process. The File Locate command line utility offers a simple, faster way to find lost files—even system or hidden files DOS's DIR command won't list—and print a catalog of files.

► Type `FL` at the prompt to locate (and display) all files on the current disk. (Pressing Space Bar will pause and resume the file name scrolling on your screen.)

► You can include a drive letter, file name, or partial file name with wild cards in the command line. For example, typing `FL S*` will locate all files starting with S on the current drive.

Typing **FL D:\STEVE.DOC** would locate any file named STEVE.DOC on drive D.

▶ Typing **FL > PRN** at the DOS prompt prints a catalog of all files on the current disk.

Table B.4 summarizes the switches you can include with the File Locate command line.

Table B.4   *File Locate Command Line Switches*

Switch	Function
/A	Searches all drives
/F[n]	Lists only the first *n* matching files located instead of all the files located
/P	Pauses after each screenful of file names is displayed
/T	Searches the directories listed in the AUTOEXEC.BAT PATH statement only
/W	Lists the files in wide format on-screen

357

File Size (FS.EXE)

Rather than using the FILEFIND utility (see Chapter 3) to check file sizes, you can use the File Size command line utility to check the size of a single file or a group of files. If you want to copy the specified files to another disk, the File Size utility lets you check to see if there's enough room.

In addition, the File Size utility reports the *slack* in the amount of space occupied by the specified file(s). That is, when a computer stores a file on disk, the smallest storage area it uses is called a *cluster*. When a file is not large enough to fill out a cluster, the remaining space is the slack. So, if one disk uses larger cluster sizes than another, the files stored on the disk with the larger cluster sizes could appear to occupy more disk space than they would occupy on the disk using smaller cluster sizes if you simply checked the file sizes using DOS's DIR command.

Typing **FS** at the DOS prompt lists the sizes of files in the current directory, the amount of disk space occupied by the files, the amount of slack space created, and the amounts of used and unused space on the drive. Table B.5 summarizes the other options for using the File Size command line utility.

Table B.5   *File Size Command Line Options*

Include	To	Command Example
drive\directory\ filename	List the size of the specified file(s)	FS C:\JEN*.TXT
drive\directory\ filename	Determine whether there is room to copy the file(s) indicated to the target drive	FS C:\STEVE*.TXT A:
/P	Pause after each screenful displayed	FS /P
/S	Also list sizes for files in subdirectories of current directory	FS /S
/T	Display directory and disk totals only	FS /T

Line Print (LP.EXE)

Rather than pulling up a word processing program or other text editor to print a text file, you can print directly from the DOS prompt using the Line Print command line utility. Line Print can print to any printer (such as LPT1) or device (such as COM1). By default, Line Print divides the file into pages headed with the file name, current time and date, and page number.

If you don't want to use the default printing format and have embedded printer setup strings in the file you want to print, use the /SET switch with the LP command. To simply print the specified document to the default printer attached to your system, type **LP** *drive\directory\filename*. Table B.6 explains the additional switches you can use with the Line Print command line utility.

Table B.6   Line Print Command Line Switches

Include	To
output	Specify a device or printer other than the default (such as LPT2)
/132	Printer in 132-column width on an IBM-compatible printer
/B*n*	Specify a bottom margin of *n* lines (3 is the default)
/H*n*	Specify a page height of *n* lines (66 is the default)
/HEADER0	Print the file without page headers
/HEADER1	Print with the default headers
/HEADER2	In addition to the current date and time, print the file date and time on the second header line
/L*n*	Specify a left margin of *n* characters (5 is the default)
/N	Print line numbers
/P*n*	Specify *n* as the starting page number (1 is the default)
/PS	Print to a PostScript printer
/R*n*	Specify a right margin of *n* characters (5 is the default)
/S*n*	Specify line spacing of *n* lines (1 is the default)
/T*n*	Specify a top margin of *n* lines (3 is the default)
/TAB*n*	Space tab stops at *n* characters (8 is the default)
/W*n*	Specify a page width of *n* characters (85 is the default)
/WS	Print WordStar files

359

Text Search (TS.EXE)

The Text Search command line utility is useful for finding text contained in a file. This utility also searches for text on areas of a disk containing only erased files. (You can then copy the found data to a new file.) Include the text you want to search for in quotation marks when you enter the Text Search command, as in TS "Find me". By entering a drive, directory, and file name (complete or using wild cards) with the TS command, you can search only the specified file(s) for the text string you enter. For example, typing

```
TS C:\PHYLLIS\*.DOC "Series Ideas"
```

at the DOS prompt would search for the words "Series Ideas" in all files with the .DOC extension in the PHYLLIS directory of drive C.

Each time Text Search finds the string of characters it's looking for, it displays several lines of the text around the located string and the full path name of the file containing the located text, and asks whether you'd like to continue the search. Table B.7 summarizes the Text Search options.

Table B.7   Text Search Command Line

Include	To
/A	Make the search automatic (assumes a "Yes" answer to all prompts)
/C*n*	Begin the search at cluster *n* of the disk
/CS	Make the search case-sensitive
/D	Search the whole disk
/E	Look for the text string on only the erased portion of the disk
/LOG	Output results in a log format you can print or save in a file
/S	Search all subdirectories of the current directory
/T	Give only summary information of the search
/WS	Omit characters in the IBM PC extended character set from the search

Index

363

365

N

O-P

369

370

371

372

Sams' First Books Get You Started Fast!

"The First Book Series ... is intended to get the novice off to a good start, whether with computers in general or with particular programs ...."

The New York Times

The First Book of WordPerfect 5.1
Kate Miller Barnes
275 pages, 7 3/8 x 9 1/4, $16.95 USA
0-672-27307-1

Look For These Books In Sams' First Book Series

The First Book of C
Charles Ackerman
300 pages, 7 3/8 x 9 1/4, $16.95 USA
0-672-27354-3

The First Book of dBASE IV 1.1
Steven Currie
300 pages, 7 3/8 x 9 1/4, $16.95 USA
0-672-27342-X

The First Book of DeskMate
Jack Nimersheim
315 pages, 7 3/8 x 9 1/4, $16.95 USA
0-672-27314-4

The First Book of DrawPerfect
Susan Baake Kelly & James Kevin Kelly
340 pages, 7 3/8 x 9 1/4, $16.95 USA
0-672-27315-2

The First Book of Fastback Plus
Jonathan Kamin
275 pages, 7 3/8 x 9 1/4, $16.95 USA
0-672-27323-3

The First Book of GW-BASIC
Saul Aguiar & The Coriolis Group
275 ppages, 7 3/8 x 9 1/4, $16.95 USA
0-672-27316-0

The First Book of Harvard Graphics
Jack Purdum
300 pages, 7 3/8 x 9 1/4, $16.95 USA
0-672-27310-1

The First Book of Lotus 1-2-3/G
Peter Aitken
350 pages, 7 3/8 x 9 1/4, $16.95 USA
0-672-27293-8

The First Book of Lotus 1-2-3 Release 2.2
Alan Simpson & Paul Lichtman
275 pages, 7 3/8 x 9 1/4, $16.95 USA
0-672-27301-2

The First Book of Microsoft Excel for the PC
Chris Van Buren
275 pages, 7 3/8 x 9 1/4, $16.95 USA
0-672-27322-5

TheFirst Book of Microsoft QuickPascal
Elna R. Tymes & Fred Waters
275 pages, 7 3/8 x 9 1/4, $16.95 USA
0-672-27294-6

The First Book of Microsoft Windows 3
Jack Nimersheim
275 pages, 7 3/8 x 9 1/4, $16.95 USA
0-672-27334-9

The First Book of Microsoft Word 5.5, Second Edition
Brent Heslop & David Angell
320 pages, 7 3/8 x 9 1/4, $16.95 USA
0-672-27333-0

The First Book of Microsoft Word for Windows
Brent Heslop & David Angell
304 pages, 7 3/8 x 9 1/4, $16.95 USA
0-672-27332-2

The First Book of MS-DOS
Jack Nimersheim
272 pages, 7 3/8 x 9 1/4, $16.95 USA
0-672-27312-8

The First Book of MS-DOS 5
Jack Nimersheim
275 pages, 7 3/8 x 9 1/4, $16.95 USA
0-672-27341-1

The First Book of Norton Utilities
Joseph Wikert
275 pages, 7 3/8 x 9 1/4, $16.95 USA
0-672-27308-X

The First Book of Paradox 3
Jonathan Kamin
275 pages, 7 3/8 x 9 1/4, $16.95 USA
0-672-27300-4

The First Book of PC-Write
Rebecca Kenyon, Ph.D.
350 pages, 7 3/8 x 9 1/4, $16.95 USA
0-672-27320-9

The First Book of PC Paintbrush
Deke McClelland
289 pages, 7 3/8 x 9 1/4, $16.95 USA
0-672-27324-1

The First Book of PFS: First Publisher
Karen Brown & Robert Bixby
308 pages, 7 3/8 x 9 1/4, $16.95 USA
0-672-27326-8

The First Book of PC Tools Deluxe, Second Edition
Gordon McComb
304 pages, 7 3/8 x 9 1/4, $16.95 USA
0-672-27329-2

The First Book of Personal Computing
W.E. Wang & Joe Kraynak
275 pages, 7 3/8 x 9 1/4, $16.95 USA
0-672-27313-6

The First Book of PROCOMM PLUS
Jack Nimersheim
250 pages, 7 3/8 x 9 1/4, $16.95 USA
0-672-27309-8

The First Book of PS/1
Kate Barnes
300 pages, 7 3/8 x 9 1/4, $16.95 USA
0-672-27346-2

The First Book of Q&A
Brent Heslop & David Angell
275 pages, 7 3/8 x 9 1/4, $16.95 USA
0-672-27311-X

The First Book of Quattro Pro
Patrick Burns
300 pages, 7 3/8 x 9 1/4, $16.95 USA
0-672-27345-4

The First Book of Quicken in Business
Gordon McComb
300 pages, 7 3/8 x 9 1/4, $16.95 USA
0-672-27331-4

The First Book of UNIX
Doglas Topham
300 pages, 7 3/8 x 9 1/4, $16.95 USA
0-672-27299-7

The First Book of WordPerfect Office
Sams
275 pages, 73.8 x 9 1/4, $16.95 USA
0-672-27317-9

SAMS

To order books, call 1-800-428-5331.

Sams—Covering The Latest In Computer And Technical Topics!

Audio

Audio Production Techniques for Video	$29.95
Audio Systems Design and Installation	$59.95
Audio Technology Fundamentals	$24.95
Compact Disc Troubleshooting and Repair	$24.95
Handbook for Sound Engineers:	
The New Audio Cyclopedia	$79.95
Introduction to Professional Recording Techniques	$29.95
Modern Recording Techniques, 3rd Ed.	$29.95
Principles of Digital Audio, 2nd Ed.	$29.95
Sound Recording Handbook	$49.95
Sound System Engineering, 2nd Ed.	$49.95

Electricity/Electronics

Basic AC Circuits	$29.95
Electricity 1, Revised 2nd Ed.	$14.95
Electricity 1-7, Revised 2nd Ed.	$49.95
Electricity 2, Revised 2nd Ed.	$14.95
Electricity 3, Revised 2nd Ed.	$14.95
Electricity 4, Revised 2nd Ed.	$14.95
Electricity 5, Revised 2nd Ed.	$14.95
Electricity 6, Revised 2nd Ed.	$14.95
Electricity 7, Revised 2nd Ed.	$14.95
Electronics 1-7, Revised 2nd Ed.	$49.95

Electronics Technical

Active-Filter Cookbook	$19.95
Camcorder Survival Guide	$ 9.95
CMOS Cookbook, 2nd Ed.	$24.95
Design of OP-AMP Circuits with Experiments	$19.95
Design of Phase-Locked Loop Circuits	
with Experiments	$19.95
Electrical Test Equipment	$19.95
Electrical Wiring	$19.95
How to Read Schematics, 4th Ed.	$19.95
IC Op-Amp Cookbook, 3rd Ed.	$24.95
IC Timer Cookbook, 2nd Ed.	$19.95
IC User's Casebook	$19.95
Radio Handbook, 23rd Ed.	$39.95
Radio Operator's License Q&A Manual, 11th Ed.	$24.95
RF Circuit Design	$24.95
Transformers and Motors	$24.95
TTL Cookbook	$19.95
Undergrounding Electric Lines	$14.95
Understanding Telephone Electronics, 2nd Ed.	$19.95
VCR Troubleshooting & Repair Guide	$19.95
Video Scrambling & Descrambling	
for Satellite & Cable TV	$19.95

Games

Beyond the Nintendo Masters	$ 9.95
Mastering Nintendo Video Games II	$ 9.95
Tricks of the Nintendo Masters	$ 9.95
VideoGames & Computer Entertainment	
Complete Guide to Nintendo Video Games	$ 9.50
Winner's Guide to Nintendo Game Boy	$ 9.95
Winner's Guide to Sega Genesis	$ 9.95

Hardware/Technical

Hard Disk Power with the Jamsa Disk Utilities	$39.95
IBM PC Advanced Troubleshooting & Repair	$24.95
IBM Personal Computer	
Troubleshooting & Repair	$24.95
IBM Personal Computer Upgrade Guide	$24.95
Microcomputer Troubleshooting & Repair	$24.95
Understanding Communications Systems, 2nd Ed.	$19.95
Understanding Data Communications, 2nd Ed.	$19.95
Understanding FAX and Electronic Mail	$19.95
Understanding Fiber Optics	$19.95

IBM: Business

Best Book of Microsoft Works for the PC, 2nd Ed.	$24.95
Best Book of PFS: First Choice	$24.95
Best Book of Professional Write and File	$22.95
First Book of Fastback Plus	$16.95
First Book of Norton Utilities	$16.95
First Book of Personal Computing	$16.95
First Book of PROCOMM PLUS	$16.95

IBM: Database

Best Book of Paradox 3	$27.95
dBASE III Plus Programmer's Reference Guide	$24.95
dBASE IV Programmer's Reference Guide	$24.95
First Book of Paradox 3	$16.95
Mastering ORACLE	
Featuring ORACLE's SQL Standard	$24.95

IBM: Graphics/Desktop Publishing

Best Book of Autodesk Animator	$29.95
Best Book of Harvard Graphics	$24.95
First Book of DrawPerfect	$16.95
First Book of Harvard Graphics	$16.95
First Book of PC Paintbrush	$16.95
First Book of PFS: First Publisher	$16.95

IBM: Spreadsheets/Financial

Best Book of Lotus 1-2-3 Release 3.1	$27.95
Best Book of Lotus 1-2-3, Release 2.2, 3rd Ed.	$26.95
Best Book of Peachtree Complete III	$24.95
First Book of Lotus 1-2-3, Release 2.2	$16.95
First Book of Lotus 1-2-3/G	$16.95
First Book of Microsoft Excel for the PC	$16.95
Lotus 1-2-3: Step-by-Step	$24.95

IBM: Word Processing

Best Book of Microsoft Word 5	$24.95
Best Book of Microsoft Word for Windows	$24.95
Best Book of WordPerfect 5.1	$26.95
Best Book of WordPerfect Version 5.0	$24.95
First Book of PC Write	$16.95
First Book of WordPerfect 5.1	$16.95
WordPerfect 5.1: Step-by-Step	$24.95

Macintosh/Apple

Best Book of AppleWorks	$24.95
Best Book of MacWrite II	$24.95
Best Book of Microsoft Word for the Macintosh	$24.95
Macintosh Printer Secrets	$34.95
Macintosh Repair & Upgrade Secrets	$34.95
Macintosh Revealed, Expanding the Toolbox,	
Vol. 4	$29.95
Macintosh Revealed, Mastering the Toolbox,	
Vol. 3	$29.95
Macintosh Revealed, Programming with the Toolbox,	
Vol. 2, 2nd Ed.	$29.95
Macintosh Revealed, Unlocking the Toolbox,	
Vol. 1, 2nd Ed.	$29.95
Using ORACLE with HyperCard	$24.95

Operating Systems/Networking

Best Book of DESQview	$24.95
Best Book of DOS	$24.95
Best Book of Microsoft Windows 3	$24.95
Business Guide to Local Area Networks	$24.95
Exploring the UNIX System, 2nd Ed.	$29.95
First Book of DeskMate	$16.95
First Book of Microsoft QuickPascal	$16.95
First Book of MS-DOS	$16.95
First Book of UNIX	$16.95
Interfacing to the IBM Personal Computer,	
2nd Ed.	$24.95
Mastering NetWare	$29.95
The Waite Group's Discovering MS-DOS	$19.95
The Waite Group's Inside XENIX	$29.95
The Waite Group's MS-DOS Bible, 3rd Ed.	$24.95
The Waite Group's MS-DOS Developer's Guide,	
2nd Ed.	$29.95
The Waite Group's Tricks of the MS-DOS Masters,	
2nd Ed.	$29.95
The Waite Group's Tricks of the UNIX Masters	$29.95
The Waite Group's Understanding MS-DOS,	
2nd Ed.	$19.95
The Waite Group's UNIX Primer Plus, 2nd Ed.	$29.95
The Waite Group's UNIX System V Bible	$29.95
The Waite Group's UNIX System V Primer,	
Revised Ed.	$29.95
Understanding Local Area Networks, 2nd Ed.	$24.95

Understanding NetWare	$24.95
UNIX Applications Programming:	
Mastering the Shell	$29.95
UNIX Networking	$29.95
UNIX Shell Programming, Revised Ed.	$29.95
UNIX System Administration	$29.95
UNIX System Security	$34.95
UNIX Text Processing	$29.95
UNIX: Step-by-Step	$29.95

Professional/Reference

Data Communications, Networks, and Systems	$39.95
Gallium Arsenide Technology, Volume II	$69.95
Handbook of Computer-Communications Standards,	
Vol. 1, 2nd Ed.	$39.95
Handbook of Computer-Communications Standards,	
Vol. 2, 2nd Ed.	$39.95
Handbook of Computer-Communications Standards,	
Vol. 3, 2nd Ed.	$39.95
Handbook of Electronics Tables and Formulas,	
6th Ed.	$24.95
ISDN, DECnet, and SNA Communications	$44.95
Modern Dictionary of Electronics, 6th Ed.	$39.95
Programmable Logic Designer's Guide	$29.95
Reference Data for Engineers: Radio, Electronics,	
Computer, and Communications, 7th Ed.	$99.95
Surface-Mount Technology for PC Board Design	$49.95
World Satellite Almanac, 2nd Ed.	$39.95

Programming

Advanced C: Tips and Techniques	$29.95
C Programmer's Guide to NetBIOS	$29.95
C Programmer's Guide to Serial Communications	$29.95
Commodore 64 Programmer's Reference Guide	$19.95
DOS Batch File Power	$39.95
First Book of GW-BASIC	$16.95
How to Write Macintosh Software, 2nd Ed.	$29.95
Mastering Turbo Assembler	$29.95
Mastering Turbo Debugger	$29.95
Mastering Turbo Pascal 5.5, 3rd Ed.	$29.95
Microsoft QuickBASIC Programmer's Reference	$29.95
Programming in ANSI C	$29.95
Programming in C, Revised Ed.	$29.95
QuickC Programming	$29.95
The Waite Group's BASIC Programming	
Primer, 2nd Ed.	$24.95
The Waite Group's C Programming	
Using Turbo C++	$29.95
The Waite Group's C++ Programming	$24.95
The Waite Group's C: Step-by-Step	$29.95
The Waite Group's GW-BASIC Primer Plus	$24.95
The Waite Group's Microsoft C Bible, 2nd Ed.	$29.95
The Waite Group's Microsoft C Programming	
for the PC, 2nd Ed.	$29.95
The Waite Group's Microsoft Macro	
Assembler Bible	$29.95
The Waite Group's New C Primer Plus	$29.95
The Waite Group's QuickC Bible	$29.95
The Waite Group's Turbo Assembler Bible	$29.95
The Waite Group's Turbo C Bible	$29.95
The Waite Group's Turbo C Programming	
for the PC, Revised Ed.	$29.95
The Waite Group's TWG Turbo C++Bible	$29.95
X Window System Programming	$29.95

For More Information, Call Toll Free

1-800-257-5755

All prices are subject to change without notice.
Non-U.S. prices may be higher. Printed in the U.S.A.

Reader Feedback Card

Thank you for purchasing this book from SAMS FIRST BOOK series. Our intent with this series is to bring you timely, authoritative information that you can reference quickly and easily. You can help us by taking a minute to complete and return this card. We appreciate your comments and will use the information to better serve your needs.

1. Where did you purchase this book?

☐ Chain bookstore (Walden, B. Dalton)
☐ Independent bookstore
☐ Computer/Software store
☐ Other _____

☐ Direct mail
☐ Book club
☐ School bookstore

2. Why did you choose this book? (Check as many as apply.)

☐ Price
☐ Author's reputation
☐ Quick and easy treatment of subject

☐ Appearance of book
☐ SAMS' reputation
☐ Only book available on subject

3. How do you use this book? (Check as many as apply.)

☐ As a supplement to the product manual
☐ In place of the product manual
☐ For self-instruction

☐ As a reference
☐ At home
☐ At work

4. Please rate this book in the categories below. G = Good; N = Needs improvement; U = Category is unimportant.

☐ Price
☐ Amount of information
☐ Examples
☐ Inside cover reference
☐ Table of contents
☐ Tips and cautions
☐ Length of book
☐ How can we improve this book?_____
☐ _____

☐ Appearance
☐ Accuracy
☐ Quick Steps
☐ Second color
☐ Index
☐ Illustrations

5. How many computer books do you normally buy in a year?

☐ 1–5   ☐ 5–10   ☐ More than 10
☐ I rarely purchase more than one book on a subject.
☐ I may purchase a beginning and an advanced book on the same subject.
☐ I may purchase several books on particular subjects.
☐ (such as _____)

6. Have your purchased other SAMS or Hayden books in the past year? _____
If yes, how many _____

7. Would you purchase another book in the FIRST BOOK series? _____

8. What are your primary areas of interest in business software? _____

- ☐ Word processing (particularly _____)
- ☐ Spreadsheet (particularly _____)
- ☐ Database (particularly _____)
- ☐ Graphics (particularly _____)
- ☐ Personal finance/accounting (particularly _____)
- ☐ Other (please specify _____)

Other comments on this book or the SAMS' book line: _____
_____

Name _____
Company _____
Address _____
City _____ State _____ Zip_____
Daytime telephone number _____
Title of this book _____

Fold here

- -